# JOHN SCOTT, LORD ELDON, 1751–1838
## The Duty of Loyalty

John Scott, Lord Eldon (1751–1838) was a dominant figure in Georgian public life, and ranks amongst the most important Lord Chancellors in the long history of that office.

This biography – the first for 150 years – also surveys Eldon's earlier career as an MP and law officer. As a lawyer entering Parliament, he encountered both prejudices against 'learned gentlemen' and opportunities for advancement. Once in office, he swiftly made his presence felt, drafting the Regency Bill of 1788, and conducting the government's legal campaign against republicanism.

Retiring at last in 1827, Eldon spent his final years opposing political reform. Labelled by many as a relic of 'Old Toryism', Eldon's views of government, politics, and the constitution represent an important strand in Georgian political thinking, and his career illuminates the work of the major legal offices of British government.

R. A. Melikan is a Fellow and College Lecturer at St Catharine's College, University of Cambridge.

# CAMBRIDGE STUDIES IN ENGLISH LEGAL HISTORY

Edited by

## J. H. BAKER

*Fellow of St Catharine's College, Cambridge*

*Recent series titles include*

Sir William Scott, Lord Stowell
Judge of the High Court of Admiralty 1798–1828
HENRY J. BOURGUIGNON

Sir Henry Maine
A Study in Victorian Jurisprudence
R. C. J. COCKS

Roman Canon Law in Reformation England
R. H. HELMHOLZ

Fundamental Authority in Late Medieval English Law
NORMAN DOE

Law, Politics and the Church of England
The Career of Stephen Lushington 1782–1873
S. M. WADDAMS

The Early History of the Law of Bills and Notes
A Study of the Origins of Anglo-American Commercial Law
JAMES STEVEN ROGERS

The Law of Evidence in Victorian England
C. J. W. ALLEN

Steel engraving of Eldon, aged 74, by H. Robinson, after T. Lawrence

# JOHN SCOTT
# LORD ELDON, 1751–1838

## THE DUTY OF LOYALTY

R. A. MELIKAN

CAMBRIDGE
UNIVERSITY PRESS

PUBLISHED BY THE PRESS SYNDICATE OF THE UNIVERSITY OF CAMBRIDGE
The Pitt Building, Trumpington Street, Cambridge, CB2 1RP, United Kingdom

CAMBRIDGE UNIVERSITY PRESS
The Edinburgh Building, Cambridge, CB2 2RU, United Kingdom
http://www.cup.cam.ac.uk
40 West 20th Street, New York, NY 10011-4211, US
http://www.cup.org
10 Stamford Road, Oakleigh, Melbourne 3166, Australia

© R. A. Melikan 1999

First published 1999

Printed in the United Kingdom at the University Press, Cambridge

Typeset in Imprint on 10/12 pt   [CE]

*A catalogue record for this book is available from the British Library*

*Library of Congress cataloguing in publication data*
Melikan, R. A
John Scott, Lord Eldon 1751–1838: the duty of loyalty / R. A. Melikan.
p.    cm. – (Cambridge studies in English legal history)
ISBN 0 521 62395 2 (hc.)
1. Eldon, John Scott, Earl of, 1971–1838.
2. Judges – Great Britain – Biography.
3. Great Britain. Lord Chancellor's Departments – History.
4. Law and politics – History.
I. Title. II. Series.
KD621.E43M45   1999
347.41′014′092 – dc21   98-42867   CIP
[B]

ISBN 0 521 62395 2 hardback

FOR MY PARENTS

# CONTENTS

*List of illustrations*       *page* x
*List of tables*       xi
*Preface*       xiii
*List of abbreviations*       xvii

1   A man of laws       1
2   An independent learned gentleman       20
3   A government retainer       38
4   Formal politics       61
5   Engagement       82
6   Setbacks       99
7   Resolution       119
8   Pater familias       139
9   Upright intentions       152
10   The King's man       167
11   The practice of patronage       190
12   Cut and thrust       212
13   A servant may serve two masters       230
14   Reform and revolution       250
15   The Speaker speaks       271
16   Lord Endless       295
17   Faithful defender       326
18   Twilight of the State       348

*Bibliography*       357
*Index*       366

# ILLUSTRATIONS

*Frontispiece*
Steel engraving of Eldon, aged 74, by H. Robinson, after
T. Lawrence (courtesy of Professor J. H. Baker)

*Between pages 174 and 175*

1 Engraving of the Scott home, and Eldon's birthplace, in Newcastle

2 Encombe, in Dorset, purchased by Eldon in 1807 (by kind permission of Mr David Scott)

3 Steel engraving of Sir John Scott, aged 48, by E. Finden, after T. Lawrence (courtesy of Professor J. H. Baker)

4 Stipple engraving of Eldon, by T. Wright, after A. Wivell, one of a series of drawings of the principal participants in Queen Caroline's trial in 1820 (courtesy of Professor J. H. Baker)

5 John Bull evinces little sympathy for Eldon and the Duke of Wellington, following their resignations in the spring of 1827 (courtesy of Professor J. H. Baker)

6 Detail of the memorial to Eldon, Lady Eldon and the Hon. John Scott, MP, by F. Chantrey, in the parish church of Kingston, Dorset (by kind permission of the rector of Kingston)

# TABLES

| 1.1 | John Scott's Northern Circuit fees, 1785–1788 | *page* 4 |
|---|---|---|
| 1.2 | John Scott's annual fees, London practice, 1785–1799 | 5 |
| 1.3 | Chancellor's fees, County Palatine of Durham, 1787–1799 | 6 |
| 1.4 | Attorney General's annual fees, 1793–1799 | 7 |
| 1.5 | John Scott's total annual earnings, 1793–1799 | 8 |
| 3.1 | John Scott's government legal opinions, 1788–1799 | 44 |
| 11.1 | Early-nineteenth-century legal patronage of the Lord Chancellor | 191 |
| 11.2 | Early-nineteenth-century ecclesiastical patronage of the Crown and Lord Chancellor | 192 |
| 11.3 | Changes in legal and judicial appointments, 1818–1819 | 201 |
| 11.4 | Chancery offices in the gift of the Lord Chancellor in the early nineteenth century | 211 |
| 11.5 | Church of England patronage in the early nineteenth century | 211 |
| 16.1 | Chancery business, 1745–1755 and 1800–1810 | 311 |

# PREFACE

I was introduced to John Scott, Lord Eldon, a decade ago in Professor Emmet Larkin's Modern British History seminar at the University of Chicago. Since then I have regularly been asked to explain my focus upon him. As my recent work has developed out of a doctoral dissertation, I have tended to reply with the reasons that founded my original study. First, I preferred to concentrate on a person rather than a trend or general phenomenon. Secondly, I was interested in the late eighteenth and/or early nineteenth century. Thirdly, I wanted to study a person whose work linked the worlds of law and politics. Fourthly, I hoped to find a suitable subject whose life had not been both recently and ably studied. Fifthly, my subject must have produced and prompted a reasonable cache of accessible materials. The combination of these factors produced Lord Eldon, although I must admit to an early indecision involving his brother, Lord Stowell, happily resolved by the appearance of Henry Bourguignon's book in 1987.

While inevitably the task of research tends to focus one's mind on the more prosaic of the above criteria, the first has imposed the most significant limitations upon my study of Eldon. Disraeli described biography as 'life without theory', and while I think it is both difficult and undesirable to aspire to the complete exclusion of theory, I have attempted to concentrate on Eldon rather than larger legal or political themes. As a result, I do not deal with Eldon's professional work as Lord Chancellor, with the exception of considering how this work led to complaints about the conduct of business in Chancery and the House of Lords. I base this omission on the belief that, while his judicial career was important to Eldon's life, it would not sit comfortably in a representation of his life. Since it has never been my aim to use Eldon to illustrate the development of particular doctrines or practices in the court of

Chancery, any discussion of the court would have had to be justified as a means of enriching my presentation of *him*. Such are the complexities of the doctrines of equity and Chancery practice, however, that they would have required substantial explanation before their significance to Eldon could have been made out. The inevitable hiatus in Eldon's story occasioned by that explanation was not, in my opinion, justified.

This does not mean, however, that I am not interested in the professional dimension of Eldon's public life. In some phases, and in certain aspects of his work, I found it possible to discuss explicitly professional activities – for example, in his legal opinions, criminal prosecutions, and during his tenure in the court of Common Pleas. In each context, however, my decision was based on the relationship between the technical demands of the material, and the likely illumination of Eldon's character. In particular, the demands of this exercise focused my work, albeit not exclusively, upon the constitutional aspects of Eldon's legal career. By 'constitutional' I mean the opportunities he had as a lawyer to affect the working of the state: as a draughtsman, prosecutor, royal adviser, and parliamentary leader.

To the extent that I have used Eldon to illustrate a particular theme, it is the nature of the British constitution during the period *c.*1790–1830. Eldon is, I believe, uniquely suited to this purpose, on account of the length of his official career, and the range of responsibilities that devolved upon him as a consequence of his ability and temperament. Such a purpose, however, ranks a distinct second to the primary purpose of my study. Primarily I am interested in Eldon the individual long important in public life, and not as the illustration of some aspect of public life. I see this as an inevitable consequence of Eldon's own historiography. Horace Twiss' biography, written under the eye of Eldon's grandson, was published in 1844. Surtees and Townsend produced shorter pieces in 1846, and Lord Campbell included Eldon in his *Lives of the Lord Chancellors* in 1847. The picture that emerges from these texts is balanced only in the sense that extremes of virtue and vice create an overall moderation. Scholars have tended to ignore Campbell, and to rely on Twiss particularly as a compendium of Eldon's personal correspondence. With little else upon which to base Eldon's character, he has become relegated to generalisation, if not caricature. He personifies High

Toryism; he is 'Old Bags', George IV's henchman; he grinds down the litigants in the interminable *Jarndyce* v. *Jarndyce*. Undoubtedly, Eldon is an important political and constitutional figure in the first decades of the nineteenth century. His career spanned the ministries of the Younger Pitt and Lord Liverpool. He played important roles during the illnesses of George III, and the divorce of George IV, and his name is inextricably linked with the repeal of the Test and Corporation Acts and Catholic Emancipation. He held the office of Lord Chancellor longer than any man in history. His significance cannot be assessed, however, until his work and achievements are addressed in their own terms, and not simply as incidental illustrations of a larger study. I hope that the following goes some way to address that need.

I owe a significant debt of thanks to several people, who have helped me produce this book. Because it grew out of my Cambridge PhD thesis, I would first like to thank my supervisors, Professor G. H. Jones and Dr A. J. B. Hilton, for their advice, support, and encouragement. More recently I have also benefited from discussions with and comments from Dr Hilton, Professor A. W. B. Simpson, Professor J. H. Baker, and Dr M. E. C. Perrott. I would also like to thank the following for their support and friendship: Dr J. W. F. Allison, Dr J. D. Ford, Mr M. Kitson, Mr F. D. Robinson, and Dr W. D. Sutcliffe.

For their help in providing access to manuscripts, and for kind permission to quote from and cite relevant materials I wish to thank the following: the Archbishop of Canterbury and the Trustees of the Lambeth Palace Library; the Archifdy Meirion Archives (Gwynned); the Bedfordshire and Luton Archives; the Beineke Rare Book and Manuscript Library (Yale University); the British Library; Cambridge University Library; Marquess Camden; the Centre for Kentish Studies; the William L. Clements Library (University of Michigan); the Controller of Her Majesty's Stationery Office; the Cumbria Record Office (Carlisle); the Devon Record Office; the Dorset Record Office; the Gloucestershire Record Office; the Earl of Harewood; the Hartley Library, (Southampton University); the Inner Temple; the Earl of Lonsdale; the Masters of the Bench of the Honourable Society of the Middle Temple; the Trustees of the National Library of Scotland; the Newcastle-upon-Tyne City Library; the Northumberland Record Office; the Free Library of Philadelphia; the Public

Record Office; the Rare Book, Manuscript, and Special Collections Library, Duke University; Lord Redesdale; Lord Ridley; the late Colonel H. E. Scott and Mr David Scott; the Scottish Record Office; Lord Sidmouth; the East Sussex Record Office; Mr S. C. Whitbread; and the Warden and Fellows of Winchester College.

My greatest thanks, however, goes to my husband, Quentin, on whose help, support, and encouragement I have consistently relied. Moreover, he has never known me without Lord Eldon, yet has behaved magnanimously toward his venerable rival.

# ABBREVIATIONS

| | |
|---|---|
| AMA | Archifdy Meirion Archives (Gwynedd) |
| BL | British Library |
| BLA | Bedfordshire and Luton Archives |
| CRO | Cumbria Record Office (Carlisle) |
| CUL | Cambridge University Library |
| DevRO | Devon Record Office |
| DorRO | Dorset Record Office |
| ER | *English Reports* |
| GRO | Gloucester Record Office |
| LCS | London Corresponding Society |
| LDA | Leeds District Archives |
| NCL | Newcastle-upon-Tyne City Library |
| NLS | National Library of Scotland |
| PRO | Public Record Office |
| SCI | Society for Constitutional Information |
| SRO | Scottish Record Office |
| SUL | Southampton University Library |

# A MAN OF LAWS

John Scott was born on 4 June 1751 in Newcastle-upon-Tyne, the youngest of the six surviving children of William Scott and his second wife, Jane. William Scott enjoyed a prosperous career as a 'hostman' or coal factor, and at his death in 1776 was the owner of several coal barges and a public house. John began his education at the Newcastle Free Grammar school and then proceeded to Oxford University. He had been intended for the family business, but his brother William,[1] then a tutor at University College, intervened on his behalf with their father.[2] Accordingly, John matriculated at Oxford University and entered University College on 15 May 1766, shortly before his fifteenth birthday. The following year he was awarded a college fellowship. He received his Bachelor of Arts degree in February 1770 and his Master of Arts degree three years later. While not known as a particularly brilliant scholar at Oxford, he did win the Chancellor's prize in English in 1771 for an essay entitled, 'On the Advantages and Disadvantages of Travel in Foreign Countries'.

Scott had almost completed his MA and was intending to pursue a career in the Church when he took the precipitous step of eloping with Elizabeth Surtees on 18 November 1772. Whatever its attractions for the young couple, the marriage was not immediately popular with either family. In particular Aubone Surtees, a

---

[1] William Scott (1745–1836) had a similarly distinguished career. An MP from 1790–1820, he also had important legal and judicial appointments. He held the posts of Advocate General (1782–8) and King's Advocate (1788–98), and served as Register of the Court of Faculties (1783–90), judge of the Consistory Court of London (1788–1820), and judge of the High Court of Admiralty (1798–1828). He is most famous for his admiralty decisions, and he is regarded, *inter alia*, as having established the modern law of prize.

[2] H. Twiss, *The public and private life of Lord Chancellor Eldon*, 2nd edn, 3 vols. (London, 1844), I:48.

wealthy Newcastle banker, had greater aspirations for his daughter than that she become the wife of a curate.[3] Both fathers did, however, establish trusts for their children in the amount of £3,000, which provided them with a degree of immediate financial security.[4] Unfortunately, Scott's long-term prospects were rendered more precarious by marriage, because it disqualified him for his fellowship. Although entitled to a one-year grace period, during which he could accept any college living that fell vacant, he lacked any other connection to whom he might turn if without a place at the end of that time. With the knowledge of that possibility Scott decided, in January 1773, to enrol as a student at the Middle Temple and study for the bar.

His first task, once he had settled on a legal career, was to qualify himself for it. Inspired by his new responsibilities, Scott devoted himself to his studies. In August 1773 he described himself to his cousin, Henry Reay, as one 'whose every hour is dedicated to learned dullness, who plods with haggard brow o'er the black-lettered page from morning to evening, and who finds his temper grow crabbed as he finds points more knotty'.[5] The following year he secured employment as deputy to Sir Robert Chambers, then Vinerian Professor of Common Law. Chambers had just been appointed Chief Justice of Bengal, and Scott was hired to deliver his lectures. For this he received £60, and was entitled to take up Chambers' residence at New Inn Hall. Financial worries returned in 1775, however, when Scott moved his wife and infant son to London.[6] It was common for law students to undertake pupillages of one to three years in order to learn such practical skills as conveying property, legal draughtsmanship, and the process of litigation. The price commanded by eminent practitioners could approach £100 guineas

---

[3] *Ibid.*, I:78; 'John Scott, Earl of Eldon', *Oxford University Record* (1951–52), 16–25, 19.

[4] William Scott senior established a trust in favour of his son and daughter-in-law in the amount of £2,000. Aubone Surtees further agreed to give them £1,000. Abstract of marriage settlement of John Scott and Elizabeth Surtees, 7 January 1773, Encombe (Scott papers). The principal of the Scott trust appears to have been paid out on 17 August 1781. At that time Aubone Surtees settled a further £1,000 on John and Elizabeth Scott, although he had not yet paid out the original £1,000. He had paid interest at 5 per cent.

[5] John Scott to Henry Reay, 20 August 1773, NCL (Scott papers). See also *The Legal Observer* 1 (1831), 193.

[6] On John Scott (1774–1805), see chapter 8.

per year.[7] Scott was fortunate in making the acquaintance of Matthew Duane, a well-respected conveyancer. Duane took on the impoverished Scott for six months without charge, an act of kindness which the beneficiary described to his brother Henry as having 'taken a great load of uneasiness off my mind, as in fact our profession is so exceedingly expensive, that I almost sink under it'.[8]

Scott was called to the bar in February 1776. His legal career during the next ten years consisted of circuit, parliamentary, and London practice. His progress in the first was not immediate. He attended the Northern Circuit, which included Northumberland, Cumberland, Westmoreland, and Lancashire. In a letter to Henry, William Scott wrote in October 1776: 'My brother Jack seems highly pleased with his circuit success. I hope it is only the beginning of future triumphs. All appearances speak strongly in his favour.'[9] On the other hand, Scott would later claim to have attended the Cumberland assizes for seven years before getting a brief, while the local newspapers rarely mention him in their accounts of the assizes – and then not prior to 1783.[10] Scott's fee books only contain records of his assize earnings for the period 1785–88, the last four years he attended the circuit.[11] By that time, however, he had become one of its leaders. The fees are set out in Table 1.1.

In the spring of 1777 Scott became embroiled in Newcastle politics, when he represented Andrew Robinson Bowes upon the latter's petition contesting his defeat in the recent parliamentary

---

[7] John Jeaffreson, *A book about lawyers*, 2 vols. (New York, 1867), II:195, 197.

[8] J. Scott to Henry Scott, 5 December 1775, Twiss, *The public and private life*, I:113.

[9] William Scott to H. Scott, 22 October 1766, W. E. Surtees, *A sketch of the lives of Lords Stowell and Eldon* (London, 1846), 32.

[10] Lord Eldon, J. Scott, *Lord Eldon's anecdote book*, ed. A. L. J. Lincoln and R. L. McEwen (London, 1960), 44; see, e.g., the *Cumberland Pacquet*, 2 September 1783, which contains one of the few references to Scott. In an undated letter written in January 1779 William thus confided to Henry Scott: 'Business is very dull with poor Jack, very dull indeed; and of consequence he is not very lively. I heartily wish that business may brisken a little, or he will be heartily sick of his profession. I do all I can to keep up his spirits, but he is very gloomy.' Twiss, *The public and private life*, I:113.

[11] These and all subsequent figures for Scott's earnings are compiled from his fee books, in the collection of Scott papers held by the Middle Temple Library, cited by kind permission of the Masters of the Bench of the Honourable Society of the Middle Temple.

Table 1.1. *John Scott's Northern Circuit fees, 1785–1788*

| Year | Spring | Summer | Total |
|------|--------|--------|-------|
| 1785 | £148.01.00 | £271.19.00 | £420.00.00 |
| 1786 | £181.13.00 | £322.07.00 | £504.00.00 |
| 1787 | £152.05.00 | £369.12.00[a] | £521.17.00 |
| 1788 | £187.19.00 | £372.05.00[b] | £560.04.00 |

[a] Newcastle £60.18.00; Carlisle £103.19.00; Appleby £11.11.00; Lancaster £193.04.00.
[b] Newcastle £59.07.00; Carlisle £114.09.00; Appleby £31.10.00; Lancaster £166.19.00.

by-election.[12] Nor was this petition Scott's sole experience as a parliamentary advocate. When Bowes was returned for Newcastle in 1780, Scott helped to defeat the petition filed against him. Friendship with Lloyd Kenyon gained Scott briefs in the Clitheroe election petition in March 1781, and in support of the Duke of Northumberland's claim to the office of Lord Great Chamberlain, argued before the House of Lords in May of that year. Together with Arthur Pigott, Scott represented Peter Perring, a member of the council at Fort St George, when he became the subject of parliamentary investigation in the summer of 1782. Perring and Sir Thomas Rumbold, the former governor of Madras, were accused of corruption and with having brought about the Mahratta war in 1780. The Commons proceeded against the pair by means of legislation. In the event, however, no evidence was taken against Perring, and he was dropped from the Bill in early 1783.[13]

In 1788 Scott, by then a leading member of the Chancery bar, asserted that 'practice began by some fortunate chance and then went on'.[14] Indeed his own London practice is said to have sprung from his successful efforts in *Ackroyd* v. *Smithson* in March 1780, a case concerning the devolution of property where circumstances

[12] T. R. Knox, ' "Bowes and liberty" ': the Newcastle by-election of 1777', *Durham University Journal* 77(2) (1985), 149–64, 149.
[13] See J. Phillips, 'Parliament and southern India, 1781–3: the secret committee of inquiry and the prosecution of Sir Thomas Rumbold', *Parliamentary History* 7(1) (1988), 81–98.
[14] I. S. Lustig and F. A. Pottle (ed.), *Boswell: the English experiment 1785–1789* (London, 1986), 219.

Table 1.2. *John Scott's annual
fees, London practice, 1785–1799*

| Year | Amount |
| --- | --- |
| 1785 | £5486.05.00 |
| 1786 | £6147.14.00 |
| 1787 | £6957.10.00 |
| 1788 | £7472.10.00 |
| 1789 | £9433.05.00 |
| 1790 | £9084.15.00 |
| 1791 | £9605.13.06 |
| 1792 | £8823.09.00 |
| 1793 | £6890.07.04 |
| 1794 | £8138.08.00 |
| 1795 | £6985.00.00 |
| 1796 | £7031.16.08 |
| 1797 | £6739.00.10 |
| 1798 | £6373.07.00 |
| 1799[a] | £2287.00.05 |

[a] January to April fees only.

had frustrated the wishes of the testator.[15] Scott argued the case
on appeal, and convinced Lord Chancellor Thurlow to reverse the
decision of the trial judge and to alter his own first impression of
the matter. A commentator has noted: 'This most able argument
confirmed the increasing reputation of Mr Scott, which quickly
led him, under the well-merited high estimation of Lord Thurlow
and his contemporaries, through successive honours.'[16] The first
of these occurred on 4 June 1783, when Scott received a patent of
precedence, a rank equivalent to that of King's Counsel.[17] Thereafter his London practice continued to expand, as his fee books
indicate (the diminution of fees from 1793 probably reflects the
pressure of his workload as a law officer). His annual fees are set
out in Table 1.2.

Shortly after he gained his patent of precedence Scott entered

[15] 1 *Brown's Chancery Reports* 503–15, 28 *English Reports* 1262–9.
[16] 1 *Brown's Chancery Reports* 514, 28 *English Reports* 1269.
[17] A patent of precedence could be regarded as more desirable. A King's Counsel
could not appear against the Crown without a licence to do so, and as the office
of King's Counsel was paid, appointment vacated a seat in Parliament. A patent
of precedence conferred equivalent rank without these disabilities. W. S. Holdsworth, *A history of English law*, 17 vols. (London, 1903–72), VI:476.

Table 1.3. *Chancellor's fees, County Palatine of Durham,*
*1787–1799*

| Year | Spring | Summer | Total |
|------|--------|--------|-------|
| 1787[a] | – | £121.00.00 | £121.00.00 |
| 1788 | £117.00.00 | £130.00.00 | £247.00.00 |
| 1789[a] | £126.05.00 | – | £126.05.00 |
| 1790 | £138.00.00 | £112.00.00 | £250.00.00 |
| 1791 | £117.00.00 | £137.00.00 | £254.00.00 |
| 1792 | £142.00.00 | £115.00.00 | £257.00.00 |
| 1793 | £120.00.00 | £130.00.00 | £250.00.00 |
| 1794[a] | £139.00.00 | – | £139.00.00 |
| 1795 | £160.00.00 | £126.00.00 | £286.00.00 |
| 1796 | £140.00.00 | £114.00.00 | £254.00.00 |
| 1797[a] | £132.00.00 | – | £132.00.00 |
| 1798[a] | – | £156.00.00 | £156.00.00 |
| 1799[a] | £90.00.00 | – | £90.00.00 |

[a] Indicates a single sitting.

Parliament, thanks to the good offices of the Lord Chancellor, and in March 1787 Thurlow's brother, the bishop of Durham, named Scott chancellor for the county palatine. Scott held that post for twelve years, resigning in July 1799. He generally visited Durham twice a year, usually in April and August. His main purpose was to hold sittings of his court, which operated for the county as the High Court of Chancery operated for the nation. In addition to his sittings he undertook administrative duties, including witnessing documents, especially patents of appointment, signing warrants issued *per curiam* during the assizes, and authorising commissions to take affidavits for cases in his own court.[18] The fees of approximately £125 for each sitting of his court constituted Scott's remuneration for his efforts. The fees are set out in Table 1.3.

Scott was a back-bench member of Parliament for five years before being appointed Solicitor General and knighted in June 1788.[19] In February 1793 he was appointed Attorney General, an office which he held until July 1799, when he resigned to

---

[18]  PRO, DURH.3 (131), (132); DURH.3 (198). Scott also acted as a general legal adviser to the bishop. For his correspondence with Thurlow's successor, Shute Barington, see Northumberland Record Office, 384/16–23.

[19]  During his first thirteen years in Parliament, Scott represented Weobley in Herefordshire. In May 1796 he was returned for Boroughbridge, Yorkshire, and continued to represent that constituency until July 1799. See chapter 2.

Table 1.4. *Attorney General's annual fees, 1793–1799*

| Year | Amount |
|------|--------|
| 1793 | £2847.04.00 |
| 1794 | £3314.12.00 |
| 1795 | £3878.16.05 |
| 1796 | £4854.19.00 |
| 1797 | £3990.04.08 |
| 1798 | £4028.10.00 |
| 1799[a] | £1394.10.07 |

[a] Earnings for January–April only.

become Chief Justice of the court of Common Pleas. At the same time he was elevated to the peerage as Baron Eldon. His tenure in the Common Pleas was brief, for in April 1801 he became Lord Chancellor in the government formed upon the resignation of William Pitt. He remained in office when Pitt returned in 1804, but resigned upon Pitt's death in January 1806. He resumed the Great Seal in 1807. This second Chancellorship lasted twenty years, and spanned the governments of the Duke of Portland, Spencer Perceval, and the Earl of Liverpool. In 1821 George IV conferred upon his 'dear friend' the titles of Earl of Eldon and Viscount Encombe, the latter referring to an estate in Dorset purchased in 1807. The cabinet split occasioned by the advancement of George Canning also brought about the Chancellor's resignation in the spring of 1827. Thereafter he remained a semi-active member of the House of Lords almost to the time of his death, on 13 January 1838. Out of office, he was particularly inspired by the great issues of religious and electoral reform.

Throughout this public phase of his professional career Scott's income continued to grow. His fee books record the fees he collected for his work as Attorney General, and are shown in Table 1.4. These, together with his various private fees from the same period, comprise his total earnings through the spring of 1799. Table 1.5 shows his total earnings.

Even taking into account the likely diminution of his private practice after he became a law officer in 1788, Scott's earnings compare favourably with those of some of the leading barristers of

Table 1.5. *John Scott's total annual earnings, 1793–1799*

| Year | Amount |
|------|--------|
| 1793 | £9987.11.04 |
| 1794 | £11592.00.00 |
| 1795 | £11151.16.05 |
| 1796 | £12140.15.08 |
| 1797 | £10261.05.06 |
| 1798 | £10557.17.00 |
| 1799[a] | £3771.11.00 |

[a] Earnings for January–April only.

the period.[20] In taking up the judicial post in the Common Pleas, he did suffer a substantial loss in income, as an annual salary of £3,500, together with patronage worth approximately £1,100, certainly did not compensate for the loss of fees.[21] His tenure as Lord Chancellor was far more lucrative. In addition to an annual salary of £5,000, he received fees and perquisites that probably placed his annual income at £15–20,000.[22] To provide some context for these figures, Massie estimated in 1759 that seventy families earned annual incomes of £8,000 or greater. Colquhoun's income table, based on the census returns of 1801 and the pauper returns of 1803, is topped by the 287 families comprising the temporal peerage, whose average income was £8,000. In contrast, persons engaged in the law, including judges, barristers, solicitors, clerks, and others, on average earned annual incomes of £100 in 1759 and £350 in 1800.[23]

This impressive record of professional achievement owed a great deal to Scott's undoubted mental capacity. Whatever the

[20] D. Duman, *The judicial bench in England 1727–1785: the reshaping of a professional elite* (London, 1982), 106.

[21] *Ibid.*, 114, 120.

[22] Scott's patent, dated 18 April 1801, describes the various fees and grants to which he was entitled as Lord Chancellor and Speaker of the House of Lords. Encombe (Scott papers). For a discussion of Scott's fee income as Lord Chancellor, see chapter 16. In addition to his salary and emoluments, the Lord Chancellor controlled a vast legal and ecclesiastical patronage. On the latter, see chapter 11.

[23] R. Porter, *English society in the eighteenth century* (London, 1982), 386, 388. At his death Eldon left an estate sworn at less than £700,000, which included his properties in Dorset and Durham. *The Legal Observer* 15 (1838), 311.

caveats regarding procrastination which dogged his work in later life, contemporaries consistently praised the intellectual ability he brought first to the bar and then to the bench. Of Sir John Scott, the law officer and barrister, it was said:

He branches forth his arguments into different heads and divisions; and pursues the respective parts through all their various ramifications, with such methodical accuracy, that arguments rise out of argument, and conclusion from conclusion, in the most regular and natural progression; so that those who are not acquainted with his practice, would suspect he had studied and prepared his speeches with the most diligent attention; while others, who are better acquainted with the business of the courts, feel their admiration and surprise increased, from the knowledge that a man of his extensive business, so far from studying what he shall say, can scarce find time to glance his eye over the numerous papers that come before him.[24]

This ability also enabled him to respond forcefully to an opposing position. 'His systematic mind seems to methodize with inconceivable rapidity, the arguments of his opponents. In the short space of time between the pleadings of his adversary, and his reply, every thing seems digested and disposed, and his mode of replication seems planned in the nicest order.'[25] Lord Abinger recalled that, as Chief Justice of Common Pleas, Scott 'investigated every case to the bottom, considered every argument advanced by counsel, and every other topic besides, that the cause suggested'.[26] James Boswell and Sir Samuel Romilly offered similar assessments of Scott as Lord Chancellor. Boswell was reported as describing him as 'superior in legal knowledge to any other person in the Court of Chancery, & the greatest Lawyer that has sat in that Court since Lord Hardwicke presided in it'.[27] Romilly, a severe critic, acknowledged that 'in point of learning in every part of the profession, and in talents, he [Scott] had hardly been surpassed by any of his predecessors'.[28]

Scott's intellectual abilities did not extend naturally either to a love of or a marked proficiency in public oratory. His forensic skills at the bar were described as being 'of that subtle, correct,

---

[24] E. Wynne, *Strictures on the lives and characters of the most eminent lawyers of the present day* (Dublin, 1790), 203–4.

[25] Ibid., 204–5.

[26] P. C. Scarlett, *A memoir of the right honourable James, first Lord Abinger* (London, 1877), 89.

[27] J. Farington, *The Farington diary*, ed. James Greig, 8 vols. (London, 1924), VIII:239.

[28] Sir S. Romilly, *Memoirs of Sir Samuel Romilly*, 3 vols. (London, 1840), II:369.

and deliberate kind, that has more the appearance of written than of oral eloquence'.[29] Far from evidencing a natural affinity for oral argument, Scott's shyness in this regard had the effect that, in the first few years following his call, 'he shunned, as much as possible, appearing even at the Chancery bar as a pleader' but rather confined himself to drafting documents.[30] His 'crimson timidity was so confirmed, that he seemed even to shun the brilliant allurement of profit, when it could only be acquired through the medium of public pleading', and he only overcame his lack of 'impudence' through an act of will.[31] Lord Abinger's assessment of the mature speaker was similarly temperate. 'As a speaker he was elaborate and ingenious, and possessed a turn for grave humour that sometimes relieved his tedious discourses.'[32] The early tendency to nerves, moreover, remained. On the occasion of his taking his seat as an earl, the attention paid him by fellow peers made Scott 'nervous and somewhat agitated'.[33] He admitted before a speech to the annual goldsmiths' dinner in 1822: 'I am always a little nervous before I make this sort of address, and ... though I could talk before a parliament with as much indifference as if they were all cabbage plants, a new audience has ever borne an appalling appearance.'[34]

The generally sensitive nature of Scott's temperament was manifest in other, sometimes contradictory ways. He was possessed both of a light-hearted, teasing nature, and a tendency to gloomy, self-indulgent introspection. On the one hand, he enjoyed making light of his troubles, and on those occasions when he suffered illness or infirmity, he tended to explain them away with a self-deprecating joke. Having mentioned attacks of 'giddiness and swimming in my head' to his brother Henry, Scott went on to describe himself as carrying on with 'what little business I can do with blisters on the outside of me and enormous quantities of medicine in the inside'.[35] On another occasion he suffered marked

[29] Wynne, *Strictures*, 203.      [30] Ibid., 201.

[31] J. Williams, *Satires and biography* (London, 1795), 62.

[32] Scarlett, *A memoir*, 89.

[33] Eldon to Lady Frances Bankes, 10 July 1821, Twiss, *The public and private life*, II:426.

[34] Eldon to Bankes, 27 April 1822, *ibid.*, 448.

[35] J. Scott to H. Scott, 2 February 1781, Surtees, *A Sketch*, 78. Attacks of giddiness, accompanied by dimness of vision, continued to plague Scott in later life. See, e.g., Eldon to Richard Richards, 3 September 1817, AMA Caerynwych

shortness of breath, but upon his restoration of health opined to his brother William: 'I hope, with care, to be yet able to make long speeches, if not good ones, a faculty which I was in danger of losing.'[36] Recovering from a fall from a horse, Scott expected 'to be well enough in a very few days, to be able if a fit and decorous opportunity offered, to trip it on the light fantastic tac'.[37] The gout provided frequent opportunities for rueful humour. As early as 1790 he lamented to Henry:

How hard it is upon me that I, the youngest, and most temperate and abstemious of the three, should, the first of all the brothers, arrive to this dignity! I hope most heartily you may escape; because, between the pain felt and the pain of being laughed at, the complaint is quite intolerable.[38]

After more than twenty years of the affliction, the sufferer could still write as a postscript to a friend: 'I had almost forgot your lameness and to mention my gout. My foot presents its compliments to your leg, and borrowing the idea from a celebrated author, hopes you improve there when I do in understanding.'[39] On the other hand, he readily admitted to gloom and lowness of spirits, often vividly expressed. The press of work and its attendant responsibilities could make him 'deplorably hysterical'.[40] During his years as Lord Chancellor, the combination of physical exhaustion and suspicion could prove particularly debilitating. He frequently considered himself undervalued by his political allies, and misrepresented by his political opponents. When corresponding with old friends, Scott could become not merely nostalgic, but extremely morose. Writing to boyhood friend Samuel Swire more than twenty years before retiring from public office, he expressed the hope that:

I may yet spend some happy day under your roof, secluded for awhile from a selfish, ambitious, interested, luxurious world, that hath not an

(Richards) papers, Z/DA/64 SA21; Eldon to Stowell, undated [*c*. September 1823], Twiss, *The public and private life*, II:484; Eldon to Robert Peel, 7 September 1823, BL (Peel papers), Add. MS 40315 f. 91.

[36] J. Scott to W. Scott, undated, Encombe (Scott papers).
[37] Eldon to Miss Mary Farrer, undated, *ibid.*
[38] J. Scott to H. Scott, undated [*c*. December 1790], Twiss, *The public and private life*, I:205.
[39] Eldon to William Bond, undated [*c*. 1827], DorRO (Bond of Tyneham papers), D. 1141:1/14.
[40] Eldon to Lord Redesdale, 9 June 1804, GRO (Mitford papers), D2002/1/23. See also Eldon to Redesdale, undated [early 1806], *ibid.*

idea of the comforts of a college commons, or the repast of a parsonage dinner, when the landlord and his host meet, with the same ideas upon all things, unaffected by the changes and chances of life, which governed them both in the same staircase in college.[41]

To long-time friend and colleague John Mitford he confessed that a letter describing his 'miseries' was interrupted by tears.[42] Indeed, Scott's public display of emotion in Parliament and in the courtroom became a topic for hostile political cartoons.[43] The poet Shelley made it the focus of his portrait of the Chancellor in *The Mask of Anarchy*:

> Next came Fraud, and he had on,
> Like Eldon, an ermined gown;
> His big tears, for he wept well,
> Turned to mill-stones as they fell.

In the same way, Scott's relations with others were characterised both by a genial manner and strict standards of conduct. His early correspondence with his cousin Reay, for example, is marked by jokes, puns, and small witticisms. In September 1771 he gave the following account of a visit to Cambridge.

Flow on! my beloved Isis, I will not pollute thy crystal wave, by drawing a comparison between it & the muddy, stagnate waters of thy sister Cam. Lift up your heads ye obnoxious piles! & shame those things called buildings at Cambridge! ... The public buildings, their senate & library are shabby beyond his conception, who has seen a Theatre, a Bodleian, Radclivian, Christchurch, or All Souls Library ... Trinity College it is true is a noble one, yet tho the quadrangle is certainly larger than that at Christchurch, if you compare their libraries & halls, Oxford outshines them even here. The celebrated King's College Chapel is a gothic structure, stupendous & magnificent as to the stone work, perhaps so beyond all description. Yet this venerable edifice ... is fitted up with stalls so exceedingly shabby, that it has more the appearance of a stable than a place of worship. In short, may I be a stewed prune if ever I march thro' Cambridge again. I should not forget to tell you, that their various coloured gowns are infinitely less pleasing than our black ones. I did not see a single academic who looked like a gentleman.[44]

---

[41] Eldon to Samuel Swire, 10 July 1805, Twiss, *The public and private life*, I:495–6.

[42] Eldon to Redesdale, 9 June 1804, GRO (Mitford papers), D2002/1/23.

[43] See, e.g., the depiction of Scott in William Hone's pamphlet, 'The political showman – at home!' in *Radical squibs and loyal ripostes*, ed. E. Rickword (Bath, 1971), 276.

[44] J. Scott to Reay, 2 September 1771, Encombe (Scott Papers). Scott prefaced his commentary with the observation: 'with all my Oxford prejudices about me, you

While his mature epistolary style lost some of this exuberance, his private letters retained a gentle humour. Describing to his brother-in-law the King's review of various volunteer corps, Scott wrote,

As a non-effective in an awkward squadron, I had the modesty not to show myself in arms, though I have military character enough to attend the drill occasionally in a more private scene. Your friend Major Sir W. Scott's corps, not having been bold enough to attempt the strong measure of firing, were also absent.[45]

A letter to his daughter describing the marriage of Princess Mary concluded, 'Even the tears trickled down *my* cheeks; and, as to Mamma, she cried all night, and nine-tenths parts of the next day, so that, do you see, your wedding is a mighty merry affair.'[46]

With ladies, whether old or young, Scott indulged in the language of light-hearted flirtation, increasingly when his own years took away any hint of improper gallantry. Recalling a meeting with two young cousins, he wrote to one of them: 'I hope you have all been well, since I had the sweet little conversation with you on the King's highway. I think his Majesty would have given me his gracious pardon, if I had robbed Mrs Farrer of both of you.'[47] Shortly before the marriage of his son to Miss Henrietta Ridley, he wrote to Lady Ridley:

A thousand thanks to you for your postscript which brings me *Miss R's best love:* were I again but just arrived at the years of discretion ... I am tempted to think that I might use her so ill as to tell her that, if she pleased, we would struggle together through five-and-twenty such years as I have gone through: – which assure her, I would not do to attain any earthly object, short of the comfort of convincing a person, whom I much

will not perhaps give my remarks all that credit which might be claimed by an uninterested observer.' See also Scott's letters to Reay written in the summer and autumn of 1771, Encombe (Scott papers), and in late 1772 and spring 1773, NCL (Scott papers).

45 J. Scott to Matthew Surtees, 6 June 1799, Encombe (Scott papers).
46 Eldon to Miss Frances Jane Scott, 25 July 1816, Twiss, *The public and private life*, II:284.
47 Eldon to Miss Frances Farrer, undated [*c.* 1804], Encombe (Scott papers). See also Eldon's undated letter to Mary Farrer, in which he claimed the privilege of addressing her as 'dear'. '[I]t is a privilege, which we, who sustain grave characters, have to be allowed to express ourselves to young ladies, in the language which our affections dictate, without being supposed to trespass beyond the bounds of propriety.' Encombe (Scott papers).

loved, that, if I prevailed upon her to act very foolishly for my sake, there was nothing which I would not endure for hers.[48]

He once composed a poem on the occasion of observing a friend's daughters playing on a swing and noting their display of ankle.

> In days of yore, as Roman poets tell,
> *One* Venus lov'd in myrtle groves to dwell:
> In modern days no less than *four* agree
> To consecrate to fame our oaken tree –
> Blest Tree! The monarch shelter'd by thy arms!
> The goddess from thy boughs displays her charms.[49]

As an old man he ruefully described a dinner party to his daughter: 'My seat was between Lady L[ondonderry] and the marchioness of Hertford. There was a great demand upon me for small talk, but I don't think I flirted with my usual success.'[50] Nor was Scott's 'small talk' reserved solely for the amusement of ladies. He was a great teller of jokes and droll stories, particularly detailing incidents from his professional life. With these he might enliven a dinner party or a less convivial occasion. Charles Greville recalled 'the many tedious hours the Prince Regent kept the Lords of the Council waiting at Carlton House, that the Chancellor used to beguile the time with amusing stories ... which he told extremely well'.[51] In later life Scott made a compilation of these stories for the amusement of his grandson entitled, *Lord Eldon's Anecdote book*. More than one contemporary remarked upon Scott's kindliness upon the bench. In an era when Chancellors like Thurlow were remarkable for their gruff, surly manners, the bar regarded Scott with considerable affection.[52]

Despite this playful, flirtatious, courteous side, however, Scott had a strong sense of propriety, as well as precise notions of entitlement. Taken together, these demanded that he refrain from

---

[48] Eldon to Lady Ridley, undated [*c.* summer 1804], Twiss, *The public and private life*, I:465.

[49] Surtees, *A Sketch*, 172.

[50] Eldon to Bankes, undated [*c.* spring 1825], Twiss, *The public and private life*, II:547.

[51] P. W. Wilson (ed.), *The Greville diary*, 2 vols. (London, 1927), I:182.

[52] See, e.g., the observations in *ibid.*, I:183; Scarlett, *A memoir*, 90; Romilly, *Memoirs*, II:369, and H. Brougham, Baron Brougham and Vaux, *Sketches of statesmen of the time of George III*, 3 vols. (London, 1855), I:186. For Eldon's delight in punning while on the bench, see J. Grant, *The bench and the bar*, 2 vols. (London, 1837), II:294–9.

thrusting, or giving the appearance of thrusting, himself forward, but once advanced to stand firm upon all rights and privileges associated therewith. Early in his career he declined to accept the offered patent of precedence until his seniority over Thomas Erskine and Pigott was recognised. Both Scott's juniors at the bar, they actually had received their patents prior to his decision to accept. Called before the Lords Commissioners of the Great Seal, Scott maintained: 'what I had understood to have been handsomely, and voluntarily, and without request offered, should either be handsomely conferred, or should not be accepted.'[53] The validity of his claim was acknowledged, albeit grudgingly, and after 'some noise' Scott received a patent that maintained his proper seniority. In 1809 his name was put forward as a candidate for the Chancellorship of the University of Oxford in opposition to Lord Grenville. Following confusion between the government and the Court, the Duke of Beaufort was also proposed, but Eldon declined to withdraw. Acknowledging that the presence of both himself and Beaufort would perhaps fatally divide their supporters, Eldon maintained that, having agreed to stand, he could not give way to a later entrant.[54] In the same way, when he was created an earl, he felt obliged to submit to the College of Heralds the question whether his grandson, as heir presumptive, was entitled to a courtesy title. He took this step despite the fact that he does not seem to have delighted much in the affirmative answer he received.[55]

Scott's attitude toward rank was ambivalent. There is little doubt that he took a certain delight in his elevation to the peerage in 1799, evident in the expressions of gratitude to family and friends and in the conferences with his brother upon a suitable motto and title. Moreover, once his protests against an earldom were overcome, his pleasure crept out. To his daughter he confided: 'I must say, notwithstanding he would not let me off, the King was very gracious. He seals *my* patent first, with some special recital in it, which I have not yet seen.'[56] Despite his far from disdainful response to ennoblement, however, he scorned the

[53] Eldon, *Anecdote book*, 5.
[54] Lord Grenville was duly elected. See chapter 12.
[55] Eldon was concerned that receipt of a title might cause his grandson, then aged 16, to cherish an unduly exalted opinion of himself. See chapter 8.
[56] Eldon to Bankes, 7 July 1821, Twiss, *The public and private life*, II:421.

practice of merely cutting a figure in consequence. Professing a preference for titles progressively acquired over several generations rather than a series of dignities descending upon family members 'without efforts on their part to obtain them', he argued that:

if a Peer does not do credit to his titles, his titles will confer no credit upon him ... if it is a blessing to receive distinctions, which furnish the opportunities and means of doing public good, he is altogether inexcusable, who, possessing those distinctions, disgraces them and himself by neglecting to promote the interests of the public, by availing himself of such means and such opportunities ... [I]f rank engenders pride, if it produces haughtiness in conduct to those with whom we have associated and do associate, if it considers well-regulated condescension and kindness of manners as what needs not anxiously to be attended to, it becomes inexpressibly odious.[57]

While the above could be explained as the cautious advice of a grandfather, it does not differ significantly from the sentiments he had expressed as a younger man. When discussing the purchase of an estate with his cousin Reay, Scott scorned the idea of purchasing beyond one's means merely to acquire the status of a landowner.

Now as to you, my dear Sir, what is the object you propose to yourself by buying, which appears to you so valuable, as to induce you ... to take the chance in case of accident to you, of throwing all these works of time and labour upon your boy? Is it the merely having the estate? That can hardly be – what object then have you in taking upon you the character of a debtor for £40,000 in order that you may say you are the owner of this estate?[58]

He likewise declined to promote his son as MP for the county of Northumberland rather than 'a poor little beggarly township', when this was suggested to him. Pointing out that 'a man ought to have a certainly continuous income, very large indeed, who can have a son, in his lifetime, living as the member of a county', he concluded that 'I could do nothing so unjust' to his son 'as as to involve him in a program of certain, heavy expenditure to promote a very uncertain undertaking'.[59]

[57] Eldon to J. Scott, 4 October 1821, *ibid.*, 438.
[58] J. Scott to H. Reay, 2 January 1799, NCL (Scott Papers). Scott had acted with a comparable prudence in 1792 when he acquired Eldon, his estate in southern Durham, for £20,000. He paid the full amount at the time of purchase and so could immediately devote all his rents to improving the property. E. Foss, *Judges of England*, 9 vols. (London, 1864), IX:43.
[59] J. Scott to W. Scott, undated [*c.* September 1801] Encombe (Scott papers).

In the proper regulation of his conduct, Scott was guided by what he habitually described as his 'duty'. The source of this obligation to duty was Scott's Christian faith. Throughout his life his attitude toward the practice of organised religion was ambiguous. His identification with the struggle to maintain the political privileges of the Anglican Church, and the well-known tag that he was less a pillar than a buttress of the Church because he habitually supported it from the outside, suggests a less than enlightened spirituality. The reality was probably not so simple.[60] His own creed, if such a term can properly be applied to a loose pattern of belief and conduct, seems to have been based on the public expression of Christian obligation. All fortune was the consequence of Divine Providence. Where Providence ordained good fortune, therefore, such as the receipt of high office, the recipient ought to acknowledge it gratefully and undertake to perform any tasks attendant thereto as part of a sacred trust. On being raised to the peerage and appointed Chief Justice of Common Pleas, Scott wrote to his mother: 'I feel that under the blessing of Providence I owe this ... I hope God's grace will enable me to do my duty in the station to which I am called.'[61] When he became Lord Chancellor two years later he professed himself prepared 'for a conscientious and most anxious discharge of my duty', and ready to scorn any office 'not attained by such means as are consistent with the principles of honour, morality, and religion'.[62] Likewise, in the event of bad fortune, God's judgment must be endured. In a letter consoling his brother Henry on the death of his sister-in-law, Scott wrote: 'the event must be submitted to the providence of HIM who knows best what is expedient for us.'[63] He struggled to exhibit a similar

---

[60] Twiss, *The public and private life*, III:489. For a discussion of Eldon's attitude toward Catholic Emancipation and repeal of the Test and Corporation Acts, see chapter 17.

[61] J. Scott to Mrs W. Scott, 19 July 1799, Encombe (Scott papers). Commenting upon the frustration of the Cato Street conspiracy, which aimed at the assassination of the members of the Cabinet, Eldon wrote: 'as to the future, I trust ... that we may all fully depend upon that Providence to which we are so largely indebted.' Eldon to Mrs Farrer, undated (February 1820), Twiss, *The public and private life*, II:362.

[62] Eldon to Swire, 15 April 1801, Twiss, *The public and private life*, I:371.

[63] J. Scott to H. Scott, 22 December 1791, *ibid.*, 211. See also Eldon to the Revd Henry John Ridley (on the occasion of the death of Ridley's father), 15 October 1825, *ibid.*, pp. 560–1.

fortitude on the death of his own son. To his cousin Reay he affirmed:

I am plunged in despair and affliction, which I know not how to bear. But I must not open my mouth – God has done it, and his will be done. I can await his command for my own departure without uneasiness, as far as respects myself – but I had vainly hoped that he, that is gone, might have protected those I might leave behind me. Heaven has told me I ought to have looked elsewhere for their protection.[64]

After the first, bitter grief had faded, he attempted to find something of value in the loss he had suffered. Reflecting that he was then entering upon the twilight of life in which one's thoughts turned naturally to eternity, he asked: 'May it not be a blessing, that, at the beginning that period which I am to employ better, I am awakened to a sense of duty, by a judgment as awful as that which, in my loss, has been poured out upon me?'[65] Apart from such moments of extreme unhappiness, however, Scott believed that: 'A truly religious temper is a cheerful temper.'[66] Moreover, the servant of God ought to be executing his duties among his fellow men. 'We can never be justified in supposing that we are doing our duty to God, whilst we are neglecting, or incapacitating ourselves for, the discharge of our duties to our neighbours in this life.'[67] He disliked the gloomy introspection that he associated with Evangelicalism, and was quick to distance himself from anything that might be so described. While mentioning to his grandson the spiritual advantages to be gained by attending his college chapel, he hastened to add: 'don't suppose that I recommend or approve that morose, canting, fanatical temper.'[68] In the same way he concluded a letter setting forth his views on Unitarianism with the caveat: 'Though I write in this style, and have been very unwell ... and however grave you may think me, don't think me "a Saint": I mean a "modern Saint". The more I see of that character, the less I like it.'[69] For Scott the demand of the spiritual life rested not so much in inquiry, as in performance. Secure not only in his belief in Anglican doctrine, but in his belief that further analysis of that doctrine would not resolve its apparent

---

[64] Eldon to H. Reay, 12 January 1806, NCL (Scott papers).
[65] Eldon to Swire, undated [received 31 May 1806], Twiss, *The public and private life*, II:4–5.
[66] Eldon to Encombe, undated [received 11 May 1824], *ibid.*, 516.
[67] *Ibid.*      [68] *Ibid.*      [69] Eldon to Swire, 7 August 1808, *ibid.*, 64.

ambiguities, he did not feel the need to question or criticise his core beliefs. Rather, his duty lay in defending and submitting to what had been ordained, whatever the circumstances. This outlook conferred upon him a degree of moral confidence that transcended merely spiritual matters, and informed his public career.

## 2

## AN INDEPENDENT LEARNED GENTLEMAN

In his analysis of why men went into Parliament, Sir Lewis Namier has identified several different groups that together comprised the House of Commons in the late eighteenth century.[1] The manner in which each group functioned was a result of their particular interests. For example, squires or country gentlemen typically lacked political ambition beyond the honour of membership in the national legislature. Accordingly, they remained aloof from party or faction. In contrast, professional men regarded a seat in Parliament as a means of advancing their careers. Lawyers could aspire to any of the several legal appointments available to a government, from borough recorder to Lord Chancellor of England. In Namier's analysis these two groups had little in common – the one anxious to avoid party intrigue, and the other conscious that from a judicious political alliance could come great professional rewards. In fact, at least a *reputation* for independence, the supreme virtue among Namier's country gentlemen, undoubtedly held some attraction for the lawyers, towards whom a deep and well-established hostility existed in the House. In earlier times a habit of poor attendance, and of claiming preaudience in the courts as a parliamentary privilege, had led to several formal and informal attempts either to exclude them completely or to prevent them from practising in the courts while Parliament was in session.[2] In the late eighteenth century criticism tended to focus on two points, the employment of technical legal jargon to confound debate, and the eager pursuit of appointments. Consequently, the lawyer or 'learned gentleman' eager to succeed

---

[1] Sir L. Namier, *The structure of politics at the accession of George III*, 2nd edn (London, 1957), chap. 1, especially 4–7, 42–4.

[2] E. Porritt, *The unreformed House of Commons*, 2 vols. (Cambridge, 1909), I:512–17.

in the House had to defeat prejudices that could preclude a fair assessment of his abilities. A studied, if not a genuine, assertion of independence, so long as it did not leave him stranded on the back benches, could prove a valuable asset.

Such was the challenge facing Scott when he entered Parliament in the summer of 1783, and his record over the following five years indicates how he attempted to achieve a balance between isolation from, and subservience to, the political leaders of the day. His object does not appear to have been merely professional recognition. As early as March 1784 the King recognised Scott as 'the fittest man' for the office of Solicitor General, and his appointment remained a matter of speculation until it finally came to pass in June 1788.[3] During his years as a private member, however, Scott would have been aware of two important legal appointments having been made on the basis of personal friendship or political expediency, in the persons of Richard Pepper Arden and Archibald Macdonald. Arden had been made a law officer and brought into Parliament by his friend William Pitt, and Macdonald owed his appointment as Solicitor General to his marriage into an important political family.[4] Such advancement is unlikely to have appealed either to Scott's sense of propriety or to his own ambitions. Only proof of his merit both as lawyer and as parliamentarian would establish a correct and sufficient foundation for a public career at the highest level.

Scott came into Parliament through the intercession of a formidable lawyer-politician, Lord Chancellor Thurlow, who proposed Weobley, a Herefordshire borough controlled by Thomas Thynne, Lord Weymouth.[5] From the outset, Scott expressed

---

[3] George III to William Pitt, 28 March 1784, A. Aspinall, *The later correspondence of George III*, 5 vols. (Cambridge, 1962), I:46; on 10 February and 26 December 1786, and again on 28 April 1788, *The Times* reported that Scott had either been offered or would soon be appointed to the post either of Attorney General or Solicitor General.

[4] Nathaniel Wraxall wrote that 'no part of Pitt's ministerial machinery exposed him to comments so severe or to ridicule so pointed as the selection of Arden and Macdonald for the posts of Attorney and Solicitor General'. *Historical and posthumous memoirs*, ed. H. B. Wheatley, 5 vols. (London, 1884), IV:151.

[5] In Scott's day the Weobley electorate amounted to approximately 100 voters. During the first half of the eighteenth century the electoral interest had been divided and elections highly contested. Between 1750 and 1754, however, Lord Weymouth had secured the dominant interest, and thereafter Weobley became a pocket borough of his family. Sir L. Namier, and J. Brooke, (eds.), *The history of*

concern for his independence under Lord Weymouth's patronage. Weymouth had controlled Weobley since the middle of the century, and it had not recently returned any notable MPs. Scott did not, therefore, immediately accept when offered the seat in May 1783. Thurlow described the situation in a letter to Lloyd Kenyon:

I have offered Scott a seat in Parliament for Weobley. He hesitates. As I know his delicacy, I am apprehensive that he fancies it is likely to fetter him; you know my sentiments on that subject perfectly well. If he were embarged [sic] in any of these confederacies, by which knots of men propose to struggle in a body for places, &c., I do not think he would do well to take this, or, indeed, be at liberty to do so. On the other hand, it would be an impudent thing to propose such a circumstance as a place in parliament to a man of sense and honour, as the price of acting for another man's opinion against his own.[6]

Scott, however, was still new to appeals of this sort. Thurlow admitted to Kenyon: 'I could not enter into this sort of explanation with him, because it seemed to be indelicate even to suppose that there was any thing to be explained.'[7] Scott did overcome his 'delicacy', but it is an indication of his political naïveté that, although the seat was uncontested, he felt obliged to present himself to the voters in Weobley on election day and deliver a speech. He was perhaps chagrined when told by one of his audience that 'they had not heard from the hustings for 30 years'.[8] Moreover, despite his hopes, he did not escape identification with his patron. In a letter to his brother, the Earl of Upper Ossory, in November 1783, Richard Fitzpatrick described Scott simply as 'Lord Weymouth's lawyer'.[9]

---

Parliament: the House of Commons 1754–1790, 4 vols. (London, 1964), I:305. From May 1796 to July 1799 Scott sat for Boroughbridge, Yorkshire, a borough consisting of approximately 64 voters, the interest of which was divided between the Duke of Newcastle and the Wilkinson family. R. G. Thorne (ed.), *The history of Parliament: the House of Commons 1790 – 1820*, 5 vols. (London, 1986), II:443 – 4

[6] Edward Thurlow to Lloyd Kenyon, 31 May 1783, Historical Manuscripts Commission, *14th Report Appendix, Pt IV (the manuscripts of Lord Kenyon)* (London, 1894), 516. See also *The Times*, 9 March 1787, 2, col. 3.

[7] Historical Manuscripts Commission, *Kenyon papers*, p. 516.

[8] Lord Eldon, J. Scott, *Lord Eldon's anecdote book*, eds A. L. J. Lincoln and R. L. McEwen (London, 1960), 61.

[9] R. Fitzpatrick to Earl of Upper Ossory, 21 November 1783, Lord J. Russell (ed.), *Memorials and correspondence of Charles James Fox*, 4 vols. (London, 1853), II:212.

When the House convened in the autumn of 1783, the coalition ministry of Charles Fox and Lord North regarded reorganisation of the East India Company as one of its principal tasks. Despite Treasury aid, the Company was in financial difficulties. Moreover, recent unrest had raised fears for the general security of the region, and neither the Company officials in London nor those in Bengal were regarded as capable of governing the territory effectively. Finally, there was a growing concern for the native Indian population, whose interests were being sacrificed for the sake of profit.[10] The Bill introduced by Fox proposed fundamental changes in the Company's structure. It vested authority for all territorial possessions in a board of seven commissioners. A further nine assistant commissioners, chosen from the holders of £2,000 of Indian stock, would manage the commercial business. The commissioners would serve four years, with vacancies filled by the Crown, while the assistant commissioners would serve for five years, with subsequent appointments made by open voting among the stockholders.[11] The most serious practical problem with the Bill was its attempt to solve the problem of local disorganisation and insubordination by strengthening the Company structure in London. Of more immediate political importance, however, was the proposed appointment of sixteen ministerial supporters to the supreme offices of the Company. The distrust engendered by this move would bring down the ministry in mid-December.[12]

Not surprisingly, given the prominence of Indian affairs, Scott's first speeches concerned the India Bill. He made his maiden speech on 21 November 1783, when the Bill came up for its second reading. In this rather colourless effort Scott emphasised the independence of his deliberations and tried to appear open-minded about the measure. Because he was 'attached to no particular party', he intended to vote 'as justice seemed to direct'. He had not yet formed an opinion on the Bill, but he intended to do so, 'and he would ensure the House, he would form it elaborately, and when he gave it, it should be an honest one'. At present he would say only that the Bill 'seemed to him rather of a

[10] J. S. Watson, *The reign of George III, 1760–1815* (Oxford, 1960), 261.
[11] W. Cobbett (ed.), *The parliamentary history of England ... to 1803*, 36 vols. (London, 1806–20), XXIV:62–3.
[12] Watson, *Reign of George III*, 264.

dangerous tendency'. Nevertheless he would not declare himself against it, but would 'rather wait till he had got more light thrown upon the subject'.[13] In general the speech was not badly received. Fox, who followed Scott, 'expressed a high opinion of his [Scott's] abilities and his goodness'.[14] The *Whitehall Evening Post* called it 'one of the most correct speeches we ever heard in Parliament'.[15] Nathanial Wraxall probably expressed a more honest opinion when he recorded in his diary: 'Scarcely any impression of the speech pronounced by Scott remains on my mind or memory.'[16]

Scott's next speech, two and a half weeks later, was far more ambitious. Having resolved against the India Bill, he expressed his objections to the third reading in an unhappy combination of measured criticism and wild rhetoric. He began cautiously, explaining that he felt that interference with the East India Company's charter was not presently justified, and that this Bill would significantly increase the influence of the Crown.[17] As he continued, however, he interspersed classical, historical, and Biblical allusions, and the abrupt shifts in language and tone that they occasioned upset considerably the balance of the speech. For example, after having stated that the Company's bankruptcy had not been established and warranted further inquiry, he quoted Desdemona's plea from *Othello*, 'Kill me not tonight, my lord! – let me live but one day – one hour!'[18] Even more surprising than that quotation, however, was the fact that Scott turned immediately to his next objection, that the respectability of the proposed commissioners did not sufficiently ensure the security of the Company's affairs.[19] The climax of the speech came when Scott quoted from the book of Revelations, which prompted Wraxall to inquire: 'Will it be believed that the "Apocalypse" of St John furnished images, which ... were made to typify Fox, under the form of "The Beast that rose up out of the sea, having *seven* heads"?'[20]

Wraxall's incredulity notwithstanding, the general response to the speech is difficult to gauge. The *London Chronicle* recorded it

[13] Cobbett, *Parliamentory history*, XXIII:1239–40      [14] *Ibid.*, col. 1240.
[15] *Whitehall Evening Post*, 20–22 November 1783, 3, col. 2.
[16] Wraxall, *Historical and posthumous memoirs*, III:162.
[17] Cobbett, *Parliamentory history*, XXIV:34.      [18] *Ibid.*, col. 36.      [19] *Ibid.*
[20] *Ibid.*, cols. 34–5. N. Wraxall, *Historical memoirs of my own time*, ed. R. Askham (London, 1904), 603.

without comment, while the *Whitehall Evening Post* reported that the Revelations metaphor 'struck the House in a very forcible manner', and that Scott added other quotations 'with great dexterity and pertinence'.[21] The *Public Advertiser* described the speech as 'very able', and, having noted that the 'House laughed very heartily' at the passage from St John, failed to explain whether this merriment was at Scott's or Fox's expense.[22] Fox graciously observed that the opposition 'had placed a learned and eloquent member (Mr Scott) in the front of the battle, and he had certainly acquitted himself ably'.[23] Several other speakers on both sides of the House also ornamented their remarks with colourful allusions. General Burgoyne compared the nabobs amassing fortunes in India with characters condemned to Tartarus in the *Aeneid*, and Sir Richard Hill likened Fox's treachery to the constitution with that of Brutus to Caesar.[24] Richard Rigby found it extraordinary 'to have heard a quotation from Scripture through the mouth of a lawyer', but R. B. Sheridan foiled Scott more cleverly by quoting other Biblical passages whereby he 'metamorphosed the beast with seven heads, with crowns on them, into seven angels, clothed in pure white linen'.[25]

Having at least made himself known in the House by these speeches, Scott retreated somewhat, and in the next weeks limited his remarks to modest contributions in support of the new ministry led by William Pitt. On 17 December 1783 the House of Lords had rejected the India Bill, after the King had indicated that he would regard a favourable vote as hostile to him. As soon as the Bill had been defeated, the King dismissed his ministers and sent for Pitt. On 12 January 1784 Scott declared his 'entire disapprobation' of the opposition motion that the King's name had been used unconstitutionally to affect parliamentary deliberations and that the new ministry lacked the confidence of the House.[26] Two days later, however, he urged that the conduct of the Duke of Portland be 'minutely examined' in the wake of allegations that the former First Lord of the Treasury had tried to

[21] *London Chronicle*, 6–9 December 1783, 658, cols. 2–3; *Whitehall Evening Post*, 6–9 December 1783, 3, col. 4.
[22] *Public Advertiser*, 9 December 1783, 2, col. 3.
[23] Cobbett, *Parliamentory history*, XXIV:47.     [24] *Ibid.*, cols. 30, 41.
[25] *Ibid.*, cols. 50, 51.     [26] *Ibid.*, col. 305.

purchase a member's support.[27] On 18 February 1784, the opposition moved to defer consideration of the Mutiny Bill to indicate their displeasure at the King's refusal to dismiss his ministers. At the same time, it was suggested that ministers should resign in favour of persons more acceptable to the majority of members. In a short speech Scott opposed the motion. He added that, if resignation would actually facilitate negotiations to strengthen the government, he would not be sorry. Having hinted, however, that it would not have that effect, he advised against any changes on the Treasury bench.[28] Surely these speeches helped to establish the view of Scott as a Pitt supporter which emerged at this time. In his memorandum in the autumn of 1783 on attitudes toward a dismissal of Fox and North in favour of Pitt, political manager John Robinson had listed Scott as 'hopeful'.[29] In his December memorandum this had changed to 'favourable'.[30] By March 1784 John Stockdale included Scott as one of those opposed to Fox, and Robinson's memorandum for the spring elections contained the following notation for Weobley: 'Lord Weymouth, the same or as good friends, it is apprehended.'[31]

While apparently content for a time to remain a 'good friend', Scott indicated his willingness to oppose Pitt in his next significant speech, on the Westminster election scrutiny in March 1785. In the previous year Fox had narrowly defeated Sir Cecil Wray at the poll. The returning officer had thereupon granted a scrutiny to Sir Cecil and declined to make a return, thus leaving the borough unrepresented. The Act of 10 & 11 Will. III c. 7 required a returning officer to make his return by the date specified in the writ authorising him to conduct the election. Nevertheless, Pitt had supported the scrutiny, keen to oust Fox from the popular

---

[27] J. Debrett (ed.), *The parliamentary register ... 1780–1799*, 54 vols. (London, 1782–99), XII:567. Philip Yorke charged that Hew Dalrymple had informed him that a Scottish member, Dalrymple's uncle John Hamilton, had offered a place worth £500 per annum on behalf of the Duke of Portland if Dalrymple would support him. On 29 January a letter was read to the House from Hamilton declaring that he had no authority to make any such offer, and the matter was dropped. Namier and Brooke, *History of Parliament*, II:295.

[28] Cobbett, *Parliamentory history*, XXIV:616.

[29] W. T. Laprade (ed.), *Parliamentary papers of John Robinson, 1774–1784* (London, 1922), 65.

[30] *Ibid.*

[31] L. G. Mitchell, *Charles James Fox and the disintegration of the Whig party 1782–1794* (Oxford, 1971), Appendix 1; Laprade, *Parliamentary papers*, 87.

constituency. On 8 March 1785, this hope had been disappointed by a vote of 162–124 against the scrutiny.[32] The government had, however, prevailed against a motion condemning the returning officer, and on 9 March 1785 sought to retain the earlier resolution to proceed with the scrutiny as part of the parliamentary record. Arden, the Attorney General, and Kenyon, Master of the Rolls, supported the government's position on the record and on the scrutiny itself.

In response to Kenyon, Scott gave what the *Public Advertiser* described as 'a long speech full of legal arguments, in which he laid down as doctrine the illegality of the scrutiny'.[33] Unfortunately, this portion of Scott's speech is only alluded to in the printed debates. While it is impossible to recreate his argument, it seems clear that precedent at least militated against, if it did not absolutely forbid, the returning officer's conduct. John Simeon's *Treatise on the Law of Elections*, published in 1789, states that if the officer cannot make the return by the prescribed date he must simply state that 'no choice, or a doubtful one, is made', whereupon the elections committee of the House of Commons would investigate the matter.[34] Simeon repeated Scott's point, that Parliament would never meet if returning officers could ignore the return date. Scott also scorned the notion that the House should protect the conscience of the returning officer. The existing rule imposed no unreasonable moral burden, while the conscience of this particular officer 'was not of the most delicate texture'. Despite his original scruples he had responded promptly to the command he had received the previous week, and Scott observed: 'He did not require, it seemed, much time to make up his mind when the House ordered him.'[35]

Fox, speaking later in the debate, was lavish in his tribute to Scott's contribution:

One learned gentleman in particular (Mr Scott) had entered into the whole of the case with a soundness of argument, and a depth and closeness

---

32 Cobbett, *Parliamentory history*, XXV:105. Fox could not have been excluded from the House by means of the scrutiny as he had also been returned for the Orkney and Shetland Islands.

33 *Public Advertiser*, 10 March 1785, 3, col. 2.

34 J. Simeon, *A treatise on the law of elections in all its branches* (London, 1789), 145.

35 Cobbett, *Parliamentory history*, XXV:121.

of reasoning, that perhaps had scarcely been equaled [*sic*] in the discussion of any topic within these walls, that turned at all on the statute and common law.[36]

Fox was probably less impressed with Scott's next effort, when he returned to Pitt's side in May to support the ill-fated commercial treaty with Ireland. Pitt had proposed to allow Irish ships to participate fully in the English colonial trade and to establish a system either of free trade or identical duties in the Anglo–Irish market. In return, the Irish would contribute to the British naval expenditure. These conditions had caused a great outcry among those who feared the consequences of Irish competition upon local and colonial English commerce. In the face of this opposition, Pitt had given way and offered to protect interests such as the West Indian sugar growers and the East India Company.[37] On 24 May 1785, the House went into committee to consider whether the Irish should be bound by the Navigation Acts. During the debate, Fox opposed the proposition at length arguing, *inter alia*, that it was degrading to Ireland.[38] Scott's answer is only summarised in the printed debates, but he is described as having 'defended this proposition from the charges Mr Fox had brought upon it ... He warmly approved the whole of the resolutions, as a system calculated to produce amity between the two nations.'[39]

Scott does not seem to have participated again in debate until February 1787, when he supported the commercial treaty with France, which Pitt proposed after the failure of the Irish negotiations.[40] Both England and France sought to restore their finances, strained during the American war, through increased trade. They agreed to reduce the duty on many staples and manufactured items, and to protect particular domestic products by maintaining prohibitive duties or simply excluding a product from export.[41] On 21 February 1787, the House considered whether to present an address to the throne signifying support for the treaty. While most of the members spoke to the treaty itself, several directed

[36] *Ibid.*, col. 129.     [37] Watson, *Reign of George III*, 276–7.
[38] Cobbett, *Parliamentory history*, XXV:686, 690–1.
[39] *Ibid.*, col. 696. The House not only voted to bind Ireland to the Navigation Acts, but to require the Irish to contribute to the British naval expenditure even when their budget was in deficit. Not surprisingly, the Irish Parliament refused to accept these terms, whereupon Pitt declined to continue negotiations. Watson, *Reign of George III*, 277.
[40] 27 Geo. III c. 13.     [41] Watson, *Reign of George III*, 289.

their remarks to the propriety of an address on such a matter. John Anstruther and Philip Adam both argued that the address would oblige members to approve the treaty as it then stood, and so deprive the House of its authority to deliberate fully on each provision.[42] In reply, Scott addressed both the substance of the treaty and the propriety of an address. Of the treaty itself he was extremely laudatory: he asserted that it 'promised this country a great accession of wealth, and held out the most liberal encouragement to her artizans, whose industry, perseverance and skill, joined to their prodigious capital, must ever insure them the superiority'.[43] He rejected the arguments against the address, and scorned the opposition as disingenuous, charging that they had clearly favoured a treaty when in office.[44] Something of the tone of Scott's remarks emerges from the account of Sir James Erskine's reply, reported in the *Morning Chronicle*:

Sir James charged Mr Scott with having resorted to ridicule to make up his deficiency in reason and argument. He said, he [Scott] had drawn a most false and extravagant conclusion from the premises laid down by Mr Anstruther, and had misrepresented what Mr Adam had said, on purpose to warrant an ungrounded conclusion.[45]

Raillery also played a significant part in Scott's speech in April 1787 on a private member Bill to prevent vexatious suits in the ecclesiastical courts.[46] This measure, brought in by John Pollexfen Bastard, restricted ecclesiastical jurisdiction over actions for defamation. Bastard argued that the ecclesiastical courts were superfluous because their only sanctions – penance and excommunication – were ineffectual. In their defence, Kenyon pointed to the narrow definition of defamation at common law, which prevented many deserving suitors in those courts from benefiting from the broader sanctions.[47] Common law judges construed words in a non-defamatory sense when possible, and ordinarily considered proof of special temporal damages as a necessary element of the prosecution's case.[48] The debate on 20 April 1787

---

[42] Cobbett, *Parliamentory history*, XXVI:493–4, 499–502.
[43] *Ibid.*, cols. 505–6.    [44] *Ibid.*, col. 505.
[45] *Morning Chronicle*, 22 February 1787, 3, col. 1.    [46] 27 Geo. III c. 44.
[47] Cobbett, *Parliamentary history*, XXVI:1005.
[48] Common law judges had, since the sixteenth century, applied the rule of *mitior sensus*. Moreover, the plaintiff had to show that as a natural and necessary consequence of the offensive words he had suffered some pecuniary loss. W. B. Odgers and R. Ritson, *Odgers on Libel and Slander*, 6th edn (London, 1929), 63,

centred on whether a cause of action in the ecclesiastical courts should be barred after six months or, as the government advised, after two years.

Scott used the occasion of this debate to entertain the House. He began by criticising his fellow lawyers, which in itself was likely to gain him a friendly hearing. He called some of the technical distinctions drawn by lawyers 'enough to draw the profession into contempt' and asserted that many 'ludicrous' decisions had been rendered 'by the wisdom of our judges' in cases of common law defamation.[49] Thereupon he quoted several cases to provide examples of the restrictions in that branch of the law. He mentioned a man wrongly accused of murder who could sue because murder constituted a felony, whereas a man merely accused of having split another's head open with a cleaver had no remedy because his alleged act did not constitute a felony. Similarly, a girl whose fiancé ended their engagement after she was falsely accused of being pregnant could maintain an action for the value of the lost marriage. A girl who was not engaged, however, could not sue, although the damage to her reputation could conceivably preclude any future offer of marriage.[50] Suitors, argued Scott, should not be restricted to a court capable of rendering such decisions. In the end, the House voted for the six-month period, after an extremely clumsy speech by the Attorney General elicited not only anti-lawyer but anti-Roman comments.[51] That Scott's speech was a personal success, however, is indicated by its favourable presentation in the press. The *Gentleman's Magazine* described it as one of 'infinite pleasantry and good-humour' while the *London Chronicle* reported that Scott was 'extremely humorous, and kept the House in a roar of laughter'.[52] Only *The Times* took a dim view of his levity, noting that 'Mr Scott's picture of the Common Law was not in the best manner of that celebrated artist'.[53]

In February 1788, Scott turned his attention to a more serious

---

95–6. The ecclesiastical courts did not apply these rules, so while their sanctions were limited, they did grant relief in a wider variety of cases. R. H. Helmholz (ed.), *Select cases in defamation: to 1600* (London, 1985), xlvi.

[49] Cobbett, *Parliamentory history*, XXVI:1006.     [50] *Ibid.*, cols. 1006–7.

[51] *Ibid.*, cols. 1007–8.

[52] *Gentleman's Magazine*, October 1787, 887; *London Chronicle*, 19–21 April 1787, 6, col. 2.

[53] *The Times*, 27 April 1787, 2, col. 4.

issue, the impeachment of Sir Elijah Impey. The principal charge
against Impey, the former Chief Justice of the Supreme Court of
Bengal, amounted to judicial murder. The background to the case
was as follows. In 1775 the Council of Bengal, then at odds with
Governor General Warren Hastings, had heard accusations of
corruption against Hastings by Nand Kumar, a Brahman money-
lender and one-time Company hireling.[54] Hastings had responded
by bringing his own charges of conspiracy. Nand Kumar was at
that time involved in a lengthy civil action for forgery, and the
Governor's counter-attack had encouraged Nand Kumar's opponents in the suit to move against him. They had had him arrested
and tried before Impey on a charge of forgery. He had been
convicted and executed. The Council, meanwhile, had decided
not to pursue Nand Kumar's allegations against Hastings. In
February 1788, on the eve of Hastings' own impeachment, Impey
was charged with having conspired with him to eliminate an
embarrassing troublemaker.[55]

Even before the matter reached the floor of the House, Scott
had indicated his support for Impey's conduct, which *The Times*
regarded as significant. 'The lawyers are divided as to the conduct
of Sir Elijah Impey ... Mr Scott's doubts are in favour of Sir
Elijah's decision; and such an opinion is in itself so powerful as to
go a great way in aiding the business of the accused magistrate's
justification.'[56] His contributions to the debates in February 1788,
however, consisted largely of procedural points. On 7 February
1788, Philip Francis moved that Impey be required to produce a
paper he had previously read to the House as part of his defence.
This document, asserted Francis, reflected upon the integrity of
the Council of Bengal, and, as one of its members, Francis asserted
his right to see the paper to answer its charges.[57] Scott, along with

---

[54] Until 1772 the East India Company had administered its territories via native
deputies under Company supervisors. This had proved ineffective, and Hastings
had been ordered to put an end to it. Thereupon he had dismissed two deputies
and had them tried for peculation. Nand Kumar had been involved in these
proceedings on behalf of the Company. W. Holdsworth, *A history of English
law*, 17 vols. (London, 1903–72), XI:170, 193.

[54] *Ibid.*, 193, 202; Watson, *Reign of George III*, 311–12. Unlike Hastings, whose
impeachment would drag on for the next seven years, the charges against Impey
would soon be dropped.

[56] *The Times*, 25 December 1787, 2, col. 2.

[57] Cobbett, *Parliamentory history*, XXVI:1418–19.

several other prominent lawyers in the House, disputed the propriety of requiring Impey to surrender a document essential to his defence, particularly as it was the only copy in existence. They argued that Impey must be permitted to decline, acknowledging that if he did so the House must take no notice of its contents.[58] Scott went on to say that Francis ought first to deny the charges levelled against *him* before he called for papers and could not resist inquiring 'whether the conduct of the council, as mentioned in Sir Elijah's defence, was not equally deserving of impeachment with that of the judge'.[59]

Five days later Scott again took exception to the conduct of the proceedings. Following a motion that Thomas Farrer, formerly the counsel to Nand Kumar, be examined before a committee of the House, Scott and others objected to Farrer's proposal that he relate his information as a narrative, after which he would answer members' questions. Scott wanted to confine Farrer to answering the questions put to him. This led to a lengthy 'contest' only briefly summarised in the printed debates, in which Fox and others argued in favour of a narrative. Their position was ultimately accepted, and Farrer continued his account.[60] Presently, however, Scott objected again, this time to Farrer's reading of a document containing hearsay. Scott maintained: 'The paper just read would not have been received in any court in the kingdom'; and he urged 'the necessity of adhering to the established law of evidence in all proceedings of any sort leading to a judicial determination'.[61] Several other prominent lawyers supported Scott, and this led Fox to rebuke them 'with a great deal of warmth and asperity' for trying to impose legal rules upon the House.[62] Pitt, like Fox, believed the document properly admitted, but he defended the lawyers, and Scott in particular, from Fox's 'unseemly wrath'.[63] *The Times* reported: 'The Chancellor of the Exchequer vindicated, with great warmth, the character of the profession, and paid a most flattering panegyric on the abilities, character, and integrity of the learned gentleman, Mr Scott.'[64]

---

[58] *Ibid.*, cols. 1419, 1422, 1423.    [59] *Ibid.*, col. 1423.
[60] *Ibid.*, XXVII:37.    [61] *Ibid.*, cols. 37–8.
[62] *Ibid.*, col. 38. Fox agreed that the document was not good evidence, but his justification of its usefulness suggested that he did intend to use it for the truth of the matter stated therein. *Ibid.*
[63] *Ibid.*, col. 39.    [64] *The Times*, 12 February 1788, 2, col. 4.

Scott established a stronger link between himself and the Pitt government one month later when he firmly defended and, at least one commentator suggests, drafted the East India Company Declaratory Bill.[65] This measure stated that, in creating the Board of Control to supervise the Company, the Act of 24 Geo. III c. 25 had enabled the Board to make the Company liable for troops sent to India that it had not requisitioned. The Bill was the result of a series of conflicts between the government and the directors of the Company over the military in India. In November 1787 the Board of Control had proposed sending four regiments, both to respond to a French threat and to increase the British military presence relative to that of the Company. After having acquiesced, the directors had rejected the deployment of additional troops and refused to pay for them.[66]

Until the Impey impeachment debates Scott had not suffered much from the anti-lawyer prejudices of his fellow members. A commentary from the *The Times*, however, indicates how easily these could be aroused:

The uniform opinion of the lawyers, on a late question, operated too forcibly in favor [*sic*] of Sir Elijah Impey, not to give his enemies the alarm. – That Mr Bearcroft and Mr Scott should dare to know more of the law than those wits who never looked into a law book, but to laugh at it, will not be easily forgiven. A large quantity of sarcasms with strong points, are manufacturing for the next attack.[67]

Possibly with these sarcasms in mind Scott entered the 5 March debate on the Declaratory Bill with considerable caution. His introduction was described by *The Times* as intended 'chiefly to deprecate the unjust prejudice of some who might impute improper motives to his thus giving his opinion'.[68] He particularly asserted that he did not wish to enter into a political discussion, but as the matter was essentially a legal one, he felt obliged to express his opinion. '[I]t would not be denied him the right of standing upon his integrity, and uniformly acting upon what he conscientiously considered to be a sense of duty.'[69] Only then did he turn to the several objections made against the Bill. He dealt summarily with a constitutional point. Critics had charged that

---

[65] 28 Geo. III c. 8. See J. Williams, *Satires and biography* (London, 1795), 63.
[66] C. H. Philips, *The East India Company 1784–1834* (Manchester, 1961), 54–60.
[67] *The Times*, 15 February 1788, 2, col. 3.     [68] *Ibid.*, 6 March 1788, 2, col. 2.
[69] Cobbett, *Parliamentory history*, XXVII:87.

the Bill would permit the Crown to raise a large standing army outside Parliament's control because it would be paid for by the East India Company. Scott dismissed this as 'so absurd, that he was ashamed at having heard it urged as a serious objection'.[70] He explained how funding was a function of size and not the reverse. In the annual Mutiny Act, Parliament authorised an army of a particular size and thereupon allocated sufficient funds. It did not merely sanction 'an army' whose size was determined by the money available. Consequently, a new source of funding would not entitle the Crown to increase the army because its legitimacy depended on the direct Parliamentary sanction of its size.[71] He similarly rejected a financial objection to the Bill. It had been claimed that the obligation imposed by the Bill would reduce Indian revenues and consequently reduce profits for the Company and the public. Scott pointed out that an analysis of the Company's balance sheet should begin not with certain profits but with necessary expenditures. Maintaining that there was no 'law that there always should be a surplus of the revenues of India', he stressed that, rather than considering expenditure as a diminution of potential profit, it should be regarded as the necessary basis upon which profits might be acquired.[72] Scott's discussion of whether the proposed Bill fairly construed the existing law has not received detailed treatment in the printed debates. Nevertheless the probable gist of his argument is not difficult to surmise. The Act of 21 Geo. III c. 65 obliged the Company to pay for troops sent by Britain to India 'on the requisition of the said United Company'. The Act of 24 Geo. III c. 25 established a six-member Board of Control to 'superintend, direct, and control' all activities related to the civil or military government of the Company's possessions. Furthermore, it required the Company to 'pay due obedience to, and be governed and bound by' the orders of the Board. Clearly the Act of 21 Geo. III c. 65 implied that the Company had no liability for expenses incurred by troops it did not request. While the later Act did not explicitly repeal, it rendered its predecessor largely irrelevant in the instant case because the Board of Control had the authority to order the Company to request soldiers.

Despite his efforts to avoid hostility on account of his profes-

---

[70] *Ibid.*, cols. 85, 88.     [71] *Ibid.*, col. 88.     [72] *Ibid.*, col. 89.

sion, or perhaps because of the way he did so, Scott found much of the opposition's remarks directed against lawyers in general and himself in particular. Philip Francis was the most scathing:

Can anything be more preposterous, than for us, who pretend to be legislators, to submit to ask lawyers, what was our own act and deed? Learned gentlemen have engrossed the question, as if it belonged solely and exclusively to their department, and as if we had nothing to do with it but to find, if we can, some determinate sense in their discordant opinions, or to reconcile if that were possible, their flat contradictions of one another.[73]

After having described Scott as 'the great luminary of the law, whose opinions are oracles, to whose skill and authority, all his own profession look up to with reverence and amazement', Francis criticised Scott for having 'almost stultified himself, for the purpose of proving his integrity' and then failing to make a convincing argument. 'I defy any man living, not a lawyer, to recite even the substance of that part of his argument. The truth is, he left the main question exactly where he found it.'[74] While Scott may not have impressed Francis, Pitt was more than willing to support him. He began his speech on 5 March noting that, had he intended to speak generally on the Bill, 'he should be perfectly willing to forego that intention in a very great measure in consequence of the very able argument of his learned friend near him'. As regards the construction of the Bill, he was 'willing to rest it upon his learned friend's reasoning'.[75] Scott's support was of particular importance to the government, as suspicion about ministers' desire to increase East Indian patronage had translated into reduced majorities. Moreover, on this occasion both Pitt and Henry Dundas were apparently not in a condition to debate effectively.[76] While certainly the ultimate success of the measure is not attributable to Scott, his contribution played no small share in it, and possibly gained for him the office of Solicitor General.[77] Writing shortly after Scott's appointment Wraxall paid him this

---

[73] Cobbett, *Parliamentory history*, XXVII:203.     [74] *Ibid.*, cols. 203–5.

[75] *Ibid.*, col. 90.

[76] In a letter of 10 March 1788 to Lord Buckingham, Lord Bulkeley noted how Pitt and Henry Dundas had been feeling the effects of the previous night's revels. Buckingham and Chandos, Richard Grenville, Duke of Buckingham and Chandos, *Memoirs of the court and cabinets of George III*, 4 vols. (London, 1853–5), I:360.

[77] Although Scott was not actually appointed Solicitor General until June 1788, a

tribute. 'His [Scott's] rise resulted from a combination of talent, labour, and character. Neither noble birth, nor favour, nor alliances produced it. Pitt's friendship he indeed acquired and enjoyed, because he earned it by great exertions.'[78]

As an old man looking back on his career Scott would write 'Politicians are fond of representing lawyers as most ignorant politicians – they are pleased, however, to represent politicians, as not being ignorant lawyers, which they most undoubtedly generally are.'[79] This comment suggests something of the uneasy atmosphere that existed when Scott entered the House of Commons. Politicians did not enjoy receiving lectures on the law. Lawyers, on the other hand, were drawn to legal issues, especially when incompetently treated by politicians. Moreover, the particular way for a lawyer to advance was to establish himself as an expert on legal matters and attach himself to a leading politician or faction. Scott was fortunate in that he enjoyed such a reputation early in his parliamentary career. The *Gentleman's Magazine* thus described the House's response to his speech on the Westminster scrutiny:

Mr Scott (member for Weobley) rose, and the whole House was struck with solemn silence. He first stated the grounds of the law, and the constitutional principles on which he had formed his opinion ... He went over the outlines of the whole proceeding, was well heard, and gave his full voice for the motion.[80]

Moreover, he strove to maintain a certain distance from the Pitt government even though his professional stature could have earned him an appointment had he shown himself a more complete supporter early on. A conscious assertion of independence was both natural for Scott and prudent. He was extremely sensitive about possible aspersions upon his integrity, and his speeches indicate when he felt himself harassed on account of the 'excessive skill and cunning of his profession'.[81] On such occasions he endeavoured to placate his audience with assurances of his good intentions and political independence. It is not surprising, therefore, that he would hesitate to expose himself to charges of place-

letter of 29 April 1788 from William Windham Grenville to Buckingham mentions the appointment as settled. *Ibid.*, I:378. See Williams, *Satires*, 63.
[78] Wraxall, *Historical and posthumous memoirs*, IV:130.
[79] Eldon, *Anecdote book*, 137.          [80] *Gentleman's Magazine*, June 1785, 442.
[81] Cobbett, *Parliamentory history*, XXVII:204.

hunting. Furthermore, by serving a period of parliamentary apprenticeship before accepting an appointment, Scott could establish himself as a House of Commons man rather than merely a government representative on legal affairs. At the same time, he could prove to ministers the value of his support and demonstrate that he need not depend on them for his political existence. William Wilberforce later recalled of Scott: 'he never fawned and flattered as some did, but always assumed the tone and station of a man who was conscious that he must show he respected himself if he wished to be respected by others.'[82] Having accepted the position of Solicitor General in 1788, Scott must have judged the preceding five years in the House as a success.

[82] R. Wilberforce and S. Wilberforce (eds.), *The life of Samuel Wilberforce*, 5 vols. (London, 1838), V:214.

# 3

# A GOVERNMENT RETAINER

In June 1788 John Scott became Solicitor General, one of the principal lawyers employed by the Crown and commonly known as the government's junior law officer. He remained in post for almost five years, before advancing to the senior office of Attorney General, where he remained for a further six. During that eleven-year period, Scott worked first with Archibald Macdonald, and later with John Mitford. Scott's years as a law officer were onerous ones for him. He had considerable responsibilities in three important areas: parliamentary debate, civil and criminal prosecution, and executive consultation and administration. Not only was the actual volume of work large, but the nature of the work placed pressures upon him as a result of the peculiar characteristics of the posts.

The offices of Attorney and Solicitor General had a long history. At least since the reign of Henry III, English monarchs followed the growing practice of appointing one or more legal representatives, first for particular tasks and then in anticipation of whatever matters might arise to which the monarch could not personally attend. Persons who acted for the Crown in a legal capacity were described as King's Attorneys. 'Attorney' not yet having come to designate a separate professional class, it merely described a legal representative. The earliest use of the title 'attorney general' actually referred to individuals appointed by the Duke of Norfolk in 1398. Gradually the practice evolved of appointing two King's Attorneys, and from 1472 the post was held singly. The first recorded mention of a Solicitor General dates from 1462. Although the designation 'Solicitor' may have reflected a particular professional emphasis, the post was primarily that of an assistant Attorney. From the sixteenth century an appointment to the former had become the usual means of attaining the latter, and at least by the eighteenth century it had become common for both law officers to succeed to judicial appointments.[1]

The responsibilities of the law officers in public life were complex, and require further explanation. Their original advisory role brought them into contact with Parliament. In particular, the Attorney's habit of attending the sovereign in the House of Lords resulted in his mediating between the two Houses. As a consequence of this work, the Attorney was barred from membership in the House of Commons until the early eighteenth century. A comparable ban did not extend to the Solicitor, and individuals occupying that post were regularly returned from the middle of the sixteenth century.[2] In Parliament, the law officers were primarily considered government speakers, and were expected to explain the government's policies as these touched on legal issues. Back-bench and opposition members, however, also felt entitled to call upon the law officers for objective advice on legal questions, particularly as these affected the interests of the House. A further expression of this parliamentary responsibility was the authority of either House to direct the Attorney to undertake prosecutions on its behalf for breaches of privilege. For the most part, however, the law officers appeared in court on behalf of the Crown. They conducted criminal prosecutions, and intervened to enforce or protect royal or governmental interests. It was the privilege of the Attorney and Solicitor to conduct Crown litigation in person, or to delegate that responsibility to qualified barristers. The law officers also advised the Crown on a range of legal matters, from the legality of a proposed policy, to the drafting of important pieces of legislation. By the late eighteenth century, however, the focus of the law officers' work had shifted from the sovereign to his ministers. The Attorney and Solicitor were not privy counsellors, and did not regularly attend meetings of the Cabinet. Queries might reach them in the name of the King, but the recipient of their advice was the relevant minister or department.

---

[1] H. Bellot, 'The origin of the Attorney-General', *Law Quarterly Review* 25 (1909), 400–11.

[2] J. L. J. Edwards, *The law officers of the crown* (London, 1964), 33–8, 42–3. See also Sir R. Chambers and Sir S. Johnson, *A course of lectures on the English law delivered at the university of Oxford 1767–1775*, ed. T. M. Curley, 2 vols. (Oxford, 1986), I:138.

Within the executive, the law officers occupied a rather unique niche. In Scott's day, they were among the few senior government officers who could boast relevant professional qualifications for their job – in their case evidenced by a substantial legal practice prior to appointment. In an era of government by amateurs, they rightly regarded themselves as experts.[3] Physical circumstances and habits of practice contributed to a sense of aloofness following appointment. They were neither absorbed into a government bureaucracy, nor given charge over a clerical staff or a library of government materials.[4] On the contrary, they retained their own chambers, and continued to advise private clients. Moreover, when ministers or departments sought the law officers' advice or expertise, they obtained a personal interview or framed a written question, and for such advice they paid an appropriate fee. These fees, and not the nominal salary, constituted the bulk of law officers' remuneration.[5] Finally, as other ancient offices were gradually affected by the principle of 'economical reform', whereby practices such as deputisation and payment by fees were abolished, the privileges of the law officers remained unaffected.[6]

Just as a largely lawyer–client relationship existed between the law officers and the government, professional attitudes seem to have characterised the relations among the various men of law in the government. The principal lawyers of the Crown occupied their separate domains of English common law and equity (the Attorney and Solicitor General), civil, ecclesiastical, and maritime law (the Advocate General), Scots law (the Lord Advocate), and Irish law (the Irish Attorney and Solicitor General). They each clung to their particular assignments and areas of expertise, and treated each other with distant courtesy.[7] The most common

---

[3] For information on the prior careers of law officers during the eighteenth and early nineteenth century, see R. A. Melikan, 'Mr Attorney General and the politicians', *Historical Journal* 40(1) (1997), 41–69, 44.

[4] Scott and Macdonald shared the services of an assistant draftsman. In 1798 Mitford requested that he and Scott be given a second assistant. Mitford to Henry Dundas, 30 July 1798, SRO (Melvile papers), GD51/1/282/1.

[5] Scott received an annual salary of £70 as Solicitor General and £81.06.08 as Attorney General. Posting Book, July 1781–October 1805, PRO, E403(2681). He did not keep detailed accounts for the fees he collected as Solicitor; see chapter 1, Table 1.4, p. 7 above, for the fees collected as Attorney.

[6] Melikan, 'Mr Attorney General', 55–6.

[7] Scott had almost no professional contact with the Lord Advocate; he and Mitford were offended by the suggestion that they had once deferred to the Irish law

integration consisted of joint legal opinions by the Attorney, Solicitor, and Advocate General, but these were not undertaken as a matter of course.[8] As departmental legal staffs developed, they mediated between ministers and the law officers, much as private solicitors would act for clients with barristers. To a certain extent the law officers could impose slightly on these individuals – desiring them to pass on to their chiefs an explanation of why a report was not forthcoming, or engaging them to conduct a mundane inquiry or investigation.[9] The most important administrative link, however, existed in the person of the Treasury Solicitor, and while he regularly received instructions from the law officers, their actual authority over him is unclear.[10]

Certain professional conventions also attached to the official relationship between the Attorney and Solicitor. Primarily it was hierarchical – senior and junior counsel, and leading and seconding speaker. Individual preferences could overcome conventions. For instance, Mitford led the prosecution of Horne Tooke for treason in 1794 while Solicitor General, and Scott, in the same office, drafted the Regency Bill in 1788. Personal friendship, moreover, could play a part in making professional relations more

officers on a question of English law. J. Scott and Mitford to the Duke of Portland, 14 May 1799, PRO, HO48(8).

[8] This was true even during the period when the Advocate General was Scott's brother, William. See, e.g., J. Scott to Dundas, 26 September 1793, PRO, HO48(3).

[9] See, e.g., J. Scott, 25 January 1796, PRO, PC1/34/A90; J. Scott to William Fawkener, 4 January 1794, PRO, PC1/20/A31; J. Scott, August 1796, PRO, CO323(92). The law officers were occasionally loaned the services of the law clerk of the Privy Council or the solicitor to the India Board to assist them in drafting particular documents. Fawkener to Archibald Macdonald, J. Scott, 11 February 1789, PRO, BT3(2); Stephen Cottrell to Macdonald, 9 April 1791, PRO, BT3(3).

[10] In a private letter Samuel Romilly suggested that Scott and Mitford did not expect much deference from Joseph White. 'He [Mitford] says you are very much mistaken in supposing that a mere hint from him would have any weight with W. The fact he says is so different that he believes if he were to send to W. to beg he would let him see the draft with the answer written by him and the [Attorney General] would refuse it. I could not press him further to expose himself to this refusal.' Samuel Romilly to Jeremy Bentham, 19 May 1797, A. T. Milne (ed.), *Correspondence 1794–1797*, vol. V of *The collected works of Jeremy Bentham*, general eds. J. R. Dinwiddy and F. Rosen, 10 vols. (London, 1981), 367–8. The draft to which Romilly referred was of Bentham's Bill to establish a national penitentiary. For an example of the law officers' official authority over Mr White, see J. Scott and Mitford to Portland, 4 April 1797, PRO, HO48(6).

informal. While certainly no evidence exists that Scott and Macdonald normally conducted themselves with rigid formality, Scott
and Mitford were close friends – Mitford stood godfather to
Scott's fourth son – and their professional correspondence indicates a fair degree of intimacy with regard to their work.

Before looking at the more glamorous jobs of prosecutor and
parliamentarian, it is worth examining Scott's other important
work as a law officer, the drafting of legal opinions for the
government. Unfortunately, his actual performance in this respect
is somewhat difficult to assess. First, the opinions themselves do
not provide clear evidence. Unlike his parliamentary or courtroom
speeches, many of the opinions were signed by two and sometimes
three people, so that conclusions about Scott's particular contribution to any such document must remain tentative. Secondly, little
secondary evidence exists. Because opinions were not widely
available for scrutiny, they provoked relatively few contemporary
comments. Within limitations, however, a certain amount of
information is available. The opinions indicate the kind of questions Scott and his colleagues answered, the conventions they
observed, and the attitudes they displayed toward the law, politics,
and the government. In this context Jeremy Bentham's *Panopticon*
correspondence does provide some insights into Scott's conduct.
From 1791 to 1810 Bentham harassed various officials, including
Scott and Mitford, to approve his national penitentiary, and he
recruited Samuel Romilly and William Wilberforce to assist him.
Scott's delayed, drawn-out review of the contract and Bill proved
a considerable hindrance. In April 1797, Romilly wrote to
Bentham that, while Scott had not neglected the Bill, 'he has done
what will probably be as injurious to you. He has so fully
considered it, that he has a thousand difficulties which it will take
a long time to get over.'[11] William Lowndes, the parliamentary
draughtsman, had previously remarked that 'the Att[orne]y
Gen[era]l is always raising foolish objections – '.[12] Finally, an
exasperated Bentham asserted to Wilberforce in May 1798 that
Scott's only use was 'to extract doubts from which none could
have been extracted by any body else – '.[13] Undoubtedly,

---

[11] Romilly to Bentham, 26 April 1797, Dinwiddy and Rosen, *Bentham collected works*, V:365–6.

[12] George Wilson to Bentham, 5 May 1795, *ibid.*, V:135.

[13] Bentham to William Wilberforce, 22 May 1798, J. R. Dinwiddy (ed.), *Corre-*

Bentham's was an exceptional situation, and Scott probably did not regard the chivvying of a private individual as comparable to an urgent request from a minister. Nevertheless, that Romilly, Lowndes, and Bentham should each allude to Scott's thoroughness and intractability suggest that these were characteristic of his work.

Several hundred official opinions and related pieces of correspondence exist from June 1788 to July 1799, which Scott authored either alone or with Macdonald, Mitford, William Scott or John Nicholl.[14] The 314 opinions form 10 general subject-matter categories: crime, colonies, trade, the militia, international affairs, local government, finance, Ireland, the military, and miscellanea. See Table 3.1.

The opinions on criminal matters, the largest category, primarily concerned either prisoner petitions or criminal investigations.[15] A detailed survey of the colonial opinions follows later in this chapter. Of the remaining eight categories, the opinions relating to trade were the most numerous, and typically concerned either the bounties sought by shippers and whalers, or the duties owed to the Customs Office. Many of the 37 opinions on the militia addressed one statute, the Augmentation Act of 37 Geo. III c. 107. Occasionally the law officers addressed more diverse matters, such as whether militia officers must pay highway tolls, and whether a Roman Catholic could hold a commission. By contrast, the opinions relating to the regular army and navy generally concerned jurisdiction, and discussed such issues as the authority of a naval court martial over army personnel, and the

---

 *spondence 1797–1800*, vol. VI of Dinwiddy and Rosen, *The collected works of Jeremy Bentham,* (Oxford, 1984), pp. 35–6.

[14] Official requests for legal advice came primarily from the Home Office, but also from the Foreign Office, the Board of Trade, the Customs Office, the Treasury, and the Privy Council. While some material has been located in private papers, most comes from the official records of the relevant department. This collection, therefore, probably gives a reasonable picture of the number and range of assignments given to these Crown lawyers, and particularly to Scott with either Macdonald or Mitford. The requests for opinions are typically recorded in departmental letter books, so it is unlikely that any significant number of such documents have been ignored. While the collection of materials issuing from the law officers is less complete, it does consist of those documents judged by the various departments as sufficiently important to keep.

[15] Many of the latter specifically involved investigations of treasonous or seditious activities, and as such are discussed in chapters 5 to 7.

Table 3.1. *John Scott's government legal opinions, 1788–1799*[a]

| | 1788 | 1789 | 1790 | 1791 | 1792 | 1793 | 1794 | 1795 | 1996 | 1997 | 1998 | 1999 | Undated | Total |
|---|---|---|---|---|---|---|---|---|---|---|---|---|---|---|
| Military | – | – | – | – | – | 1 | – | 2 | 2 | 1 | 3 | 1 | – | 10 |
| Colonies | – | 3 | 3 | 5 | 2 | 4 | 9 | 2 | 3 | 4 | 5 | 7 | 1 | 48 |
| Crime | 5 | 1 | 1 | 1 | 2 | 14 | 7 | 8 | 5 | 17 | 13 | 5 | 1 | 80 |
| Finance | – | 2 | 1 | – | 1 | – | 2 | 2 | 1 | 1 | 2 | 4 | 1 | 17 |
| International | – | – | 3 | – | 2 | 7 | 1 | 1 | 6 | 4 | 2 | 5 | 1 | 32 |
| Ireland | – | – | 1 | – | – | 3 | 1 | 1 | – | 3 | 2 | 4 | – | 15 |
| Local government | – | – | – | – | 1 | 6 | 1 | 6 | 7 | – | 1 | – | – | 22 |
| Militia | – | – | – | 1 | – | 1 | 4 | 4 | 3 | 10 | 12 | 2 | – | 37 |
| Miscellaneous | – | – | – | 3 | – | 1 | 1 | – | 2 | 3 | – | 2 | 1 | 13 |
| Trade[b] | 2 | 10 | 7 | 2 | 3 | 8 | – | 2 | 6 | – | – | – | – | 40 |
| Total | 7 | 16 | 16 | 12 | 11 | 45 | 26 | 28 | 35 | 43 | 40 | 30 | 5 | 314 |

[a] The figures do not include those drafted by Macdonald alone or Mitford alone in response to queries directed to them individually.
[b] No letter books from the Board of Trade, the source of most queries and opinions regarding trade, exist for the period 1797–9.

division of booty between British and East India Company forces. War also influenced the body of opinions written on international affairs. These tended to address such questions as whether a foreign-born individual, usually a French refugee, could be considered a British subject, or what law applied in a captured territory. Several opinions addressed the rights of neutrals, most notably the United States of America. Opinions on financial matters covered a broad spectrum, from the problems of individual businessmen unable to operate abroad, to advice to the First Minister on proposed tax legislation. Matters of local government directed to the law officers typically consisted of petitions from towns alleging various rights and privileges. Questions relating to the governance of the Isle of Man were also frequently raised. Irish affairs were largely outside the sphere of the English Attorney and Solicitor General. They were, however, asked to review Irish legislation, and public documents such as pardons, warrants, and proclamations having special application to Ireland. Finally, the law officers also provided advice on such miscellaneous topics as patents, peerage claims, and royal marriages.

Government queries to the law officers were of two types: 'Cases' and 'Letters'. Cases consisted of precisely framed questions, and included relevant factual and legal details. Their level of sophistication probably indicates the work of the Treasury Solicitor or a nascent departmental legal staff. Most queries, however, appeared in the form of Letters, apparently casual, offhand requests that the law officers 'take into your immediate consideration' a particular matter. In fact, however, even these documents demonstrate a certain degree of formality. First, the question posed never officially originated with the author of the letter. While this may have been accurate where a clerk or secretary passed on the requirements of his superiors, it was a convention when written by a minister. Secondly, the question might not even have originated in the relevant department. In the spring of 1795 Scott wrote a note to John King, the Under-Secretary of State for the Home Department stating: 'I think this question will do, "what descendants of natural born subjects of His Majesty, are by law deemed natural born subjects, though born abroad?" ' That Scott was drafting a question to himself is evident from the fact that on 2 April 1795 a letter from the Duke of Portland asked

Scott precisely that question with reference to officers in the Irish Brigade.[16]

The style of the request dictated the style of the response, so these were also of two types. The opinions answering questions posed in Cases were usually brief and informally written, often on the back of the Case itself. Letters, by contrast, received far more studied replies. An opinion of this kind repeated the entire Letter before providing the answer. The document typically concluded either 'All which is humbly submitted to Your Majesty's royal wisdom' or 'We have the honour to be your most obedient servants'. The choice of conclusion depended upon the source of the query, because the law officers directed their opinions to their true, rather than their ostensible questioner. For example, they replied to the Board of Trade rather than to its secretary. They wrote directly to ministers, but if ministerial queries also conveyed royal commands, they would address their opinions to the King. The very formal Letter style of these law officers contrasts with the opinions written by their close contemporaries. In particular, Richard Pepper Arden, who served in the Shelburne and Pitt ministries, and John Nicholl, Advocate General from 1798 to 1809, seem to have been far less concerned with verbatim transcripts of the questions presented to them. Rather they tended briefly to summarise the questions in the context of their analyses.

Certain conventions also applied to the presentation of the opinion. The majority of requests for legal advice in Scott's time were addressed to both the Attorney and Solicitor General, and in almost all of these situations the men concerned drafted their opinions as joint statements.[17] If an opinion expressed doubts or concerns, they were joint doubts and concerns; an opinion would not normally indicate a divergence of thought or even that the two authors had considered the matter independently. A few opinions to the Customs Office do contain independent statements instead of the usual combined effort. One such document provides an

---

[16] J. Scott to John King, undated, PRO, HO48(5); Portland to J. Scott, 2 April 1795, PRO, HO49(3).

[17] Particular matters, such as prisoner petitions, seem to have been the sole province of the Attorney General. A series of requests for the attendance of the law officers at meetings of the Board of Trade also indicates that the presence of both was preferred, but one would suffice. See, e.g., Cottrell to Macdonald, 8 June 1791, PRO, BT3(3); Fawkener to J. Scott, 1 May 1794, PRO, BT3(5). The law officers did write separate opinions to the Customs Office.

interesting example of the individual styles of Scott and Mitford. In March 1793 they each drafted brief comments upon an opinion written by Macdonald in February of that year. The opinion concerned whether the Customs Commissioners should pay the usual bounty to a grain exporter. The exportation was contrary to an Order in Council, but the Customs officials had mistakenly allowed it to proceed. A subsequent statute, moreover, had rendered suspect the legal authority of the Order, and in one section had declared it unjustified by law. Macdonald had described the question as 'very doubtful' and advised obtaining a judicial opinion. Both Scott and Mitford disagreed, but they expressed themselves very differently. On 14 March Scott wrote:

The strong inclination of my opinion is that the exporter is entitled to the bounty; and with great deference to the opinion above stated, I rather think if the law is that the exporter is entitled, or if it be probable that such would be the decision that the taking the opinion of a court of law would be inexpedient.

Two weeks later Mitford, the newly appointed Solicitor General, penned a far more confident report:

The exportation was clearly legal; if it is true, as stated in the Act of Parliament, that the Order in Council could not be justified by law, I think it too late now to enquire whether that recital in the Act is true; and I must presume the exportation was legal, not having been lawfully prohibited. The consequence seems to me clear, that the exporter is entitled to the bounty, the subsequent Act doing no more than justifying the officers, who obeyed the Order in Council, without affirming the Order, or attributing any fault to those who disobeyed it.[18]

Another pair of law officers, Edward Thurlow and Alexander Wedderburn, in office together in the early 1770s, had written some of their opinions separately. As the two are known to have disliked each other, it is tempting to account for their individual submissions as resulting from personal preference. Similarly, the occasional references to their work indicate a fairly close collaboration between Scott and Mitford, which would accord with the more prevalent style of joint opinions. Scott concluded an informal note in March 1795 to John King: 'Be so good as to direct your references to the Solicitor General as I am under the

---

[18] Macdonald to Customs Commissioners, 9 February 1793, PRO, CUST41(11). Appended to this document are the separate remarks of Scott, dated 14 March 1793 and Mitford, dated 27 March 1793.

necessity of going out of Town for a few days, but I shall leave my opinion with him.'[19] Romilly thus described Scott and Mitford reviewing the draft of Bentham's Bill: '[T]hey promised to settle it before they parted, and I left them with the Bill before them, and pens in their hands.'[20] Nevertheless, neither Scott, Macdonald, nor Mitford regarded his contribution as equivalent to that of his colleague. This is evident from their strict adherence in their opinions to the manner in which queries were phrased. While a request to both the Attorney and Solicitor General would produce an opinion which did not distinguish the individual authors, both would have contributed to it. Consequently, if one had to draft the document alone, he would indicate whether he had at least consulted with his absent associate. In October 1791, Macdonald thus concluded an opinion: 'This report has been seen & approved by Mr Solicitor General, whose absence prevents his subscribing it.'[21] Occasionally Mitford answered queries without having previously obtained Scott's view. This typically occurred when Scott visited Durham to fulfil his duties as Chancellor of the County Palatine, as Mitford would make clear. He thus prefaced an opinion to Lord Grenville in October 1795:

I have not had any opportunity of communicating with the Attorney General on the subject; but apprehending that your Lordship might be desirous of my separate opinion, as the obtaining the opinion of the Attorney General must be attended with delay, I have thought it most adviseable to submit immediately my sentiments for your Lordship's consideration.[22]

In the same way, one law officer would not normally contribute to a report upon a question directed only to his colleague. Scott answered alone all inquiries directed specifically to him as Attorney General. While certainly he may have mentioned these matters informally to Mitford, the opinions give no indication of this. Macdonald had followed a similar practice.

Official queries and opinions comprise the bulk of the correspondence between ministers and the law officers. William Pitt

---

[19] J. Scott to King, March 1795, PRO, HO48(5).

[20] Romilly to Bentham, 2 May 1797, Dinwiddy and Rosen, *Bentham collected works*, V:367.

[21] Macdonald to George III, 8 October 1791, PRO, HO48(1).

[22] Mitford to Lord Grenville, 19 October 1795, C. Parry (ed.), *Law officers' opinions to the Foreign Office*, 97 vols. (London, 1970–73), I:282–5.

did occasionally discuss legal matters casually. In an undated note Scott offered an apology for overwhelming the First Minister with materials.

Dear Sir,
   I fear you will be considerably alarmed by the bulk of the papers which I send you: but they will not employ, in your way of reading, a quarter of an hour: and I think myself bound to have the benefit of your advice both with respect to the particular proceeding, & to give you the opportunity of seeing how much may be done to prevent fraud by a little of regulation. You will recollect that I mentioned the subject to you a few days ago.[23]

If ministers regularly requested information informally, however, the evidence has not survived. Scott's few informal replies to ministerial queries indicate that he rendered them, not because such had been solicited or because he felt such informality appropriate, but because he could manage nothing better. Nor would he fail to acknowledge the lack of a formal opinion. While on a forced absence in Wales in September 1792 he attempted to answer a query from the Home Secretary. After apologising for being unable to consider the matter fully, he added that he hoped Mr Dundas would excuse the form 'because tho I would not have it considered, & indeed it cannot be considered as an official act, I should be sorry to be thought without a real anxiety to consider the subject and to form an opinion upon it'.[24] Scott and his colleagues seem to have felt far more comfortable writing informally to persons holding lesser offices. This distinction between the tone taken with ministers and with less exalted government personnel is found in the official correspondence of several of the law officers of George III.
   Taken together, the opinions provide certain insights into how Scott, Macdonald, and Mitford regarded their authority with respect to the senior officials. In addition to formality, the opinions display considerable respect towards their recipients and other responsible persons. In general, these law officers did not easily criticise such individuals. After mentioning the failure of some local officials to interpret a statute correctly, Scott and Mitford described the measure as 'perhaps so ambiguously ex-

---

[23] J. Scott to William Pitt, undated, PRO (Chatham papers), 30/8 321:153.
[24] J. Scott to Dundas, 19 September 1792, PRO, HO48(2). See also J. Scott [probably to Dundas], undated [probably December 1793], PRO, HO48(3).

pressed as to excuse the mistake'.[25] They likewise hesitated when their opinion might create a conflict:

> At the same time, as our opinion appears to be in contradiction to that of Marquis Townshend, & the late Lord Amherst ... we cannot entertain this opinion without great diffidence, or without fearing that something has escaped our attention which induced persons so eminently informed on the subject to entertain a different opinion.[26]

If, however, they conceived that they had been treated negligently, the Crown lawyers were much offended. Scott and Mitford complained bitterly of incomplete instructions, unusually phrased requests, and the lack of necessary documentation. Once they rebuked Portland for having sent them 'only the printed copy of the articles of constitution referred to by Your Grace's letter, and that copy ... only in the Italian language'.[27] Angry upon learning that one of their opinions had been shown to private persons, Scott and Mitford had to be assured that henceforth access would be limited to 'members of the cabinet or official persons of such a description as are admitted to the perusal of the most confidential papers'.[28] Even reports to the King could mention failings, albeit with considerable deference. In June 1792 Macdonald and Scott pointed out that 'the papers above mentioned do not afford such information as we humbly submitted in our former report to be necessary, before we presumed to offer an opinion'.[29]

In the area of professional discretion the opinions likewise suggest a generally docile attitude on the part of Scott and his associates, not unmixed with a degree of spirit. The question of discretion typically arose when they addressed issues related to, but not strictly part of, the questions posed. As might be expected from persons who began most of their opinions by repeating verbatim the query they had received, Scott, Macdonald, and Mitford were very careful, almost pedantic, in establishing precisely the question they should answer. On being asked by Portland in March 1799 to prepare the draft of a proclamation, Scott

---

[25] J. Scott and Mitford to Portland, 31 May 1797, PRO, HO119(1). See also Macdonald and J. Scott to Grenville, 15 January 1790, PRO, HO48(1).

[26] J. Scott and Mitford to Portland, 27 November 1797, PRO, HO48(6).

[27] J. Scott and Mitford to Portland, 12 September 1794, PRO, HO48(4). See also J. Scott and Mitford to Portland, 17 December 1796, PRO, HO119(1).

[28] W. Wickham to J. Scott and Mitford, 15 May 1799, answering J. Scott and Mitford to Portland, 14 May 1799, PRO, HO119(1), HO48(8).

[29] Macdonald and J. Scott to George III, 22 June 1792, PRO, HO48(2).

and Mitford produced the instrument with the observation: 'We presume, from the terms of Your Grace's letter, that the necessity of the case, & the urgency of the occasion, have induced Your Grace to order us to prepare the proclamation, without requiring our opinion as to the legality of the measure.'[30] Only upon receiving a further request for such an opinion did they provide it. Having decided to render an opinion, however, the law officers were not averse to enlarging the scope of their discussion to include somewhat peripheral matters. They usually felt obliged, however, to justify what they had done as helpful or proper.[31] When they ventured into matters of policy, they became even more guarded. Officially, they did not give advice on political questions. When Scott argued against a proposed Order in Council in January 1796 he added: 'If my doubt did not arise upon a point of law, I should not presume to suggest it.'[32] He and his colleagues did not actually avoid the political dimension of questions, however, they merely claimed to do so. A disclaimer such as 'We do not presume to submit any thing with respect to the propriety of authorizing ...' frequently prefaced their suggestions. These were usually brief, but probably did not leave the reader in doubt of the author's views. On being asked whether the government should bring forward legislation to avoid the harmful consequences of enforcement of a colonial statute, Scott and Mitford raised with Portland the practical considerations of asserting parliamentary sovereignty:

we presume your Grace did not mean to require of us an opinion on matter of political expediency but to require our opinion as to the legal operation of such an Act. Upon this subject we beg leave to submit to Your Grace's consideration, whether any law to be passed by Parliament here would not be an interference with the internal legislation of the colonies, which Parliament has of late not been disposed to exercise.[33]

A closer examination of the opinions in a particular area will provide a better sense of the kind of work Scott and his fellow law officers performed. Colonial matters frequently occupied their attention. Scott contributed to forty-eight colonial opinions, and

---

[30] J. Scott and Mitford to Portland, 15 March 1799, PRO, HO48(8).
[31] See, e.g., J. Scott and Mitford to Portland, 27 February 1797, PRO, HO48(6) and J. Scott and Mitford to Portland, 3 February 1798, PRO, HO48(7).
[32] J. Scott (probably to Cottrell), 25 January 1796, PRO, PC1/34/A90.
[33] J. Scott and Mitford to Portland, 11 March 1799, PRO, HO48(8).

the departmental letter books contain a further twenty-seven queries from the period for which no written answer exists. The opinions concern seventeen different colonies and treat a variety of questions, although they tend to address issues of local rather than imperial significance. Most originated with a colonial authority: the governor, agent, or commanding military officer. That individual posed a question to the Home Secretary, who in turn directed the matter to the law officers. Not surprisingly, colonial administrators tended to seek answers to problems particular to themselves. Less frequently the law officers received queries which originated, as far as can be determined, from the government in London. These were typically broader in scope or concerned matters of appointment. Very occasionally the personal query of a private individual, a colonist or military officer, was directed to the Crown lawyers.

In contrast to their general attitude towards receiving advice from other government lawyers, Scott, Macdonald, and Mitford took advantage of available resources when making recommendations on colonial matters. When possible they conferred with former colonial legal officials.[34] They also tended to defer to local authorities, particularly colonial law officers and members of the judiciary. In November 1789, Macdonald and Scott declined to serve as counsel in the proceedings brought by the former lessees to Crown lands in Quebec against their successors to secure compensation for improvements, because the Crown might prove an interested party. At the same time, however, they observed:

His Majesty's Attorney General of the province of Quebec may probably have a more intimate knowledge of the subject in question than we are able to form, & may therefore if our reasons are stated, be able to satisfy your lordships in an answer to them that we have not formed accurate notions upon the subject.[35]

In May 1797, Scott and Mitford acknowledged the doubts expressed by the civil authorities on St Christopher with regard to their capacity to institute criminal proceedings against a suspected

---

[34] See, e.g., William Scott, Macdonald, J. Scott to George III, 4 March 1791, PRO, HO48(1); John Nicholl, J. Scott, Mitford to Portland, 20 March 1799, PRO, HO48(8).

[35] Macdonald and J. Scott to the Lords of the Treasury, 9 November 1798, PRO, T64(189). See also W. Scott and Mitford (concurrence of J. Scott noted) to Dundas, 22 June 1794, PRO, HO48(4).

murderer on the island of Antigua. Professing to have no information themselves, they were content to leave the matter in the hands of the Solicitor General of Antigua, having 'signified our approbation of the measures recommended by Mr Burke, in confidence that he is fully informed upon the subject'.[36]

The fact that the bulk of queries really came from remote colonial officials rather than ministers may in part account for an interesting feature of colonial opinions – the length of time the law officers took to produce them. The differences in sample size and the impossibility of calculating the response time in all instances precludes a direct comparison between the colonial opinions and those on other matters. Nevertheless, many colonial opinions were produced in a month, and two to six months was not exceptional, while most queries on other matters seem to have required less than a week. It is possible that the frequent inclusion of the Advocate General in colonial opinions also resulted in delay. Furthermore, despite their reliance on the colonial legal community, the Attorney and Solicitor probably found answering these queries far from simple. Long after he had ceased to be a law officer, Scott would recall a conversation in which he had explained to the King some of the burdens imposed on himself and Macdonald:

I stated to him that the attention of his law officers was called to matters of international law, public law, and the laws of revenue and other matters, with which, not having been previously familiar they were obliged to devote to them a vast deal of time, and to withdraw it from those common matters of business.[37]

Implementation of the Canada Act, 31 Geo. III c. 31, was one of these 'uncommon matters' which occupied Scott's time as a law officer. Passed in 1791, this statute divided the country into two provinces, Upper and Lower Canada. Under the supreme authority of the Governor General, the Lieutenant Governor of each province was assisted by an appointed legislative council and an elected assembly. The statute also provided for an endowed Anglican church. Although Scott occupied the junior legal post in January 1793, the meditative style of the opinion signed by

---

[36] J. Scott and Mitford to Portland, 8 May 1797, PRO, HO48(6).
[37] Lord Eldon, J. Scott, *Lord Eldon's anecdote book*, ed. A. L. J. Lincoln and R. L. McEwen (London, 1960), 116.

himself, his brother, and Macdonald on the potential disabilities of Canadian legislators reads very much like Scott's work. The three lawyers had been asked whether particular individuals were disqualified from serving in the Council or Assembly of Lower Canada, and, if so, whether this could be overcome now and avoided in future.[38] The opinion began with the pointed observation that a lack of sufficient information prevented a determination of the precise circumstances of the individuals involved. Apparently they had either departed Quebec with the French troops or resided in France at the time of the cession of Canada. In either case they would not come within the requirements of the Canada Act.

The law officers enlarged the scope of their discussion when they came to offer recommendations. They noted first that in the present case the statute provided that the Council would decide all questions of eligibility of its own members, with appeal to the King in Parliament. Three possible means of avoiding future problems, however, did present themselves. The British Parliament might pass a corrective statute. This the law officers hesitated to endorse, as it raised the thorny question of 'how far a constitution once given to a colony by the Parliament of Great Britain can in any respect be altered by Act of Parliament'. Moreover, even if they supposed that parliamentary sovereignty permitted interference with the domestic affairs of the colony, section 46 of the Canada Act, which reserved to the British Parliament the right to legislate with regard to commerce and navigation, might imply 'that any further power of the legislation in the British Parliament except in the reserved cases, is acknowledged not to exist'. They next raised the possibility of a statute passed by the colonial legislature, but quickly rejected it, as that body had no authority to make laws repugnant to the Canada Act. The third and most complicated alternative gained their qualified support. An Act of the British Parliament could lift the above-mentioned restriction on the Canadian legislature to enable it to act contrary to the Canada Act on this occasion. The law officers desired further consideration of the matter, made no claims for the expediency of their proposal, and only submitted whether it

[38] Dundas to W. Scott, Macdonald, and J. Scott, 28 December 1792, PRO, HO49(1).

'might not be practicable'. Perhaps this lukewarm endorsement helped dissuade Dundas, the Home Secretary, from pursuing any course of action in this matter.[39]

Scott probably would have felt less pleased to be held responsible for an opinion from the summer of 1793, in which he, William Scott, and Mitford erred in answering a slightly different question from the one asked. In July 1793, Dundas inquired whether the patent appointing the new Bishop of Quebec might also state that the Bishop and his successors 'shall be entitled to be summoned to the legislative council' of the province.[40] The law officers answered that 'His Majesty cannot grant that the said Dr. Mountain and his successors to the said see shall be summoned to the legislative councils', which was not precisely what Dundas wished to include. Moreover, they failed to mention that section 6 of the statute actually included the right to be summoned among those vested in the Bishop; they said only that His Majesty could order the Governor to grant a writ of summons to the Bishop to attend the Council.[41] On this small, technical question, the law officers seem here to have been rather careless.

In their opinion of May 1794 they showed greater attention to the statute, this time in the face of possible political pressure. Dundas requested that they review a draft of proposed additional instructions to the Governor General, Lord Dorchester, enabling him to appoint members of the Council.[42] While this measure apparently originated with Dorchester,[43] Dundas seems not to have regarded it as inappropriate. Rather, he asked whether members appointed by virtue of these or any instructions proposed by the law officers would have the same authority as those appointed by His Majesty. Scott, William Scott, and Mitford did not hesitate to condemn the extension of Lord Dorchester's authority to appoint members to the Council; that authority rested

---

[39] W. Scott, Macdonald and J. Scott to George III, 8 January 1793, PRO, HO48(3). The law officers made a comparable recommendation for the Assembly, as the Canada Act did not provide for any mode of determining cases of disability with respect to it.

[40] Dundas to W. Scott, J. Scott and Mitford, 5 July 1793, PRO, HO49(1).

[41] W. Scott, J. Scott and Mitford to Dundas, 16 July 1793, PRO, HO48(3).

[42] Dundas to W. Scott, J. Scott and Mitford, 25 May 1794, PRO, HO49(1).

[43] In their opinion the law officers alluded to complaints mentioned by Lord Dorchester. W. Scott, J. Scott and Mitford to Dundas, 5 June 1794, PRO, HO48(4).

only with the King. Alluding to complaints by Lord Dorchester of the difficulties engendered by this regulation, they offered no solace beyond appointment by the King of auxiliary councillors upon whom the Governor could call as vacancies occurred.[44]

Nor was this the only instance when the law officers declined to approve a proposal having government support. Their careful attention to the law resulted in extremely cautious advice with regard to plans to reorganise or extend colonial judiciaries in the West Indies, Australia, and India. In the summer of 1794, John Scott, William Scott, and Mitford successfully resisted the plan to alter the manner of prize adjudication in the West Indies. It was proposed that the commissions for adjudicating prize cases be withdrawn from the vice-admiralty courts on the several islands. In their place two prize courts would be established, one for Jamaica and the other for the Leeward and Windward Islands.[45] The law officers foresaw two basic problems with the plan. First, it failed to deal adequately with the existing court structure. General practice and the recently enacted Prize Act, 33 Geo. III c. 66, dictated that commissions for prize cases issue only to admiralty courts. The proposed court in Jamaica, therefore, would have to be designated a vice-admiralty court, and it was not clear how this tribunal would differ from the existing vice-admiralty court on that island. The proposed court for the Leeward and Windward Islands, moreover, would have to be designated a court of vice-admiralty for all the islands, in order to exercise prize jurisdiction throughout that region. In both Jamaica and the Leeward and Windward Islands the creation of these new courts would have the likely effect of superseding the existing vice-admiralty courts and causing 'serious difficulties' for the cases depending therein. Secondly, the proposed courts were unlikely to prove effective. '[T]he High Court of Admiralty itself, and the Lords Commissioners of appeal in prize cases, have experienced considerable difficulties in executing their processes in the said islands', consequently one court, lacking both a venerable reputation and a local presence, could hardly be expected to execute justice effectively across several islands. In effect, the law officers

---

[44] W. Scott, J. Scott and Mitford to Dundas, 5 June 1794, PRO, HO48(4).
[45] Portland to W. Scott, J. Scott and Mitford, 25 July 1794, PRO, HO49(1).

pronounced themselves dissatisfied with the proposal and politely returned it to Portland:

Considering the momentous changes proposed to be made in the judicial establishments of so important a part of the empire, we venture to suggest to your Grace the necessity of affording us more precise information of his Majesty's intentions before we can venture to give such an opinion as your Grace's letter appears to us to require upon the mode to be adopted for carrying such instructions into execution, & especially before we can proceed to prepare any instruments which may be necessary for such purpose.[46]

In July 1794 Portland requested that the Attorney and Solicitor review the draft of a warrant for a commission to establish a court of criminal judicature on Norfolk Island, located off the coast of Australia.[47] In their answer they advised against issuing the commission, because they were uncertain how to interpret the underlying statute. It was intended that the court on Norfolk Island should exercise a jurisdiction equivalent to that of the criminal court in New South Wales. The latter tribunal was authorised by the Act of 27 Geo. III c. 2, which stated that the court would pronounce judgment of death,

if the offence be capital, or of such corporal punishment, not extending to capital punishment, as to the said court shall seem meet; and in cases not capital, by pronouncing judgment of such corporal punishment, not extending to life or limb, as to the said court shall seem meet.

The Act of 34 Geo. III c. 45 authorised the establishment of the court on Norfolk Island, but it stated that the court would pronounce judgment of death 'if the offence be capital, or of such corporal punishment, not extending to capital punishment, as to the said court shall seem meet'. Scott and Mitford asserted that this statute might not in fact establish a court with discretionary power in capital cases as well as the power to inflict corporal punishment in non-capital cases, as the Act of 27 Geo. III c. 2 did. Rather, it might only authorise punishment in capital cases. Until the correct interpretation of the statute was determined, the commission should not issue, because it might grant unwarranted, and therefore illegal, powers to the court.[48]

Portland acknowledged the uncertainty they had mentioned,

---

[46] W. Scott, J. Scott and Mitford to Portland, 9 August 1794, PRO, HO48(3).

[47] Portland to J. Scott and Mitford, 12 July 1794, PRO, HO49(1).

[48] J. Scott and Mitford to Portland, 18 August 1794, PRO, HO48(4).

which had resulted from a copying error. Nevertheless, he asked Scott and Mitford if this problem could not be overcome:

At the same time, it being very desirable that a commission for a court of criminal judicature at Norfolk island should be framed, pursuant to the said Act, I am to desire that you will reconsider the same with that view, and report to me, for His Majesty's information, your opinion whether the Act as it stands, does not give a discretionary power, in non-capital cases, to the court proposed to be established under the same.[49]

Scott and Mitford, however, hesitated to comply with this request. They believed 'this imperfect Act' did indeed only authorise the court to award punishment in capital cases. An analogous power in non-capital cases might be implied, but they found such a construction doubtful. They repeated their advice against issuing the commission in the terms of that for New South Wales, which specifically authorised corporal punishment in non-capital cases. Instead, they suggested that the proposed court might rely upon the general enabling language of the statute, authorising the court to punish crimes according to the law of England. 'If this should produce any inconvenience, we think it unavoidable until the defect in the Act shall have been remedied by Parliament. The expediency of sending to the country a commission under such circumstances we humbly submit to His Majesty's wisdom.'[50] In the event Parliament repealed the 34 Geo. III c. 45 the following year and enacted the 35 Geo. III c. 18, which tracked precisely the 27 Geo. III c. 2. Scott and Mitford thereafter approved the draft of a commission for Norfolk Island based on that statute.[51]

In October 1798 Scott and Mitford received a request from Dundas to prepare a warrant for a charter to create new Crown courts in India.[52] Since 1773 India had had a Supreme Court in Calcutta. In 1797, in an attempt to professionalise the judiciary and establish a system of Crown courts distinct from those of the East India Company, Parliament had enacted the 37 Geo. III c. 142. This abolished the existing Mayor's courts in Madras and Bombay and replaced them with Recorder's courts. These tribu-

---

[49] Portland to J. Scott and Mitford, 19 August 1794, PRO, HO49(1).

[50] J. Scott and Mitford to Portland, 30 August 1794, PRO, HO48(4).

[51] Portland to J. Scott, 4 May 1795, PRO, HO49(3); J. Scott and Mitford to Portland, 8 May 1795, PRO, HO48(5).

[52] J. Scott and Mitford to Dundas, 9 January 1798, PRO, CO323(92).

nals would consist of the mayor, three aldermen, and a recorder appointed by the Crown, and would exercise civil, criminal, admiralty, and ecclesiastical jurisdiction, with appeals to the Supreme Court in Calcutta. Scott and Mitford expressed reservations about the ultimate success of their undertaking. While not discussing these in detail, they found fault with both the underlying statute and its implementation. They found the 37 Geo. III c. 142 confusing. Moreover, they were not satisfied with the charter authorising the court in Calcutta, but felt obliged to draft the proposed charter in conformity therewith:

fearing that the introduction of new provisions or any attempt to express with more clearness & precision the provisions adopted from the Calcutta charter might have the effect, not only of introducing some difference in the administration of justice in the three settlements but also of raising doubts with respect to the construction of the Calcutta charter, & the authorities given by it to the Supreme Court thereby established.[53]

Before the charter could be executed, however, an additional complication arose. Thomas Strange, the newly designated Recorder for Madras, was desirous of departing for India and taking up his post. He wanted the warrant for that tribunal immediately, without provision for the court in Bombay, for which no recorder had been named. In an undated letter, probably to Dundas, Scott advised that such was not permitted under the Act of 37 Geo. III c. 142. The language of the statute, he explained, granted to the King the power of creating two courts by a single charter, not by different charters at different times, and with possibly different powers. He added:

this seems consistent with what has been done in all former charters, and it is very important, because, if the doubt be well founded, not only the charter, which is now granted for Madras only, & all acts done under it, would be void, but that, which shall hereafter be granted for Bombay, would be liable to the same objection.

Scott requested that his concerns be passed on to the Lord Chancellor, but he was not inclined to alter his opinion for the benefit of Mr Strange, except to suggest that he might merit some compensation:

If this doubt turns out of importance enough to prevent Mr S. from going out by the present ship in consequence of the non-appointment of a

[53] *Ibid.*

Recorder for Bombay, it will be a hardship upon him which will meet with due consideration, no doubt, on the part of Government.[54]

Such provision did not prove necessary, however, as Strange received his commission on 20 February 1798. It is unclear whether that document reflected Scott's concerns.

Taken together, these legal opinions provide a particular insight into the status of the law officers within the executive government. While common authorship frequently complicates the task of identifying a particular contributor, these documents do have the benefit of a single audience. In these private opinions the law officers did not have to take into account the effect of their remarks upon the House of Commons or the general public. As a result, the substance and tone of the recommendations probably reflect their authors' place in the executive hierarchy. The most obvious feature of the opinions is their formality. Their precise language and generally deferential tone suggest that, at least officially, the law officers saw themselves as providing a service and regarded ministers, their usual clients, as entitled to considerable respect. Beneath this layer of submission, however, lay a certain independence. They too occupied offices meriting respectful treatment, and ministers did not encounter servility in the Attorney and Solicitor General. About the extent of their actual authority the Crown lawyers were less certain. In legal matters they asserted themselves quite openly, frequently declining to amend their advice to suit the government. In political matters they were not so confident. They did speak out, but attempted to insulate themselves, both from possible impropriety and from responsibility for potentially unwise remarks. When drafting documents purely for perusal within the confines of government this was not so difficult. Scott would find the task of balancing his political and professional duties more onerous when he had to perform in a public setting.

[54] J. Scott (probably to Dundas), undated [probably January–February 1798], PRO, CO323(92).

# 4

# FORMAL POLITICS

John Scott was not, during his years as Solicitor General, one of the more prolific speakers in the House of Commons. On the contrary, he addressed the House on only fifteen different occasions. This level of participation, however, was not unusual for a junior law officer. Of those of his immediate predecessors who held office for a substantial period, only Alexander Wedderburn spoke much more frequently; James Wallace spoke twice in two years. As regards substance, Scott contributed several modest, rather colourless efforts which suggest little more than a workmanlike adherence to his duty to support the Attorney General and the government. In May 1792 he defended Archibald Macdonald's decision not to indict Birmingham magistrates for failing to prevent or control recent rioting there.[1] In December he spoke on behalf of the Bill to regulate the presence of aliens in England.[2] In May 1789 he had supported an inquiry into the slave trade, possibly out of friendship for the inquiry's principal advocate William Wilberforce.[3] Not all of Scott's speeches were of this sort, however. During the debates on the King's illness in the winter of 1788–9, the Hastings impeachment in 1790, and the Libel Act the following year, Scott played a far more significant role. Since they contributed to the survival of the government, Scott's efforts during the Regency crisis were the most immediately important. Nevertheless, in all three situations he demonstrated a growing ability to exploit the political dimension to parliamentary discussion, which generally increased his own value to the government.

[1] W. Cobbett (ed.), *The parliamentary history of England ... to 1803*, 36 vols. (London, 1806–20), XXIX:1455–6.
[2] J. Debrett (ed.), *The parliamentary register ... 1780–99*, 54 vols. (London, 1782–1799), XXXIV:237.
[3] *The Times*, 27 May 1789, 2, col. 4.

In November 1788, the King suffered a complete mental break-down that rendered him incapable of participating in the administration of the government. As soon as it became clear that he was unlikely either to die or recover immediately, politicians began to speculate on the likely consequences of a prolonged incapacity. It was generally accepted that some kind of Regency must be established, with its powers exercised by the Prince of Wales.[4] Moreover, it was widely understood that, were he to find full prerogative powers at his disposal, the Prince would not only dismiss Pitt in favour of Charles Fox, but he would use royal patronage to fortify Fox's ministry against the anticipated hostility of the King, in the event of his recovering.[5] Under the circumstances, therefore, while the opposition hoped for the Prince's swift accession to full political power, it was in the interest of ministers both to delay the Regency and restrict the scope of its authority.[6]

The legal status of the King, Regent, and Parliament in the event was not obvious. Neither law nor precedent clearly established what authority, if any, remained in an insane King, or how and to what extent a Regent could supply any deficiency. During the debates in December, however, both the government and opposition positions on these issues emerged. Briefly, the opposition argued that insanity, so long as it lasted, was equivalent to the death of the sovereign. Consequently, royal powers passed by right to the heir apparent during incapacity just as they did upon a demise of the Crown.[7] Ministers, on the other hand, maintained

---

[4] Apparently Pitt briefly considered asking the Queen when it was reported in early December that the Prince of Wales would decline a limited Regency. J. Derry, *The regency crisis and the Whigs* (Cambridge, 1963), 12.

[5] Writing well after the fact, Scott suggested that the opposition had been suspected of far darker intentions: 'I well remember, that it was the universal persuasion that, if a Regency was once appointed his Majesty never would be restored to his throne, tho' he might be restored to his mental health.' Lord Eldon, J. Scott, *Lord Eldon's anecdote book*, ed. A. L. J. Lincoln and R. L. McEwen (London, 1960), 119–20.

[6] In a letter to his cousin Henry Reay on 25 December 1788 Scott indicated his feelings about the political situation: 'You will see I have been doing my best – I have prepared myself for political death – for a month I have had one foot in the grave – but I feel no disposition but to act gracefully & firmly in the hour of my exit. We have seen stranger scenes, but as yet I think not so strange as those we shall see.' NCL (Scott Papers).

[7] See, e.g., Fox's speeches of 10 and 12 December 1788. Cobbett, *Parliamentary history*, XXVII:706–7; 720–2.

that insanity had no such effect, either upon the sovereign or the heir apparent. The King had lost the physical ability and not the right to exercise royal authority, and the appointment of a Regent to act on his behalf was an expedient rather than an application of the constitution.[8]

At the outset of the crisis, victory by the opposition seemed inevitable. In the weeks that followed, however, they were obliged steadily to retreat, so that when the King's recovery in February 1789 finally determined the issue, it marked the end of an unexpectedly successful government campaign. On 10 December 1788, Fox proclaimed the Prince's hereditary right to full royal authority, describing it as 'what no man had a right to take from him, what the law and the constitution had given him a right to take, without waiting for a declaration of either House of Parliament'.[9] Whether an impetuous gaffe or a considered opinion, this speech committed the opposition to an extreme position.[10] Instead of convincing the House speedily to entreat the Prince to accept an immediate, unrestricted Regency, moreover, it struck members as advocating hereditary royal power at the expense of Parliament. Pitt called Fox's assertions 'little less than treason to the constitution of the country', and successfully urged the House to consult precedent to determine how best to proceed.[11] On 16 December

[8] See, e.g., Pitt's speech of 10 December 1788. *Ibid.*, cols. 708–9.

[9] *Ibid.*, cols. 712–13.

[10] L. Mitchell, *Charles James Fox and the disintegration of the Whig party* (Oxford, 1971), 123–4, 128–9, has argued that two explicit positions existed among the opposition leadership in late November and early December. R. B. Sheridan, who represented the first, wanted to secure office quietly and negotiated with Lord Chancellor Thurlow to that end. Lord Loughborough and Edmund Burke, on the other hand, believed that the administration of the government should come to the Prince of Wales as a matter of right. In Mitchell's view, Fox adopted the latter position, convinced of its validity by Burke and eager to avoid an alliance with Thurlow. C. Hobhouse, *Fox* (London, 1934), p. 212, on the other hand, has seen Fox's speech of 10 December 1788 as a passionate outburst, while J. Derry, *Charles James Fox* (London, 1972), 264, 267, adopts a middle course, asserting that, while Fox's speech was a result of frustration at Pitt's attempts to procrastinate, he might have adopted Loughborough's theory to convince him that he had not been abandoned.

[11] Cobbett, *Parliamentary history*, XXVII:708, 716. The committee appointed to search for precedents consisted of W. Pitt, W. Ellis, R. P. Arden, F. Montagu, A. Macdonald, R. Vyner, H. Dundas, T. Powys, J. Scott, R. B. Sheridan, W. Hussey, I. Campbell, Marquis of Graham, Lord Belgrave, Sir G. Cooper, W. Wilberforce, W. Windham, P. Yorke, G. G. L. Gower, W. W. Grenville, and E. Burke.

1788, Pitt asserted that no person exercising royal authority on behalf of an infant, insane, or absent King had ever acted other than upon parliamentary appointment. Fox's response was unpersuasive, and the House voted 268 to 202 in favour of Pitt's resolution that Parliament had the power 'to provide the means of supplying the defect of the personal exercise of the royal authority'.[12] Six days later, a further resolution that Parliament should enact legislation creating a Regency won acceptance; an opposition amendment calling for an address to the Prince was defeated, 251 to 178.[13] Having been defeated in December on the issue of hereditary right, in January the opposition abandoned its claim for an unconditional Regency. Thereafter, Pitt successfully limited the Regent's powers with respect to patronage, disposal of royal property, and management of the royal household. By the end of the month gloom had replaced confidence among opposition members; their only consolation lay in the knowledge that the Prince, albeit constrained, would still be Regent. Worn out by a long illness,[14] Fox retired to Bath to finalise the membership of his prospective cabinet, but by the time he returned to London on 21 February 1789 the King was in a state of convalescence.

While the failure to anticipate the mood of the House had contributed to the opposition's discomfiture, so too did Pitt's careful attention to precedent and constitutional theory when framing his own position. An important document in this respect was the fragment of Sir Matthew Hale's 'Incepta de Juribus Coronae' which studied the problem of royal incapacity and made a series of recommendations.[15] The King, it asserted, had a natural and a political capacity, the one adhering to him as an individual and the other endowed upon him by the constitution. So long as he lived, the King retained this political capacity. Particular physical infirmities might render the exercise of his political duties difficult or even impossible, but they did not affect his legal capacity to perform them. As a practical matter, certainly, someone must undertake to exercise essential political duties on behalf of an infirm King. It rested with Parliament, as the remaining branch of the legislature, to appoint the person or

---

[12] *Ibid.*, cols. 746–7.     [13] *Ibid.*, col. 852.

[14] Fox had contracted dysentery during his return journey from Italy, where word of the King's illness had reached him.

[15] 'Incepta de Juribus Coronae', PRO (Chatham papers) 30/8 228(2), 210–25.

persons, having first determined what quantity of royal authority to delegate. Pitt obtained this document in mid-November, and he began his first important speech on the Regency echoing its precepts.[16] He also had a series of memoranda summarising the important events during the incapacities of Henry VI and showing how Parliament and the Council had appointed Protectors on these occasions. Although unsigned, these documents appear to be in Scott's handwriting.[17]

In addition to such advisory work, Scott also explained the government position in debate. His most important contribution came in his defence of the rather elaborate legal foundations of the proposal to create the Regency by Act of Parliament. On 22 December 1788, Scott explained how Parliament could enact legislation permitting the Regent to exercise royal authority, when the hitherto suspended royal authority was itself necessary to enact the proposed legislation. His solution was to place the Great Seal in commission and attach it to the two necessary documents – the letters patent opening the new session of Parliament, and the Bill appointing the Regent – and to ignore the fact that the King had not actually given the assent indicated by the affixing of the Seal. Despite the lack of a genuine royal assent, this solution maintained the formal rules of the constitution, and for Scott this was enough. '[B]e it remembered that upon the preservation of the forms depended the substance of the constitution.'[18]

Scott's attention to the requirements of form did not result merely from 'constitutional pedantry'.[19] He pointed out that, if the House ignored the formal requirements of the constitution such as royal assent, they would produce measures that were *prima facie* invalid. This could throw the legal system into confusion as judges, hard pressed to accept these enactments as authoritative, would abandon their proper function of declaring the law in

[16] Cobbett, *Parliamentary history*, XXVII:732–3.
[17] Unsigned memoranda, PRO (Chatham papers) 30/8 228(1), 129–32, 140–5, 146–80; *ibid.*, 228(2), 181–5.
[18] Cobbett, *Parliamentary history*, XXVII:826.
[19] J. S. Watson, *The reign of George III, 1760–1815* (Oxford, 1960), 305, uses this expression to describe the behaviour of politicians in general during the crisis. W. Holdsworth, *A history of English law*, 17 vols. (London, 1903–72), X:444, speaks slightly more generously of 'the feeling of very many lawyers and statesmen that the technical forms and rules of the constitution must at all costs be maintained'.

favour of personal interpretation. On the other hand, if an enactment contained every indication of regularity, its authority would
be unquestionable. The presence of the Great Seal on a commission, 'notwithstanding that it was not the immediate order of the
King', precluded any inquiry into how the Seal had been affixed,
because 'on the face of the proceedings, everything seems to be
taken for granted to be regular'.[20] Elsewhere, however, Scott's
defence of fictitious assent became somewhat vague, as when he
dismissed the idea that future ministers might use it to eliminate
the sovereign from the legislative process. 'The right which
necessity creates – necessity limits – and, that right of the
Commons is an exercise of their duty, and whenever they go
beyond that right, they go beyond their duty, and consequently
abuse their right.'[21] Similarly, his conclusion that fictitious assent
in the present case was a 'wholesome fiction, inasmuch as it saved
the constitution from danger, and proved that so admirably
constructed was that constitution, that it contained in itself a
provision for cases of the greatest emergency'[22] suggests that the
'neatness' of this solution had a particular attractiveness for Scott
quite apart from its constitutional validity.

*The Times*, firmly behind the government during the crisis,
warmly applauded Scott's efforts. On 26 December 1788 it
proclaimed: 'Sir John Scott, unquestionably the First Authority
of the time, has fully asserted his pre-eminent claims, and fully
proved that perfect Legal Science, and Constitutional Zeal, are
indissolubly united.'[23] The opposition, of course, was far from
convinced. Fox charged that Scott's 'whole train of reasoning' was
'enveloped in a nice kind of legal metaphysics, admirably calculated to confound the plain understandings of unlearned men, but
which, when stripped of its covering, would appear to be totally
inapplicable to the subject'.[24] William Windham complained:
'That wonder-working machine, the political capacity of the
Sovereign, was the grand spring of all the arguments, on which
the gentlemen of a certain profession relied.'[25] To these objections
Scott responded with assurances of the legality of his proposals
and the absence of lawful alternatives.

[20] Debrett, *Parliamentary register*, XXV:132.   [21] *Ibid.*

[22] Cobbett, *Parliamentary history*, XXVII:1157.

[23] *The Times*, 26 December 1788, 3, col. 2.

[24] Cobbett, *Parliamentary history*, XXVII:835.   [25] *Ibid.*, col. 1159.

[T]hey were then discussing no question of politics, nor question of party; they were all agreed as to the object; their sole object was to make the Prince of Wales regent, on the terms of the resolutions. The only difference of opinion was, which were the most safe, legal, and constitutional means of attaining their common object. He must contend, that the mode proposed in the resolution was the only legal one.[26]

Nathaniel Wraxall wrote of the confrontation between Scott and the opposition:

Scott, the Solicitor-General, opposed to these shafts of oratorical declamation the arms of legal metaphysics, endeavouring, not without success, to demonstrate that the fiction ... was dictated and justified by necessity. Fox, who well knew how to appreciate talents, and who respected Scott's abilities, which were of another order from those of Arden and of Macdonald, replied to him, putting out all the energies of his mind against an adversary so worthy of his exertions.[27]

On this occasion, however, Fox's energies proved insufficient.

Not all of Scott's remarks during the Regency debates were pitched at such a technical level. Nor did he eschew blatant political point-scoring. In his speech of 19 January 1789 he defended the fourth proposition in the Regency Bill, which made the Queen responsible for the King's person and the royal household, by appealing to patriotism. At the outset of the crisis Pitt had established himself as the defender of Parliament; speeches such as this one promoted the government's unblemished loyalty to the Crown. Remembering 'the respect due to the sovereign whom they all loved', Scott argued that the King must be maintained in circumstances commensurate with his dignity, and which enabled him easily to resume his royal authority upon his recovery.[28] The public, he warned, would find it scandalous if Parliament failed in this duty.

But let the sense of the People be taken ... in any other way, the language which they would undoubtedly hold would be, 'What, could you not do your duty for three short months? Were you so hasty to dethrone the King, your lawful Sovereign, to whom you have all sworn allegiance, that you treated him with the grossest disrespect, and stript him of every mark of Regal dignity and distinction, after he had been ill no longer than a month?'[29]

---

[26] *Ibid.*, col. 1156.

[27] N. Wraxall, *Historical and posthumous memoirs 1772–1784*, ed. H. B. Wheatley, 5 vols. (London, 1884), V:234.

[28] Cobbett, *Parliamentary history*, XXVII:1024.

[29] Debrett, *Parliamentary register*, XXV:272.

The most appropriate way to uphold the regal dignity was to entrust it to the Queen, said Scott, and he hinted that the opposition cared more for office than public good. He found it 'a gross and indecent reflexion on the high and exalted character' of the Queen to imply that she would attempt to thwart the government of her son, and dismissed the idea that the lack of patronage from the royal household could hamper him.[30] 'Was it possible, that these gentlemen could seriously argue, that the Regent, with the army, the navy, the Church, and all the officers of the public revenue at his command, could not carry on a vigorous and effectual government?'[31] Surely, asked Scott, the opposition did not mean that without additional patronage the Regent could not obtain the services of able politicians? 'Was there no man who would act from the impulse of an higher feeling, from a sense of duty, and from what they owed to their character, and to their country?'[32] Fox replied that Scott was 'labouring to enfeeble the arm of government', but the House rejected an amendment to limit the duration of the Queen's authority, 220 to 164, and approved the original proposal.[33]

While he clearly provided important legal expertise and, to a lesser extent, political rhetoric in aid of the government during the Regency crisis, Scott's participation in the Hastings impeachment debates is harder to assess. Certainly Scott was definite in his opinions and sometimes combative in his presentation, but the relationship between his statements and government policy in March and December 1790 is not clear. This uncertainty results primarily from the difficulty in determining Pitt's attitude. The opposition supported fully the impeachment of the former Governor General of India. Edmund Burke and Philip Francis were convinced that Warren Hastings was personally responsible for a corrupt and oppressive Indian administration. Others, such as Fox, fastened onto the impeachment as a means of vindicating their own conduct and embarrassing Pitt. In the condemnation of Hastings, Fox could show that his own India Bill, which had cost him high office and severely damaged his political reputation, had been necessary. Moreover, the impeachment of the foremost servant of the East India Company would force Pitt to decide

---

[30] Cobbett, *Parliamentary history*, XXVII:1025.     [31] *Ibid.*     [32] *Ibid.*
[33] Fox's remark is at *ibid.*, col. 1028.

between the powerful East India interests and his own professed support for reform.[34] Pitt's response has received different interpretations. Commentators have seen his criticism of both Hastings and the impeachment managers variously as an attempt to profit politically from either a conviction or acquittal, and as a decision to support the will of the House while ensuring fair treatment for the accused.[35] Whatever may have been the goals of the First Minister, Scott's remarks, at least in the spring of 1790, seem designed to harass the impeachment managers. It seems unlikely, moreover, that he would have pursued such a course if it conflicted directly with government policy.

The debates of mid-March 1790 concerned an alleged atrocity committed by a British soldier in 1781 during a rebellion in Oudh, an autonomous state north-west of Bengal allied with the East India Company. Trouble had begun when the Company levied additional taxes upon its dependencies to help pay for the war with France. Chait Singh, the zamindar of Benares,[36] had been assessed £50,000 a year in addition to his existing annual tax of approximately £230,000. He had failed to pay, however, and in July 1781 Hastings had had him arrested and fined £500,000.[37] This step had precipitated a rebellion, which had begun with Chait Singh's liberation and quickly spread across Oudh. In the following weeks the revolt had been put down by the Company and the Nawab of Oudh, who had a number of British officers in his service. One of these, Captain David Williams, had taken charge of the fort of Gorrukpore shortly after the fighting there ceased. Upon arrival, he had received an order from his commanding

---

[34] Mitchell, *Fox*, 106–7.

[35] *Ibid.*, 110–11, argues that Pitt determined to associate himself sufficiently with the prosecution to prevent the opposition from receiving all the glory if it succeeded, but not so much that he or his supporters would be blamed if it failed. To this end he voted against Hastings on the Benares charge, thus ensuring that the impeachment would succeed, but thereafter steadily voted against the managers on almost every occasion. J. Ehrman, *The younger Pitt: the years of acclaim* (London, 1969), 448–50, maintains that Pitt considered the charges against Hastings on their merits and gave his vote accordingly. Thereafter his government followed a decidedly non-political course.

[36] Zamindars were territorial magnates. In 1775 the Bengal Council forced the Nawab of Oudh to cede Benares, extremely wealthy as a pilgrimage city, to the Company. Watson, *Reign of George III*, 310, 317; C. C. Davies, *Warren Hastings and Oudh* (Oxford, 1939), 120–1.

[37] Watson, *Reign of George III*, 317.

officer to execute Mustapha Cawn, said to be a notorious robber who had participated in the attack on the fort. Captain Williams' compliance with this order had subsequently led to his implication in Hastings' impeachment. The so-called Benares charge, which held Hastings responsible for the rebellion and the manner in which it had been quelled, stated that 'Captain Williams, or some other British officer' had committed an atrocious murder upon a native prince.[38] Although the charge had been framed in 1786, Captain Williams had apparently not become aware of it until four years later, whereupon he had petitioned the House to undertake an inquiry whereby he might clear his name. Francis, an enthusiastic supporter of the Benares charge, had little sympathy for Captain Williams. As the recipient of Captain Williams' petition, however, he had moved an inquiry on 8 March 1790.

The motion was debated on 15 March 1790 and provoked a very rancorous discussion. General John Burgoyne spoke of the 'perversion and prostitution of honourable discipline', which had permitted British officers 'to become subject to the vilest employments of the most abominable misgovernment'.[39] Alluding to Hastings' agent, Fox wondered whether someone 'capable of making it a constant practice ... to traduce the managers of the prosecution, ought to be suffered to continue a member of that house'.[40] Scott was equally provocative. He argued that Parliament should leave this matter to the courts in order to preserve the 'constitutional security of the subject', which in the instant case meant protection against malicious prosecution. An individual maliciously prosecuted in the courts had the remedy of an action for calumny. Captain Williams, by contrast, would be crushed by the 'weight and authority' of a parliamentary inquiry without recourse. Scott identified Francis as Captain Williams' chief tormentor. The fairer course of action under those circumstances, according to Scott, would have been for Francis to prosecute

---

[38] On 8 March 1790, Francis explained that the allegation against Captain Williams had not been made for the direct purpose of incriminating him, 'but to show how horribly the country was treated by persons appointed and supported by Hastings, and to make him answerable for the consequences of his own evil government.' Cobbett, *Parliamentary history*, XXVIII:495.

[39] *Ibid.*, col. 535.

[40] *Ibid.*, col. 546. Hastings' agent was Major John Scott (1747–1819), an officer in the Bengal army. His name has been omitted in the text to avoid obvious confusion.

Captain Williams himself. 'If he was confident of what he asserted, why would not he, in a manly way, stand forward, and encounter the risk of engaging in a prosecution for which he must be personally responsible?'[41]

The suggestion of a private prosecution caused tumult on both sides of the House. Richard Pepper Arden, the Master of the Rolls, doubted whether the instant case could be prosecuted at all, let alone by a private individual: he moved to defer debate on the motion.[42] This led Pitt to withdraw his support for the inquiry, at least until they had established its legal basis.[43] Notwithstanding Scott's protest that he did not mean to imply that malice existed in this case, Francis not unreasonably charged Scott with having 'exerted his utmost efforts' to involve him in a prosecution 'for the generous purpose of exposing him to a subsequent action for damages, on a presumption, most liberally taken for granted by the learned gentleman, that it would turn out a malicious prosecution'.[44] Remarking that, far from wishing to force an inquiry, he had only acted at Captain Williams' behest, he added: 'I do not wonder that the learned gentleman [Scott] should forget the principal fact in this transaction, for facts, I know, are not in the learned gentleman's department.'[45]

An adjournment, however, was agreed to, and the debate resumed on 29 March 1790. Once more temper played a part. Arden began the discussion by asserting that the 33 Hen. VIII c. 23, which alone conferred authority to try an individual for murder outside of the realm, only applied to crimes committed against British subjects. Even if the Act could admit of a more expansive interpretation, the courts were unlikely to read it as conferring jurisdiction in the present circumstances, since it had never yet formed the basis of a prosecution.[46] He advised, therefore, that they let the matter rest. Far from convinced, Burke demanded how anyone could advocate inaction in a case 'affecting our humanity, our charity, and the laws of nature and of nations'.[47] He went on to criticise the torpor of the law officers for, instead of urging reform, 'they always appeared very reluctant, and seemed rather desirous, when the law was impotent, that

---

[41] *Ibid.*, col. 550. Scott's argument is found at cols. 549–51.
[42] *Ibid.*, cols. 552–3.    [43] *Ibid.*, col. 554.    [44] *Ibid.*, col. 559.
[45] *Ibid.*    [46] *Ibid.*, col. 561–2.    [47] *Ibid.*, col. 564.

it should remain so'.[48] The Attorney General declined to be drawn. Eschewing the role of law reformer, he remarked that he could not justify further inquiry because 'whatever might be Capt[ain] Williams' offence, he [Macdonald] was satisfied the law of the country would not reach it'.[49] Scott did not adopt a similar tone. While acknowledging that his former application of the 33 Hen. VIII c. 23 to the instant case had been 'rash', he remained doggedly opposed to the inquiry.

[H]e was well known to be fond of forms, and it had been more than once imputed to him as a matter of blame. He owned that he loved the common and ordinary forms of justice, as administered in the courts of law, and whenever a subject could be tried in those courts, that House ought not to deprive the subject of the advantages which he might derive from that situation.[50]

Then, as though determined to provoke a further confrontation, he turned to the fact that the impeachment managers had seen fit to accuse Captain Williams of a serious crime although they had not uncovered his actual role until four years after the event. Under those circumstances, 'Capt[ain] Williams was most unjustly dealt with to have had his name mentioned as at all connected with the imputation of atrocious murder'. Moreover, 'if a private individual had stated that "Capt[ain] Williams, or some other British officer" had committed an atrocious murder, without being in full possession of proof to bring the fact home to him, justice would have reached that individual'.[51]

Not surprisingly, this prompted an angry retort from Burke, who charged that, while Scott might love forms, 'respect for that house was not one of the forms he loved, since he had cast a slur upon the Commons of England and upon their most important proceedings, thereby sullying the justice of the country and stopping its course'.[52] The Speaker finally succeeded in calling him to order, whereupon Pitt asserted that he agreed with Scott, and that 'nothing which his learned friend had said, could justify the hot, intemperate, and unparliamentary- manner in which the right hon[ourable] gentleman over the way had thought proper to treat his learned friend's argument'.[53] Scott offered a token

[48] *Ibid.*, col. 566.    [49] *Ibid.*, col. 567.
[50] Debrett, *Parliamentary register*, XXVII:335.
[51] Cobbett, *Parliamentary history*, XXVIII:573.    [52] *Ibid.*, col. 574.
[53] *Ibid.*, col. 580.

apology for his contribution to the fray. He had not intended 'the smallest offence whatever against the managers; possibly his observations might as well have been spared'.[54] He declined to retract those observations, however, and actually repeated them. Francis tried to return to the issue of the inquiry, but the House had become impatient, and when Burke rose again members called for the question. In the vote that followed, the motion for the inquiry was defeated, 61 to 22.[55] Scott, however, had not yet ceased to be an irritant. On 11 May 1790, Burke wanted the House to signify their intention to persevere in the impeachment out of a sense of honour and duty, and he introduced a motion to that effect. Scott opposed it, 'as conveying an insinuation adverse to the party upon his trial, which he [Scott] did not think sufficiently grounded by anything he had heard'.[56] He thereupon divided the House, but was defeated, 48 to 31. Burke accused him of having attempted to obtain an unfair advantage by calling for a vote immediately after many members had left the House. Scott defended himself, and the Speaker was obliged to step in and adjourn the debate.

In December Scott argued against the First Minister, as well as Burke, Fox, and the other leaders of the opposition on the possible abatement of the impeachment. Like the other prominent lawyers in the House, Scott maintained that the dissolution of Parliament in June had had the effect of quashing or suspending the impeachment. Politicians on both sides of the aisle rejected this interpretation. It has been suggested that Pitt approved of the concept of non-abatement not so much on the basis of its constitutional validity as on its political utility. The impeachment having become 'a tedious and embarrassing inconvenience for the opposition' he had no wish to provide them with an easy means of escape.[57] Scott's participation, although he supported abatement, is actually not inconsistent with such a policy. Accepting it as unlikely that Scott, or any government lawyer, would have been asked to argue a legal issue contrary to his professional judgment, Scott certainly did not support abatement with much vigour. His speech on 17 December 1790 was heavy with platitudes in favour

---

[54] *Ibid.*, col. 584.
[55] Scott's remarks are found particularly at *ibid.*, cols. 573, 584.
[56] *Ibid.*, col. 794.     [57] Mitchell, *Fox*, 112.

of recognised legal principles. He did offer some specific arguments in support of his position. In each case, however, he did little more than echo Thomas Erskine, the leading speaker in favour of abatement. Fox complained that with the remarks of the Solicitor General they had heard an argument repeated for the third time.[58] Nor did the politicians find that argument persuasive. On the contrary, they responded with derogatory comments about the lawyers' failure to respect parliamentary practices. Fox described the legal members of the House as 'acting, as it were, under an *esprit de corps*, forming themselves into a sort of phalanx to set up the law of the ordinary courts of Justice as paramount to the law of Parliament'.[59] Scott, however, responded mildly to such taunts. 'He had precedents uniform and concurring to the support of his arguments, except in the solitary instance of 1678. If he was wrong in drawing the conclusions which he did from them, he could not help it, he had done it to the best of his judgement.'[60] When Burke accused the lawyers of treating the Commons merely as a stepping-stone to judicial appointments and peerages, Scott remained silent.[61] Nor did he interfere in the subsequent exchange between Burke and Erskine – Erskine remarking that Burke seemed to have forgotten who were his friends, and Burke exclaiming that he 'approved of the country being governed by law, but not by lawyers'.[62] While not about to hinder potentially divisive squabbling among the opposition, Scott declined to let his own remarks become emotional.

The vote of 143 to 30 in favour of non-abatement revealed the hopelessness of the lawyers' position, but it was not a defeat that would have unduly bothered Scott.[63] A restrained advocacy permitted him to retain his professional integrity and not unduly inconvenience the government. This interpretation of Scott's

---

[58] Debrett, *Parliamentary register*, XXVIII:279. The *General Evening Post*, 23–25 December 1790, 2, col. 4, reported of Fox: 'He was particularly severe on the Solicitor General, who, he said, had contented himself with a hacknied repetition of the arguments of those who had gone before him on the same side of the question.'

[59] Debrett, *Parliamentary register*, XXVIII:282–3.      [60] *Ibid.*, 276.

[61] *Ibid.*, 259.      [62] This exchange is found at *ibid.*, 291–2.

[63] *Ibid.*, 293. Parliament thereafter established that prorogation and dissolution do not affect impeachments. Sir T. E. May, *Erskine May's treatise upon the law, privileges, proceedings and usage of Parliament*, ed. Sir Charles Gordon, 20th edn (London, 1983), 273.

participation is supported in the attitude of the press towards the debate. *The Times* strongly approved of the outcome, asserting: 'The law makers are and ought to be superior to the cold letter of legal distinctions.'[64] Scott, however, not only avoided criticism, but won muted praise. *The World* remarked of his arguments that 'if they had not their intended effect, it must be acknowledged were acute, and conceived with much legal ingenuity'; while *The Times* admitted that 'Sir John Scott was logical in his arguments in the Impeachment'.[65]

Scott adopted a similarly mild approach in the spring of 1791 during the debates on the Bill to amend the law of criminal libel. He opposed the principal aim of the Bill, to expand the power of juries in libel trials. Such a view could easily have been perceived as an attack upon the almost sacred institution of trial by jury, and so created considerable hostility. That it did not, and that Scott succeeded in carrying his point, resulted from the coincidence of two factors. First, no leading politician gave his uncompromising support to the Bill. Secondly, Scott did not attack the Bill blatantly. Instead he disguised his opposition as simple technical objections, and so gained the advantage on lightly defended ground.

Libel of government had become a troublesome area of the criminal law by the late eighteenth century. One commentator has defined it as 'written censure upon public men for their conduct as such, or upon the laws, or upon the institutions of the country'.[66] Criminal liability, accordingly, resulted not only from publishing with the specific intent to bring public men or the institutions of government into disrepute, but also from knowingly publishing material that did in fact criticise the laws or government. This conception of libel, which regarded any criticism of legitimate political authority as wrong, conflicted with the post-Revolution acceptance of the public's right to reform the government, and inhibited serious political discussion.[67] Increasingly, during the

---

[64] *The Times*, 27 December 1790, 2, col. 2.

[65] *The World*, 24 December 1790, 3, col. 2; *The Times*, 27 December 1790, 2, col. 2.

[66] J. F. Stephen, *A history of the criminal law of England*, 3 vols. (London, 1883), II:348.

[67] Commentators have offered different analyses of the pre-1792 law of libel. Holdsworth, *History*, X:673–4, has argued that, while legally correct, the interpretation espoused by the courts in the late eighteenth century no longer

eighteenth century, critics of the existing law had urged that good faith political commentary should not constitute a crime. Until the passage of the Libel Act,[68] however, their arguments had been unavailing.

Failure had not been from lack of effort. Diligent defence counsel had frequently claimed that the prosecution must prove that the defendant actually intended to disparage the subject of the publication.[69] They were encouraged to raise this point by the habit of prosecutors to emphasise the wicked, ill-disposed tendencies of the accused.[70] This convention, however, was not incorporated into the established law of libel, which considered only the published material, and not the particular motivations of the defendant. A panel of high court judges asked to state the law in 1791 remarked:

The criminal intention charged upon the defendant in legal proceedings upon libel is generally matter of form, requiring no proof on the part of the prosecutor and admitting of no proof on the part of the defendant to rebut it. The crime consists in publishing a libel. A criminal intention in the writer is no part of the definition of libel at the common law.[71]

conformed with generally held views on political commentary. P. Hamburger, 'The development of the law of seditious libel and the control of the press', *Stanford Law Review* 37 (1985), 661–765, maintains that judges manipulated the law of libel to control sedition following the abolition of the Licensing Act in 1695. Finally M. Lobban, 'From seditious libel to unlawful assembly: Peterloo and the changing face of political crime c.1770–1820', *Oxford Journal of Legal Studies* 10 (1990), 307–52, 311, points out that libel and sedition addressed fundamentally different issues – the former being concerned with the legal significance of printed material, and the latter with the effect of a publication on society. The attempt to combine these two crimes, one of which required legal analysis and the other of which involved factual analysis, made the law generally unworkable even before the Libel Act.

[68] 32 Geo. III c. 60.

[69] For example, in December 1789 Erskine defended John Stockdale's publication of the allegedly libellous 'Review of the principal charges against Warren Hastings Esq.' by arguing the *bona fide* motivations of the author, the Revd John Logan, and pointing to the failure of the prosecution to show that Stockdale had published the pamphlet with any different purpose. T. J. Howell (ed.), *A complete collection of state trials and proceedings for high treason and other crimes and misdemeanours*, 33 vols. (London, 1816–26), XXII:263.

[70] The information submitted by Macdonald and Scott in the *Stockdale* case described the accused as being 'a wicked, seditious, and ill-disposed person', and accused him of 'most unlawfully, wickedly, and maliciously devising, contriving, and intending to asperse, scandalize, and vilify the Commons of Great Britain'. *Ibid.*, col. 240.

[71] The complete recommendations of the judges are found at *ibid.*, cols. 296–304.

Specific intent might be relevant when the criminality of a writing was not apparent from the document alone. A writer's use of irony or metaphor, or the distribution of the document among persons upon whom it had a particular effect, might necessitate a more expansive scrutiny.[72] Occasionally, a jury was asked to interpret a potentially libellous writing. For the most part, however, they operated in a far more restricted sphere. Judge and jury divided the decision-making function in a libel case as follows: the jury found whether the accused had knowingly published the relevant material, and the judge determined whether it constituted a libel. The jury's verdict, therefore, was 'special', being based only on a factual finding. Critics argued that a libel jury had the right to give a general verdict that reflected every aspect of the crime, as they did in other criminal trials.[73] It was hoped that a jury would feel less obliged to uphold outmoded conceptions of the law than a judge, and if able to decide the entire issue would apply a more liberal rule. This too, however, the courts refused to sanction, precedent having clearly determined the proper province of judge and jury.[74] Likewise, efforts to introduce legislation to enable juries to render verdicts which took into account the purpose as well as the fact of publication had failed.[75] In 1791 Fox entered the controversy. He brought in a Bill whereby a libel jury could render a general verdict on 'the whole matter put in issue.' While not directly altering the basis of the crime from general to specific intent, the Bill did establish that juries need not convict merely on

---

[72] Lobban, 'Seditious libel', 315, particularly points to *Rex* v. *Horne*, Howell, *State trials*, XX:651, as supporting this view.

[73] Holdsworth, *History*, VIII:337–45, observes that the practice of special jury verdicts resulted from libel having originally been the province of the court of Star Chamber. Since that tribunal did not employ juries, it did not have to formulate firm distinctions between issues of law and fact. Only when the common law courts began to hear libel cases did it become necessary to resolve how seditious intent related to the fact of publication.

[74] Lord Chief Justice Mansfield explained in *Rex* v. *Shipley*, 'It is almost peculiar to the form of a prosecution for libel, that the question of law remains entirely for the court *upon record*, and that the jury cannot decide it against the defendant … It finds all which belongs to a jury to find; it finds nothing as to the question of law. Therefore when a jury have been satisfied as to every fact within their province to find, they have been advised to find the defendant *guilty*, and in that shape they take the opinion of the Court upon the law.' Howell, *State trials*, XXI:1034–5 (emphasis in original).

[75] Holdsworth, *History*, X:688–90.

proof of publication and the sense ascribed to the published material in the indictment.[76]

Although Fox introduced the Bill, its leading proponent was Erskine. Probably the foremost advocate of the day, he had represented several defendants in libel trials, and his recent courtroom experiences were evident in his passionate support of the Bill. Fox, however, did not support him wholeheartedly. Whether on the grounds of expediency or misunderstanding of the details, Fox did not undertake to retain the original wording of the Bill in every particular. This became clear on 29 May 1791, during the discussion on the Bill's second reading. Scott entered the debate tentatively, fortifying his position by 'professing a most religious regard for the institution of juries, which he considered as the greatest blessing which the British Constitution had secured to the subject'.[77] Alluding to the long-established precedent against general verdicts in libel, he asked that the House not move so quickly to overturn it:

Surely, then, it would be conceded to him, that a Bill which was to unsettle the doctrines of the courts of law, after they had obtained for a whole century, and had been sanctioned by the greatest law authorities which this country could boast, ought not to be carried with precipitation through parliament.[78]

In that context he mentioned that he thought the Bill's preamble too expansive. This apparently mild objection was immediately opposed by Erskine, who exclaimed that he would sooner abandon the Bill altogether than consent to give up the preamble.[79] Fox thereupon proceeded to undercut his colleague's position:

With respect to the preamble, he did not agree with his learned friend that it was so essentially necessary to the Bill, that if one was not carried the other ought to be given up; he would be glad to carry both through; but if he could so far satisfy the scruples of some gentlemen by giving up the

---

[76] The 32 Geo. III c. 60 states in pertinent part: 'That on every such trial, the jury ... may give a general verdict of guilty or not guilty upon the whole matter put in issue upon such indictment or information; and shall not be required or directed by the court ... to find the defendant or defendants guilty, merely on the proof of the publication by such defendant or defendants of the paper charged to be a libel, and of the sense ascribed to the same in such indictment or information.'

[77] Cobbett, *Parliamentary history*, XXIX:592.        [78] *Ibid.*

[79] *Ibid.*, col. 593.

preamble, as to prevail upon them to vote for the Bill, he felt himself very much disposed to make that compromise . . .[80]

While Fox had thus indicated that he would accept alterations, Scott remained cautious. When debate resumed on 31 May 1791 he offered an explanation for his objection based on the form rather than the substance of the Bill. He argued that the preamble had the effect of equating libel with other crimes, when the Bill maintained procedural differences between them. The relevant difference, from Scott's perspective, was that in other crimes the jury had absolute authority to acquit or convict. If a jury convicted against the manifest weight of the evidence, the defendant could only seek a royal pardon. This Bill, however, provided that an accused might by-pass the jury at two stages of the trial. He could either keep the issue of libel from the jury completely in favour of a determination from the bench, or he could submit the matter to the judge after the jury had rendered its verdict.[81] Therefore the Bill did not envisage unfettered discretion on the part of the jury, and the preamble failed to make this clear.

That Scott's real objection lay more with juries rendering general verdicts than with the incongruity between the preamble and the body of the Bill is indicated by his proposed solution. He moved an amendment to the preamble as follows:

And whereas doubts have arisen whether on the trial of an indictment, or information, for the making or publishing any libel, it be competent to the jury *with the assistance and direction of the judge in matters of law* to take into their consideration the whole matter of the charge contained in such indictment or information.[82]

This amendment did not make the preamble any clearer on the ostensible issue that Scott raised. Rather, it created a new tension with the body of the Bill because it implied that judges ought to provide direction to the jury on whether the publication constituted a libel. After having offered his amendment, Scott attempted to recede casually from the debate. He remarked that: 'These were the remarks that had occurred to him, and if they were worth any thing they would be attended to, and if not, he did not wish that any notice should be taken of them.'[83] This did not deceive

[80] *Ibid.*, col. 594.   [81] *Ibid.*, cols. 594–6.
[82] *Ibid.*, col. 595 (Scott's amendment in italics).
[83] *Ibid. The World*, 1 June 1791, 2, col. 3, reports Scott as explaining that: 'Although he had thrown out those remarks, he trusted no Gentleman would

Erskine, however, who quickly realised Scott's true intentions. He claimed that the amendment would have the practical effect of narrowing the rights of juries in all areas, by officially sanctioning judicial commentary.[84] Fox too objected to the amendment as likely to result in continued confusion, if not on the proper provinces of judge and jury, then on the distinction between law and fact. Although he seems to have hit upon the precise aim of Scott's amendment, Fox possibly felt himself slightly out of his depth. He had prefaced his remarks with the admission that he 'was persuaded there was much more difficulty in wording a Bill of this sort, than many gentlemen imagined; and therefore he was obliged to the learned gentleman [Scott], and to any other member, who could give him such assistance as might tend to render the Bill as perfect as possible'.[85] So, while unhappy with Scott's amendment, Fox was neither combative nor insistent. Instead, he agreed to a proviso 'that there was nothing in the present Bill which was intended to preclude the judges from giving their opinion', which he thought might meet Scott's objection.[86] Scott promptly agreed to withdraw his amendment and moved the not dissimilar proviso: 'That on every such trial, the court or judge, before whom such indictment or information shall be tried, shall give their or his opinion and directions to the jury, according to their or his discretion, in like manner as in other criminal cases.'[87]

This development also worked an apparent change on the First Minister. He had previously expressed approval of the Bill, but in the wake of Scott's proviso he moved that they omit the Bill's entire first paragraph. This stated in pertinent part that the jury 'have always had, and by the law and constitution of England were intended to have, and in their discretion to exercise, a jurisdiction over the whole matter put in issue between them'.[88] Like Scott's amendment and proviso, the omission suggested by Pitt had the effect of weakening the claim that a libel jury could deliver verdicts independently from the judge. Far from acknowledging such a purpose, however, Pitt merely said: 'it was proper to avoid

consider him at all averse to the Bill: but exceptions having arose in his mind, he thought it his duty to state them to the House.'
[84] Cobbett, *Parliamentary history*, XXIX:598.     [85] *Ibid.*, col. 596.
[86] *Ibid.*, col. 599.      [87] *Ibid.*, col. 602
[88] Debrett, *Parliamentary register*, XXIX:591.

any general proposition in the preamble, which was not necessary to introduce the enactment of the Bill.'[89] Fox did not object; the House was satisfied; and the Bill was approved in its altered form.

These speeches reveal two important features of Scott's parliamentary work as Solicitor General. The first is his reliance on form. He might point out the justice or fairness of a particular course of action, but the stronger and more frequent justification was that it coincided with established legal rules and practice. Such advocacy does not seem to have been essentially an affectation on Scott's part. Rather, he was convinced that in matters of state, where motives and consequences were uncertain, the safest course lay in adhering to formal legal requirements. That way alone preserved the constitution, in whose ultimate justice one's confidence *could* firmly rest. If that were the only facet to his public character, however, Scott would have been little more than a conservative technician, and his speeches merely narrow legal statements. In fact, however, neither was the case. A well-established predilection for formal procedures could occasionally mask other less readily admitted goals, and Scott's speeches contain examples of this. An ability to manipulate his own parliamentary persona is part of the second feature of these speeches – their political sensitivity. Scott was not a brilliant orator. A contemporary writer said of him: 'he can never hope to charm a popular assembly, or command the applause of the Senates – He wants warmth and animation, the bold declamatory vehemence, that distinguish the senatorial from the forensic orator.'[90] He therefore had to gain his end in spite of his unsympathetic style; and he did so by taking advantage of his profession. He could calm the House or disrupt the opposition by appealing to formalism, to the procedures that made novelty comfortable, and to the regulations that exposed, or suggested, disrespect. In this way he demonstrated a political shrewdness which his colleagues might not have expected from a 'mere lawyer'.

---

[89] *Ibid.*
[90] E. Wynne, *Strictures on the lives and characters of the most eminent lawyers of the present day* (Dublin, 1790), 212–13.

# 5

# ENGAGEMENT

A wide variety of subjects occupied Scott's time as Attorney General, with criminal law being just one. In Parliament he spoke on a number of other issues, including an annuity for the Prince of Wales, cash restrictions granted to the Bank of England, and legacy and inheritance taxes. He appeared in the House of Lords on peerage claims, reviewed the government Bills to be presented to the Irish Parliament, and recommended when the Crown should grant patents for useful inventions and procedures. The majority of the legal opinions he wrote also concerned other than criminal matters. Nevertheless criminal administration, particularly administration of the law on crimes against the state, was the most important work that Scott performed during this period. As Attorney General he helped shape the official response to what many perceived as the internal threat of republicanism during the 1790s. First as a draughtsman and then as one of the leading government speakers in the House of Commons, he helped determine the extent of the legislative response. Furthermore, he not only advised *when* the Crown should undertake public prosecutions, but he often determined *how* the Crown ought to prosecute individuals for treason and sedition. Because of its overwhelming importance for this phase of his career, therefore, it is important to concentrate on Scott's administration of the law of treason and sedition, and the evolution of his attitude toward legislation and prosecution as the best method of enforcement.

By the time war with France commenced in February 1793, English attitudes toward their adversary had been transformed by recent events. For the most part, the French Revolution had been welcomed in England. Some had likened it to the Glorious Revolution of 1688, and British political clubs had begun corresponding with their French counterparts. Those less interested in political reform in France had at least found satisfaction in the discomfiture of an old enemy. As late as February 1792 William Pitt had concluded that French weakness justified a reduction in British military expenditure.[1] While a few individuals such as Edmund Burke had warned of the likely consequences of democratic upheaval in France, it was not until the middle of 1792 that significant numbers had begun to fear French radicalism. At that point, conservative and loyalist associations such as the Association for Preserving Liberty and Property against Republicans and Levellers had been formed to combat the perceived threat to England from French ideas. The more reactionary of these groups had countered radical rhetoric with their own pamphlets, and had encouraged the harassment of individuals professing Jacobin sympathies. Advocates of democratic reform in the British Isles, however, had continued to support the French. Foremost among these in England had been the Society for Constitutional Information (SCI), an offshoot of the County Association movement which had advocated 'economical reform' in the 1770s and 1780s. In the 1790s the SCI, and newer societies such as the London Corresponding Society (LCS), had begun to advocate reform of the legislature to the extent of universal manhood suffrage and annual Parliaments. They had quoted with approval Thomas Paine's *The rights of man*, and the SCI had begun a campaign for its widespread distribution. In Scotland similar societies had been founded in several cities, with the lead in Edinburgh being taken by the Society of the Friends of the People. In Ireland, the Society of United Irishmen had also adopted a programme of manhood suffrage, reform of electoral districts, and annual Parliaments.

From Pitt's early complaisance, the government had become increasingly alarmed at events in France and their apparent effect in England. In May 1792, a royal proclamation against seditious activities had followed hard upon addresses to the nation issued by the LCS. A further proclamation in autumn had ordered the embodiment of the militia, after British radicals presented congratulatory addresses to the French National Convention.[2] The response of the Edinburgh authorities to a convention of Scottish

---

[1] I. R. Christie, *Wars and revolutions: Britain 1760–1815* (London, 1982), 212, calls this 'one of the most inept forecasts ever made by a statesman of the first rank'.

[2] *Ibid.*, 226.

societies had been to disperse the meeting and arrest its leaders. In England Paine had been tried and convicted *in absentia* of seditious libel for publishing the second part of *The rights of man*, an act which Attorney General Archibald Macdonald had described as evidencing the author's 'deliberate design to calumniate the law and constitution under which we live, and to withdraw men's allegiance from that constitution'.[3]

Interestingly, amid the passionate and divergent attitudes inspired by the recent events in France, Scott presents a blank front prior to 1793. If he was touched by the Revolution, the evidence has not survived. Nor is such a gap altogether surprising. He had never travelled to France, nor had he demonstrated any interest in the administrative or political reforms discussed by the politically conscious during the 1780s. Professional concerns had probably consumed his time; neither was his a temperament suited to philosophical speculation. The outbreak of the war, therefore, could very well have given him his first opportunity to consider the new regime across the Channel, because the war obliged him to act against it – not on the battlefield, but in Parliament and in the courtroom. Scott became Attorney General in the same month that war was declared. Foremost in his mind must have been the dangers posed and the responsibility placed on him to defeat them. At that moment, therefore, republicanism became real for him, and he saw it simply as a destructive force, bent on rending the very fabric of the English government, constitution, and society.

From February 1793 most of the British radicals severed ties with France and proclaimed that their loyalty was in no way affected by their political outlook. That outlook, however, remained sinister to the authorities, especially when contemplating war with an old and now unpredictable enemy. The threat of subversion from English Jacobins, therefore, was a matter of grave concern. The government acted quickly to prevent further direct

---

[3] T. J. Howell (ed.), *A complete collection of state trials and proceedings for high treason and other crimes and misdemeanours*, 33 vols. (London, 1816–26), XXII:384. As Solicitor General Scott participated in this trial, as well as the other significant prosecution undertaken by Archibald Macdonald involving seditious libel, that of John Stockdale, who was acquitted in December 1789 of having libelled the House of Commons. Whatever may have been Scott's role in preparing these cases, he contributed relatively little during the actual trials.

contact with France. On 15 March 1793, the new Attorney General introduced a Bill to prevent 'traitorous correspondence', by making criminal particular transactions that could assist the French, including the sale or delivery to the French government or army items of military value, and the purchase of lands in France. It also required British subjects and residents to obtain a licence from the Secretary of State before travelling to France or entering England from France, and it prohibited the insurance of vessels or cargoes going to or coming from France.[4] Criticism of the Bill came immediately from an outraged opposition. Charles Fox 'could not omit even this first opportunity' to express his disapproval of a 'useless, unjust, and impolitic' measure.[5] He asserted that the Bill had been introduced 'with no other view than to disseminate through the country false and injurious ideas of the existence of a correspondence between some persons and France, and alarms of dangers where there were no dangers at all'.[6] Thomas Erskine agreed that the Bill reflected the government's unreasonable fears and suspicions. These defamed the people of England, whom Erskine described as 'stigmatized by distrust, and libelled by suspicions of treason and rebellion'.[7]

For the most part Scott ignored jibes such as these. His demeanour during the debates expressed both commitment and accommodation. He remained firm on the principles of the Bill, describing it as meeting a crisis 'when the very existence of the constitution was endangered'.[8] 'It was a fact that the most dangerous doctrines had gone forth; doctrines the operation of which could not be checked but by declaring them liable to the penalties of treason.'[9] On the regulatory details, however, he was willing to bend. He agreed to exemptions for British subjects and resident aliens who already possessed estates in France and wished to sell their produce.[10] He quietly added a proviso limiting the Bill's application to England, thus avoiding a potentially embar-

---

[4] 33 Geo. III c. 27.

[5] W. Cobbett (ed.), *The parliamentary history of England ... to 1803*, 36 vols. (London, 1806–20), XXX:583.

[6] *Ibid.*, col. 586.    [7] *Ibid.*, col. 590.    [8] *Ibid.*, col. 603.

[9] *Ibid.*, col. 604.

[10] J. Debrett (ed.), *The parliamentary register ... 1780–1799*, 54 vols. (London, 1782–99), XXXV:142, reports that Scott thanked Colonel Thomas Maitland for reminding him of the existence of the Alien Act, which made this provision unnecessary.

rassing situation posed by Fox whereby the Bill might hold an
Irishman in England liable for acts done in Ireland that were not
illegal there.[11] Scott's flexibility on details is hardly surprising.
His previous responsibilities had not extended to introducing and
conducting a piece of legislation through the House, and he could
hardly have avoided a degree of reservation. Moreover, support
for the Bill was far from certain. Even the third reading passed by
only a single vote, 154 to 153, and cautious MPs had to be
convinced of the prudence as well as the necessity of the measure.
Under these circumstances Scott was wise to avoid heavy-handed
tactics.[12]

*The Times* of 16 March 1793 quoted Scott as saying that he
believed the Traitorous Correspondence Bill 'would have a considerable tendency to put a speedy end to the war'.[13] He seems to
have enjoyed a similar confidence in the efficacy of prosecuting
individuals for seditious expressions during wartime. As Attorney
General he received information about possible criminal activity
and determined whether the case warranted further investigation
or prosecution. In each of the five cases thus submitted to him in
the autumn of 1793 he advised prosecution. While the size of the
sample discourages firm conclusions, these materials do tend to
show that Scott did not shy away from prosecution. He supported
the prosecutions of George Wilkinson and John Kirby for seditious words.[14] In the case of a handbill posted in Norwich, Scott
regarded its author as at least liable for a misdemeanour, 'and it
seems to me that it may be proper … further to consider whether
a charge of a higher nature can be supported against him'.[15] While
hesitating until an inquiry could determine the reliability of the
depositions accusing members of a reform society in Coventry of
seditious expressions, he added that he was ready to 'take such

---

[11] Cobbett, *Parliamentary history*, XXX:623–4.
[12] *St James' Chronicle*, 23–26 March 1793, 3, col. 2. was fulsome in its praise of the
Bill and its author: 'The crimes it provides against are of a serious and flagitious
nature; yet, numerous as they are, they have been so admirably discriminated
and arranged by the Law-Officer who introduced it, that we hope future
Attorney Generals will profit by the brevity and perspicuity he has observed on
this occasion.'
[13] *The Times*, 16 March 1793, 2, col. 3.
[14] J. Scott to Henry Dundas, 4 November 1793, SRO (Melville Papers) GD51/1/
234; J. Scott to Dundas, 12 October 1793, PRO, HO48(3).
[15] Scott to Dundas, 8 October 1793, PRO HO48(3).

measures as may be necessary to bring those persons to punishment'.[16] Similarly, he wondered whether the fact that Edward
Higgins was being pressed into the Navy when he uttered
allegedly seditious expressions might evoke sympathy in a jury,
but this fact did not discourage him:

> At the same time it must be farther observed that the language of this
> person is highly criminal, &, in my humble opinion, it is of great
> importance to have it fully understood that the law will not endure that
> any person should utter such language with impunity.[17]

Scott's prosecutorial work was not merely advisory, of course,
and during 1793 he conducted four prosecutions himself: John
Frost for seditious words, and Daniel Isaac Eaton, Daniel Holt,
and John Lambert, James Perry, and James Gray for seditious
libel. Frost was convicted and Holt's conviction affirmed, while
the others were acquitted. The libel trials are immediately notable
as applications of the new law on the subject. In establishing that a
libel jury need not consider only the fact of publication when
rendering its verdict, Fox's Libel Act[18] had introduced the issue
of the author or publisher's intent into the analysis of the crime.
Just as Scott had opposed the Libel Act itself, so here he zealously
attempted to avoid it.[19] In each of these cases he argued, if not for
the pre-Libel Act standard of knowing publication by the defendant of what proved to be seditious material, at least for a less
rigorous standard than actual seditious intent on the part of the
defendant.

In May 1793 Scott undertook the prosecution of John Frost.
Frost, an attorney, had a considerable involvement in radical
politics. He had been a prominent member, along with William
Pitt and the Duke of Richmond, of the society for parliamentary
reform that had met at the Thatched House tavern in the early
1780s. He had enthusiastically supported the French Revolution.
In 1792 he had helped to form the LCS and had become its
secretary. That autumn the SCI had chosen him to deliver an
address to the French Convention stating that the British people
would not fight a war against liberty. On 6 November 1792,
however, Frost had had a brief exchange with some of the patrons

---

[16] Scott to Dundas, 24 November 1793, *ibid.*
[17] Scott to Dundas, 5 October 1793, *ibid.*     [18] 32 Geo. III c. 60.
[19] See chapter 4.

in a London coffee house, during which he had remarked that he advocated equality and did not believe in a monarchy. His arrest had followed, and a grand jury had returned an indictment against him in February 1793. His trial, before Lord Kenyon, took place on 27 May 1793.

Scott's strategy in this case was to avoid the problem of proving seditious intent by raising an inference of intent that Frost would find difficult to rebut. Scott argued that some words in of themselves sufficed as *prima facie* evidence of that intent. If a defendant had uttered those words, he bore the responsibility of coming forward with evidence to show that he had not spoken with such an intention.[20] Under this interpretation of the law, therefore, a defendant who could not establish his good intent could be convicted merely upon proof of utterance. Scott based his interpretation on a reference to treason in Sir Michael Foster's *Discourses upon a few branches of the Crown law*:

As to meer [*sic*] words supposed to be treasonable, they differ widely from writings in point of real malignity and proper evidence. They are often the effect of meer [*sic*] heat of blood, which in some natures otherwise well disposed, carrieth the man beyond the bounds of decency or prudence. They are always liable to great misconstruction from the ignorance or inattention of the hearers, and too often from a motive truly criminal.[21]

From the reference to persons 'otherwise well disposed', Scott read Foster as saying that a person who utters words whose nature is *prima facie* criminal may yet be well disposed, but it rests with him to prove it. Scott avoided saying directly that the simple utterance was sufficient proof of guilt. In his reply he told the jury: 'if you should be of opinion, that Mr Frost did not utter the words advisedly and knowingly, and with an intention to work the mischief this record imputes to him, I do not desire this conviction.'[22] A few moments later, however, he indicated that absent evidence of Frost's good intent, simple utterance *would* supply the requisite criminal intent.

[20] Howell, *State trials*, XXII:519.
[21] Sir M. Foster, *A report of some of the proceedings of the commission of oyer and terminer and gaol delivery for the trial of the rebels in the year 1746 in the county of Surrey, and in other crown cases to which are added discourses upon a few branches of the crown law* (London, 1762), 200.
[22] Howell, *State trials*, XXII:512.

But if you are of opinion that these words were advisedly spoken, if the words themselves import that seditious intent which this record ascribes to them, I say … that it would be competent to the defendant to give evidence of his general demeanor as a good subject of the country, to show that he had not that meaning, which is the *prima facie* sense of the words.[23]

Since Frost had not provided such evidence, Scott argued, his conviction was appropriate. Scott also sought to enhance his characterisation of Frost's statements by referring to the situation in France. He equated Frost's advocacy of 'no King' with French republicanism, which he described as contrary to moral and political nature.[24] He further pointed out that, when Frost uttered his remarks, Parliament had just enacted a statute that made treasonable any statement that denied the right of the legislature to regulate the royal succession. Scott doubted that under such circumstances, 'it shall be innocent for men to say that the King and parliament of this country have no right to continue any government in this country'.[25]

In his summing up, Lord Kenyon generally supported the prosecution. He remarked that Foster was not directly on point, since the passage concerned treason rather than sedition, but his advice to the jury suggests that he regarded the negating of criminal intent implied by the utterances as the responsibility of the defence:

If these words were spoken, if they were spoken in a connexion which tends to explain them, and to do away the *prima facie*, obvious intention of them, – I say, if they were spoken in a context which tends to explain them, and show they were inoffensive words – let the context be received, let the favourable construction be put on them; but if in your opinion there is no context to explain them, it is your duty undoubtedly, by weighing and deliberating upon the question, to decide as your judgment shall lead you.[26]

He adopted an even stronger line with regard to the relevance of external circumstances. He suggested that circumstances could render words more blameworthy, if in their context the words were likely to inspire dangerous behaviour:

[U]ndoubtedly, if you think those words were spoken in seasons, when seditious words might be the forerunners of seditious acts, and that men's

---

[23] *Ibid.*, col. 513.    [24] *Ibid.*, col. 478.    [25] *Ibid.*, col. 481.
[26] *Ibid.*, col. 517.

spirits were inflamed, and might from small beginnings take fire, and might be brought into action, it adds most immensely to the criminal construction you ought to put upon the words.[27]

Fortified with such instructions the jury retired and convicted Frost after deliberating for an hour and a half.

Scott was less successful in his next prosecution, which charged Daniel Isaac Eaton with publishing a seditious libel. Eaton, a bookseller, had sold Paine's 'A letter addressed to the addressers on the late proclamation'. Even before this trial began, the prosecution had encountered difficulties. In June 1793 Eaton had been tried for seditious libel for selling the second part of *The rights of man*. This case, which neither of the law officers had prosecuted in person, had originated in a grand jury indictment and been tried at the Old Bailey before the Recorder of London. The jury had returned the verdict of guilty of publishing, but without a criminal intention. Thereupon Scott had successfully moved that the twelve high court judges determine the effect of such a verdict in the following term. In the meantime, he had proceeded with the second prosecution of Eaton by means of an information filed in his capacity as Attorney General.[28] This case came on before Lord Kenyon on 10 July 1793.

Scott continued to manipulate the concept of intent in this case. He did not attempt to show libellous intent on the part of Eaton, merely pointing out that he had continued to publish the pamphlet long after Paine had been convicted for his earlier work, and after having himself been warned by the chief magistrate of London.[29] Scott's main point, however, was that Paine had intentionally written what he believed to be treason, and Eaton had knowingly published it, so that Paine became the central figure in the prosecution. Scott said he would not ask for a verdict if the jury felt that 'the author, with the knowledge he necessarily must have of the nature of the constitution of this country, meant fairly to represent the constitution of this country'.[30] Confident that he could show specific criminal intent on the part of Paine, Scott pressed for the pre-1792 standard of intent for Eaton –

---

[27] *Ibid.*, col. 518.

[28] The Attorney General was permitted to file *ex officio* informations for misdemeanours affecting public stability or the governance of the country in the court of King's Bench on the Crown's behalf.

[29] Howell, *State trials*, XXII:794.     [30] *Ibid.*, col. 795.

knowing publication of material that was in fact seditious – without showing a positive intent to publish contumacious material. In setting out his standard Scott quoted directly from Sir William Blackstone: '[E]very freeman has an undoubted right to lay what sentiments he pleases before the public, but if he publishes what is improper, he must take the consequence of his temerity.'[31]

Lord Kenyon addressed more particularly than counsel on either side whether the writing constituted a seditious libel, and if so whether Eaton specifically intended to publish such. With respect to the first point, his approach was balanced. He explained that, if the passages identified by the prosecution conveyed a different meaning in isolation from that conveyed by the work generally, and if in that larger context the work was blameless, then the jury must acquit.[32] With respect to criminal intent, however, Lord Kenyon adopted a position which seems completely at odds with the Libel Act. He maintained that proof of wicked intention was not required 'where the intention goes to constitute the offence'.[33] Using the example of a murderer who acted to relieve suffering in the world, Kenyon said that in such a case 'we must refer to the act the party has done and ascribe to that the intention of doing good, of doing evil, or of doing neither good nor evil'.[34] While he did not make the parallel directly, his example encouraged the jury to liken the individual who disseminated dangerous pamphlets to the murderer. While both might actually have benevolent motives, the consequences of their actions justified an inference of criminal intent. This advice, however, did not sufficiently sway the jury, and despite prompting from the bench, they refused to render a verdict beyond simple publication.

Undaunted by the outcome of the *Eaton* trial,[35] Scott appeared

---

[31] *Ibid.* See Sir W. Blackstone, *Commentaries on the law of England*, 4 vols. 1st edn facsimile (Chicago, 1979), IV:151.

[32] Howell, *State trials*, XXII:821.  [33] *Ibid.*  [34] *Ibid.*

[35] Scott was not immediately satisfied with the outcome of the *Eaton* trial. Following the verdict he moved for an order to show cause why it should not be entered according to its legal import, which suggests that he wanted to argue that, because the jury found that Eaton had published the relevant material, this was equivalent to a conviction. The motion was granted, but the case does not seem to have been argued. Rather, Scott seems to have come, quite properly, to regard the jury's verdict as a *de facto* acquittal.

before the court of King's Bench in November 1793 to affirm the conviction of Daniel Holt for seditious libel. Holt had been convicted at the Nottingham Assizes for selling Paine's 'Address to the addressers' and Major Cartwright's 'An address to the tradesmen etc. on parliamentary reform'. On appeal Erskine argued three points on Holt's behalf, with the most important being that the trial court had wrongly refused to admit the prior publication of the Cartwright pamphlet to support Holt's position that he did not intend to publish seditious material.[36] Both Scott and the court dealt severely with the argument that prior publication could negative specific intent. If the writing constituted a seditious libel, said Scott, the fact that a previous publisher had escaped prosecution could not immunise Holt.[37] Scott even used the fact of republication to hint at a direct accusation of seditious intent. He strongly criticised Holt for republishing ten-year-old complaints about Parliament without indicating their context, at a time when he could have expected that such criticisms would cause unrest:

> The defendant, after seeing the effect of publishing and disseminating these pernicious doctrines all over the kingdom, comes forward with this paper, to assist the spirit that was then raised, without having the fairness to state that it was a paper published ten years ago. What has been the conduct of the defendant? Why, that of maliciously stirring up and reviving doctrines that were dangerous to the constitution, at a time when it was likely that, if spread, they would do much mischief.[38]

Not only did the court agree with Scott on the irrelevance of prior publication, in affirming the conviction Mr Justice Ashhurst made clear his opinion on the dangers associated with Holt's activities:

> Was it not enough that such a horrid production had been once stifled in the birth? and must you foster and nourish the unnatural and diabolical offspring, and give it fresh life and existence? Though the nation in general had shown their abhorrence and detestation of the doctrines contained in this publication, yet you were determined to cram it down the throats of his majesty's subjects.[39]

Finally, in December 1793 Scott conducted the unsuccessful prosecution of John Lambert, James Perry, and James Gray for seditious libel. The trial followed Scott's *ex officio* information against Lambert the printer, and Perry and Gray the proprietors,

---

[36] For Erskine's several arguments, see Howell, *State trials*, XXII:1205–22.
[37] *Ibid.*, col. 1231.     [38] *Ibid.*, cols. 1230–1.     [39] *Ibid.*, col. 1236.

of the *Morning Chronicle* newspaper, for their publication of an advertisement purporting to have been issued by a political society in Derby. The advertisement announced the aims of the Derby society, which were 'the pursuit of truth in a peaceable, calm, and unbiased manner', and noted the society's opposition to taxes, war, the loss of annual parliaments, the system of poor relief, and the game laws.[40]

The question of intent remained a thorny one for the prosecution. Scott flirted with an accusation of specific intent to publish seditious material, but largely undid any effect this might have had on the jury by his remarks in support of the defendants' personal *bona fides*. The only evidence of actual seditious intent lay in the time of publication. The advertisement had purportedly been written in July 1792, yet it had appeared in the *Morning Chronicle* five months later. All the other advertisements included in that edition dated from December 1792. This suggested to Scott that, while the defendants had not written the Derby advertisement, they had had some particular interest in it, and had published it when they did for political effect.[41] Scott gave more attention, however, to indirect allegations. In both his opening statement and reply he stressed that, where the crime involved the commission of an act with criminal intent, certain acts in of themselves provided legal indicia of that intent. So, while mere publication did not indicate seditious intent, the jury:

may draw the inference of guilty intention, if they discover in the contents of the paper a wicked and malicious spirit, evidently pursuing a bad object by unwarrantable means ... In all cases of publication, containing any thing improper, the bad intention of the person publishing was clear, unless on his own part he could prove the contrary.[42]

In the instant case the defendants bore responsibility for what they published, and the writing in question had implications of seditious intent. Scott located these implications in the fact that the writing expressed only criticisms of the British government and constitution and ignored all their benefits. Expanding on a point he had first made in the *Holt* appeal,[43] he maintained that unbiased political analysis had merit, but he implied that all

[40] *Ibid.*, cols. 955–6.    [41] *Ibid.*, col. 990.    [42] *Ibid.*, col. 1013.
[43] Scott had observed to the bench during the *Holt* trial: 'If persons will publish commentaries on parliament, let them do justice to its character and to the different men in it; and let them make a jury believe that when they discuss any

honest criticism included praise where deserved. If a writer omitted such praise, he must have evil intentions:

> I never will dispute the right of any man, fully to discuss topics respecting government, and honestly to point out what he may consider as a proper remedy of grievances ... But when men publish on these points, they must not, as in the present instance, do it unfairly and partially; they must not paint the evil in the most glowing colours, while they draw a veil over the good.[44]

Lord Kenyon summed up very aggressively in favour of the prosecution, justifying himself by informing the jury that the present law of libel obliged him to state his opinion.[45] He then affirmed what Scott had argued with respect to evil intent being evidenced by the contents of a writing: '[I]f an evil tendency is apparent on the face of any particular paper, it can only be traced by human judgment *prima facie* to a bad intention, unless evidence is brought to prove its innocence.'[46] In this case he not only failed to find evidence of a benevolent intent, but he considered the reforms advocated in the advertisement positively dangerous.[47] With respect to the time of publication, he noted a great 'gloominess' in the country, when foreign agents had been spreading 'horrid doctrines'. Consequently, he felt himself bound to say: '... I think this paper was published with a wicked, malicious intent, to vilify the government, and to make the people discontented with the constitution under which they live.'[48] Despite such strongly worded remarks, the jury did not share Kenyon's opinion, however, and acquitted the defendants.

These cases show Scott to have been rather an aggressive prosecutor in 1793. He was a firm advocate of litigation, and his interpretation of the law of libel shows him willing to hold defendants to an extremely strict and arguably incorrect standard. Moreover, in the *Eaton* and *Morning Chronicle* cases he proceeded on his own authority by information, preferring his own opinion to that of a grand jury, and in *Eaton* this followed a *de facto* acquittal on a comparable charge. He was also willing to postpone

---

public matter, they discuss it temperately, and then a question will never arise between any defendant and myself before your lordships.' *Ibid.*, col. 1232.

[44] *Ibid.*, col. 992.

[45] *Ibid.*, col. 1016. Kenyon's assertion that he was obliged to give his opinion had been predicted by Erskine as the likely and undesirable consequence of the proviso contributed by Scott to the Libel Act. See chapter 4.

[46] Howell, *State trials*, XXII:1018.      [47] *Ibid.*, col. 1017.      [48] *Ibid.*

the trial of Lambert, Gray and Perry in the hope of getting a more sympathetic jury. Their trial was originally set for the Easter term. Having successfully moved for a special jury, whose members were drawn from higher ranks than ordinary jurors, Scott declined to proceed when an insufficient number presented themselves. In the Michaelmas term he tried to secure a new special jury, and only when the court disallowed this did the trial commence with a panel of eight of the original special jurors and four talesmen.[49] In other respects, however, Scott demonstrated a degree of even-handedness and even magnanimity that might seem surprising. When he argued that Frost must produce evidence of his good intentions, Scott urged the jury not to regard such evidence sceptically:

[I]f you shall find, upon a due consideration of this case, that this is a hasty, an unguarded, and unadvised expression of a gentleman otherwise well disposed, and who meant no real mischief to the country, you will be pleased, with my consent, to deal with the defendant as a person under those circumstances ought to be dealt with.[50]

He even went so far as to assure the jury that 'the crown, upon the temperate consideration of what the jury does, will not be dissatisfied with that verdict, let it be what it may'.[51] In the case of *Frost*, the Crown had no cause for dissatisfaction with the jury's work. In the *Morning Chronicle* case, however, Scott probably contributed to the acquittal by his remarks on the defendants' behalf. In his reply he made this observation to the jury:

I think it a duty which I owe to the defendants, to acknowledge, that in no one instance before this time were they brought to the bar of any court, to answer for any offence either against government or a private individual – This is the only solitary instance in which they have given occasion for such charge to be brought against them. In every thing, therefore, that I know of the defendants, you are to take them as men standing perfectly free from any imputation but the present, and I will also say, from all I have ever observed of their morals in the conduct of their paper, I honestly and candidly believe them to be men incapable of wilfully publishing any slander on individuals, or of prostituting their paper to defamation or indecency.[52]

---

[49] A talesman was a person summoned to act as a juror from among the court bystanders.

[50] Howell, *State trials*, XXII:481–2.     [51] *Ibid.*, col. 481.

[52] *Ibid.*, col. 1012.

With such a testimonial coming from the Attorney General, it is not surprising that the jury acquitted the defendants.

Scott's conduct in this instance could be explained by the fact that he was prosecuting the leading opposition newspaper, and he would have wanted to avoid charges of taking improper advantage of his office. This does not explain his remarks in the *Frost* case, however, nor his support of Holt's tardy motion for a new trial:

My lords, if the defendant thinks that any serious mischief will result to him from the verdicts that have been given under the idea that he had been illegally convicted; I do not wish that the Court should be troubled with hearing this argument; but shall think it a substantial ground for saying, that I conceive it to be my duty to permit the defendant to bring it again before the Court.[53]

An explanation of the seeming incongruity in Scott's courtroom demeanour, which combined principled severity and practical liberality, may come in his view of his responsibilities. He observed during the *Eaton* trial:

[I]t has always appeared to me that the duty of a counsel for the prosecution consists in stating facts fairly to the jury, and reasoning with candour on those facts. I should betray that important and sacred trust which has been reposed in me, and should no longer desire to be continued in the discharge of the duties of that situation which I unworthily fill, if I departed from those sacred principles which actuate my conduct in this place, as the servant of the crown, prosecuting a subject of the crown, well knowing that I am bound by the duty of my office to do justice to that subject equally as much as to the crown itself.[54]

This was Scott's general definition of a prosecutor. Moreover, a deep concern for the qualities of honesty, independence, and humility was ever at the forefront of his mind. During the *Eaton* libel trial he complained: 'it has so happened that every question of this kind is generally made rather the trial of the officers of the crown, instead of the defendant, by the imputation of unworthy motives to that officer of the crown in instituting this species of trial.'[55] During the *Frost* case he maintained that a law officer had the obligation:

to regulate his judgment by a conscientious pursuance of that which is recommended to him to do. And if any thing is recommended to him, which is thought by other persons to be for the good of the country, but which he thinks is not for the good of the country, no man ought to be in

---

[53] *Ibid.*, col. 1205.    [54] *Ibid.*, cols. 813–14.    [55] *Ibid.*, col. 813.

the office who would hesitate to say, My conscience must direct me, your judgment shall not direct me.[56]

He closed his reply in the *Morning Chronicle* case deferring openly to the jury:

I had no other view than the public advantage; and should you be of opinion that the defendants ought to be declared not guilty, I trust you will acquit me of any intention of acting either impertinently with respect to you, or oppressively to the defendants. I shall then retire conscious of having done my duty in having stated my opinion, though inclined, in deference to your verdict, to suppose myself mistaken.[57]

However appropriate in an era of general domestic tranquillity, this attitude was somewhat at odds with Scott's particular obligation, to defend the nation against republicanism. With the very survival of the nation at stake, was the nation's prosecutor justified in maintaining this air of detachment? Such was Scott's predicament. He recognised the current danger as extremely grave, and he possessed the legal acumen to construct arguments that were both strict and harsh. When it came to pressing these arguments against individual defendants, however, his nerve failed him. Instead, he tended to fall back on the habits that characterised his general conception of a prosecutor. As 1793 drew to a close, an alteration in Scott's official burdens did not appear likely. Contrary to government hopes, the war had not been brought speedily to a close, and on the domestic front the war-related dangers seemed very real. In October the Master General of the Ordnance had requested additional infantry and cavalry to oppose possible French landings in Kent, Sussex, and Hampshire.[58] At about the same time Scottish reformers had convened a British Convention in Edinburgh to discuss a plan of campaign for legislative reform. Once again the authorities had broken up the meeting and prosecuted the leaders for sedition. Undaunted, the English societies resolved in January 1794 to hold their own Convention. The prospect of such activity in England raised the possibility of a heightened response by the English Attorney General, who had heretofore confined himself to more isolated sources of trouble. Scott once remarked that, while he did not enjoy taking the lead in supporting an unpopular measure, 'when he was called upon by

[56] *Ibid.*, col. 510.      [57] *Ibid.*, col. 1015.
[58] C. Emsley, *British society and the French wars, 1793–1815* (London, 1979), 23.

reason, by conscience, by his duty to his country, to perform the task, he would do it boldly'.[59] The events of the next year and a half would show to what extent such a statement was wishful thinking on Scott's part.

[59] Cobbett, *Parliamentary history*, XXXI:1154.

# 6

# SETBACKS

In the autumn of 1794 Scott took the next significant step in his work of administering the criminal law – prosecuting two leading members of the London Corresponding Society (LCS) and the Society for Constitutional Information (SCI) for high treason. In several ways the proceedings represented a formidable undertaking. They concerned a heinous crime and a complicated, controversial legal argument, and they were commenced after a period of mounting tension and suspicion between the government and the radicals. For Scott, the immediate result of his labour was failure, as both defendants were acquitted following lengthy and exhausting trials. The experience of the trials and their aftermath, however, have a wider significance. They influenced what would become Scott's ultimate attitude toward his own and the government's role in safeguarding the nation.

Events during the first part of 1794 showed the government and the English radicals proceeding steadily toward a collision. With their president, Maurice Margarot, awaiting trial in Scotland for his allegedly seditious participation in the Scottish National Convention, the LCS began the year in a defiant mood. In January they resolved to hold an English Convention if Parliament introduced any measures 'inimical to the liberties of the people', which included the landing of foreign troops, the suspension of the Habeas Corpus Act, the imposition of martial law, or a ban on political assemblies.[1] From the perspective of the LCS, therefore, the actions of the government in the first months of the year were extremely provocative. In February they proposed to quarter

---

[1] The resolutions adopted at the 20 January meeting, in the form of an address to the people, are reprinted as Appendix B in C. B. Cone, *The English jacobins* (New York, 1968), 229–34.

Hessian soldiers briefly in England until they were sent abroad, and the opposition failed to convince the House that such an action would be unconstitutional.[2] The following month the House likewise declined to support opposition calls for reform of the Scottish criminal law, in light of the recent convictions of Thomas Muir and Thomas Palmer for sedition. Leading government speakers on Scottish and legal matters described parliamentary interference as neither appropriate nor necessary. Scott argued that the Act of Union prohibited the wholesale alteration of Scottish law, and he professed astonishment 'that the patriots of England and Scotland never should have found out till lately that all the criminal proceedings of that country were a nuisance'.[3]

Meanwhile, a Convention was becoming a topic of discussion among radicals in London and elsewhere. On 28 March 1794, the SCI approved the idea, and while its position would subsequently become unclear, organisations in other parts of the country resolved to send delegations.[4] In April, the LCS held an open-air meeting in the outskirts of the capital, where they passed resolutions stating that the constitutional rights of the people had been violated, and asserting the authority and obligation to assemble a Convention to consider the consequent state of affairs.[5] Similar meetings were held in Sheffield and Halifax. On 2 May 1794 the SCI marked its fourteenth anniversary with a celebratory dinner, during which the 300 or so participants heard a number of violent speeches and drank inflammatory toasts. Precisely what the LCS and other radical societies actually intended by their calls for a Convention never became clear. The LCS always said that they looked for political reform through the agency of Parliament. On the other hand, they asserted that the authority to govern was not

---

[2] The motion for the previous question passed 184 to 35. W. Cobbett (ed.), *The parliamentary history of England ... to 1803*, 36 vols. (London, 1806–20), XXX:1391.

[3] *Ibid.*, XXXI:81. William Adam's motion to appoint a committee to consider Scottish criminal law reform was defeated by a vote of 77 to 24. *Ibid.*, col. 83.

[4] The SCI had early enjoyed a certain prestige within the radical community. Gradually, however, its place was taken by the LCS. In the spring of 1794 the SCI was far more tentative, and Cone, *English jacobins*, 191, argues that the organisation did not unequivocally favour a Convention.

[5] The Chalk Farm resolutions are reprinted in the first report of the Committee of Secrecy. Cobbett, *Parliamentary history*, XXXI:706–8. Cone, *English jacobins*, 192–3, argues that the LCS did not, in these resolutions, explicitly propose a Convention.

an inalienable right of the propertied minority but a trust granted by the majority, and as such was subject to their revocation.[6] While there is no evidence that the LCS ever wanted to supplant Parliament absolutely, far more modest aims could have been, and probably were, regarded as a challenge to parliamentary authority.[7]

Certainly the authorities did not regard the societies with equanimity. On the contrary, as early as February 1794 information regarding their activities had been collected and transmitted to the law officers.[8] Finally, on 12 May 1794 ministers decided to move against the radical leadership. Among those arrested in the next few days were Thomas Hardy, the corresponding secretary of the LCS, and John Horne Tooke, a founding member of the SCI. The papers of their respective societies were also seized, and the Home Secretary, Henry Dundas, presented these to the House. A Committee of Secrecy undertook to study the papers.[9] On 16 May 1794 the Committee submitted its first report, which concluded that a plot existed to overthrow the legislature, and most recently this had come to include armed force.[10] William Pitt warned that there was 'not one moment to be lost in arming the executive power with those additional means, which might be sufficient effectually to stop the farther progress of such a plan, and to prevent its being carried into final execution'.[11]

The particular means Pitt sought was suspension of the Habeas Corpus Act. This statute made mandatory a judicial review for imprisoned persons whose warrants of committal did not assign the legal cause, and provided for speedy trials in cases of treason and felony.[12] When the Habeas Corpus Act was suspended, therefore, an individual could be arrested and kept in custody without

---

[6] J. S. Watson, *The reign of George III, 1760–1815* (Oxford, 1960), 358, has described the ideas of the LCS as 'those of Locke spiced with Rousseau'.

[7] See *ibid.*, 359.

[8] For a study of government methods and sources see C. Emsley, 'The Home Office and its sources of information and investigation 1791–1801', *English Historical Review* 94 (1979), 532–61.

[9] The twenty-one member committee consisted of W. Pitt, H. Dundas, W. Ellis, W. Windham, J. Scott, J. Mitford, I. Campbell, T. Grenville, T. Steele, R. Arden, R. Jenkinson, H. Hoghton, Lord Upper Ossory, T. Powys, Lord Mornington, Lord Mulgrave, H. Browne, J. Anstruther, T. Stanley, C. Townshend, and E. Burke.

[10] The report is found at Cobbett, *Parliamentary history*, XXXI:475–497.

[11] *Ibid*, col. 497.    [12] 31 Car. II c. 2.

the power either to obtain bail or a prompt adjudication of his case. However confident of support in the House, no minister could lightly undertake to suspend action of that 'most celebrated writ in the English law'.[13] On this occasion, Pitt enjoyed over-whelming support and, despite lengthy opposition speeches, the Bill's progress was cushioned by extremely comfortable majori-ties.[14] Nevertheless, government speakers were eager to assure the House that the proposed legislation was both proper and urgently necessary. Scott 'thanked God that he had from circumstances been placed in the situation of attorney-general of England at this time, and he was certain that nothing would be done that was not consistent with the most perfect justice'. As to the necessity of suspension: 'So great was the combination of those people who had formed the plan of subverting the constitution, that he was free to say, that upon this measure depended the salvation of our inestimable constitution, and the preservation of the happiness and liberty of this country.'[15]

Having won approval for that measure, ministers did not relax their vigilance. Interrogation of the prisoners took place before the Privy Council.[16] In late May 1794 Scottish authorities uncovered plans for an armed insurrection which appeared to have links with the proposed English Convention.[17] This Scottish link was noted in the Committee of Secrecy's second report of 6 June 1794, which asserted that the peaceful reform frequently professed by the English radicals cloaked a deeper plan to displace the govern-ment by violence.[18] The report also referred to the activities of the Loyal Lambeth Association, whose members allegedly undertook to learn military drill, and who, 'If they could not obtain a reform in parliament in any other way, they meant to have recourse to arms'.[19] Finally, the report noted the French policy of destabi-

[13] Sir W. Blackstone, *Commentaries on the laws of England*, 4 vols. 1st edn facsimile (Chicago, 1979), III:129.

[14] The House granted permission to bring in the Bill by a margin of 201 to 39, and approved the first and second readings after votes of 197 to 33 and 186 to 29, respectively. Cobbett, *Parliamentary history*, XXXI:521, 523–5.

[15] *Ibid.*, col. 521.

[16] John Thelwall recalled his interview by Pitt, Lord Loughborough, and Scott in the *Tribune*, 4 April 1795, section 3.

[17] Dundas' letters to Pitt on the subject are found at Cobbett, *Parliamentary history*, XXXI:696–702.

[18] The second report (with appendices) is found at *ibid.*, cols. 688–879.

[19] *Ibid.*, col. 693.

lising countries which they intended to invade by an 'incitement to internal commotions', and asserted that French agents had recently undertaken to discover what assistance they might expect in Britain and Ireland.[20] Ten days later, the Commons agreed to second the Lords' loyal address to the throne. Scott's reply summed up the attitude of the government toward the radicals. Far from merely 'not quite laudable', their principles 'tended to the destruction of the whole government of England', while they themselves 'wished to subvert the constitution, to destroy the monarch, and, under the name of liberty, to tyrannize over the people'.[21]

In the wake of the findings of the Secret Committee, the law officers set about preparing the next action against the radicals – prosecution of their leaders for treason.[22] Their first challenge lay in interpreting the relevant statute. The Treason Act proscribed 'compassing and imagining' the death of the sovereign.[23] As a practical matter, this crime came within judicial cognisance when demonstrated by an overt act. In his treatise on Crown law, Sir Michael Foster had explained how to frame an indictment for treason under the statute:

---

[20] *Ibid.*, cols. 733–4. In early May the cabinet had begun questioning William Stone about his possible participation in the mission of an Irishman, the Revd William Jackson, to discover the level of likely support for a French invasion. Stone was later tried for treason and acquitted. See chapter 7.

[21] Cobbett, *Parliamentary history*, XXXI:930.

[22] Writing many years later Scott would observe that he could have charged Hardy and Tooke with the lesser offence of sedition and been more confident of obtaining convictions, but that the many prior references in and out of Parliament to the projected trials as trials for treason had obliged him to prosecute for that offence. Moreover, if he had opted for sedition, he could not have been sure that evidence of greater criminal activity might not have emerged. If that had proved sufficient to make out a case of treason, the defendants would have been acquitted of the lesser charge, 'and then the country would not have tolerated, and ought not to have tolerated that, after such an acquittal, their lives should have been put in jeopardy by another indictment for high treason'. Lord Eldon, J. Scott, *Lord Eldon's anecdote book*, ed. A. L. J. Lincoln and R. L. McEwen (London, 1960), 55–6.

[23] 25 Edw. III c. 2. The statute principally declares the following to be acts of treason: 'When a man doth compass or imagine the death of our lord the King, or of our lady his Queen, or of their eldest son and heir; or if a man do violate the King's companion, or the King's eldest daughter unmarried, or the wife of the King's eldest son and heir; or if a man do levy war against our lord the King in his realm, or be adherent to the King's enemies in his realm, giving to them aid and comfort, in the realm, or elsewhere.'

It must charge that the defendant did traiterously *compass and imagine* &c. and then go on and charge the several overt-acts as the means employed by the defendant for executing his traiterous purposes. For the compassing is considered as the treason, the overt-acts as the means made use of to effectuate the intentions and imaginations of the heart.[24]

Identifying a sufficient overt act, however, was more difficult. Following its enactment in the fourteenth century, the Treason Act had come to be regarded as insufficient alone to protect the sovereign. Particularly between the middle of the fifteenth and the late sixteenth century, statutes had been enacted that made treasonous such acts as alleging that the King was a heretic or praying to God to shorten the Queen's life.[25] Near the end of the reign of Elizabeth, however, jurists had begun to argue for a wider interpretation of the Treason Act itself.[26] Gradually judges had come to regard acts which placed improper restraints upon the sovereign, but which fell far short of direct physical attacks upon him, as legally sufficient to demonstrate a treasonous intention under the statute of Edward III. Sir Edward Coke had noted:

He that declareth by overt act to depose the king, is a sufficient overt act to prove that he compasseth and imagineth the death of the king. And so it is to imprison the king, or to take the king into his power, and manifest the same by some overt act.[27]

Matthew Hale had argued that a conspiracy to imprison or depose the sovereign had the same effect:

Tho the conspiracy be not immediately and expressly the death of the king, but the conspiracy is of something that in all probability must induce it, and the overt-act is of such a thing as must induce it; this is an overt-act to prove the compassing of the king's death.[28]

The constitution of the legally sufficient overt act had been further extended in the late seventeenth century and especially

---

[24] Sir M. Foster, *A report of some of the proceedings of the commission of oyer and terminer and gaol delivery for the trial of the rebels in the year 1746 in the county of Surrey, and in other crown cases to which are added discourses upon a few branches of the crown law* (London, 1762), 193–4 (emphasis in original).

[25] 5 & 6 Edw. VI c. 11; 1 & 2 Phil. & Mary c. 9.

[26] For an explanation of this change in attitude, see W. Holdsworth, *A history of English law*, 17 vols. (London, 1903–72), VIII:310.

[27] Sir E. Coke, *The third part of the institutes of the laws of England* (London, 1797), 6.

[28] Sir M. Hale, *Historia placitorum coronae: the history of the pleas of the crown*, ed. G. Wilson, 2 vols. (London, 1778), I:109.

after the Glorious Revolution.[29] Foster, writing in 1762, had remarked:

The care the law hath taken for the personal safety of the King is not confined to actions or attempts of the more flagitious kind, to assassination or poison, or other attempts directly and immediately aiming at his life. It is extended to every thing wilfully and deliberately done or attempted, whereby his life may be endangered. And therefore the entering into measures for deposing or imprisoning him, or to get his person into the power of the conspirators, these offences are overt-acts of treason within this branch of the statute.[30]

Contrary to what Sir James Stephen has argued, 'Compassing and imagining' the King's death was probably not demonstrable in 1794 by 'anything whatever which under any circumstances may possibly have a tendency, however remote, to expose the king to personal danger'.[31] Indeed, the question remained open, given the evolution of the law, how far a court and jury would extend the idea of a threat to the sovereign so as to convict an individual of treason on the strength of a given act.

A second question inherent in the Treason Act also stood unanswered – what was the legal relationship between the treasonous intention and the overt act which expressed it? Jurists linked certain actions to an intent to kill the sovereign because these typically involved a threat to his safety. As Foster had noted: 'experience hath shewn that between the prison and the graves of princes the distance is very small.'[32] But neither Coke, Hale, nor Foster had indicated whether they considered a particular act like imprisoning as dispositive evidence of the intent to kill. If so, the actual existence in a particular defendant of an intent to kill ceased to be a question of fact, and treason consisted simply of committing the legally sufficient overt act. In the late eighteenth century both interpretations of the Treason Act – expanding the constitution of the overt act, and conferring a greater legal status upon it – had acquired the label of 'constructive treason' because they established the crime by a complex legal argument.

---

[29] Holdsworth, *History*, VIII:316–17, lists only two recognised limitations: mere words, except when uttered in direct relation to actions, and unpublished writings could not constitute overt acts under the statute.

[30] Foster, pp. 195–6.

[31] J. F. Stephen, *A history of the criminal law of England*, 3 vols. (London, 1883), II:268.

[32] Foster, *Report*, 196.

Representing, as it did, an extension of the plain meaning of the Treason Act, constructive treason was regarded popularly with suspicion.[33]

On 2 October 1974 the law officers produced an indictment for treason against thirteen members of the LCS and the SCI.[34] The indictment charged them with four types of overt act: conspiring to depose the King, conspiring to levy war against the King, producing and distributing arms in aid of the conspiracies, and producing and distributing pamphlets encouraging participation in them.[35] Ten days later, a grand jury approved the charges against all but one of the men, following an address by the presiding judge, Sir James Eyre, Chief Justice of the court of Common Pleas, which described further judicial inquiry as a public service. He regarded organisations such as the LCS and the SCI with grave scepticism. While they might have been founded with benign intentions, the wickedly inclined could easily pervert them. 'If we suppose bad men to have once gained an ascendancy in an assembly of this description, popular in its constitution, and having popular objects; how easy is it for such men to plunge such an assembly into the most criminal excesses?'[36] Sir James also criticised severely the proposed national Convention. He maintained that such a body must undoubtedly have attempted to alter the character of Parliament; therefore the plan to assemble the Convention was:

at best, a conspiracy to overturn the government in order to new model it, which is, in effect, to introduce anarchy, and that which anarchy may choose to settle down into; after the King may have been brought to the scaffold, and after the country may have suffered all the miseries which discord and civil war shall have produced.[37]

Consequently, he advised that if the grand jury found that the accused had tried to assemble people against Parliament's

---

[33] See Stephen, *History*, II:272.

[34] The following persons were indicted: John Baxter, John Augustus Bonney, Thomas Hardy, Richard Hodgson, Thomas Holcroft, Jeremiah Joyce, Steward Kyd, John Lovett, Matthew Moore, John Richter, John Thelwall, John Horne Tooke, and Thomas Wardle. The grand jury subsequently dismissed John Lovett.

[35] T. J. Howell (ed.), *A complete collection of state trials and proceedings for high treason and other crimes and misdemeanours*, 33 vols. (London, 1816–26), XXIV:238.

[36] *Ibid.*, col. 206.     [37] *Ibid.*, col. 208.

authority, or over-awe the legislature and compel it to pass certain reform legislation:

perhaps it may be fitting that, in respect of the extraordinary nature and dangerous extent and very criminal complexion of such a conspiracy, that case, which I state to you as a new and a doubtful case, should be put into a judicial course of inquiry, that it may receive a solemn adjudication, whether it will, or will not, amount to high treason.[38]

Hardy's was the first 'new and doubtful case' to be heard, when his trial commenced on 28 October 1974. Because little direct evidence existed to link him with actual armed force, Scott based the prosecution on the reputation of the LCS. He portrayed the LCS as consisting of dedicated republicans, and he introduced considerable documentary evidence in support thereof, including their professions of friendship with the French National Convention, their toasts and songs ridiculing the King, and their resolutions in support of the political ideas of Thomas Paine.[39] Scott dismissed their support for moderate reform as attempts to conceal plans for revolutionary change, and he attempted to demonstrate how their Convention would have necessarily threatened the Crown. Hardy and the LCS, claimed Scott, had wanted to alter the entire form of government by transferring legislative authority to the Convention. If the King had refused to accept this he would have been removed, while his agreement to treat with that self-appointed body would have violated his coronation oath and so deprived him of royal authority. Consequently, the plan to hold a national Convention had consisted of a conspiracy to depose the King, and this brought its participants within the ambit of the Treason Act.[40] Scott reviewed Coke, Hale, and Foster, noting that they cited with approval cases in which conspiracies to depose, imprison, or oblige the king to change his ministers had resulted in convictions for treason. The case against Hardy, Scott argued, should be understood in the light of those precedents.[41]

---

[38] *Ibid.*, cols. 209–10.
[39] *Ibid.*, cols. 281–368. Scott did attempt to link Hardy to individuals in Sheffield who had manufactured pikes and models of a device to be used against cavalry, and to the Lambeth Loyal Association. He did not, however, devote much time to either point. *Ibid.*, cols. 367–9.
[40] *Ibid.*, col. 265.       [41] *Ibid.*, col. 251.

For all that he tried to portray this case as unexceptional, Scott's analysis extended the concept of 'compassing and imagining' in two ways. First, while he denied that he was construing the conspiracy to depose as dispositive evidence of treason, in fact he was doing just that. Nowhere in his argument did he offer to show that Hardy had actually intended to kill the King. Rather, Scott inferred that from proof of the conspiracy to depose. Secondly, his allegation that the proposed Convention would have deposed the King required a considerable extension of the definition of 'depose'. Scott described his analysis as 'perfectly obvious'.[42] That a body which never actually met, however, should be presumed to have overturned Parliament and either removed the King or obliged him to act unconstitutionally if it *had* met, did not impress everyone as quite so apparent.

Certainly Scott's analysis did not find a receptive audience in Erskine, Hardy's defence counsel. He, not surprisingly, characterised it as constructive treason and argued that it did not accurately apply the Treason Act. Compassing and imagining the King's death, he said, meant nothing less than 'a traitorous intention against his natural life',[43] and he relied on the same passages from Coke, Hale, and Foster to support his view. Erskine regarded all overt acts other than actual attempts on the sovereign's life as competent, but never dispositive evidence of a treasonous intent. He told the jury: 'it is to be submitted to your consciences and understandings, whether, even if you believed the overt act, you believe also that it proceeded from a traitorous machination against the life of the king.'[44] In the instant case, of course, Erskine did not believe the overt act. He argued that Hardy had pursued only moderate and legitimate goals. He had no ulterior motives against the King or the House of Lords. Rather he sought only that reform which the LCS had taken pains to make known – a more equitable representation in the House of Commons through universal manhood suffrage and annual elections.[45] Erskine played down any links between Hardy and the LCS and their more notorious associates, and pointed out that, during the period of correspondence between the LCS and the

---

[42] *Ibid.*, col. 255.    [43] *Ibid.*, col. 883.    [44] *Ibid.*, col. 895.
[45] *Ibid.*, col. 912.

French National Convention, the latter had maintained friendly diplomatic relations with England.[46]

In his summing up, Chief Justice Eyre maintained much of the bias that he had displayed in his charge to the grand jury.[47] He stated categorically that certain acts short of direct attacks on the King's person conclusively established the intent to kill him:

The conspiracy to depose the king is evidence of compassing and imagining the death of the king, conclusive in its nature, so conclusive that it is become a presumption of law ... admitting of no contradiction. Who can doubt that the natural person of the king is immediately attacked and attempted by him who attempts to depose him[?][48]

Moreover, his description of the important events in the case could have left none of the jurors unaware of his views. He remarked on the similarity between the Scottish Convention and the French National Convention, and argued that the Edinburgh delegates had posed a serious threat to the government.[49] Given that danger, only recently thwarted, the LCS ought to have taken all necessary steps to avoid arousing fears about the nature of their activities. Instead, they had resolved to call another Convention and had put forward a manifesto 'in a still more questionable shape than the former'.[50]

Thus primed, the jury retired. They deliberated for just over three hours which, by the standards of the trial, was prompt. The trial itself had lasted seven days, with daily sessions of ten to twelve hours. In part this had resulted from the considerable forensic displays of the leading protagonists. Scott's opening statement had taken nine hours to deliver, while Erskine had spoken for over seven. Chief Justice Eyre had required a day and a half merely to sum up the evidence for both sides. The jury, however, did not need nearly so long to return a verdict of not guilty.

If they were disappointed by the outcome Scott and John Mitford gave no indication. Instead they turned almost immediately to the prosecution of Horne Tooke, which commenced on 17

---

[46] *Ibid.*, col. 947.

[47] Compare A. Goodwin, *The friends of liberty: the English democratic movement in the age of the French revolution* (London, 1979), 352, and Holdsworth, *History*, XIII:162, both of whom regard the Chief Justice's performance as able.

[48] Howell, *State trials*, XXIV:1361.      [49] *Ibid.*, col. 1373.

[50] *Ibid.*, col. 1376.

November 1974. During this trial both prosecution and defence changed their tactics and, more significantly, a change in attitude occurred on the part of the court. The result, however, was the same. After a trial of six days, the jury would need less than ten minutes to acquit Tooke.

Tooke's trial started on a different footing from Hardy's, with the prosecution's opening statement coming from the Solicitor General. Mitford was a much more decisive speaker than Scott, and in his hands the legal and factual material became an argument rather than an exposition. This shift in emphasis also resulted from Mitford's greater selectivity with respect to background material, so that he spent much less time explaining. Instead of reading into the record lengthy documents containing suspicious or inflammatory language, Mitford made bold assertions. Parliament's opposition to electoral reform made all professions of moderate, peaceful reform by Tooke and the SCI unbelievable. The SCI had undertaken their petition campaign in full knowledge that it would fail, and hopeful that such failure would sufficiently inflame the public to support a Convention. Moreover, the SCI had purposely raised other issues such as tithes, enclosures, and the public debt, to appeal to anyone not interested in representative government.[51] Mitford thus described the SCI and LCS, over both of which Tooke allegedly exerted influence:

their force can never be calculated, but they are a united body, acting in perfect order, acting as a corporation, as a state within a state itself, and having all the force and compactness of a state, and subject to no control whatever.[52]

For the defence Erskine maintained his position on the law, arguing that the prosecution must prove that Tooke had acted 'with the fixed and rooted *intent in the mind*, that this convention, when it got together, whatever might be external pretext, should depose the king, AND PUT HIM TO DEATH'.[53] Where he had defended Hardy as a member of the LCS, however, now he defended Tooke as an individual. He referred to Tooke's personal association with the Duke of Richmond, pointed out how Tooke had never joined any SCI or LCS resolutions that criticised the

---

[51] *Ibid.*, XXV:32–3, 39, 51–2.      [52] *Ibid.*, col. 37.
[53] *Ibid.*, col. 263 (emphasis in original).

King or the House of Lords, and related how Tooke had consistently rejected universal manhood suffrage.[54]

In his cross-examination and reply, Scott attempted to show that Tooke's activities were at variance with those of his 'moderate' friends as well as with his own supposed political creed.[55] When the SCI had received from the radical Joel Barlow an address 'which recommended most distinctly the destruction of monarchy in the country', Tooke had approved a vote of thanks to Barlow and publication of the address.[56] Tooke's claims of moderation constituted 'a case of fraud against the public security and happiness', and an attempt to avoid detection by placing others between himself and the acts for which he bore responsibility.[57] While Scott thus remained adamant, however, Chief Justice Eyre had undergone a change of heart since the beginning of the trials. In his summing up, he indicated to the jury that he believed the prosecution had failed to make out a case of treason. He accepted their interpretation of the relevant law, but thereafter he viewed their case with scepticism. If the aim of the Convention had been to depose the King, the plan to hold the Convention would have been a treasonous conspiracy. The prosecution had not sufficiently proved that intention, however, and such could not be made out merely by 'nice and verbal criticism'.[58] He accepted, moreover, that both the LCS and the SCI had been founded with the legitimate goal of parliamentary reform, and he particularly rejected the idea that from the beginning either organisation had operated according to a hidden agenda orchestrated by Tooke.[59] While the SCI had published the works of dangerous radicals and composed addresses to the French Jacobins 'of a very doubtful complexion', there was insufficient evidence of any darker scheme.[60] '[H]ere, I think, he [Scott] must leave his case, for I do not see myself that he has carried it any farther than to show that the conduct of these societies has been the conduct of determined republicans.'[61] In voting to acquit, the jury indicated a similar assessment of the case.

The Crown's immediate interest in the LCS and the SCI came to an end with the acquittal of Tooke.[62] Nor was the consequent

---

[54] *Ibid.*, cols. 275–7.    [55] See, e.g., *ibid.*, cols. 405–6.    [56] *Ibid.*, col. 518.
[57] *Ibid.*, col. 500.    [58] *Ibid.*, cols. 727–9.    [59] *Ibid.*, col. 730.
[60] *Ibid.*, cols. 732–3.    [61] *Ibid.*, cols. 738–9.
[62] The prosecution of John Thelwall did proceed, but the law officers did not

break from prosecution an unwelcome one for Scott. Not only had these been difficult cases to argue, but the public response had made the task extremely wearing. Large numbers had gathered outside the Old Bailey each day, and they had cheered the defence counsel and booed the law officers as they entered or left the court. One evening Scott had been obliged to pacify a crowd to avoid being attacked, and following Hardy's acquittal Erskine had used his influence to protect his late adversary.[63] Scott's mood during the trials had been evident in his frequent justifications of his conduct, by way of invocations of duty, assurances of good faith, and expressions of modest confidence in his professional competence. Sometimes the combination of these had resulted in statements of considerable circumlocution, as when Scott had explained his objection to a defence question during Hardy's trial.

[Y]our lordship will recall that I stand here as the prosecutor for the public, if I were in my own cause I could sacrifice, at my own pleasure, principles which appear to me to be the principles of public justice; but in the situation in which I stand, I do not know how I can regulate my conduct better towards the public, and towards the prisoner, than by acting upon the principles of law, as I understand them, admitting at the same time, that no man is more likely to be mistaken: but this I will say distinctly, that I would not trouble your lordship with the objection that I am now stating, if I were not perfectly convinced, upon the best judgment I can form, that the question cannot be put to a witness.[64]

So too his exchanges with opposing counsel had showed his nerves to be on edge. For the most part, he had displayed his usual generous courtroom demeanour, making no objection when Erskine had wished to introduce material during Hardy's trial without a prior showing of its relevance, or when Tooke's defence had been mistakenly closed before Hardy's acquittal had been

---

conduct it. After he too was acquitted, the charges against the remaining defendants were dropped. After being discharged, Thomas Holcroft published *A narrative of facts relating to a prosecution for high treason* (London, 1795), which was highly critical of Scott.

[63] Eldon, *Anecdote book*, 101. Erskine is reported to have told the crowds, eager to bear him away in triumph: 'I will not go on without the Attorney-General.' H. Twiss, *The public and private life of Lord Chancellor Eldon*, 3 vols. (London, 1844), I:271.

[64] Howell, *State trials*, XXIV:814. Stephen, *History*, II:276 footnote 1, observes that Scott 'repeats himself in all sorts of forms of words, and with endless precautions and qualifications, and in sentences which neither begin nor end for many pages'.

offered as evidence.[65] Scott's temper had flashed, however, when he had felt Erskine to be pursuing his case too aggressively, or unfairly attempting to present Hardy as a pathetic figure.

I wish my learned friend would at once either decline talking of the difference between a poor shoe-maker and men of higher rank, or that he would state the facts upon which he thinks it fit to hold that sort of language ... [S]peaking for myself, I desire to be disgraced from this moment, if in the course of this trial, I either have conducted myself, or can conduct myself in such a manner as not to do that justice to this prisoner which the law means should be done to him.[66]

Even more off-putting had been the participation of Tooke. He had been permitted to sit beside his counsel, and he had conducted much of his defence himself. Witty and intelligent, he had affected not to understand the rules of oral argument, and under that pretext had delivered rather improper but effective quips at the prosecution's expense. As a result, Scott had frequently interrupted, convinced that Tooke had or would shortly commit some irregularity, only to be obliged to apologise.[67] When Scott himself spoke unguardedly, moreover, Tooke had been more than ready to take advantage of any gaffe.[68]

In the immediate aftermath of the trials, Scott did not make his feelings known, but over the course of the next year he had several opportunities to discuss not only these but prosecutions in general. The first opportunity occurred in January 1795, when he brought in a Bill to continue suspension of the Habeas Corpus Act.[69] Like its predecessor, this measure proceeded easily through

---

[65] After listening to Erskine's vague references on the former point, Scott interrupted: 'I do not know what it is Mr Erskine is now alluding to; but if he will state to me that it is a proceeding of the House of Lords of this Kingdom, which he conceives can be of use to a subject of this Kingdom standing at that bar, let it be what it will, if it be a proceeding of the House of Lords, I will not object to it.' Howell, *State trials*, XXIV:1060. When Erskine asked whether he might re-open Tooke's defence, Scott replied, 'Notwithstanding Mr Tooke has closed his evidence too early, he has my consent, as far as that will go, to offer any thing he pleases in evidence. With respect to this evidence of the acquittal of Hardy, I have no objection in the world to that – I leave it to the Court.' *Ibid.*, XXV:448.

[66] *Ibid.*, XXIV:1084. See also cols. 681–2.     [67] See, e.g., *ibid.*, XXV:342.

[68] When Scott asserted that the King must die before violating his coronation oath, Tooke inquired whether this statement did not amount to treason by the Attorney General. Scott pretended to be affronted by the interruption so as to give himself time to recast his remark. *Ibid.*, col. 508.

[69] 35 Geo. III c. 3.

the House on the strength of large majorities.[70] The opposition
protested that the treason trials had proven the absence of any
substantial danger.[71] While it failed to block the Bill, this argument prompted Scott to explain why the recent acquittals had not
determined the issue. According to him, the trials were essentially
irrelevant to the present Bill. The latter had not been proposed, he
pointed out, because of the guilt of any particular person, but
'upon the existence of a conspiracy'. That juries had acquitted
specific individuals of participation in that conspiracy did not
mean that it did not exist.[72] Furthermore, because an individual
was acquitted did not mean that he was not 'morally guilty', since
a prosecution might fail for reasons other than the proven innocence of the accused. Scott gave far more weight to the grand
jury's determination that a criminal conspiracy existed, in justifying the government's current response.[73] Nor did he hesitate to
discuss his own conduct in the trials. He pointed out how he had
paid all due attention to his obligations as a prosecutor:

> The duty which had been thrown upon him was to conduct a great public
> prosecution, in such a manner as to render it effectual; but it was also his
> duty not to render it effectual by violating any one of the rules of law or of
> justice. He hoped, in this particular, his conduct was not liable to censure;
> of this he was sure, that he had acted strictly according to the dictates of
> his conscience.[74]

Moreover, he defended the prosecutions as having disrupted the
activities of the radicals and prevented them from completing
more dangerous undertakings. *The Times* quoted Scott as asserting
that, even if no plot had actually existed, 'yet it was evident that
matters were rapidly tending toward that point, and but for the
timely interference of Government, we might have had melancholy proof of it'.[75] His similar claim that 'if government had not
acted with the vigour which it had done, if it had suffered the
British Convention to have met, in all probability he should never

---

[70] On 15 January, leave was granted to bring in the Bill after a vote of 71 to 13; it
received its first reading the following day. On 29 January the House voted 239
to 53 in favour of a second reading, and thereafter approved the measure, 62 to
4. Cobbett, *Parliamentary history*, XXXI:1145, 1191–3.

[71] *Ibid.*, cols. 1149–53.    [72] *Ibid.*, col. 1155.

[73] J. Debrett (ed.), *The parliamentary register ... 1780–99*, 54 vols. (London:
1782–1799), XL:258–60.

[74] Cobbett, *Parliamentary history*, XXXI:1153.

[75] *The Times*, 24 January 1795, 2, col. 2.

have had an opportunity of discussing this measure in parliament' appeared in the *Gentleman's Magazine*.[76]

Scott resumed his defence of the treason trials when the House considered the Treasonable Practices Bill in November. This measure, the first of the so-called 'Two Acts',[77] made it treason to:

compass, imagine, invent, devise, or intend death, or destruction, or any bodily harm tending to death or destruction, maim or wounding, imprisonment or restraint, to the person of his Majesty, or to depose him, or to levy war against him, in order, by force or constraint, to change his measures or counsels, or in order to put any force or constraint upon, or to intimidate or overawe both houses or either house of parliament ...

The above were demonstrated by printing, writing, or other overt act. Publishing or uttering words tending to inspire hatred of the King or government became a misdemeanour. Pitt had introduced the Bill following what some believed had been an attempt on the King's life in October.[78] The Bill's ultimate success was never in question, judging by the substantial majorities on each vote.[79] The House took its time, however, and considered the measure for over three weeks. Debate centred on two points, whether publication of allegedly treasonous materials warranted legislation, and whether the Bill merely applied the existing law of treason or altered it to enshrine the constructive treason analysis. Discussion of the first point led inexorably to the significance of the treason trials. Scott considered references to the failed prosecutions as personal criticism, and his explanations of his conduct became increasingly strident. He called it 'unfair' that he should be the subject of an 'attack' when he had undertaken the prosecutions only after the grand jury had approved the charges laid in the indictment.[80] '[I]f he had not done his duty, let it be made the

---

[76] *Gentleman's Magazine*, May 1795, 396.

[77] The 'Two Acts' were the Treasonable Practices Act, 36 Geo. III c. 7, made perpetual as to treason by 57 Geo. III c. 6, and the Seditious Meetings and Assemblies Act, 36 Geo. III c. 8. The latter forbade meetings of more than fifty persons, other than those meetings convened by responsible authorities, without prior notice and permission from those responsible authorities.

[78] A crowd surrounded the King's carriage in St James Park as he was on his way to open the new session of Parliament. Just outside the House of Lords a window in the carriage was broken, either by a stone or a bullet.

[79] The vote in favour of the first reading was 170 to 26, and the margin for the second reading was 151 to 25. Final approval of the Bill was given by a vote of 226 to 45.

[80] Cobbett, *Parliamentary history*, XXXII:369.

grounds of a motion against him. He could easily withdraw from a public to a private situation.'[81] Nor did he confine his remarks to the treason trials. He also felt called upon to defend his conduct in other state prosecutions:

> He had heard over and over again of the cruelty of the prosecutions, and the severity of the punishments for sedition. He could with confidence declare that there had never been a case in which he had been called upon to prosecute, that he did not state to the jury that he would rather have the gown stripped from his back than to ask them to give a verdict contrary to their consciences.[82]

The fault, according to Scott, lay not with his prosecutions, but with the state of the law on treason and sedition, which the instant Bill would correct by removing all existing doubts as to the correct interpretation of the Treason Act.[83] Turning to the Bill's second focus, Scott spoke emotionally of the great increase in the publication of libels, and of his own inability to check their progress by prosecution. 'Gentlemen would ask, why those libels were not prosecuted? To this he would answer, because they were so numerous, so intricate, and so dextrous, that no individual prosecution was sufficient to answer the wholesome purposes to be derived from such a proceeding.' He could not combat this 'infernal poison' produced by persons intending 'to degrade and destroy every principle of virtue and all natural religion and political order'.[84] He acknowledged that some might regard the Bill as an infringement of their liberty. Rather than debating this point, he argued the prudence of surrendering a portion of that liberty to ensure the safety of the whole, for 'If ... the sovereign was to be libelled and degraded with impunity, the mischief would soon rise to that excess, that the House would wish, when too late that they had applied a timely remedy to the evil.'[85]

While obviously disturbed by the repeated references to the treason trials, Scott was far from overborne by them. He gave evidence of his resilience when the House interrupted debate on the Treasonable Practices Bill to consider an opposition motion that he prosecute John Reeves for a libel of Parliament.[86] Reeves,

---

[81] *The Times*, 17 November 1795, 2, col. 4.
[82] Cobbett, *Parliamentary history*, XXXII:512.     [83] *Ibid.*, col. 483.
[84] *Ibid.*, col.488.        [85] *Ibid.* See also col. 371.
[86] See chapter 7 for Reeves' trial.

the founder of the reactionary Association for Preserving Liberty and Property Against Republicans and Levellers, had published a letter which allegedly described the legislature as the inferior element of government. The motion proved very popular, and many members expressed outrage at the publication. For most of the debate Scott did not contribute, explaining that he must not prejudice any official actions he might be called upon to undertake.[87] Instead, he confined himself to the occasional mischievous comment, as when he reminded the now eager opposition of the hazards of prosecution by an oblique reference to the trials. 'It had been found, in former instances of complaints sent from the House, that a jury, after a long investigation of the facts charged, differed in opinion and acquitted the party prosecuted.'[88] Later he included more than a hint of irony in his acceptance of Reeves' likely prosecution. '[H]e always conceived it an unfortunate circumstance, when a jury felt themselves obliged to pronounce a different opinion from that of the House of Commons. However they were to decide the question; and if he was ordered to prosecute, he would discharge his duty faithfully.'[89]

Many years after the event, Scott would explain that a significant influence upon his conduct in the trials had been his desire to inform the public of the danger posed by the radical societies. He had produced extensive documentary evidence relating to the radicals, believing it 'more essential to securing the public safety that the whole of their transactions should be published, than that any of these individuals should be

---

[87] Mitford explained that, when the Attorney General prosecuted on his own authority, he proceeded according to his own discretion. When instructed by the House to prosecute a case of privilege on its behalf, however, he must submit to their judgment as to the merits of the case. Consequently, he did not feel competent to interfere in their deliberations. Erskine, however, argued that in remaining silent the law officers were abrogating their responsibility to provide legal advice to the House. *Morning Chronicle*, 27 November 1795, 2, col. 3.

[88] Cobbett, *Parliamentary history*, XXXII:627.

[89] *Ibid.*, col. 634. In A. V. Beedell, 'John Reeves's prosecution for a seditious libel, 1795–6: a study in political cynicism', *Historical Journal* 36(4) (1993), 799–824, Beedell argues that Pitt's denial of Reeves – a government placeman and pamphleteer – indicates the breadth of 'liberal' Whig views in the Commons, to which Pitt was obliged to submit in order to secure passage of the Two Acts. If this reading of Pitt's conduct is correct, Scott's remarks suggest either an independence similar to that of William Windham, or a wish on the part of the government to curb the opposition's satisfaction engendered by the success of the motion.

convicted'.[90] If such had indeed been his motivation, he learned the danger of using the courtroom as a venue for proving general conclusions. As the political opposition cited the acquittals in condemnation of the government's analysis of the radical threat, Scott saw that the result of a prosecution was critical to the reception of any ancillary aim. Moreover, failure could reflect badly upon the prosecutor, a subject upon which Scott was far from indifferent. The failure of the prosecutions might have signalled the demise of the theory of constructive treason. At least immediately, however, this was not the case. In a personal letter written just after Hardy's acquittal, Henry Addington asserted that the jury had merely found insufficient evidence of an overt act, and had been 'wholly uninfluenc'd by Erskine's strange doctrines of the law of treason'.[91] More significantly, one year after the trials, Parliament enacted the Treasonable Practices Act, which fully sanctioned the constructive treason analysis. The enactment of that statute provided a clear contrast to the trials, as in several weeks the government achieved what it had failed to do in as many months. Having been fully involved in each, Scott cannot have been unmoved by the different effects of the legislative and prosecutorial responses. Moreover, the experiences of those twelve months between the trials and the Treasonable Practices Act would remain with him when he returned to the courtroom.

[90] Eldon, *Anecdote book*, p. 101. F. K. Prochaska describes Scott as believing that he had a 'delegation from society' to preserve it from evil. 'English state trials in the 1790s: a case study' *Journal of British Studies* 13(1) (1973), 63–82.

[91] Henry Addington to Hiley Addington, 8 November 1794, DevRO (Sidmouth Papers) 152M/OZ43.

# 7

# RESOLUTION

John Scott's last years as a law officer were characterised, not by a single dramatic event such as the Regency crisis or the treason trials, but by a constant press of work. This was particularly true in matters of criminal law, which kept him busy in chambers, in court, and on the floor of the House of Commons. Political unrest, and ministerial fear of it, continued, and fuelled a range of activities for the law officers in respect of conduct possibly amounting to treason and seditious libel. A definite trend too, emerges in Scott's work during this time, which was openly to favour legislation over litigation. Stephen Watson has identified an actual shift in policy and associated it with William Pitt.[1] Of comparable, if not greater, importance in this matter must have been the attitude and conduct of the Attorney General. His post uniquely qualified him to assess the costs and benefits of different government responses, and his professional reputation and standing in the government afforded him considerable authority. Moreover, the other 'elements' of a successful prosecutorial regime were lacking. The replacement of Henry Dundas with the Duke of Portland at the Home Office did not provide either vigour or guidance, and the acquittals of Hardy and Tooke demonstrated that the English bench was not bound to act in accordance with the government's wishes. In the absence of either a strong-willed Home Secretary or a deferential judiciary, Scott was well-placed to re-direct the course of criminal administration in accordance with his own views and sensibilities.

In the first half of 1796, Scott unsuccessfully prosecuted two cases of treason and one of seditious libel. In January a jury acquitted William Stone of conspiring to obtain information for

---

[1] J. S. Watson, *The reign of George III, 1760–1815* (Oxford, 1960), 360.

the French regarding an invasion of England, and in May Robert Crossfield was found not guilty of conspiring to procure a model of a device to assassinate the King. John Reeves, charged with publishing a libel of Parliament, was similarly acquitted. The cases are noteworthy because they demonstrate Scott's unwillingness to press forcefully prosecutions with which he had incomplete sympathy. Stone, Crossfield, and Reeves were all awkward defendants – the first two because the criminality of their conduct was unclear, and the third because the government's attitude toward the prosecution was equivocal. Scott presented restrained, even reluctant, cases against each man, and, when the juries acquitted, they might be described as having acted with Scott's acquiescence. Consequently, those gains which the government or Parliament might have achieved from convictions, in terms of punishment and deterrence, were lost, at least in part, through the scruples of their chief prosecutor.

Whatever William Stone's intentions, he had been involved in a plot to assist a potential French invasion. In January 1794, William Jackson had come to England to obtain information on the likely support for such a venture.[2] He had contacted Stone, whose Francophile brother had notified him of Jackson's business. As requested, Stone had questioned various businessmen and politicians and learned that any invasion would be resisted absolutely, and he had duly passed this assessment on to Jackson. The two men had continued to correspond when Jackson went to Ireland in February to meet the leaders of the United Irishmen. Shortly thereafter, however, Jackson's work had come to a premature end. The English and Irish authorities had had him under observation, and they had intercepted a communication from the United Irishmen that Jackson had despatched to the French government. His arrest had taken place on 26 April 1794, and his conviction for treason had followed one year later.[3]

The case against Stone rested on his relationship with Jackson. Stone had carried on a correspondence with Jackson, and he had

---

[2] Jackson's mission is summarised in M. Elliott, *Partners in revolution: the United Irishmen and France* (New Haven, 1982), 62–5. See also H. Boylan (ed.), *Dictionary of Irish biography*, 2nd edn (Dublin, 1988); and R. Hayes, *Biographical dictionary of Irishmen in France* (Dublin, 1949).

[3] Jackson committed suicide by swallowing poison before sentence could be passed.

both ignored the advice of opposition politicians to cease his inquiries and failed to alert the Home Secretary.[4] According to the Crown, such conduct implied a sympathy with Jackson's aims. The theory of the prosecution, however, differed considerably from its tone. Throughout the proceedings Scott demonstrated sympathy for Stone's situation. He did not oppose the defence's request to postpone the trial, and, when the case was finally argued, he said much that was favourable to the accused. The jury, said Scott, should not convict unless satisfied of Stone's evil intentions. Moreover, no one could demand that Stone ought to have severed all ties with his brother, and Scott admitted that conducting any correspondence with that brother in perfect safety would have been difficult.[5] The defence took advantage of Scott's attitude. In his affidavit, Stone referred to 'the Attorney General, who never pressed beyond the line of his duty', while Thomas Erskine maintained in his closing statement: 'If the Attorney-general had done as some officers of the crown in former times have done, he might have conducted his case very differently, and more unfavourably for the prisoner; but he could not so conduct it, because he can do nothing that is unworthy.'[6]

The case of Robert Crossfield presented Scott with a prosecution made particularly awkward by factual uncertainty.[7] In September 1794 Crossfield and two others had made inquiries of several London metal-workers about the manufacture of a device not unlike an air gun. Drawings of such a device had subsequently been found in the possession of one of the men, Thomas Upton, who had informed the Privy Council of a conspiracy to assassinate the King by shooting a poisoned dart at him. Thereupon Paul Le

---

[4] T. J. Howell (ed.), *A complete collection of state trials and proceedings for high treason and other crimes and misdemeanours* 33 vols. (London, 1816–26), XXV:1182–8, 1204–5.

[5] *Ibid.*, cols. 1323, 1330.

[6] *The Times*, 20 November 1795, 3, col. 3. Howell, *State trials*, XXV:1376. Reporting Stone's acquittal, *The Times* stated on 1 February 1796, 2, col. 3: 'here then is another instance of the mildness of our laws, and of the purity of British jurisprudence; and after such repeated instances of their excellence, those who may hereafter offend, deserve to be punished with every possible severity. Mr Stone's trial will however, we hope, be productive of some good. It has unmasked, and exposed to public light the meddling spirit of a certain class of men, whose politics are not viewed in a very favourable light.'

[7] Even accounting for prosecutorial bias, the clearest account is given by Scott in Howell, *State trials*, XXVI:18–23.

Maitre, John Smith, and George Higgins had been arrested, and Crossfield sought for questioning. Crossfield, however, had not been discovered and in January 1795 he had obtained employment as a surgeon on a merchant ship and left England. In February this vessel had been captured by the French. Three months later Crossfield had returned to England under a false name with other English prisoners. Upon reaching Cornwall, several of his companions had informed a magistrate of claims he had made regarding a plot to kill the King with an air gun, and he had been arrested.

The case was much more complex than these facts suggest. Almost every person involved proved unreliable. The primary prosecution witness, Upton, had disappeared. The prosecution maintained that he was dead, but the defence charged that he had absconded after accusing Le Maitre, Smith, and Higgins, against whom he bore a grudge.[8] Peregrine Palmer, who had visited the metal-workers with Upton and Crossfield, proved such a recalcitrant witness for the Crown that Chief Justice Sir James Eyre commented on the irregularity of his examination by the prosecution.[9] Of the persons who gave accounts of Crossfield's shipboard and subsequent behaviour, one allegedly disliked him, another apparently tried to influence witnesses on his behalf, and a third's supposed belief in witches rendered his opinions suspect.[10] Crossfield's character was also difficult to evaluate. He had made frequent provocative and potentially damning remarks both before and after his arrest. On the other hand, several witnesses mentioned his light, careless, talkative nature, and his tendency to drink.[11] Scott's response was to treat the various problematic individuals with overt scepticism. He stressed that he had carefully avoided relying upon any declarations made by Upton, and warned the jury:

you should not only believe that he has said nothing more; but such is the

---

[8] *Ibid.*, cols. 17, 123.      [9] *Ibid.*, col. 37.

[10] *Ibid.*, cols. 77–8.

[11] While at sea Crossfield had not only sung republican songs and spoken against the King, he had frequently mentioned the air gun and an assassination plot. Many of the details of the plot, however, had altered with each telling. *Ibid.*, cols. 58–9, 66–7, 71–4, 78. The constables who conducted him to London testified that Crossfield had tried to convince them to help him escape, suggesting that they kill the driver and post boy if necessary. They also reported that he might have been drunk at the time, and that he had fallen asleep soon after he had presented his proposals. *Ibid.*, col. 81.

nature of the proof in this case, that you should even act upon the supposition that if he had been here present, in order to be examined, he might have spoken favourably for the prisoner.[12]

He further noted that he would have been obliged to issue a warning if Upton *had* testified:

that his evidence ought to have been received with great jealousy and with great attention; that you ought to protect against such a witness, a prisoner, put upon his deliverance before you, till your unwillingness to receive his testimony had been subdued by a conscientious conviction, arising out of all the circumstances of the case, not only that he was as guilty as he admitted himself to be, but that other persons represented by him to be equally guilty with himself actually were so.[13]

With respect to James Winter, whose reliability was tarnished by his accounts of supernatural experiences, Scott acknowledged: 'if this case depended upon Winter's testimony I should think it an extremely hazardous thing to come to a conclusion against the prisoner upon his evidence alone.'[14]

Finally, in the case of John Reeves, Scott undertook a prosecution for which he had little sympathy in principle.[15] In 1795 Reeves had published the first of a series of letters, 'Thoughts on the English government, addressed to the quiet good sense of the people of England'. One passage had described the King and his ministers as the most fundamental components of the English government, with Parliament and juries as adjuncts. The monarch had been further designated the 'ancient stock' and the Lords and Commons 'goodly branches' of the tree of government. While these branches might be 'lopped off' the tree would remain:

The kingly government may go on, in all its functions, without Lords and Commons: it has heretofore done so for years together, and in our times it does so during every recess of parliament; but without the king, *his* parliament is no more.[16]

Following members' complaints, the House of Commons had appointed a committee to examine the document, and on their report the House had voted an address to the King requesting that Reeves be prosecuted for seditious libel. On 8 January 1796 Scott had received the King's instructions to undertake the prosecution.

In essence, the contest between prosecution and defence rested

---

[12] *Ibid.*, col. 172.    [13] *Ibid.*, col. 17.    [14] *Ibid.*, col. 180.
[15] See chapter 6.
[16] Howell, *State trials*, XXVI:530–531 (emphasis in original).

on the interpretation of the single passage. The prosecution argued that Reeves demeaned the legislature, by denominating it as merely an advising and consenting, but not a correcting, body. Moreover, Reeves claimed that the King could lawfully exercise all aspects of government although Parliament was abolished, whereas in fact the Bill of Rights permitted only a prorogation or suspension, and required that the King's ministers regularly account to Parliament for any and all actions taken.[17] Even as he presented his case, however, Scott took pains to distance himself from the decision to prosecute and from a final evaluation of the letter. Having designated himself merely as an agent of the House, Scott reminded the jury that they must not merely consider one particular passage, but that 'it was their duty to consider the work from the beginning to the end of it, to take every part of it as a context to the part charged in the information'.[18] If they found the document merely 'ill-advised' or 'ill-executed', 'it is not consonant to the lenient genuine spirit of the law under which we live, that in such a case you should press a man with the consequences of guilt'.[19] Scott acknowledged that the *prima facie* meaning of the document called for a disavowal from Reeves, but as he hastened to assure the jury: 'I am not pretending to assert before you – that is for you and not for me to decide – that the *real* meaning is so obnoxious to the constitution.'[20]

Scott's conduct in these three trials might be written off simply as the unwillingness of the professional to argue beyond the limits of his case. Undoubtedly, they were not obviously strong cases for the prosecution. On the other hand, neither were they so plainly without merit that an able prosecutor would have been expected to make as little of them as Scott did. That his conduct reflects a more general dissatisfaction becomes more likely when his subsequent work is considered. During the next three years he demonstrated distinctly different attitudes toward legislating against future criminal activity and prosecuting individual malefactors. His language in support of the former was robust, confident, even

---

[17] *Ibid.*, cols. 539, 540.     [18] *Ibid.*, cols. 535–6.     [19] *Ibid.*, col. 553.

[20] *Ibid.*, col. 582 (emphasis in original). Scott's conduct of the prosecution must further call into question the attitude of the government, and Pitt in particular, toward Reeves. See A. V. Beedell, 'John Reeves's prosecution for a seditious libel, 1795–6: a study in political cynicism', *Historical Journal* 36(4) (1993), 799–824.

combative, as he sought to convince Parliament to enact measures to curb unrest in the military, inhibit political assemblies, and restrict inflammatory publications by newspapers. When the prospect arose of an actual prosecution in any of these areas, however, he became extremely guarded in his expression, both in comments upon the likely prospects in a case, and in his actual conduct of the prosecution.

In the spring of 1797 Royal Navy seamen at Spithead and the Nore mutinied over their poor pay and working conditions. In June Parliament approved two government Bills, the first declaring that those mutineers who refused to surrender were rebels, and the second punishing anyone who attempted to seduce members of the armed forces from their duty and allegiance.[21] Scott drafted the first of these, the Ships in Mutiny Act, which also prohibited all communication with ships in a state of mutiny, upon pain of death. The measure enjoyed general support in the House, although some members found it unduly severe. Scott, however, urged the necessity of strong measures. He regarded the 'aggravated treason, piracy, and rebellion' then taking place as a dark plan to disrupt the nation. He wanted to rescue the seamen from 'the perilous situation in which a gang of conspirators had placed them' and argued that without such legislation, the 'conspirators' who had provoked the uprising would surely find the means to continue it.[22] When it came to taking direct action against individuals, however, Scott was much less strident.[23] In July he undertook the prosecution of Richard Fuller for violation of the Incitement to Mutiny Act. From the first, Scott was unhappy with the case. On 11 June 1797 he and Mitford observed in a letter to the Duke of Portland:

But we beg leave again to observe that prosecutions of government have frequently failed, where the prosecution has been compelled by the necessity of supporting magistrates who have committed persons as guilty

---

[21] 37 Geo. III c. 71; and 37 Geo. III c. 70.

[22] W. Cobbett (ed.), *The parliamentary history of England ... to 1803*, 36 vols. (London, 1806–20), XXXII:816–17.

[23] Most of the prosecutions under the Ships in Mutiny Act occurred in military courts martial in which he did not participate. He nevertheless reviewed these prosecutions, and he drafted opinions to the First Lord of the Admiralty advising pardons in cases of uncertainty or irregularity. See, e.g., Earl Spencer to George III, 11 August 1797 and 14 August 1797, A. Aspinall (ed.), *The later correspondence of George III*, 5 vols. (Cambridge, 1962), II:610, 613.

of offences, without any previous examination of the evidence which may be obtained, by the Solicitor of the Treasury, or under his direction, for the purpose of ascertaining whether the evidence which can be obtained will probably support the prosecution upon a trial.[24]

Scott soon had further cause for uneasiness. Not only had the offence followed 'very speedily' after the enactment of the statute, the defendant had also proven 'at all times weak, and very often deranged in his intellects'.[25] At Fuller's trial Scott repeatedly stressed the propriety of both indictment and conviction, but reminded the jury of the availability of a pardon. '[T]he Constitution of this country has provided that mercy may be applied for, and you perhaps may conceive with me, that it will not be applied for in vain.'[26] The jury duly convicted Fuller and recommended that he receive a pardon.

A similar divergence in Scott's attitude is evident from his involvement with the Bill to prevent unlawful oaths, which he brought before the House in early July.[27] This measure was aimed at secret political associations or *ad hoc* agreements such as those which had bound many of the mutineers. It prohibited the administering or voluntary taking of oaths to engage in mutinous or seditious activities, disturb the peace, or obey the orders of any organisation not lawfully constituted. Anyone convicted was guilty of a felony and liable to transportation for a maximum of seven years. Scott defended the measure strongly to the Commons.

[T]he common law already fixed a considerable punishment on this offence; and when it was considered how much this horrid practice had lately prevailed, to the great injury of the Government and the Country, he thought it his duty to endeavour to point out to deluded men what the nature of the crime, and the punishment attached to it, were, by introducing a statute expressly for that purpose. [H]e scarcely knew how to express his feelings at the attempts of those evil-minded persons who by such means endeavoured to subvert the constituted authorities of the country.[28]

---

[24] J. Scott and John Mitford to the Duke of Portland, 11 June 1797, PRO, HO48(6).

[25] *The Times*, 17 July 1797, 4, col. 1; see also *Rex* v. *Fuller*, *The Old Bailey proceedings*, 38 micro film reels (Brighton, 1984), 16 July 1797, Case No. 463, 447.

[26] *Rex* v. *Fuller*, 447.        [27] 37 Geo. III c. 123.

[28] J. Debrett (ed.), *The parliamentary register ... 1780–1799*, 54 vols. (London, 1782–99), XLVII:777.

When he received a query on enforcing the statute in November, however, Scott was once again luke-warm. He and Mitford expressed uncertainty at the evidence of unlawful activity, and advised that the local magistrate content himself with observing the individuals concerned until circumstances distinctly warranted intervention, '& not to hazard the loss of the advantages gained, by instituting any prosecution which may fail of success, or, if successful, may not have a considerable or extensive effect'.[29]

Neither was Scott proving eager to prosecute potentially libellous publications. Upon receipt of a query from the Duke of Portland regarding a questionable newspaper article, Scott and Mitford replied:

> whilst the paper referred to by your Grace's letter, & other publications of a similar tendency, remain unnoticed by the two houses of Parliament ... prosecutions carried on without the authority of either house of Parliament, & applied only to individuals of the probable description of the editor & publisher of the paper so referred to, are liable to objections which have a strong tendency to prevent their success, & if successful have very limited consequences.[30]

In the following April, however, he showed that such a legislative regulation of the newspapers had his very strong support. He brought in the Newspapers Regulation Bill, which passed into law that summer.[31] It restricted the production and distribution of newspapers, and required newspaper proprietors to identify themselves to the government.[32] Scott stressed the necessity of regulation, given the threat to public morals posed by 'the shameful calumny and slander which disgraces the British press'.[33]

---

[29] Scott and Mitford to Portland, 11 December 1797, PRO, HO48(6). The following summer, an individual named Heron was acquitted at the Hampshire assizes of violating the same statute. The prosecution's brief notes that the Treasury Solicitor laid the indictment before Scott, 'who had great doubts about prosecuting the prisoner capitally, but at length he directed the present indictment to be preferred, at the same time particularly enjoining the Sol[icito]r of the Treasury to acquaint the King's Counsel that in case the prisoner should be convicted special care should be taken that nothing further should be done until his case should have been represented to his Majesty'. A further comment in the margin states: 'The Att[orne]y Gen[eral] intreats that this may be particularly attended to. J. White' PRO, TS 11/834(2774).

[30] Scott and Mitford to Portland, 9 November 1797, PRO, HO48(6).

[31] 38 Geo. III c. 78.

[32] S. Lambert (ed.), *House of Commons sessional papers of the eighteenth century*, 147 vols. (Wilmington, DE, 1975–76), CXVI:287–301.

[33] Debrett, *Parliamentary register*, L:578.

I will submit to the House, whether an alarming public evil does not arise from such a deal of private slander being continually presented to our eyes? I would have you consider, whether the constant current of abuse which flows from the newspapers of all parties, has not a very great tendency to deaden that delicacy of feeling upon which the purity of morals so much depends?[34]

While acknowledging that most publishers lacked any 'malignant intention', he considered this 'not a sufficient apology' for what actually appeared in print.[35]

Given the tendency of his conduct, it should come as no surprise that Scott's next significant prosecution inspired another restrained performance. In the summer of 1798 he conducted the prosecution of James O'Coigly, Arthur O'Connor, John Binns, John Allen, and Jeremiah Leary. They were accused of having conspired to gain information to assist the French.[36] Briefly their activities had been as follows. O'Connor had come to England just before Christmas 1797. In London he had met openly with prominent opposition politicians, and had allegedly conferred privately with members of radical political groups, including the United Britons and the militant wing of the London Corresponding Society. O'Coigly had visited Ireland and England in January 1798. He had met with the United Irish leadership in Dublin and with radicals in Manchester and Liverpool. Arriving in London in February, he had met O'Connor, and the two of them had prepared to depart for the continent. John Binns had undertaken to hire a boat for the crossing either to Holland or France. After various delays he had met O'Connor and O'Coigly in Margate on 27 February 1798. The two Irishmen had travelled as army officers and under false names, and they had been accompanied by their servants Leary and Allen. The following day all five had been arrested. Constables and Bow Street officers had seized at that time and subsequently various documents, but they had found only one particularly incriminating item – an address from the United Britons to the French Executive Directory in O'Coigly's coat pocket.

The evidence of criminality was therefore strongest against O'Coigly, and the prosecution pointed out every link between

---

[34] *Ibid.*, 577.   [35] *Ibid.*

[36] See Elliott, *Partners*, 173–83, and R. A. E. Wells, *Insurrection: the British experience 1795–1803* (Gloucester, 1983), pp. 121–6.

O'Coigly and the others, to show that they had acted according to a common plan.[37] While Scott's approach cannot be described as aggressive, he did at least indicate that he had an opinion about the evidence. He began his opening address with his usual complexity:

I am bound to act according to the best sense I can form of my duty; and therefore, however painful it is to me so to state this matter to you, I hold it to be my bounden duty to state to you that I am not aware how it is consistent with possibility that, upon the trial of this indictment, you can receive such an answer from the prisoners, to the proof which I have to lay before you, as can justify you ... in pronouncing that they are not guilty.[38]

He pointed out flaws in O'Connor's story and inconsistencies in his conduct, noting that if he *had not* intended to convey information to the French, 'it never happened to an innocent man to stand in a situation which exposes him to so much suspicion of guilt'.[39] Scott still refused, however, to acknowledge 'any zeal for the event of this cause' or motivation beyond his official duty.[40] The result of Scott's conduct? An acquittal for four of the five defendants. Lord Glenbervie wrote indignantly of the prosecution:

But I believe it is not less the common than it is a just observ[atio]n that the fault of the many state acquittals in this country ought to be laid fully more to the door of the judges & the Att[or]n[e]y G[eneral] than of the juries. If the King's Prosecutor will descant in very long harangues on his own humanity & make himself (what no duty or principle or precedent requires or warrants) counsel for the prisoner ... it cannot be expected that juries will take on their shoulders the individual burden & odium of convictions.[41]

---

[37] Howell, *State trials*, XXVI:1247–59.    [38] *Ibid.*, XXVI:1245.

[39] *Ibid.*, XXVII:114.

[40] *Ibid.*, col. 92. Scott's pre-trial conduct, moreover, had been rigorously correct. When asked by Portland whether they need honour a request from O'Connor's attorney to interview Roger O'Connor, also in custody on suspicion of treason, Scott and Mitford answered that: 'We apprehend that there is no circumstance relative to the prosecution which can make it advisable to refuse Mr Simmons permission ... & on the contrary, we conceive that a refusal of such permission might have a very serious effect upon the trial of Mr O'Connor.' PRO, HO48(7). Upon being informed of a possible plan to bias three potential jurors against the defendants, Scott promised both to investigate the case, and to prevent any person from the locality in question from serving on the jury. Howell, *State trials*, XXVI:122–3.

[41] Lord Glenbervie to Lord Sheffield, 17 August 1798, East Sussex Record Office (Sheffield papers), AMS 544/322, reproduced with permission of the County Archivist, copyright reserved.

Scott's legal opinions during these years also indicate that he did not relish the prospect of litigation. He and Mitford received a number of queries regarding potentially seditious activities, and in each case they answered cautiously. Where the prospective case was merely weak they pointed this out. For instance, as regards John MacClellan, a naval surgeon described by a neighbour in Plymouth as 'an inveterate enemy to our present constitution', Scott and Mitford found insufficient evidence on which to base a prosecution.[42] They were also troubled, however, by the negative effect a failed prosecution could have on the administration of the criminal law. When a magistrate committed a person to gaol whom the Attorney General declined to prosecute, this could adversely affect the magistrate's reputation and authority. Conversely, if cases were prosecuted to validate the misguided efforts of local officials, the government could find its own reputation tarnished. With respect to John Cantelo, who allegedly supported the naval mutinies and wanted to 'shake off the arbitrary government' of the nation, Scott and Mitford wrote:

This appears to us to be a case in which if no commitment had taken place, our experience of similar cases would have led us not to advise that measure. But the magistrates having taken upon themselves to commit Cantelo to Winchester Gaol, we must submit to the direction of Government how far it is expedient to support the magistrates in what they have done, as their intentions were evidently laudable, by directing a prosecution which we think will probably fail of success.[43]

Scott was particularly anxious about precipitate actions by local officials being regarded as government acts.[44] He and Mitford thus responded to reports of individuals having undertaken to learn military drill.

It appears to be a subject of uncommon & indeed extreme delicacy; & the consequences which may follow any steps which may be taken by the magistrates, unless those steps can be fully justified by law, seem to us so important that we rather advise that no step should be taken but upon the fullest information & consideration of the particular circumstances of each particular case.[45]

---

[42] Scott and Mitford (probably to Portland), 24 June 1797, PRO, HO48(6).
[43] Scott and Mitford (probably to Portland), 14 June 1797, *ibid.*
[44] Scott to Portland, undated [prior to 12 January 1796], PRO, HO48(5).
[45] Scott and Mitford to Portland, 24 June 1797, PRO, HO48(6); see also another opinion between the same men on this subject, also dated 24 June 1797, *ibid.*

Instead of committing suspicious persons to gaol, Scott and Mitford urged magistrates 'to remonstrate with the persons concerned on the impropriety of their conduct' or to obtain apologies and security for future good behaviour.[46] When the law officers saw no way of avoiding an unattractive prosecution they undertook it grudgingly. Reporting on the case of David Norcliffe, who allegedly 'several times drank the health of Buonaparte and success to his undertaking', they wrote:

It is difficult to avoid prosecuting in this case, the words being spoken in the presence of soldiers, & the soldiers having brought the party speaking them before the civil magistrate. Enquiry should be made so as to ascertain all the particulars of the conversation in which the words were spoken in order to ascertain whether the party was sober and spoke the words deliberately. If the circumstances attending the conversation prove the words to have been deliberately spoken, it rather seems to us that the party should be prosecuted.[47]

In his parliamentary speeches during his last six months in office, Scott stated most clearly his views on administration of the criminal law. In his remarks during the debates on the Bills to suspend the Habeas Corpus Act in December 1798, and to suppress the radical societies in April 1799, he confirmed his support for legislation as against prosecution.[48] Legislation enabled the administration to prevent dangerous situations from arising. Armed with more and stronger legislation, local authorities could take steps to inhibit the growth of disloyal or criminal attitudes before they became dangerous. As he explained in December, his support for suspension of the Habeas Corpus Act resulted not from a desire to keep people in prison, but 'to prevent others from getting into prison'.[49] Presumably he meant by this that volatile or imprudent persons could either be frightened into good behaviour by the threat of confinement, or actually confined and thereby prevented from committing any act that would subject them to more severe punishment. Similarly, in April he maintained the wisdom of taking preventative action against the radical societies. If meetings were banned, misguided individuals

---

[46] Scott and Mitford to Portland, 29 June 1798, PRO, HO48(7); Scott and Mitford (probably to Portland), 31 December 1798, PRO, HO48(7).
[47] Scott and Mitford (probably to Portland), 26 February 1798, PRO, HO48(7).
[48] 39 Geo. III c. 15; and 39 Geo. III c. 79.
[49] *Morning Chronicle*, 22 December 1798, 3, col. 4.

were less likely to become involved in dangerous activities.[50] Prosecution, on the other hand, was at best a crude remedy for existing dangers. Blameworthy individuals were not brought to trial as a result of deficiencies in prosecutorial resources or inadequate evidence. 'Was it not, therefore,' asked Scott, 'rather more desirable to apply new laws, than to bring forward useless prosecutions?'[51] Even when a prosecution succeeded, the severity of the punishment afforded by the law frequently conflicted with a benevolent sensibility. Scott far preferred the 'lenient measures' of the legislature to the 'forfeiture of lives, and the imposition of rigorous penalties' by the courts.[52] Sometimes, certainly, prosecutions were necessary. Scott had by this time overcome the vexation caused by the treason trials. An account of his speech during the Habeas Corpus debates shows him apparently confident to base his arguments on that litigation.

He had heard it also alledged, that after the state trials and acquittals of 1794, that a verdict of Not Guilty negatived all ideas of the existence of a conspiracy; but we had now come back again to common sense, and did not maintain that, because there was an acquittal, there could not be any ground of accusation. The truth of the matter was, that notwithstanding the acquittal of individuals charged with High Treason, there not only might be, but there actually was, as subsequent events had shewn, a conspiracy, as dangerous to the state as any legal guilt could be.[53]

Presumably, however, if the legislature had acted firmly before the radical societies had grown so strong, the trials might not have been necessary.

Scott's actual prosecutions during his last months in office similarly demonstrate his attitude toward resolving criminal matters in the courtroom. In the trials of these relatively lesser offences he took a disinterested, and even benevolent approach where the case was uncertain or the defendant sympathetic; he became severe only when confronted by recalcitrance and invective. This distinction is most clearly illustrated by two cases of seditious libel conducted on the same day in February 1799 against John Cuthell as publisher and the Revd Gilbert Wakefield as author. The work in question was a response to a tract written by Richard Watson, the Bishop of Llandaff, defending the proposed income tax. Wakefield's piece not only criticised Watson,

---

[50] Cobbett, *Parliamentary history*, XXXIV:994.      [51] *Ibid.*, col. 995.
[52] *Ibid.*      [53] *Morning Chronicle*, 26 December 1798, 2, col. 3.

Pitt, the tax, and the war, but contained charges of civil and ecclesiastical corruption.

With respect to Cuthell, Scott stated a legal position as regards the non-author publisher that admitted no compromise. When a work sank from 'free, manly, and rational discussion' to 'abuse and invective without argument' it was a libel. If the work was libellous, the publisher was guilty, regardless of his ignorance of its contents.[54] '[E]very man who publishes a book does so at his own hazard; if it be a libel, whether he knew it or not, he is answerable criminally.'[55] While absolutely firm on the legal consequences of Cuthell's actions, however, Scott readily admitted that the 'guilt' of a negligent publisher need not condemn him to severe punishment. Cuthell's good character, Scott added, entitled him to lenity 'ten thousand times more' than that given to Joseph Johnson, who had already been sentenced to six months imprisonment for the same offence.[56] When the court came to pronounce sentence on Cuthell, Scott requested that punishment be 'as lenient as the court could order, consistently with their regard for the interest which the public has in the prosecution of libels', whereupon Cuthell received a fine of 30 marks.[57]

By contrast, Scott seems to have been goaded into what was for him an unusual severity in the trial of Wakefield, as a result of the defendant's combativeness. Scott started the proceedings by simply placing the work before the jury. He pointed out that previous juries had already found it libellous, and that Wakefield had subsequently published a third and even more objectionable edition. 'What the defendant will say in his own defence, I am really at a loss to conjecture.'[58] Wakefield did not long leave Scott in doubt. Having declined to employ counsel and so speaking on his own behalf, he began with a particularly scathing personal attack on the Attorney General. After noting that the office had long been regarded as 'essentially destructive of all honour and integrity' he asserted that Scott could not conscientiously conduct this prosecution, because he belonged to the government that Wakefield had criticised.[59] 'But now, for him to set up a claim of unprejudiced and unbiased judgment, is not only an insufferable

[54] Howell, *State trials*, XXVII:654.   [55] *Ibid.*, col. 673.
[56] *Ibid.* For the sentence passed on Johnson, see PRO, TS 11/456/1511.
[57] Howell, *State trials*, XXVII:676 (addendum).   [58] *Ibid.*, col. 703.
[59] *Ibid.*, col. 705.

insult to our understandings, but a dereliction of shame and decency in him.'[60] Nor did his criticism end there.[61] Not content merely to disagree with Scott's view on freedom of the press, Wakefield couched his position thus:

What the Attorney-general has incidentally advanced on the subject today, are the remarks of a man who is miserably unacquainted with all philosophical principles and liberal information on such points, and deserves nothing but contempt from me, as the wretched babblings of one blinded by education, or corrupted by his office.[62]

Previously, the courtroom participation of a defendant had caused Scott a certain discomfiture.[63] In the instant case, however, he responded in a controlled, dignified manner. He began his reply thus mentioning Wakefield's invective: 'With respect to the many observations which have been made upon my conduct, I am content that they also shall go to you, without any reply from me. You shall judge of my conduct yourselves, with the comment which this defendant has put upon it.'[64] He then offered a few observations on the substance of the defence, and his measured severity made Wakefield's tirade seem more unreasonable. Criticism of the government was appropriate and valuable, but Wakefield could not portray ministers as robbers and murderers and then complain if the government's chief lawyer queried whether this amounted to a libel.[65] The jury delivered a verdict of guilty without retiring. Wakefield was sentenced to two years' imprisonment, together with securities for five years totalling £1,000.

In March Scott prosecuted John Vint, George Ross, and John Parry, the printer, publisher, and proprietor, respectively, of the *Courier and Evening Standard* newspaper. The information charged them with publishing a libel on Tsar Paul I of Russia. Specifically the *Courier* article described a recent Russian edict prohibiting timber exportation as unjust to the Russian people

---

[60] *Ibid.*, col. 706.

[61] Wakefield had begun his assault on Scott before his trial. On 21 July 1798 he had published an open letter to Scott, consisting of a 33–page defence of his own conduct and an indictment of the prosecution of Johnson. Wakefield exclaimed: 'I must solemnly declare, that I look upon the conduct of you, Sir John ... so occupied as ye are in molesting and punishing your fellow-creatures; with sentiments of astonishment and horror, to which language could not easily do justice.' Gilbert Wakefield, *A letter to Sir John Scott* (n.p., 1798), 29.

[62] Howell, *State trials*, XXVII:709.    [63] See chapter 6.

[64] Howell, *State trials*, XXVII:734.    [65] *Ibid.*, col. 735.

and foolish with respect to foreign trade. As he had against Wakefield, Scott barely made an opening statement, other than to lay the article before the jury. In contrast to the *Wakefield* case, however, Scott received no further stimulus to pursue these defendants with any vigour. Instead, he responded half-heartedly to Erskine's argument for the defence. After a few remarks about 'unauthorized invectives in newspapers' Scott hinted that he did not really favour the prosecution. Moreover, he remarked that, if the jury *did* convict, the defendants need not receive a severe punishment. The Russian ambassador could help reduce the sentences. '[P]roper representations might obtain for the defendants what the law in its just administration could not possibly confer.'[66] The tone of his remarks to Erskine also shows Scott's unwillingness to regard the proceedings as an occasion for confrontational advocacy. He concluded his opening statement predicting 'a brilliant speech' containing 'plausible and ingenious arguments' from Erskine,[67] and he thus prefaced his reply:

Gentlemen of the jury; it is plain that I have not much embarrassed my learned friend by bespeaking from him a brilliant speech. After twenty years experience of him, I knew I might safely do it; I knew also his clients had bespoke it, and were not likely to be disappointed.[68]

Scott's last major prosecution was a more serious matter: a charge of riot that arose directly and immediately out of the O'Coigly case.[69] The defendants were accused of having attempted to effect Arthur O'Connor's rescue before he could be re-arrested following his acquittal. When Bow Street officers had attempted to make their way to the bench to present their warrant, a general disturbance had broken out in the court, during which O'Connor had made his way into the corridor before being stopped. As a result of these events Scott had filed an information against five persons, including O'Connor's lawyer. He and the Earl of Thanet were found guilty as charged on 25 April 1799. Despite the gravity of the case, Scott maintained his now familiar posture – offended at the crime as alleged and compelled by his office to conduct the prosecution, but indifferent as to the actual

---

[66] *Ibid.*, col. 639.    [67] *Ibid.*, col. 630.    [68] *Ibid.*, col. 638.
[69] *Ibid.*, cols. 829–35. On 21 May 1799 the Duke of Portland requested Scott to move to have O'Connor detained if he was acquitted. PRO, HO49(3). O'Connor's detention is also discussed in a letter from Portland to the King on 22 May 1799. Aspinall, *Correspondence*, III:1742.

outcome. He called the offence 'one of the most heinous the consideration of which has been offered, in the history of our law to the decision of a jury'.[70] His own role, however, was that of respectful caretaker.

[T]he duty imposed upon me is this – to take care of you – to take care of the learned judges – to take care of all who have either acted in the administration of justice; and I should have been deeply responsible if I had not instituted this prosecution, whatever may be your verdict upon the circumstances of the case, as a public lesson to all mankind that the courts of justice must be treated with respect.[71]

Remarks such as these suggest Scott's contentment as a prosecutor; yet during his last years as Attorney General he certainly demonstrated that he did not savour the prospect of a criminal brief. Six years in office had not enabled him to resolve the conflict which had made him so equivocal in that role in 1793. He could certainly make a harsh legal argument, and he could take advantage of privileges accorded to him as Crown prosecutor. He frequently proceeded by *ex officio* information, whereby he could proceed without the sanction of a grand jury.[72] He also tried hard to obtain juries likely to be favourable to the prosecution, including special juries, whose members were not only drawn from higher ranks than ordinary juries, but whose manner of selection arguably gave the Crown more control over the make-up of the panel.[73] It is also clear, however, that he could not exploit the element of personal confrontation inherent in courtroom proceedings. By his last years in office he was no longer easily flustered, but a challenging case did not inspire him to a superior courtroom performance, as it might a great criminal advocate,

---

[70] Howell, *State trials*, XXVII: 829.          [71] *Ibid.*, col. 834.

[72] The Attorney General could file an *ex officio* information in the court of King's Bench on behalf of the Crown in cases of misdemeanours affecting public stability or the governance of the country.

[73] Authorities were able to vet special jurors in advance and could delete up to twelve names from the list of forty-eight potential jurors. C. Emsley, 'An aspect of Pitt's *terror*: prosecutions for sedition during the 1790s', *Social History* 6(2) (1981), 155–84, 168. On the other hand, with a regular jury, the Crown could challenge far more extensively, since all of its challenges were for cause, and it did not have to assign cause unless the entire list of potential jurors, which could easily contain over 100 names, had been exhausted and the panel still not completed. Scott defended the use of special juries, explaining that, in a complicated case, he felt it his duty to call upon persons whose greater education and circumstances would make them 'responsible to their country and to their posterity for their verdict'. *Rex* v. *Jordan*, PRO, TS11/456(1511), 62.

while the sympathetic defendant rendered him mild and conciliatory.

The experience of office, had, however, shown Scott a way out of his difficulty, namely, to avoid prosecutions where possible. If a problem was widespread or the state of the law unclear, Scott would advise legislation.[74] In cases of limited harm or local significance he would advocate informal remedies undertaken by local authorities. He argued that such conduct insulated *the government* from the unattractive consequences of prosecution. A successful prosecution of a sympathetic defendant made the government look oppressive, while an unsuccessful prosecution rendered it ridiculous as well. Furthermore, whatever the outcome, a prosecution could necessitate the revelation of information – details of investigations that the authorities might prefer to keep secret.[75] A legislative response, by contrast, shifted the onus of a controversial decision from the government to Parliament generally, while a wholly local response meant that the decision never reached the government at all. Where prosecutions were necessary, according to this view, *government* was best served by a disinterested officer of the court, whose purpose was solely the administration of justice. If a defendant were then acquitted, the government had not been defeated, because a conviction had never been its particular aim. Responding to a query from the Lord Lieutenant of Ireland in 1797 about prosecuting Arthur

[74] In an undated letter discussing whether an English captain in the Dutch merchant marine had committed treason, Scott and Mitford felt 'it might be expedient to attempt to obtain a legislative declaration on the subject rather than to hazard the consequences of a decision on the subject'. Scott and Mitford to Henry Dundas, undated, Inner Temple Library, (Mitford Collection of Legal Manuscripts, LVIII) 58.

[75] In an opinion to Portland in July 1797, Scott and Mitford cautioned against prosecuting members of a radical society for seditious words, but rather advised 'keeping a watchful eye over the persons whose conduct appears more particularly to require attention. We are the more induced to submit this to Your Grace's consideration, as we observe in the paper No. 2 notice given of an intended meeting of all the corresponding societies; & it may perhaps be more easy to obtain intelligence respecting any such meeting by means of the open conversation which appears to take place in the public house mentioned in the papers referred to, than by any other means; especially if the institution of any prosecution should tend to put the persons concerned on their guard.' Scott and Mitford to Portland, 7 July 1797, Yale University, Beinecke Rare Book and Manuscript Library (Osborn files), 11.394.

O'Connor either for treason or sedition for an offensive publication, Scott replied:

> I have no doubt that the dignity of government is better consulted by prosecuting, as for the lower offence, what persons of great consideration may think a higher offence, than it is by prosecuting as for a higher offence, what persons, considerable in the country, may regard as not amounting to the case put upon the record.[76]

Of course, this promotion of legislation over prosecution was particularly attractive for a government in which Scott was the chief prosecutor. It insulated *him* from the dangers of prosecution, not so much the hostile comments of the political opposition, as the far more unsettling fear that he was failing in his official duties. The choice of legislation as the preferred weapon against republicanism allowed him to press his arguments as strongly as he felt necessary, without the face of a sympathetic defendant to cause him to stay his hand. This does not mean, however, that Scott's ostensible argument of governmental benefit was specious. Certainly it relied on formal distinctions – that prosecutions would reflect badly on the government but statutes would not because they were enacted by Parliament (although drafted by government lawyers, brought in by ministers, and supported by pro-government majorities). Indeed, it smacks of the very legal metaphysics in which Scott had previously been accused of indulging. For that reason, however, it is probably a genuine reflection of his views. He placed great store in the efficacy of formal compliance with rules and the recognition of formal conduct. In that way, the basic fabric of public life was maintained, and within it particular strands could be re-woven by hand to achieve the particular result desired. Not only was this the genius of the British constitution, it was essential to political practice. It was a valid reason for Scott's behaviour, but an incomplete one. He argued that prosecuting was inferior to legislation as a means of administering the criminal law, because prosecutions were so uncertain. He complained of ill-advised inquiries, dubious witnesses, or unsatisfied juries, but he failed to mention the irresolute prosecutor.

[76] Scott to Lord Camden, 15 August 1797, Centre for Kentish Studies (Camden papers), U840 add.0193/2.

# 8

# PATER FAMILIAS

On being apprised of the imminent decease of their father in the autumn of 1776, John Scott wrote to his brother, Henry:

> I must say it gives me very great concern that I should be the only one of my father's family at a distance from him at this time, and, if your letter did not preclude every hope that Providence might prolong his life till I could get down, I should suffer nothing to prevent my setting out immediately ... I must beg too that you will assure my mother that, if my presence can be any way necessary in assisting you to administer to her every comfort which her situation shall require, there is nothing that shall prevent me from coming down – I shall be happy on this occasion in joining you in the discharge of every duty to her as a parent who deserves so well of us all.[1]

Throughout his life Scott's family was very important to him. Never one to take much pleasure in travel, public entertainment, or private reading, relations within his family supplied much of what might be described as his private life. Through an active correspondence his immediate family circle was expanded to include siblings, cousins, and later the children of both. In his youth he commiserated with a cousin on the subjects of love and labour, while in old age he gave professional advice to the son of his former daughter-in-law. Eldon's family bonds were not only broad but deep, and particularly as regards his wife and brother, into whose care he placed a considerable emotional burden.

When he eloped with Elizabeth Surtees in November 1772, Scott was full of confident admiration for his bride. Describing her as 'a perfect heroine' he maintained that for her sake 'I would willingly submit to ten thousand times more uneasiness, than it

---

[1] J. Scott to Henry Scott, 8 November 1776, W. E. Surtees, *A sketch of the lives of Lords Stowell and Eldon* (London, 1846), 18–19.

will ever be in the power of man to create me'.[2] Bold words, but
he does not seem ever to have regretted them. Theirs was a long
union, lasting until her death in 1831 at the age of 76. While very
few of her letters, or between husband and wife, survive, those
that have done so indicate a loving bond that survived the
inevitable separations resulting from his public position and her
retiring nature. Obliged to be parted from her after the birth of
their third child, he sent a stream of letters to accompany her
journey from Newcastle to London. In one he assured her that: 'a
hint from you, that you wish me to come to you, will bring me
immediately'.[3] When a political crisis required a prolonged attendance at Windsor, he wrote longingly of being reunited with his
'ever dearest and most beloved' at Encombe.

He [the King] said I should not go till after his levee on Wednesday, for
he must see me there; that I might then put myself in my chaise, and
come to you without stopping, and stay with you to the end of the month.
This was our bargain at parting; and I hope, therefore, to dine with you
on Thursday. And of God I have no blessing to ask or pray for with so
much anxiety and importunity, as that nothing may interrupt this. I think
nothing will or can. O that I was with you![4]

The crisis in question concerned what ministers believed to be the
likely break-up of the government. That Lady Eldon was generally made privy to her husband's political secrets is evident from
his assurances on this occasion that such interesting details as he
'dare not commit to paper' he would soon be able to state 'in my
dearest Elizabeth's hearing'.[5] During the same negotiations Eldon
wrote:

I dare not commit to paper what passed, for fear accident should not
bring that paper to the hands of my Eliza, and though I promised her a
letter of particulars, the particulars that passed are really so very special in
their kind, that I cannot communicate them even to her except in
conversation – and would I could have that conversation![6]

A poem he composed for her on 18 November 1811, the thirty-
ninth anniversary of their elopement, attests to his constancy.

[2]  J. Scott to Henry Reay, 12 December 1772, NCL (Scott papers).
[3]  Lady Scott to Mrs H. Scott, undated [*c.* November 1791], H. Twiss, *The public
     and private life of Lord Chancellor Eldon*, 3 vols. (London, 1844), I:210–11.
[4]  Eldon to Lady Eldon, 2 October 1809, *ibid.*, II:103.
[5]  Eldon to Lady Eldon, 2 October 1809, *ibid.*, 102.
[6]  Eldon to Lady Eldon, 21 September 1809, *ibid.*, 97.

Can it, my lovely Bessy, be
That when near forty years are past
I still my lovely Bessy see
Dearer and dearer at the last?

Nor time, nor years, nor age nor care
Believe me, lovely Bessy, will
Much as his frame they daily wear,
Affect the heart, that's Bessy's still.

In Scotland's climes I gave it thee,
In Scotland's climes I thine obtained,
Oh to each other let them be
True till an heaven we have gain'd.[7]

In the early years of their marriage, straightened finances obliged Elizabeth to practise a strict economy, and this ingrained in her a habit that remained when their circumstances became comfortable, and then affluent. More than one contemporary noted the contrast between the Chancellor's wealth and the quality of his official dinners – when, indeed, he gave them. As a Cabinet member and the head of the bar, he was expected to entertain his colleagues and professional associates with some regularity, and Lady Eldon seems to have found these obligations difficult. If her husband was aware of her shortcomings, he nevertheless supported her efforts loyally. Following a Cabinet dinner in 1823 he bragged to their daughter: 'Mamma had directed things in capital style. I have seen no such doings at any other Minister's.'[8] In later life Lady Eldon suffered from a degree of ill-health which seems to have rendered her a semi-invalid. Certainly her enfeebled condition, which included severe headaches and periods of partial paralysis, featured regularly in her husband's personal correspondence. Despite her substantial withdrawal from the world, evidence exists of an everyday camaraderie between the pair. She liked to take the carriage in the afternoon to meet him upon the termination of his Chancery sittings, and if he was obliged to remain in the House until the early hours, he would often find that she had waited up for him. Eldon's description of a

[7] Encombe (Scott papers).
[8] Eldon to Lady Frances Bankes, 16 June 1823, Twiss, *The public and private life*, II:472. See too Eldon's letter to his daughter of 23 November 1820, in which he says of Lady Eldon's recent organisation of a Cabinet dinner, 'Mamma really did this most magnificently.' *Ibid.*, 409.

trivial domestic incident presents a charming picture of marital harmony:

I have the happiness of having finished my accounts with Mamma this morning, as we generally try my ability in arithmetic in an Easter week. My good father spared no expense in teaching me addition, multiplication, &c., but expense without diligence does not prevent Jack's being a dull boy or dunce, and so I remain to this day rather puzzle-pated as to figures: however, Mamma compliments me rather, I think, upon my performance this morning. I did not blunder quite so much as usual.[9]

Eldon's sentiments following a particularly severe bout of illness in 1827 are not obscured by the familiar circumlocution of its author:

As Lady Eldon has had no return of the attack, that had nearly deprived her of existence, and me of all comfort in this world, tho' she remains exceedingly weak, I venture to hope that a kind providence may yet bless me in my old age by continuing to me in the remains of life, and in my journey to the close of life, the person, who has been my companion in the last 57 years of it.[10]

If his wife provided comfort to the heart, his brother William provided support to the mind. Sir John Scott regarded Sir William Scott as 'more than a father to me'.[11] As adults they met frequently and corresponded almost daily until Lord Stowell's mental collapse in 1834. A considerable correspondence between them has survived, and this reveals a bond which, if it became more nearly equal, remained very deep. Following his resignation from office in 1827, Eldon wrote from Encombe: 'Being absent from your society I can assure you I feel very painfully; as to any other society in London, I should be quite content to have done with it entirely.'[12]

Throughout his life, the younger brother relied on his eldest brother for all manner of advice. Acknowledging that the breadth of Sir William's scholarship far exceeded his own, Sir John sought his assistance in matters classical and philosophical. The motto, *sit sine labe decus*, which he chose upon his elevation to the peerage,

---

[9] Eldon to Bankes, 7 April 1825, *ibid.*, 541.

[10] Eldon to Revd William Bond, undated [1827], DorRO (Bond of Tyneham papers), D. 1141:1/14.

[11] J. Scott to William Scott, undated [probably spring 1799], Encombe (Scott papers).

[12] Eldon to Lord Stowell, undated [*c.* late summer 1827], Twiss, *The public and private life*, III:15.

was proposed by Sir William, and the latter's knowledge of the civil law was begged to fill out the library of the new Chief Justice of Common Pleas. 'I should wish', wrote Eldon, 'to have so many (& not more) as it may be fit for me to have, *now*.'[13] When Eldon was awarded the degree of Doctor of Laws in 1801, a hurried request for 'a bit of a Latin answer' was despatched from the Lord Chancellor to the judge of the High Court of Admiralty. 'Pray, pray, give me two sentences thanking them & assuring them that to the best of that judgment (the talent they are pleased to allow me) I wish to dedicate my old age with diligentia, & more of it than adorned my adolescentia, to literis, virtuti, probitati, and pietati.'[14] Of course, the range of their correspondence was not restricted to academic matters. Particularly in their younger days they discussed family affairs, and throughout John Scott's public life he discussed politics, and more particularly his own political conduct, with his brother. So habitually did he offer up matters for brotherly scrutiny that a lapse warranted an explanation. In November 1810, the King suffered a return of his former mental illness, and in the following weeks Eldon played an important role, both in monitoring the King's condition and in formulating government policy according to his assessment of that condition. Subsequently, Eldon's conduct came under hostile scrutiny in both Houses of Parliament and, obviously aware of the political dangers associated with his actions, he resisted the temptation to involve his brother. He wrote in explanation;

I hope you are not angry with me for not seeking to see you. The fact is, that my present duties are, or are thought by me to be, so arduous and difficult, and withal so perilous, that I do not wish to ask any body's advice, or to involve those I love in the consequences of my conduct . . . I know I should be asking advice if I were with you, and I have determined rather to look for consolation to those whom I affectionately love, *after* I have acted for myself, than to pursue any other course of proceeding.[15]

Usually, however, Eldon's political hopes and fears were fully revealed in letters to his brother. Resuming office in the spring of

---

[13] See undated letters to W. Scott, the first signed J. Scott and probably dating from June 1799, and the second signed Eldon and probably dating from September 1799. Encombe (Scott papers).

[14] Eldon to Scott, undated [*c.* 15 October 1801], *ibid.*

[15] Eldon to Scott, undated [December 1810 or January 1811], Twiss, *The public and private life*, II:161.

1807 and unsure of his likely tenure, he assured his brother: 'On my own personal account, I have no wish about it – much less than I thought I should have had.'[16] In a far less phlegmatic state of mind about remaining in a possible coalition ministry in 1809 he wrote: 'If it takes place, there is something horribly offensive, shockingly degrading in it – and feeling *that* most bitterly it was, that I asked you whether I was right in doing as the King might wish ... Do you continue of opinion that that should be my *line?*'[17] And as the vexing question of resignation became a more or less constant refrain during his last years he thus scotched a rumour to Sir William: 'Whatever may be my wishes on this subject, when they become fixed purpose, as such, they would have been first communicated to my wife, to you, and the Regent.'[18]

Nor did the transmission of advice occur in a single direction. The brothers discussed legal issues arising from their different professional spheres, and the younger advised the elder on matters of professional status and protocol. On learning that Sir William had been offered a substantial gift by a group of merchants in gratitude for his professional services as an advocate, Sir John advised on how the matter should be arranged to avoid any suggestion of impropriety.[19] Likewise, when Sir William considered retiring from the Admiralty bench in 1808 to become Dean of the Arches, Eldon urged his brother to consider the actual, and not the technical, pretensions of each office.

I can't think that the retaining your present situation merely because a junior will have professional rank beyond the Judge of the Admiralty, can affect any other object. It is in that character you have so strong a claim upon the country, and that claim admits of daily manifestation by a judge of the Admiralty in these times, in a degree and with a lustre which cannot, in the nature of things, belong to the pretensions in these times of dean of the Arches and Judge of the Prerogative.[20]

[16] Eldon to Scott, 31 March 1807, *ibid.*, 31.
[17] Eldon to Scott, 25 September 1809, *ibid.*, 101.
[18] Eldon to Scott, undated [*c.* 1818], *ibid.*, 308.
[19] J. Scott to W. Scott, undated, Encombe (Scott papers). For evidence of fraternal loyalty publicly expressed, see Eldon's defence of Sir William's conduct as Admiralty judge in T. Hansard (ed.), *Parliamentary debates from the year 1803 (1st series)*, 41 vols. (London, 1812–20), XX:713.
[20] Eldon to W. Scott, undated [1808], Twiss, *The public and private life*, II:67. See also a letter from Eldon to his brother, evidently written in 1802, on the subject of an unspecified legal post that might be in the offing to Sir William. Encombe (Scott papers).

This influence, or attempted influence, with his brother also extended to personal matters, most notably health. Following a period of illness in the autumn of 1783 John Scott informed his convalescent brother: 'At present I will not trouble you with a great deal of advice which I have to give you on the means of preserving your health when it is restored but I am sure more care & attention must be paid to it than you have lately bestowed upon it.'[21] Such restraint seems to have been exceptional, as Scott's letters to his brother frequently contained not only general inquiries but specific suggestions, such as residing in the outskirts of London so as to sleep 'in better air', or bathing gouty legs 'in warm brine (not sea water) – brine that meat had been salted in'.[22] Commenting upon his brother's condition at the end of a long and less than abstemious life, however, Eldon could only admit on this subject: 'all my sage advice is thrown away upon him, though I give him plenty of it.'[23]

The middle Scott brother, Henry, died in 1799. While distance and the absence of a professional bond might have been expected to weaken fraternal feelings, this does not seem to have been the case. Throughout his life, Eldon remained keenly interested in the family in Newcastle, discussing with William such matters as the health and circumstances of their brother and sisters. In 1795 he had applied to William Pitt to obtain for Henry 'in whose welfare I am much interested' a post in the excise service at Newcastle.[24] On Henry's death, Eldon wrote to their sister Barbara: 'I have felt very acutely upon this event and my mind has been running back thro scenes of infancy, youth & manhood, which I spent with poor Harry, till my firmness has occasionally quite failed me, & my spirits have been depressed excessively.'[25] In his later years, Eldon would correspond regularly with Henry's daughter, Mary Forster, and the family of his sister Jane. In the autumn of 1834 he wrote in characteristically teasing vein to his young great niece, Ellen Forster:

21 J. Scott to W. Scott, 26 September 1783, Encombe (Scott papers).
22 Two letters from Eldon to W. Scott, undated [probably September 1799], *ibid.*
23 Eldon to Mrs Edward Bankes, undated [*c.* 1820], Twiss, *The public and private life*, II:410. Eldon remarked of his brother, 'His mornings, therefore, are spent in complaining – his evenings in laying the foundation of complaint – when he can go out'. *Ibid.*
24 J. Scott to W. Pitt, undated [*c.* 1795], PRO (Chatham papers), 30/8 132:129.
25 Eldon to Barbara Scott, undated [December 1799], Encombe (Scott papers).

When I wrote to your dear mother, I at first intended to make it a joint letter to you and her. But, seeing that all the newspapers, the Newcastle papers among the rest, represented me to be of the tender age of *ninety*, I was afraid that she might suppose that there might be more of a flirtation between two young people than she might altogether approve. I leave it therefore to your good judgment, whether you will subject this little epistle to her perusal.[26]

Scott's interest in the younger generation was not limited to his nieces and nephews. In general he was both a fond and indulgent parent. Upon his elevation to the peerage his son John succeeded him as MP for Boroughbridge, but thereafter Eldon also found seats for his younger son, William-Henry. Ill health prevented John from taking up a profession or pursuing an active public life, and his father provided him with an allowance. While not similarly disabled, William-Henry seems to have been likewise constitutionally ill-suited to work. Rather than being forced to cure himself of this failing, he was supported by his father's political patronage, though not to the extent popularly believed. He held, during his lifetime, sinecures worth approximately £3,000 per annum.[27] Of his youngest child, Frances, 'dear Fan', Eldon was particularly fond. After her marriage, he obtained for her husband the living at Corfe Castle, in Dorset, and subsequently arranged for the Revd Edward Bankes to become rector of St Mary and All Saints, Langham Place. The ostensible reason for the second manoeuvre was to facilitate the happiness of Lady Eldon, but the Chancellor's own spirits were undoubtedly lifted by the prospect of his daughter's proximity. She had already, like Sir William Scott, become her father's regular correspondent, and during a period of illness she had acted as nurse and secretary to her 'dear patriarch'.[28] In his last years, the receipt of 'my daily comfort in a letter' from Fan went some way to filling the chasm left by the death of Lady Eldon and

---

[26] Eldon to Ellen Forster, 14 November 1834, Twiss, *The public and private life*, III:237.

[27] William-Henry Scott held the following legal sinecures: Commissioner of Bankrupts (1816–21), Receiver of Fines (1816–1832), Secretary of Decrees and Injunctions (1816–21), Clerk of Patents and Registrar of Affidavits, Court of Chancery (1819–32), and Cursitor and Commissioner of Lunacy (1821–32). He was popularly believed to hold posts worth approximately £12,000 per annum. See, e.g., Eldon to Bankes, 13 March 1832, Twiss, *The public and private life*, III:170.

[28] See the letters from Frances Scott to Richard Richards, undated, AMA Caerynwch (Richards) papers, Z/DA/64 SB44, 45.

the senility of Lord Stowell. On Christmas Day 1834 Eldon wrote: 'You, under God's blessing, may prolong my life, even as long as the medical men comfortably told me it would be prolonged.'[29]

Scott bore his share of parental grief. He and Elizabeth had six children, and two of these died in infancy. Of the others, John (born 1774) and William-Henry (born 1795) died in their thirties and only Elizabeth (born 1783) and Frances Jane (born 1798) survived their father. The marriages of these two daughters caused Scott considerable disquiet. The elder married without his consent, and, despite the obvious precedent for such conduct on her part, he was not reconciled to her for almost three years.[30] The younger, Frances, separated from her husband after almost seventeen years of marriage. While Eldon wholly supported 'my truly excellent daughter', the necessity of a separation was painful for a man opposed in principle to divorce. The deaths of his sons, of course, were far more devastating for their father. The elder, John, fell ill with a chest complaint in the winter of 1805. Following a short, but very painful, illness, he died on 24 December at the age of thirty-one. Eldon's letters to his brother provide a terse account of the last days.

Monday December 23–Tuesday December 24 1805

Dear Brother,

9 o'clock Monday evening. The spasmodic affection very strong, & poor John very ill.

8 o'clock Tuesday morning. John has had an extreme bad night, & is this morning very ill. I shall keep this open till the post hour. My poor daughter in law is of course informed as favorably as possible, her own situation requiring it.

4 o'clock. The report of the physicians is that John is worse today than yesterday. They still say they will not pronounce there is danger. His pain great – his spirits sinking. May God, in mercy, give him some relief – for the continuance of this cannot be long, as it is.[31]

---

29 Eldon to Bankes, 25 December 1834, Twiss, *The public and private life*, III:240. See also Eldon to Bankes, undated [12 July 1833], *ibid.*, 206.

30 Elizabeth Scott eloped with architect George Repton, the youngest son of Humphrey Repton the noted landscape gardener, in 1817, having failed to secure her father's approval of the match. Father and daughter were reconciled in 1820, and Repton subsequently designed several structures for his father-in-law's home in Dorset. For evidence that Eldon regarded elopement a serious offence, see H. Brougham, Lord Brougham and Vaux, *Sketches of statesmen of the time of George III*, 3 vols. (London, 1855), II:413.

31 Eldon to W. Scott, 23–24 December 1805, Encombe (Scott papers).

Tuesday December 24 1805

My ever dear Brother,

with a broken heart I inform you that, before I had written the last paragraph of the letter I sent by this day's post, my poor dear, dear John was no more. I am so distressed, & all round me is such a scene of distraction & misery, that I know not what to do.[32]

In this situation, Eldon was obliged to care for his daughter-in-law, who had given birth to a son on 10 December, and his wife. He thus described their immediate condition to Sir William: 'His mother is living in my arms out of one hysteric into another; & his poor widow is in a state which can neither be conceived nor described.'[33] Lady Eldon's condition did not swiftly improve. Sir William wrote to his daughter on 31 December, of the effect upon Eldon:

It is impossible to describe the degree in which my brother is worn down by the constant attentions he is obliged to pay to her. She will hardly suffer him to be out of the room, and, during the whole time he is there, he is a witness to the indulgence of such sorrow, as it is quite impossible for any man to stand.[34]

Nor was Eldon's own suffering less intense. He described himself in a letter to his cousin Henry Reay as 'plunged in despair and affliction, which I know not how to bear'.[35] Friends and relatives sent letters of sympathy. Pitt, terminally ill himself, wrote to Sir William: 'it is with great regret that I break in upon you ... but I feel too deeply for the loss which the Chancellor & all his family have sustained, not to be anxious to enquire how he & they support themselves under this heavy affliction.'[36] The King's secretary wrote likewise to Sir William, but added:

His Majesty commands me to add that he had, when first apprised of it, intended writing himself to the Chancellor, & that he had solely been withheld from the impression that it would be more kind towards him not to disturb him in the first moments of his just grief; that he would have been very sorry if the Chancellor had distressed his feelings under the immediate pressure of so severe a calamity, by personally making this

[32] Eldon to Scott, 24 December 1805, *ibid.*      [33] *Ibid.*

[34] Scott to Marianne Scott, 31 December 1805, Twiss, *The public and private life,* I:502.

[35] Eldon to Reay, 12 January 1806, NCL (Scott papers).

[36] William Pitt to Scott, 27 December 1805, Encombe (Scott papers).

communication, & that his Majesty is truly sensitive of his attention in requesting you to convey it to him.[37]

Eldon endured the death of William-Henry Scott almost twenty-seven years later less with a sense of shock than with quiet sorrow. Eldon's own advanced years, and his knowledge that his younger son's life had been characterised by indulgence and neglected opportunities, perhaps account for this.[38]

After the death of his son John, Eldon increasingly placed his hopes for the future on his grandson and namesake. He remained on close and affectionate terms with his daughter-in-law, and co-operated fully with her and her second husband in the matter of young John's upbringing and education. The boy attended Winchester school, and its proximity to Encombe meant that holidays were often spent with his grandparents and aunt. Eldon took considerable interest in his grandson's scholarship. The importance of a disciplined approach to study was a recurring theme in his correspondence. Convinced that William-Henry had been ruinously indulged during his school and university days, he was determined that young John should not suffer under the same handicap.[39] He discussed John's progress with Hugh Gabell, the headmaster of Winchester, and to his grandson he penned regular homilies on the virtues of hard work.[40] Turning, for example, from an account of the doings of the various dogs and horses at Encombe, he inquired of the thirteen year old,

And now, my dearest John, do you ask me why I enjoy all these things so much? ... It is because one enjoys them by contrast with meritorious labour at other times: and depend upon it, neither Encombe, nor any other place, will have any lasting charms, unless in the period of life spent in education, a great stock of information is laid in in the mind,

---

[37] H. Taylor to Scott, 31 December 1805, *ibid.*

[38] See, e.g., Eldon to Stowell, 4 July 1832, Twiss, *The public and private life*, III:185.

[39] See, e.g., Eldon's observations regarding William-Henry: 'My anxieties about him are very great: the mischief, which was done to him at Eton and Oxford awaken the most painful apprehensions about him, & is not easily got over.' Eldon to Richards, 3 September 1817, AMA Caerynwch (Richards) papers, Z/DA/64 SA21.

[40] Eldon's letters to Hugh Gabell are preserved at Winchester school. See, e.g., letters 16, 26, and 28, dating from 2 February 1818, 19 August 1823, and 6 January 1824, respectively.

and a great stock of virtuous and religious feeling is implanted in the heart.[41]

Shortly after he went up to Oxford, Viscount Encombe, as he had become upon his grandfather's receipt of an earldom, was warned about natural ability impaired by over-indulgence. Musing on the public career of R. B. Sheridan, Eldon wrote:

I knew him. I often heard him speak most eloquently in Parliament. If he had applied his great talents to great and useful purposes in life, he would have been one of the most useful and considerable of the men who have lived in my time, or perhaps in any age. But he lived a life of great dissipation.[42]

Still later, the ever-vigilant grandfather turned his attention to a different danger. He observed to Fan:

John writes from Oxford that he has the honour to be a Bachelor: and Lady Londonderry has obtained him a place at Almack's which I anxiously hope may, neither too soon nor improvidently, convert him *out of* the character of bachelor; but I must read him a quiet cautionary lecture upon the arts of the world.[43]

Nor was Viscount Encombe the sole recipient of such lectures. When another grandson, George Repton, began his university career, he too received a missive extolling the virtues of disciplined study:

[A]fter long and great experience, I never knew a young man who had indulged too much in these amusements at Oxford to the neglect of very diligent, if not severe duty, who ever afterwards in life graced his friends, family, or country, as I hope and pray you may hereafter grace them; and I never knew one who signally devoted his time at Oxford to study, who did not in after life become a blessing and ornament to his family and country ... Be very select in the company you keep at Oxford, and never forget, what so many forget, that the University is not a place of amusement, but of constant study, to be interrupted only by *necessary* attention to health.[44]

In his old age, and particularly after his retirement from high office in 1827, Eldon's family would become an easily tapped source of comfort. His correspondence, increasingly with a

---

[41] Eldon to John Scott, 12 September 1819, Twiss, *The public and private life*, II:341.

[42] Eldon to Encombe, 17 March 1823, *ibid.*, 470.

[43] Eldon to Bankes, 3 May 1828, *ibid.*, III:45.

[44] Eldon to G. W. J. Repton, undated [15 February 1837], *ibid.*, 276 (emphasis in original).

younger generation to whom he could be both venerable and jovial, helped to keep him feeling part of the busy world even as his views were being publicly questioned and rejected. During the period of his own public career, however, his family played a different, and more important role. Instead of consolation, his wife, brother, and finally, daughter, provided him with necessary support. The length of Eldon's tenure in government, and the several political crises that he faced, exposed him to considerable criticism, as well as simple envy. Outlasting, as he did, not only political opponents but political colleagues, he often felt isolated and unappreciated. Moreover, his own code demanded that he both assume and fulfil public obligations as sacred trusts. Subjected, therefore, to such internal and external pressures, his need for reassurance was great, and it is not surprising that he sought it from persons well qualified to give it unfailingly. His wife, who lived cocooned from the world even by the standards of women of the time, was hardly in a position to offer criticism, while his daughter added paternal veneration to a sheltered, if less restricted, lifestyle. His brother, by contrast, was possessed of that happy combination – notable intellectual ability and substantial similarity of political outlook. Between them these people provided an unquestioning *and* informed vindication of Eldon's conduct, and must have provided him with a strong anchorage during many stormy years.

# 9

# UPRIGHT INTENTIONS

It is easy to consider John Scott's public career as falling solely into two parts: the first consisting of his work as a law officer, and the second his work as Lord Chancellor. Indeed, one might almost be forgiven for forgetting that he was also Chief Justice of the court of Common Pleas. He held the post for less than two years, from July 1799 until May 1801, and coming, as it did, between the better-known phases of his public life, it tends to be neglected.[1] While understandable, however, such a tendency is not a salutary one. Lord Eldon's Chief Justiceship was an important period of transition for him. It brought to a close eleven years of government advocacy, and receipt of a peerage ended his fifteen-year membership of the House of Commons.[2] The professional and political pressures upon him had been considerable, and on the bench he achieved a partial, if incomplete, respite from them. He also began, in this period, the process of reflection and assessment necessary to any politician whose career is to be a lengthy one. Always keenly self-conscious, Eldon's evaluation of his work as a law officer had previously, of necessity, occurred while he was fully engaged in it. His judicial appointment afforded him a certain distance, from which he could begin to view and express his attitudes toward contemporary society before these had been hardened into unshakeable tenets by the passage of time and renewed stress. Given the greater public responsibilities that were

---

[1] Eldon received the Great Seal on 14 April 1801, but he retained the Chief Justiceship until 21 May 1801. During the Easter term he occasionally presided in Common Pleas in order to participate in matters arising from causes that had been tried before him. None of his opinions from his last term in office have been reported.

[2] He was created Baron Eldon of Eldon, in the county of Durham.

shortly to descend upon him, this period of relative calm was particularly valuable.

Eldon left office in the summer of 1799 physically and mentally drained by his experiences as a law officer. He had found the sheer size of his workload as Attorney General exhausting. Moreover, he had shown himself unsuited temperamentally to the task of public prosecution, especially in such politically sensitive circumstances as he had endured in the trials for treason and seditious libel in the 1790s.[3] In June and July 1799 he had spoken of his desire to quit his 'station of great anxiety (such as I hope is unlikely to attend the office of attorney general in after times)'.[4] The move to the bench represented 'a situation of dignity and ease'.[5] To Mrs John Lee he described it as a 'retirement' through which 'I have considerably augmented my chance of happiness and comfort'.[6]

From a purely professional point of view, the move to Common Pleas was a success. Given Eldon's circumstances upon appointment to the bench, this was not a trivial achievement. He did not become a serjeant-at-law until his appointment, so he had never practised as an advocate in Common Pleas. He was, moreover, largely a Chancery lawyer, and while he had also appeared in both King's Bench and Exchequer as a law officer, and had previously enjoyed a substantial circuit practice, his appointment to a common law court could have been the occasion for professional discomfiture. In fact, however, he proved himself fully competent. While not called upon to render any landmark decisions, his opinions have been cited with approval by his successors. On three occasions he would be over-ruled, but these would represent changes of policy rather than failures by Eldon to recognise current law or practice.[7]

---

[3] See chapters 6 and 7.

[4] Lord Eldon to Matthew Surtees, 22 July 1799, Encombe (Scott papers). On 6 June 1799 Eldon had written gloomily to Surtees: 'I am likely to remain some time longer in the miseries of my office, unless I am turned out, all my superiors being in deplorably good health.' *Ibid.*

[5] Eldon to Surtees, 22 July 1799, *ibid.*

[6] Eldon to Mrs John Lee, 9 August 1799. William Clements Library, University of Michigan (Lee papers), 2:55.

[7] See *Street* v. *Blay* (1831) 109 ER 1212 (the purchaser of a defective chattel cannot return it and sue for the purchase price, but is limited to an action for the difference between the purchase price and the actual value), *contra Curtis* v. *Hannay* (1800) 170 ER 546; *Birn* v. *Bond* (1816) 128 ER 1150 (an action against a

On a personal level, however, Eldon found his new job did have its disadvantages. First, it reduced his annual income by several thousand pounds. In contrast to his fees of between £8,000–12,000 a year as Attorney General, his annual salary and perquisites as Chief Justice totalled approximately £4,600.[8] Almost immediately he began to complain jokingly of his 'poverty' to his brother, Sir William Scott. Upon requesting the latter's advice on the purchase of some law books he remarked: 'I am, moreover, drained to the bottom of my purse by return of fees, by larger fees for patents, robes, etc.'[9] Secondly, he seems to have felt somewhat isolated in his new situation, referring to Serjeants' Inn as his dungeon, and Common Pleas as 'my little obscure retreat – my hole in the wall'.[10] Common Pleas *was* generally regarded as something of a judicial backwater at this time, in comparison with the busier court of King's Bench, but Eldon was probably also unused to the company of his fellow judges, many of whom would not have spent as much time in political circles, while the atmosphere of the House of Lords undoubtedly required a certain adjustment after the Commons. When, in 1804, Spencer Perceval would consider an identical change in career, Eldon's friend Lord Redesdale could comment upon the unpleasant, but inevitable, changes in habit and association consequent upon such an undertaking. 'I know that Lord Eldon felt this very much while he was in the Common Pleas with a peerage; and I think it would have been more strongly felt by you.'[11]

In contrast to these obvious changes in work, income, and

---

sheriff for the escape of a person released without bond does not terminate when bail is obtained), *contra Allingham* v. *Flower* (1800) 126 ER 1262; *Cohen* v. *Hannon* (1813) 128 ER 625 (averments of interest in insurance policies require the same degree of precision as other contracts), *contra Page* v. *Fry* (1800) 126 ER 1258.

8 D. Duman, *The judicial bench in England 1727–1785: the reshaping of a professional elite* (London, 1982), 114, 120. See chapter 1, Table 1.3, p. 6 above, for Eldon's income as a law officer.

9 Eldon to Sir William Scott, undated [September 1799], Encombe (Scott papers). See also Eldon to Scott, 7 September 1799, *ibid.*

10 Eldon to Scott, undated [c. 24 September 1799], *ibid.* Eldon to William Wilberforce, undated [c. 27 February 1800], Rare Book, Manuscript, and Special Collections Library, Duke University (Wilberforce papers).

11 Lord Redesdale to Spencer Perceval, 26 April 1804, S. Walpole, *The life of the Rt Hon. Spencer Perceval*, 2 vols. (London, 1874), I:136. Redesdale was the former John Mitford.

associations, the more interesting aspects of Eldon's public life during this period lie slightly beneath the surface. These concern his attitudes toward his public obligations, the government, and the law. A concern to fulfil his 'duty' to family, friends, and colleagues was not new, but his changed circumstances afforded him new opportunities for its expression. That he felt the moral burden of his judicial situation is evident from the letters he wrote upon his appointment to the bench. To his mother he observed: 'I hope God's grace will enable me to do my duty in the station to which I am called.'[12] On the relationship between intellect and morality, he revealed to Sir Matthew White Ridley:

I should be pressed down with apprehensions, which I have, as to that future life, if I had not personally experienced the ample indulgence with which the public treats the efforts of what is intitled [sic] to no higher merit than such as belongs to mere assiduity, when it is disposed to believe that its exertions are regulated by the influence of upright intentions.[13]

To Matthew Surtees, Eldon observed: 'experience has proved in my own case, that much indulgence is given to men acting with upright intentions, that I occasionally indulge a hope that I may be able to execute satisfactorily the important duties of that great and important station, which an English judge holds.'[14]

These upright intentions – both consciously and unconsciously expressed – greatly affected his public demeanour. As a judge they made him mild and gentle. Far from bullying counsel or indulging in self-aggrandisement, he was more likely to acknowledge his own shortcomings. In *Morris* v. *Langdale*,[15] a slander action brought by a City trader, Eldon began his opinion acknowledging that he was largely ignorant of the role of such individuals. 'My brother Heath has indeed removed from my mind the impression which it had first received, viz., that a jobber or dealer in the funds was always to be considered as a culpable person, by shewing the necessity of such persons for the accommodation of the market.'[16] Similarly, in *Governors of Harrow School* v. *Alderton*,[17] where the defendant in an action for waste demanded judgment because

[12] Eldon to Mrs William Scott, Sr, 19 July 1799, Encombe (Scott papers).
[13] Eldon to Sir Matthew White Ridley, 9 August 1799, Northumberland Record Office, Z/RI. 25/20.
[14] Eldon to Matthew Surtees, 22 July 1799, Encombe (Scott papers).
[15] (1800) 126 ER 1284.    [16] *Ibid.*, 1286.    [17] (1800) 126 ER 1170, 1171.

the plaintiff had been awarded a derisory sum in damages, Eldon remarked: 'I confess, that when this application was first made, I was not aware, that under the circumstances of the case the defendant was entitled to demand judgment: but my brother Heath has satisfied me that the application is supported by the current of authorities.'

One criticism made of Eldon as a judge was that his own intellectual ability rendered him unable to explain the law coherently to a jury:

[H]e ... laid the whole of them before the jury in an elaborate and full summing-up which presented more points and more subtle distinctions and more ingenious hypotheses than men unaccustomed to such discussions were able to deal with, and finally after an admirable lecture for a student at law, puzzled and confounded the jury, and made it often uncertain on what ground they pronounced their verdict.[18]

The published cases tend not to record Eldon's directions to the jury in sufficient detail to evaluate the truth of this assessment. Nevertheless, some suggestion that he was aware of this tendency and sympathised with his juries is revealed in newspaper reports of two cases. *The Times*, which elsewhere described Eldon's judgments as 'elaborate' and 'of judicious eloquence',[19] quoted him as assuring the jury in a case of clerical non-residence: 'the law upon this point was so plain that his duty appeared to him easy and simple, and he had no hesitation in stating what his ideas of it were.'[20] Similarly, in *Wolf* v. *Barnard*, an action for recovery of an insurance subscription on a neutral ship and cargo, he attempted to make his remarks more palatable to the jury by informing them of what they were being spared. On the effect of the vessel having been condemned as prize by a French court, 'he was extremely happy to inform the jury, that he should give them no trouble whatsoever, and he was particularly so, that he was not bound himself to state at that moment one word of an opinion'.[21] This was not to imply that *he* had not considered this issue, for he went on to say that it required an analysis of Admiralty court decisions as well as a determination of the relationship between courts of municipal jurisdiction and the law of nations. It was with 'the most solid and substantial relief', however, that he 'was not

---

[18] P. C. Scarlett, *A memoir of James, first Lord Abinger* (London, 1877), 89.
[19] *The Times*, 15 May 1800, 3, col. 3; *ibid.*, 27 February 1800, 3, col. 3.
[20] *Ibid.*, 15 July 1800, 3, cols. 2–3.     [21] *Ibid.*, 12 July 1800, 3, col. 2.

called upon at that moment to suggest the ideas which he had to a certain degree in his mind'.[22]

Modesty, however, did not render him passive. In particular, he did not hesitate to express his views on moral issues, as these arose either in the courtroom or in the House of Lords. For example, in *Norman* v. *Cole*,[23] Eldon non-suited a plaintiff who attempted to recover money deposited to help secure a pardon. His indignation at such conduct is obvious:

> I cannot suffer this cause to proceed. I am of opinion, this action is not maintainable; where a person interposes his interest and good offices to procure a pardon, it ought to be done gratuitously, and not for money: the doing an act [*sic*] of that description should proceed from pure motives, not from pecuniary ones. The money is not recoverable.[24]

He strongly supported Lord Auckland's Adultery Prevention Bill, which passed the Lords in the spring of 1800 but was defeated in the Commons.[25] The Bill's principal feature, the making illegal any agreement by an adulterous couple to marry upon obtaining a divorce, he regarded as admirable. Of the so-called 'honourable' men who entered into such agreements he professed himself ignorant, and saw instead only their deception of 'simple and silly' women, who surrendered their virtue in reliance upon worthless promises.[26] When the Bill first came before the House, Eldon argued for a stronger measure, specifically, the criminalisation of adultery:

> The act of adultery was at present by law, only a civil trespass, and for which only damages could be given as a 'satisfaction,' as some persons called it: but he had not the mind of a man to whom civil damages could give satisfaction for such an injury; for it was a crime which not only robbed the husband of his comfort, the wife of her honour, the family of their credit, but innocent children of the invaluable blessings of a good education and virtuous example.[27]

While he felt private sympathy for an 'abandoned woman', he declined to let this affect his 'legislative judgment'. Far better that Parliament consider even 'a poor, helpless girl ... robbed of her innocence' as a prostitute, than that the social fabric be weakened

[22] *Ibid.*      [23] (1800) 170 ER 606.      [24] *Ibid.*

[25] See Eldon to Scott, 10 April 1800, Encombe (Scott papers).

[26] W. Cobbett (ed.), *The parliamentary history of England ... to 1803*, 36 vols. (London, 1806–20), XXXV:233.

[27] *Ibid.*, col. 234.

by toleration of her conduct.[28] 'It was the first policy of any state to see that children should be virtuously educated; and where was the example to be sought but in parental affection and conjugal delicacy?'[29] This abhorrence of domestic irregularity is also evidenced in his remarks from the bench. In *Ewers* v. *Hutton*,[30] a husband sought to avoid liability for necessaries furnished to his wife after her departure from the family home. Eldon held that if a husband turned his wife out or obliged her to flee for her own safety, anyone who afforded her protection commensurate with the husband's station could recover from him. Similarly, a husband was obliged to prove notice to a tradesman that his wife had a separate maintenance to avoid liability for necessaries furnished to her.[31] This contrasted sharply with Eldon's general attitude toward a tradesman's liability, whereby the master's prior conduct was sufficient 'to put the tradesman on his guard, and to make it incumbent on him to satisfy himself that the goods were really for the use of the master's family'.[32] Perhaps most striking was the case of *Bedford* v. *M'kowl*, a mother's action for damages against the man who had seduced her daughter. Here an outraged Eldon 'warned' the jury that:

such was his abhorrence of the enormity of which the Defendant had been guilty, he was afraid his feelings might make him express himself in stronger terms than justice might warrant. He felt not only as a man, but as a parent, who had daughters of nearly the same age with the Plaintiff's daughter, and he would prefer the loss of even life itself to that of one of his daughters being debauched, as this young Lady had been; under these circumstances, he conjured the Gentlemen of the Jury to consider what he should say with caution.[33]

---

[28] *Ibid.*, cols. 234–5.    [29] *Ibid.*, col. 282.

[30] (1800) 170 ER 607. Eldon dismissed the husband's claim that he and his wife had executed a separate maintenance agreement, which would insulate him from any liability for her debts. 'As to the deed of separation produced, it was waste paper – it was binding in no degree; it was executed by the husband and wife; but the wife had no will of her own; she could execute no deed; she could not covenant with her husband.'

[31] *Rawlyns* v. *Vandyke* (1800) 170 ER 605. In *dicta* Eldon opined that, if a husband allowed his children to remain with their mother, he thereby made her his agent with regard to their necessary expenses, and was liable for them, although he might no longer be liable for her necessaries. *Ibid.*, 605–6.

[32] *Pearce* v. *Rogers* (1800) 170 ER 592. To do otherwise, Eldon remarked, 'would be to put it in the power of servants and tradesmen to ruin the master'.

[33] *The Times*, 27 February 1800, 3, cols. 3–4. He went on to inform the jury that the injury done to the girl could not be compensated, and 'must be left to a bar not of this world', but that the defendant owned property, had a respectable

With this strict moral outlook so colouring his public life, it is hardly surprising that Eldon was deeply sensitive to any imputations of impropriety levelled against himself. When, therefore, Sir Francis Burdett implied during a Commons debate that Eldon had gained his appointment through subservience to the government, and was in consequence 'now on the way to the first high station in the Kingdom',[34] Eldon was sufficiently upset to write a letter of thanks to William Wilberforce, who had defended him against Burdett. '[B]elieve me I have felt deeply, gratefully & cordially the kind things you said of me in the H[ouse] of Commons ... I shall feel a glow of satisfaction in the recollection that you thought me worthy of such notice.'[35] Aspersions of this kind were doubly galling to a man of Eldon's sensibilities, given his particular situation with respect to the government. If he had been fully content to withdraw from political life, he could have laid to rest any unkind murmurs simply by disappearing into the Common Pleas. This, however, was not his particular aspiration. It is clear that from the moment of his appointment he did not regard the Common Pleas as the necessary summit of his achievements. He would later record in his *Anecdote book* that the King had consented to his appointment to the Common Pleas only on condition that he promise to accept the Great Seal if so called upon.[36] Something of this is suggested by Eldon's remark to Surtees on 22 July 1799: 'I have some reason to believe that it [the Chief Justiceship] may not eventually render more uncertain, than it was, the prospect of attaining the highest situation in the law.'[37] His peerage, moreover, which was not an essential accompaniment to his judicial appointment, had certainly been a political consideration by the government. Eldon maintained that William Pitt had withdrawn his opposition to the appointment upon Eldon's agreeing to accept a peerage.[38] Nor is there any reason

---

business, and his own children were already provided for. Damages of £400 were awarded to the plaintiff.

[34] Cobbett, *Parliamentary history*, XXXIV:1469. See also *The Times*, 14 February 1800, 2, col. 3.

[35] Eldon to Wilberforce, undated [*c.* 27 February 1800] Duke University (Wilberforce papers).

[36] Lord Eldon, J. Scott, *Lord Eldon's anecdote book*, ed. A. L. J. Lincoln and R. L. McEwen (London, 1960), 115.

[37] Eldon to Surtees, 22 July 1799, Encombe (Scott papers).

[38] Eldon, *Anecdote book*, 115. See also Eldon's memorandum of January 1825 regarding legal promotions. BL (Liverpool papers), Add. MS 38370 f. 134.

to doubt the accuracy of this recollection. While serving as a law officer Eldon had loyally and capably supported the government in debate, and it is logical that Pitt should condition an appointment that must deprive him of a supporter in the Commons upon creation of a supporter in the Lords.

Eldon's relationship with the government during his tenure in Common Pleas is not easy to assess. A certain amount of political business came his way as a privy councillor.[39] He also maintained friendly contact with Pitt.[40] A letter to Pitt on the subject of tithes illustrates Eldon's wish to act in a manner both personally satisfying and acceptable to his former colleagues. He was concerned by the President of the Board of Agriculture's having charged grand juries to state the character of lands for purposes of assessing tithes. Such charges were, Eldon felt, both unconstitutional and politically inexpedient. Having encountered this practice during his circuit, he directed the following to the Minister:

> I think it also of evil example as converting Grand Juries ... into political clubs meeting twice a year to debate politics instead of making presentments. I am not disposed to admit that the names of the York Grand Jury jurors intermeddled in this are all names of men bred in principles friendly to the Establishment, tho' this I say in confidence. You will do me the justice to believe that I should be unwilling to do any thing running counter to a measure which I could suppose has the sanction of Government. I do not imagine that this measure has. Possibly however the view in which I see it may not have occurred & some thing may have passed about it that may lead you to do me the favour to make some communication to me before I give my charge on Monday.[41]

Despite his sympathies for the government, however, Eldon was not one of its mainstays in the Lords. His level of participation in debate was not significant, probably because he considered attendance as secondary to his judicial commitments. On the

---

[39] He was, for example, a member of the committees on trade and coinage. See Lord Liverpool's letter to Eldon of 14 October 1799, *ibid.*, Add. MS 38311 f. 25b. In September of that year Eldon complained of having to attend a meeting of the council in Weymouth – 'my movement is unavoidable, the Chancellor having showed me the King's letter, in which he expressly desired my attendance' – principally because he guessed that he would be obliged to play cards with the princesses, at a cost of £15 or £20. Eldon to Scott, (postmark) 7 September 1799, Encombe (Scott papers).

[40] See, e.g., Eldon to Scott, (postmark) 24 September 1799, Encombe (Scott papers).

[41] Eldon to William Pitt, undated [summer 1800], PRO (Chatham papers), 30/8, 1332:133.

seminal issues of Irish Union and Catholic emancipation Pitt would have hoped for the support of all his friends, yet he obtained nothing from Eldon but his silence. Certainly he opposed Catholic emancipation, and did not alter his position for Pitt's sake, but he was too much Pitt's friend to oppose him publicly.[42] Similarly, he seems not to have been consulted on the Union with Ireland Act, and when he spoke in the debate on the King's Speech in February 1801, Eldon avoided mention of the Union, concentrating instead on the question of neutral shipping.[43] He did play a large part in the debates on the Bills to renew suspension of the Habeas Corpus Act in 1800, though to what extent this should be regarded as support for the government of the day is open to question.[44] Both Bills were introduced in the Commons by his friend and successor as Attorney General, Sir John Mitford, and Eldon spoke in their favour. They presumed, however, the existence of threats to public safety identified during Eldon's term of office, and thus potentially brought his official conduct at that time into question. Certainly this was the approach that Eldon took. He largely ignored current dangers or actions by the present government, in favour of a robust defence of his own prosecutorial record. He reminded peers of the trials for treason of James O'Coigly, Arthur O'Connor, and John Binns.[45] These trials, he maintained, had demonstrated not only the dangers posed by these particular men, but also the more general risk arising from the law of treason, which permitted known criminals to escape justice if the Crown could not produce two witnesses to their misdeeds.

---

[42] In an exchange of letters on the subject of Catholic emancipation, the Archbishop of Canterbury informed the King: '... I have mentioned to my friend L[or]d Ch[ief] Justice Eldon the intended Bill before-mentioned ... [a]nd I am happy to assure your Majesty that his sentiments upon it are such as I expected, & as your Majesty would wish them to be, firm & decisive against it.' The King and the Archbishop hoped that knowledge of the sentiments of such 'respectable persons' would convince Pitt to abandon his plans on the subject. Archbishop of Canterbury to George III, 29 January 1801, George III to the Archbishop of Canterbury, 31 January 1801, A. Aspinall (ed.), *The later correspondence of George III*, 5 vols. (Cambridge, 1962), III:478, 479.

[43] Cobbett, *Parliamentary history*, XXXV:886–7. See Redesdale to Eldon, 3 July 1802, Encombe (Scott papers).

[44] Mitford brought in two Bills, the first in February, and the second in December, to prolong the suspension of the Habeas Corpus Act.

[45] For Eldon's conduct of the prosecution, see chapter 7.

[C]ases might occur, in which for want of two witnesses, persons could not be legally convicted, though no doubt remained of their guilt. But would the noble lord say because in this country a person could not be put upon his trial for high treason without the testimony of two witnesses, that therefore no danger existed? [B]ecause sufficient legal proof could only be brought against one of the men who were put upon their trial, the legislature should not have endeavoured to prevent the mischief?[46]

He condemned any minister who would not take steps (as Eldon had done) to 'suspend a part of those laws that provided for the public liberty, in order to save the whole of the laws and liberties of the country'.[47] Concluding the debate on the second Bill for the government along with the Foreign Secretary, Lord Grenville, Eldon indicated that he had not forgotten the criticisms he had endured in the Commons over the Maidstone trials. He pointed out that prominent opposition members had acted 'in gross error' in supporting the Maidstone defendants, while he praised the government (and by extension its law officers) effusively – lauding their vigilance and moderation.[48] The Bill passed comfortably.[49] Certainly Eldon's remarks were not unhelpful to the government, but their primary emphasis lay not in promoting present actions, but in vindicating those which had passed, and for which Eldon himself bore significant responsibility. He maintained that for the defeat of the O'Coigly conspiracy in England 'we are indebted to the vigilance of the government, and that it was crushed by temperate means instead of arms'. If resolute ministers (like himself) had not acted decisively in such times of crisis, 'the sovereign not only would not be upon the throne, but our religion, our laws, and our freedom, would have been overturned'.[50]

In addition to this interest in vindicating his own conduct, Eldon's attitude toward the law is also evident in these debates. He advocated a practical attitude toward the Habeas Corpus Act, in which the occasional necessity of suspension did not detract from the value of the measure:

The laws of England were not founded on those speculative theories, which must ever be practically false, because they falsely assumed that all

---

[46] Cobbett, *Parliamentary history*, XXXIV:1488.
[47] *The Times*, 27 February 1800, 3, col. 4.
[48] Cobbett, *Parliamentary history*, XXXV:754.
[49] The vote on the first reading was seventeen to three. Thereafter the Bill was unopposed. *Ibid.*
[50] Cobbett, *Parliamentary history*, XXXV:753.

men were virtuous and perfect. They were the result of long experience and wisdom, and therefore suited to human wants and weakness: as men were not perfect, it was impossible the laws intended to regulate their actions could be perfect.[51]

The law tends to appear in Eldon's public remarks alongside his appeals to morality. His support of the Adultery Prevention Bill, for example, was based on the demand for civic, as well as family stability. The current practice was for parties to settle matters 'in some room in the city', and to treat the *legal* resolution of the dispute as a practical irrelevance. Thus damage awards were ignored, and cases of divorce were brought before the House of Lords without any mention of the private agreements that had already been negotiated. 'It was impossible', Eldon argued, 'to suffer the law to remain in the shameful state in which it at present stood.'[52]

This belief, that society depended upon respect for law, was central to Eldon's thinking. He was less interested either in innovation or preservation *per se*, than in sustaining the law as a valued and valuable institution. To achieve this end he would both advocate change and resist it. Respect for law entailed recognition of its structure. The constitution, and not more general ideas of justice, primarily informed his analyses and solutions of legal problems. Individual injustices, for example, were preferable to a general weakening of the constitution. In *Mainwaring* v. *Newman*,[53] he declined to allow an action on a promissory note, despite the 'highly injurious' commercial consequences, because the proper parties had not been joined. Similarly, in *Beard* v. *Webb*,[54] Eldon declined to countenance a married woman being sued as a sole trader in the courts of Westminster, while acknowledging the 'inconvenience' of his decision, and the 'prevailing fashions of the times'. His decisions do not reflect an unwillingness to change the law, but a belief in his constitutional incapacity, as a judge, to undertake it. Such was the job of Parliament, and until Parliament saw fit to act, individual suitors must be discomfited. As Eldon remarked in *Beard* v. *Webb*, 'if the policy of the law has withheld from married women certain powers and faculties, the courts of law must continue to

---

[51] *The Times*, 28 February 1800, 3, col. 4.
[52] Cobbett, *Parliamentary history*, XXXV:237.
[53] (1800) 126 ER 1190, 1194.        [54] (1800) 126 ER 1175, 1183–4.

treat them as deprived of those powers and faculties, until the legislature directs those courts to do otherwise.'[55] Where he was *not* so handicapped, as in matters of Common Pleas procedure, Eldon not only identified flaws but took steps to remove them. In *Hall* v. *Ody*, he criticised the court's approach to the allocation of costs of different actions involving the same parties. 'I find it to be the settled practice with much surprise, since it stands in direct contradiction to the practice of every other court as well as to the principles of justice.'[56] After noting that the party in the instant case had acted with full knowledge of the practice, and so had no legitimate claim to different treatment, he nevertheless opined that the court should, in future, adopt the more admirable practice of the King's Bench. Nor was this the only time he sought conformity with that tribunal. He rejected precedent from Common Pleas on the issue of whether a successful party was entitled to costs for those pleadings to which he should have raised a legal objection.

[I]f it had been followed up by a long, invariable, and known usage, the Court would have been bound to enforce that usage at least *pro hac vice*; but as it is not even pretended that any rule has been brought into familiar practice in consequence of that decision, I think we are at liberty notwithstanding that case to adopt the rule which was laid down in the King's Bench in *Kirk* v. *Nowill*, and which appears to me most conformable to justice and to the fair construction of [21] H[en] VIII.[57]

Given his position on Catholic emancipation, it is interesting to consider Eldon's opinion in *Lord Petre* v. *Lord Auckland*,[58] a case heard by all the judges in the Exchequer Chamber in May 1800. It concerned whether a Roman Catholic peer enjoyed the privilege of franking. Eldon delivered the opinion of the court, which found in favour of Lord Auckland, the Postmaster General. Eldon based the decision on the statute of 4 Geo. III c. 24. The privilege of franking, he explained, must be exercised according to the statute.

---

[55] *Ibid.*, 1184.       [56] (1799) 126 ER 1136, 1137.
[57] *DaCosta* v. *Clarke* (1801) 126 ER 1336, 1337. The Act of 21 Hen. VIII c. 19 formed the basis for an award of costs in the instant case, but did not specify whether or how the court could regulate such an award. Eldon again specifically relied on Buller's opinion in *Kirk*, which he described as 'a very considerable authority'. For further instances of Eldon's queries regarding Common Pleas procedures, see *Penson* v. *Lee* (1800) 126 ER 1309, *Rushton* v. *Chapman* (1800) 126 ER 1316, and *Vollum* v. *Simpson* (1801) 126 ER 1331.
[58] (1800) 126 ER 1202.

This measure, in its turn, regulated the privilege as it had previously been afforded to members of Parliament, and that had not included persons professing Roman Catholic beliefs. Thus, under the statute of 4 Geo. III, those persons who had previously been permitted to frank letters could continue to do so, subject to the restrictions introduced in the Act to prevent abuses. This, presumably, was all that he needed to say on the subject. Yet he continued – not to make an oblique reference to possible Parliamentary reform of the situation, to which he would not have agreed – but to point out some further features of the legal record. Roman Catholic peers, he believed, were recognised as having the privilege of peerage, but not the privilege of Parliament. In this way they were like Protestant peers during minority, who similarly could not frank. Whether the two privileges *ought* to be regarded as co-extensive he could not say. He did not believe that the instant case required resolution of that issue, 'but if it were necessary, I will not pretend to say but that there are many acts of parliament containing expressions such as "Lords of Parliament," and "Lords of the House of Parliament", which would apply to any peer before he has taken his seat'.[59] In thus mentioning this ambiguity, Eldon seems to have been motivated by the demands of his own code. Finding himself in the happy situation of deciding a case consistently with his political principles, he felt bound to demonstrate that politics had neither dictated the result nor blinded him to an ambiguity in the current law. A verbose, complex, or even weak opinion was a small price to pay for that satisfaction.

On 14 April 1801, Eldon accepted the office of Lord Chancellor in the ministry formed upon Pitt's resignation. Two occurrences at the time are illustrative of his response to the appointment. First, he obtained Pitt's blessing on his acceptance of high office in the new government, and he agreed to serve if Pitt should ever come into office again.[60] In this way he demonstrated his loyalty to his chief, yet avoided having to forego either actual or prospective employment. He displayed something more honourable than merely a politician's shrewdness in a communication with Lord

---

[59] *Ibid.*, 1207.
[60] L. V. Harcourt (ed.), *The diaries and correspondence of the Rt Hon. George Rose*, 2 vols. (London, 1860), I:310.

Kenyon, the Chief Justice of King's Bench, shortly before his appointment was made final. While lacking political clout, Kenyon was an old friend and colleague, and someone to whom Eldon had turned for advice while serving in Common Pleas. For these reasons he hastened to make clear that no want of proper courtesy had kept him from reporting a change in his circumstances.

> I feel a good deal of uneasiness to protect myself against the possibility of your Lordship's thinking that I am wanting in the respect and duty which I owe to you, and which I can truly say has ever been accompanied with the most grateful & affectionate regard. May I therefore be allowed to assure you that whatever other persons may have thought it becoming to mention in conversation regarding themselves or me, nothing has passed yet with respect to me that would warrant me, consistently with propriety, in making that communication to you, which it would be my duty to make, as I wish to make it to you, whenever the matter is settled one way or the other.[61]

Thus ambition and decency attended his elevation to the highest legal office in the government, and while his sense of duty and moral obligation would make his tenure burdensome, his drive to succeed would make him equally tenacious of office. Did he ever regret having left the relative quiet of the Common Pleas? In later years he might reflect fondly upon his period of 'retirement', but this was nostalgia coloured by the criticisms of his current professional and political conduct. He could no more have resisted the lure of high office than he could have avoided the moral conflicts with which he endowed it.

---

[61] Eldon to Lord Kenyon, 14 February 1801, Encombe (Scott papers).

# 10

# THE KING'S MAN

In the spring of 1801 Eldon changed his professional situation for the second time in two years, when he left the Common Pleas to become Lord Chancellor of England. His interlude of relative ease and independence was over, and he took up again the combined burden of professional and political duty, but with a responsibility more onerous than he had heretofore borne. The office of Chancellor was of medieval origin, and the first incumbents acted as royal secretaries. Over the centuries, however, the Chancellor had assumed a range of important functions. Professionally, he was the senior lawyer in the land, presiding in the court of Chancery. Politically, he was a privy councillor and member of the Cabinet, bringing legal and political expertise to bear on the problems of government. He was also a courtier of sorts, his particular role as keeper of the Great Seal affording him access to the sovereign whenever legislation required the royal assent. As a parliamentarian his was a guiding authority, moderating debates and litigation as Speaker of the House of Lords. The workload of the Lord Chancellor, consequently, was very considerable, but the potential conflicts of loyalty were more debilitating. He was obliged to balance the demands of his court against the time spent on political matters, his ties to ministers against his obligations to the sovereign, and his duties to the government with those to Parliament. In becoming Lord Chancellor, Eldon had reached the summit of any political lawyer's ambition, but in an office whose execution was as difficult as its achievement.

The occasion for Eldon's promotion was the change in government following the resignation of William Pitt. Several of Pitt's principal associates left office with him; while Lord Loughborough had no wish to resign the Lord Chancellorship, he was obliged to do so by the new First Lord of the Treasury,

Henry Addington. Addington's government would last for three years, and achieve for the nation a brief respite in the long war against France. For Eldon, however, this first phase of his career as a Cabinet minister was coloured by two men, neither of whom was a member of the government. The first was the King himself, whom Eldon increasingly felt obliged to protect, as well as to serve, and the second was Pitt, to whose previous and prospective ministries Eldon was inextricably linked. Upon Pitt's return to office in the spring of 1804 Eldon would retain the Great Seal and find himself enmeshed ever more tightly in royal affairs.

The transition from the government of Pitt to that of Addington was a protracted one, due to the precarious state of the King's health. Pitt resigned and Addington accepted office in early February 1801, but before the former could deliver up and the latter receive the seals of office, the King became so seriously ill that his life was feared to be in danger. It was not until 14 March 1801 that he had recovered sufficiently to confirm Addington in his new post. Eldon's own status remained unsettled rather longer, and he did not finally take up his new appointment until 15 April 1801. In part this delay was the result of Loughborough's unwillingness to leave office. More important, however, was the King's condition. Both George Rose, and the King himself in a lucid interval, warned Eldon against resigning from the Common Pleas precipitously.[1] That appointment, unlike the Chancellorship, did not depend on the longevity of the government, and therefore ought not to be surrendered lightly when further ministerial changes, perhaps even a regency, seemed possible. As Rose noted in his diary entry for 23 February 1801: 'it occurred to me that he [Eldon] might be taking steps ... such as would be irrevocable, which would necessarily leave him in an unpleasant situation if the King's malady should unhappily continue upon him.'[2] The following day, Eldon maintained that he would not accept the Great Seal unless convinced that the King was competent to bestow it.[3] As late as 5 April 1801 he was repeating this

---

[1] A. Aspinall (ed.), *The later correspondence of George III*, 5 vols. (Cambridge, 1962), III:503, footnote.

[2] L. V. Harcourt (ed.), *The diaries and correspondence of the Rt Hon. George Rose*, 2 vols. (London, 1860), I:312.

[3] *Ibid.*, 313.

assertion to Rose and, moreover, expressing 'great doubt' that the King was fit to perform any public duties.[4] Nevertheless, the day after the royal physicians dismissed the King's 'minders' Eldon became Lord Chancellor.

Almost immediately, Eldon was exposed fully to the political dangers of his position. As had been the case in 1788, opposition politicians began raising the issue of royal competence. Eldon, as the minister expected to enjoy the greatest access to the King, was subjected to close scrutiny. For him the dangers were two-fold. If he needlessly exposed the King to a period of Regency, control of the government would pass to the Prince of Wales and his friends, to whose views both the King and ministers were opposed. If, however, he improperly shielded the King, he violated his public duty, not only by permitting ministers to remain in office without legal authority, but by acquiescing in the enactment of legislation in an unconstitutional fashion. No sooner was Eldon appointed than it was suggested that his appointment was illegal. The Earl of Carlisle remarked to the Prince of Wales:

It ought to be recollected ... that it is no secret that Dr Willis' keepers were removed on the Wed[nesda]y; on the Tuesday preceding L[or]d Eldon accepted the Seals as Chancellor from the King. On the Monday following the former lamentable symptoms returned, since which time Dr Willis' keepers were again placed about the King in the room of his own domestics. In this lucid interval his M[ajest]y makes a Chancellor. What would L[or]d Eldon's answer be, as a professional man, fit as I believe him to be both from integrity & learning to be a Chancellor, were he to be asked as to the *validity of a Will made under similar circumstances; whether he, sitting in the Court of Chancery, would a moment entertain the idea of its being valid!* [5]

Eldon was also assailed by the Prince's representatives, wishing to know whether the King was able to conduct business. Foremost among these was Lord Thurlow. Two months previously, Thurlow had congratulated Eldon upon his prospective appointment, professing: 'But I congratulate still more with the House, and the country.'[6] Despite those fair words, Eldon believed that Thurlow would willingly resume office himself, were a Regency

---

[4] *Ibid.*, 340.

[5] Earl of Carlisle to the Prince of Wales, undated [late April, early May 1801], A. Aspinall (ed.), *The correspondence of George Prince of Wales (1770–1812)*, 8 vols. (London, 1967–71), IV:212 (emphasis in original).

[6] Lord Thurlow to Eldon, 18 February 1801, Encombe (Scott papers).

created.[7] Consequently, he kept aloof from his old mentor.[8] Even to the Prince, Eldon was generally unforthcoming upon the subject of the King's health.[9] That Eldon was troubled about how best to proceed with the King himself, however, is apparent. Prior to his own acceptance of office, he had criticised Loughborough for having obtained the royal assent in circumstances in which the King might not have been strictly competent.[10] After two weeks in office, however, Eldon was justifying a rather controversial interpretation of royal competence. As Rose reported in his diary for 28 March 1801:

> He [Eldon] seemed to think it not necessary that his Majesty should be in an *uninterrupted* state of health and composure to justify his being called upon to discharge the ordinary duties of the Sovereign; but that it would be sufficient for his Lordship's justification if his Majesty should, at the time of his being called upon to perform any act of sovereignty, be in a proper situation to do such an act.[11]

Whether such a plan could be executed successfully, however, was unclear. The first test occurred in mid-April, when Eldon had to obtain the King's signature to a commission. Rose advised, rather than merely assessing the King's condition through a personal interview, that Eldon should obtain from his Majesty a letter accompanying the signed commission, 'because he would then be in possession of a written testimony of his Majesty's competency'.[12] Accordingly, Eldon sought permission to send the relevant documentation rather than bringing it in person. The reason for seeking this 'indulgence', he confided, was 'its being necessary that he should, for the convenience of the suitors, if possible, attend in the Court of Chancery'.[13] The King's reply, that he would 'by no means have wished that his Lord Chancellor should have omitted sitting in the Court of Chancery tomorrow, for the mere matter of form of bringing himself the Commission' furnished Eldon with the desired proof of competence.[14]

The King's health also caused a certain ministerial friction, as

---

[7] Harcourt, *Diaries*, I:341.
[8] Thurlow to Wales, 27 April 1801, Aspinall, *Wales*, IV:210.
[9] Harcourt, *Diaries*, I:347; see Thurlow to Wales, 22 April 1801, Aspinall, *Wales*, IV:209.
[10] Harcourt, *Diaries*, I:340.      [11] *Ibid.*, 351 (emphasis in original).
[12] *Ibid.*, 350.
[13] Eldon to George III, 29 April 1801, Aspinall, *George III*, III:522.
[14] George III to Eldon, 29 April 1801, H. Twiss, *The public and private life of Lord*

Eldon resented Addington's lack of candour on the subject. Having seen the King on 22 February 1801 and found him 'much deranged on some subjects', Addington had not only attended a Cabinet with Eldon and revealed nothing, but after Eldon had received a warning about the King's fitness and attempted to learn the truth from Addington, the latter had avoided an interview.[15] Eldon explained this lack of cordiality as the consequence of his own refusal to regard himself as Addington's man. He had informed Addington that he would assume office 'only in obedience to the King's command, and at the advice and earnest recommendation of Mr Pitt', and that he would remain 'no longer than he could continue to do so in perfect friendship with the latter'.[16] Such an announcement would hardly have encouraged displays of confidence on the part of the new premier. After their initial coolness, however, the shared responsibility brought about a closeness between the two men. Certainly Eldon made a point of notifying Addington upon matters affecting the King, stating: 'I am determined that nothing shall ever pass with me that shall not, in effect, pass with you.'[17] Moreover, they informed each other of the conduct of their respective audiences with the King, and conferred about how best to approach him upon particular topics.[18] For example, at the end of May the King's physicians advised against his going to Weymouth, and urged ministers to dissuade him, if possible. It was decided between Eldon and Addington that 'one of us should write, and the other so to show', and accordingly Eldon drafted a letter to the King which Addington approved and delivered to him.[19] The deftness of the Chancellor's touch is demonstrated in the letter written on that occasion:

The Lord Chancellor, offering his most humble duty to your Majesty,

*Chancellor Eldon*, 3 vols. (London, 1844), I:372; see George Rose's diary notation of 17 May 1801, Harcourt, *Diaries*, I:352.

[15] Lord Colchester, C. Abbot, *The diary and correspondence of Charles Abbot, Lord Colchester*, 3 vols. (London, 1861), I:244; Harcourt, *Diaries*, 1:313.

[16] Harcourt, *Diaries*, I:313.

[17] Eldon to Henry Addington, 12 May 1801, DevRO (Sidmouth papers), 152M/1801/OR66.

[18] Eldon to Addington, undated [*c.* early May 1801], *ibid.*, 152M/1801/OZ91; Addington to Eldon, 21 May 1801, Encombe (Scott papers).

[19] Addington to Eldon, 30 May 1801, Encombe (Scott papers). See also Addington's two letters to Eldon of the following day, *ibid.*

presumes to submit to your Majesty's gracious consideration that it appears to him that great difficulties may arise in matters of public concern if your Majesty should be pleased during the time of its sitting, to remove to any considerable distance from your Majesty's Parliament. It cannot but happen that, before Parliament can be closed, some intelligence should be received from abroad upon which it may be absolutely necessary to learn promptly & perhaps instantly your Majesty's pleasure, and to learn it by communications more ample than your Majesty, however gracious to your servants, could probably allow to them if they were not personally attending, in the discharge of their duty, upon your Majesty. Communications from your Majesty in the form of messages to your Parliament, not admitting of delay, may also become necessary. Impressed at this moment with a deep sense that it is extremely important, on all accounts, to your Majesty's welfare that your Majesty should be graciously pleased to secure to your servants the power of personally communicating with your Majesty, at least during the short interval which must elapse before Parliament seperates [*sic*], at the close of which they may, in obedience to any commands which your Majesty may think proper to give, attend your Majesty anywhere, the Lord Chancellor ventures to hope that your Majesty will not think it inconsistent with his duty that he should have thus most humbly but most earnestly submitted to your Majesty the expression of his conscientious conviction that such a measure is of the highest expediency.[20]

The success of the letter can be judged in the King's reply: 'The King cannot allow any difficulty to stand in the way of his doing what may be most useful to the public service. He will, therefore, postpone his journey to Weymouth till the close of the session of Parliament, relying that the Chancellor and Mr Addington will bring it as soon as possible to a conclusion.'[21] The royal physicians also relied upon Eldon's personal influence with the King. On 16 May 1801 Thomas Guisborne wrote: 'Knowing at the same time the degree of attention with which his Majesty receives everything which falls from your Lordship, permit me to beg you will inform him, in your own manner, how necessary I know it to be that he should still exert himself steadily to be at quietness & repose.'[22] When Thomas Willis feared the King was becoming dangerously excited he inquired of Eldon: 'Had not your Lordship, therefore, better write to his Majesty ...?'[23]

On 21 June 1801, when the King seemed at last fully recovered,

[20] Eldon to George III, 31 May 1801, Aspinall, *George III*, III:547.
[21] George III to Eldon, 31 May 1801, Twiss, *The public and private life*, I:378.
[22] Thomas Guisborne to Eldon, 16 May 1801, Encombe (Scott papers).
[23] Thomas Willis to Eldon, 25 May 1801, Twiss, *The public and private life*, I:376.

he asserted that he 'would not do justice to the feelings of his heart, if he an instant delayed expressing his conviction of the attachment the Lord Chancellor bears him'.[24] Nor was this an isolated expression of the King's affectionate regard. Perhaps in recognition of Eldon's support during his illness, the King was very solicitous of Eldon's health. When the Chancellor was laid up with gout in the spring of 1802, the King repeatedly expressed his concern, even suggesting that Eldon defer an audience, in order to spare him the physical effort of attending. 'The King therefore strongly recommends ... not coming next Wednesday to St James's ... which will avoid the necessity of going up stairs; and Wednesday is the first day of Term, which must in itself be a day of some fatigue.'[25] The King spoke of the 'real integrity, talents, legal knowledge, and good temper' of *his* Lord Chancellor, and he commissioned Eldon to act as royal intermediary in matters of delicacy.[26] He relied upon 'an intimation' from Eldon to prevent the Earl of Berkeley from bringing his wife to court in circumstances in which the King could not recognise her, and he approved of Eldon's having sufficiently 'calmed the temper' of the Duke of Northumberland to convince him to accept the commission as Lord Lieutenant for that county.[27] Perhaps the most significant mark of esteem, however, was the King's determination to seek Eldon's advice on the proper tone to take with his unhappy daughter-in-law. Estranged from her husband, the Princess of Wales wrote to the King in the autumn of 1801, complaining of financial embarrassment. The King sent Eldon the draft of his proposed reply, and later nominated him the channel for any further correspondence.[28] He explained to the Princess that the Chancellor's 'station in my service as well as his excellent private character particularly point him out for being employed on the present occasion'.[29]

Apart from his evident attachment to the King, Eldon's poli-

---

[24] George III to Eldon, 21 June 1801, *ibid.*, 382.
[25] George III to Eldon, 30 April 1802, *ibid.*, 404–5. See also the King's letters to Eldon of 11 and 15 April, and 14 August 1802, *ibid.*, 403, 404, 408.
[26] George III to Eldon, 29 April 1801, *ibid.*, 372.
[27] George III to Eldon, 27 September 1803, Aspinall, *George III*, V:647; George III to Eldon, 12 June 1802, *ibid.*, 646.
[28] George III to Eldon, 20 November 1801, *ibid.*, 645.
[29] George III to the Princess of Wales, 23 November 1801, Aspinall, *Wales*, IV:240.

tical value to the government was less clear. In his previous incarnation as a parliamentarian, his participation in debate had been careful and self-conscious. He had spoken with moderate frequency, and particularly on legal issues. As Attorney General, he had been somewhat constrained, not only by a certain natural reserve in the company of speakers of superior ability, but also by his professional obligations to both the government and Parliament. As Lord Chancellor, his status and situation might reasonably have altered his parliamentary demeanour. He held a ministerial office which afforded him considerable political weight, and also conferred upon him great authority within the profession. He could speak, therefore, with greater confidence. Moreover, he not only appeared, but presided in the House of Lords, where debate did not generally achieve the same level of forensic ability or intensity as in the lower House. Indeed, these facts do seem to have had an effect upon Eldon's conduct during this phase of his career. He spoke frequently, often concluding debates for the government or speaking in answer to Lord Grenville, a leading government critic. He also spoke more confidently. He did not, however, become a leading or even powerful advocate for the government. This was because of his tendency to distance himself, either from the measure under consideration, or from the government itself. He urged the House to accept a Bill to clarify the legal position of newly created military units, while at the same time explaining that he did not particularly approve of legislation of this kind.[30] He supported an inquiry into administrative abuses in the navy, but was unhappy with the proposed method and scope of authority.[31] When the Earl of Carlisle complained that the government lacked public confidence, Eldon spoke at length about the strong support that ministers enjoyed in Parliament 'which represented the public'. He added, however, that *he* 'had been chosen to the situation he had the honour to fill, by the pleasure of his Majesty'.[32] This unwillingness to commit himself fully to the government is particularly noticeable in the debates on the government's most important measure, the peace

---

[30] T. Hansard (ed.), *Parliamentary debates from the year 1803 (1st series)*, 41 vols. (London, 1812–20), I:1887.

[31] W. Cobbett (ed.), *The parliamentary history of England ... to 1803*, 36 vols. (London, 1806–20), XXXVI:1145, 1146.

[32] *The Times*, 16 March 1803, 2, col. 2.

1    Engraving of the Scott home, and Eldon's birthplace, in Newcastle

2    Encombe, in Dorset, purchased by Eldon in 1807

3  Steel engraving of Sir John Scott, aged 48, by E. Finden
after T. Lawrence

4   Stipple engraving of Eldon, by T. Wright, after A. Wivell, one of a
series of drawings of the principal participants in Queen Caroline's
trial in 1820

5   John Bull evinces little sympathy for Eldon and the Duke of Wellington, following their

6 Detail of the memorial to Eldon, Lady Eldon and the Hon. John
Scott, MP, by F. Chantrey, in the parish church of Kingston, Dorset

with France negotiated in the autumn of 1801 and completed in the spring of 1802. Eldon spoke frequently on the subject, and defended the government's efforts to achieve a settlement that was in the nation's best interest. Yet even as he described criticism of the peace as unrealistic, he requested that he 'not be understood to vapour in praise of the peace, as if it was a very honourable one'.[33]

The evidence from Eldon's personal correspondence indicates that his public expressions about the peace arose from a genuine lack of ardour.[34] His more general reluctance wholeheartedly to support the government, however, reflected his enduring commitment to Pitt. This certainly did not extend to support for every measure of the late government. On the merits of Catholic emancipation, for instance, Eldon differed from Pitt, and declined to consider himself in any way bound by the position that Pitt had taken.[35] For the most part, however, Eldon's political temperament was dominated by his experiences of the 1790s. He repeatedly justified his current position by pointing to the salutary effect that similar conduct had had in warding off revolution, and by warning of social collapse if a contrary view were now adopted. Issues as diverse as tithes, divorce, and eligibility to membership of the House of Commons brought forth such arguments. '[A]lmost all the miseries of France', he assured the House, 'were produced by the very circumstance of abolishing tithes, and depriving the Clergy of their support'.[36] He believed that 'this country would never have recovered from the shock which within the last ten years she had sustained, were it not for the morality and virtue that distinguished the higher orders of the people here, from those of the same description in other countries that had become a prey to revolution and anarchy.' Consequently, uncontested actions for divorce ought to be opposed, because of the grave danger that they posed to public morals.[37] Maintenance of a separate clerical character was similarly important, and ought to take precedence over any pretensions to political equality. For this reason he supported the Bill to maintain the bar against men in

---

[33] Cobbett, *Parliamentary history*, XXXVI:171; see also *The Times*, 14 May 1802, 2, col. 3.

[34] Eldon to Sir William Scott, 2 October 1801, Encombe (Scott papers); Eldon to Lord Redesdale, 29 April 1802, GRO (Mitford papers), D2002/3/1/23.

[35] Eldon to Redesdale, 28 September 1802, GRO (Mitford papers), D2003/3/1/23.

[36] *The Times*, 7 July 1803, 2, col. 1.    [37] *Ibid.*, 20 March 1802, 2, col. 1.

holy orders standing as members of Parliament, and 'He considered it indeed as one of the most alarming signs of the times, that so much zeal should be shewn to overturn the ancient practice in this respect'.[38] Given this anxiety, it is not surprising that Eldon recalled the government's achievements in the 1790s with pride and satisfaction. He supported a Bill to indemnify the late ministers who had arrested persons during a previous suspension of the Habeas Corpus Act.[39] Speaking on the latter, he argued that it was sometimes necessary to 'confide large powers to the executive government' to counteract traitorous conspiracies. If their lordships 'had not a mind to hurl their sovereign from his throne, or turn themselves out of these doors, they would pass the Bill before them'.[40]

In addition to his formative political experiences, personal attachment linked Eldon to Pitt. Eldon maintained contact with his former chief, and was concerned to know whether he remained generally sympathetic to the current government.[41] As early as September 1802, Eldon was beginning to question whether Addington was the right man to lead the government. In a letter to Lord Redesdale he pointed to the work required of a premier, to Addington's relative inexperience, and to his disinclination 'to admit that it is too much for him', as contributing to his being 'confused, wearied, & stunned'. Eldon took comfort, on this occasion, from the fact that the government retained the 'prodigious assistance' of Pitt in the Commons.[42] He became increasingly uneasy, however, as relations between Pitt and Addington began to sour in 1803. Writing to Redesdale in October of that year, Eldon admitted that the widening breach was a source of great anxiety:

To me there is an end of all comfort in my official situation: I must do my duty, as well as I can determine what it requires of me, whilst I remain in it: but I can have no unmixed comfort, if our old Friend Mr Pitt is hostile ... and the bitterness of all this is much increased by a full persuasion that, if a discreet friend had been employed, when the attempt was made to bring back Mr P. to his situation, the attempt would have succeeded, and that even now matters might be set right, if interest and folly in those,

---

[38] *Ibid.*, 16 June 1801, 2, col. 1; Cobbett, *Parliamentary history*, XXXV:1545.
[39] *The Times*, 23 June 1802, 2, col. 2.
[40] Cobbett, *Parliamentary history*, XXXV:1538.
[41] See George Rose's diary entry of 11 June 1801, Harcourt, *Diaries*, I:355.
[42] Eldon to Redesdale, 28 September 1802, GRO (Mitford Papers), D2002/3/1/23.

who are around these two gentlemen, were not engaged in doing every thing, except what is for their true interest.[43]

Eldon's loyalty to the King and his respect and affection for Pitt produced a political crisis for the Chancellor in the spring of 1804. In mid-February the King suffered a further bout of illness. His condition was extremely grave for the first few days, and even after his physical health improved, he continued to exhibit symptoms of severe derangement. On 26 February 1804, the royal physicians published a bulletin announcing that the King's condition had become favourable, but that a full recovery could not rapidly be anticipated. The following day they reported to the Cabinet that the King was competent to conduct routine business, but that it would be prudent to spare him unnecessary mental exertions.[44] The question of the King's health, consequently, again became a matter of parliamentary interest, and in early March ministers were obliged to field questions about the possible suspension of royal functions. Eldon's views were particularly sought, as the minister responsible for obtaining the King's assent to legislation. On several occasions he was called upon to assure peers that the King was competent. Eldon expressed himself fully cognisant of his own obligations under the circumstances:

He was aware, that while he was, on the one hand, constantly to keep in view what was due from him, in point of delicacy to his Sovereign, he ought, on the other, never to forget that he had a duty to perform to the legislature and the public. He had settled in his own mind what line of conduct he was to pursue on this occasion, and kept that line exactly, which, in his own idea, appeared to be his duty.[45]

He declined, however, to enlighten the House more particularly, remarking only that, if called upon to affix the Great Seal in recognition of the King's concurrence, 'he would consider himself in breach of duty if he did not first have an interview with the King to request the royal will on the subject'.[46] In fact, Eldon did visit the King on several occasions and had the opportunity to satisfy himself as to the King's mental state.[47] He did not offer to

---

[43] Eldon to Redesdale, 10 October 1803, *ibid.*

[44] Memorandum: examination of the King's physicians, 27 February 1804, Twiss, *The public and private life*, I:421–2.

[45] Hansard, *Parliamentary debates*, I:639.      [46] *Ibid.*, col. 642.

[47] See *ibid.*, cols. 697, 808; Lord Eldon, J. Scott, *Lord Eldon's anecdote book*, ed. A. L. J. Lincoln and R. L. McEwen (London, 1960), 117–18.

satisfy Parliament, however, other than by bland assurances of his own 'delicacy, deliberation, and caution'.[48]

The King's condition was of particular importance at this time because his illness coincided with a growing political pressure on the Addington government from two sources. Grenville and Charles Fox had determined to co-ordinate their opposition, and Pitt's growing dissatisfaction was at last manifest, not in a union with Fox and Grenville, but in a separate opposition to the government. This was the decision for which Pitt's friends outside of the government had been waiting. Precisely what were the sentiments of his friends within the government is less clear. On 20 March 1804, Pitt received and accepted an invitation to dine with his former Attorney General on 24 March. While the precise nature of their discussions on that occasion is not known, it can be assumed that the political situation was foremost on the agenda. In his letter of acceptance Pitt wrote:

> whatever may be the result of our conversation I think the sooner we hold it the better. The state of public affairs makes it impossible that the present suspense should last very long, and nothing can give me more satisfaction than to put you confidentially in full possession of all the sentiments and opinions by which my conduct will be regulated.[49]

Moreover, in a letter to Lord Melville[50] on 11 April, Pitt asserted that he had 'strong grounds' to believe that Eldon was foremost among those ministers 'feeling the insufficiency of the present Government, and wishing my return to office'.[51] On 16 April, Addington made a final attempt to solicit Pitt's assistance in remodelling the ministry. When Pitt expressed a willingness to communicate his views on the establishment of a new government to a person designated by the King, Addington advised the King to commission Eldon to undertake the role of intermediary.[52]

Accordingly, on 22 April Eldon received a letter from Pitt for

---

[48] Hansard, *Parliamentary debates*, I:808.

[49] William Pitt to Eldon, 20 March 1804, Encombe (Scott papers). John Ehrman has suggested that Eldon supported Pitt's return, but hoped that Addington might be retained in a prospective Pitt government. *The younger Pitt*, vol. 3, *The consuming struggle* (London, 1996), 640.

[50] Formerly Henry Dundas. He had accepted a peerage as Viscount Melville in 1802.

[51] Pitt to Lord Melville, 11 April 1804, Earl Stanhope, *The life of William Pitt*, 3 vols. (London, 1879), III:146.

[52] See Lord Grenville to the Marquis of Buckingham, 19 April 1804, *ibid.*, 211.

delivery to the King. This was intended to convey Pitt's political sentiments prior to their being made public in the debate on the state of the nation, which Fox had put down for the following day.[53] In his answer of the same day, Eldon explained to Pitt the difficulties created by the receipt of such a commission. First, he was being asked to tender a communication hostile to the government in which he held a prominent office. 'It is impossible for me not to be aware that, in delivering any such paper to his Majesty, much may be, properly, or improperly, observed upon my conduct.'[54] Despite this, he was resolved to convey the message. Secondly, he was being asked to do so 'with as little delay as the nature of the case will admit'.[55] This wish, in Eldon's view, could not take precedence over the considerations of the King's health and the authority of the present government. The King's mental condition was sound but fragile, and required that he be spared unnecessary agitation. However, given the current state of politics, ministers must inevitably inform him of their opinions. Consequently, Eldon could not undertake to deliver Pitt's letter until after the King had recovered from the audience that Addington would have on 26 April.

[T]ill he has had the repose of a night, and I have learnt the effect of tomorrow's proceedings on Thursday morning, I cannot, according to my notions of duty to him, take any step, which must affect him so materially, as the communication of y[ou]r opinions will, & ought, to affect him.[56]

That Eldon was motivated by concern for the King, and not a particular loyalty to the government, is evidenced by the fact that he did communicate something of Pitt's views to the King on 23 April prior to Addington's audience.[57] Moreover, he delivered the letter on 27 April,[58] following Addington's audience, but before the Cabinet's decision to resign, which was not taken until 29 April.[59]

On 30 April, Eldon called on Pitt to acquaint him with the

---

[53] See Pitt to Eldon, 22 April 1804, Encombe (Scott papers); Pitt to George III, 21 April 1804, Stanhope, *William Pitt*, III: Appendix i.

[54] Eldon to Pitt, PRO (Chatham papers), 30/8 132:151.

[55] Pitt to Eldon, 22 April 1804, Encombe (Scott papers).

[56] Eldon to Pitt, 22 April 1804, PRO (Chatham papers), 30/8 132:120.

[57] Eldon to Pitt, 23 April 1804, *ibid.*, 30/8 132:145.

[58] Eldon to Pitt, 29 April 1804, *ibid.*, 30/8 132:141.

[59] Pitt to Eldon, 29 April 1804, Encombe (Scott papers); see Colchester, *Diary*, I:501.

King's request to produce a further statement of his proposals. Pitt delivered the document to Eldon two days later, and Eldon conveyed it to the King on 5 May.[60] Its contents, which included a broadly based ministry to include Fox and the Grenvilles, as well as Pitt's own particular associates, did not please the King. While not rejecting further contact, the King drafted a sharply worded reply, in which he praised Addington, criticised Pitt's views on Catholic emancipation, and expressed 'astonishment' that Pitt 'should for one moment harbour the thought' of bringing Fox into the government.[61] Pitt's reply of 6 May indicated that he regarded the King's objections as tantamount to dismissal.[62] The following day, however, Eldon conveyed to Pitt the King's message to attend him, and that meeting, which took place on 8 May, was one of extreme cordiality.[63] While the reason for this change of temperament is not clear, it is known that between receiving Pitt's letter and agreeing to see him the King had met again with Eldon.

Eldon's attitude toward Pitt's return to office was complicated by the fact that he objected to any coalition with Fox. Upon receiving Pitt's first communication to the King in late April, Eldon had stressed that he ought not to be regarded as an uncritical envoy. He expressed satisfaction that Pitt had not committed himself to an alliance, the existence of which would have rendered delivery of the message 'the most painful act of my life'.[64] When Pitt did propose an alliance with Fox, Eldon expressed his objections in a letter of 3 May.

I am indeed to be the channel of that communication, merely because I think it my duty, in the present circumstances, to submit your opinions to His Majesty's consideration, in the form in which you propose them to be conveyed, however much my own sentiments may differ from those opinions, and however unable I may feel myself to entertain a hope that I could ever induce myself to think that any useful consequences would result from the measures, which the opinions represent to be clearly beneficial.[65]

That Eldon was distinctly concerned by the likely consequences of

[60]  Pitt to Eldon, 2 May 1804, Encombe (Scott papers).
[61]  George III to Pitt, 5 May 1804, Stanhope, *William Pitt*, III: Appendix, X.
[62]  Pitt to George III, 6 May 1804, *ibid.*, xii.          [63]  Harcourt, *Diaries*, II:121.
[64]  Eldon to Pitt, 22 April 1804, PRO (Chatham papers), 30/8 132:120.
[65]  Eldon to Pitt, 3 May 1804, *ibid.*, 30/8 132:149.

a coalition, both for the King's mental stability and Pitt's reputation in the country, was made clear in an exchange of letters with
George Rose on 4 May. In answer to Rose's suggestion that he
promote the idea of such a partnership, Eldon replied that he
could only do so 'if the King's health was firm, and I could so far
forget my duty to Mr Pitt as to give him what I thought the worst
advice I could offer him'.[66] Eldon would continue to advise
caution and independence when Pitt returned to the subject in the
autumn. Not only would independence preserve Pitt's political
integrity, but it would provide the best chance of securing the
King's peace of mind.

[B]alancing all considerations, tho in some circumstances that might
happen, it might deeply affect His Majesty's welfare & happiness, yet,
upon looking round, & viewing all that may happen, I hardly know any,
in which a change would ensure him much good, or protect him from
much evil. The embarrassments of a successful negotiation will also be
very great, whatever of good it may produce: and the consequences of a
negotiation, if it does not succeed, somewhat mischievous.[67]

Pitt returned to power in May 1804 without the questionable
benefit of either a Fox or Grenville coalition, and also without the
clear benefit of the King's good health. Throughout the summer
and, indeed, for the remainder of the year, the King's health
would be a continuing cause for concern. While never reaching the
seriousness of previous periods of illness, his condition seems to
have drifted between phases of more or less normality and
disturbances of the kind that might presage another breakdown.
Not surprisingly, the resultant changes of temper made the task of
working with the King and shielding him from stress extremely
wearing for the person so employed. In December Eldon would
confide to Redesdale that: 'In some four or five months of this
expiring year no moment passed that, with reference to this
subject, was not a moment of trepidation & anxiety.'[68] By that
time, moreover, Eldon's royal responsibilities had been considerably increased by the interventions of the Prince of Wales.

On 2 June 1804 Eldon received a letter that constituted the

---

[66] See the exchange of letters between Rose and Eldon on 4 May 1804, and Rose's
diary entry for the same day, in Harcourt, *Diaries*, II:76–79, 115.
[67] Eldon to Pitt, undated [probably 21–22 October 1804], PRO (Chatham papers),
30/8 132:151.
[68] Eldon to Redesdale, 31 December 1804, GRO (Mitford papers), 2002/3/1/23.

opening gambit in a more bruising conflict of royal interests than
he had yet experienced. The Prince of Wales wished to know why
he had received no official statement respecting the King's condition, given the 'extraordinary circumstances' of his Majesty remaining under the care of his doctors while he 'has so long been
said to be well & when he is actually in the full exercise of the
Royal functions'.[69] That such an inquiry would not please ministers is hardly surprising. The Prince remained firmly tied to the
political opposition, and his relationship with his father was
sufficiently bad that they no longer corresponded. Ministers,
consequently, suspected both the Prince's motives and the authorship of his inquiries, and probably had little interest in satisfying
him. Nor, indeed, was the Prince satisfied with Eldon's polite, but
bland, responses.[70] Hinting at the impropriety of ministerial
conduct, the Prince maintained that the communications he had
thus far received fell far short 'in both form and substance' of that
which he was entitled to receive.[71] This forced the Cabinet to
assume a more aggressive posture. Eldon, juggling the almost
daily visits to Kew with his other duties, and confident that the
King was competent, if frail, was stung by the Prince's suggestion
that the constitutional issue remained open.[72] He thus concluded
his letter of 10 June 1804 to the Prince:

In consequence of one part of his Royal Highness' letter, his Majesty's
servants feel it incumbent upon them to represent to his Royal Highness
that they have not been so unmindful of their own duty or of the province
of his Majesty's physicians as to have reference to the judgment of those
physicians any legal or constitutional point. The opinion of the physicians
founded upon a knowledge of the circumstances of his Majesty's situation,
fully confirmed by their own observations, appeared to them to form the
best ground upon which they can judge of the actual state of his Majesty's
health. Thus informed it has remained for them to regulate their publick
conduct in the discharge of the trust which his Majesty has been pleased
to repose in them by a sense of what their publick duty and their

---

[69] Prince of Wales to Eldon, 2 June 1804, BLA (Whitbread papers), W I/2421.

[70] See, e.g., Eldon's letters to the Prince on 2 and 5 June 1804, *ibid.*

[71] Wales to Eldon, 7 June 1804, *ibid.*

[72] See, e.g., George III to Eldon, Twiss, *The public and private life*, I:458
[misdated, probably 6 June 1804]; Eldon to George III, 6 June 1804, Aspinall,
*George III*, 4:208, in which, *inter alia*, the King congratulated Eldon on his son's
upcoming wedding; Eldon to Redesdale, 9 June 1804, GRO (Mitford papers),
2002/3/1/23. Here Eldon admits that the *duration* of the King's recovery is still
'very, very dubious'.

allegiance to his Majesty have indispensably required of them & by those considerations they must continue to be guided.[73]

The Prince retorted that, during the five months of the King's illness, ministers had kept the matter wholly within their own circle, and had failed to inform not only the Prince, but also the Privy Council and Parliament. '[M]inisters ... appear to conceive that the trust which His Majesty has reposed in them for very different purposes empowers them to exercise their own discretion on publick interests to which that trust certainly does not extend.'[74] Armed with a further favourable report of the King's condition, Eldon reminded the Prince that, far from being kept in ignorance during the earlier stages of the King's illness, he had received daily personal attendance from the physicians, and that these had been terminated with the Prince's approbation.[75] This jibe hardly satisfied the Prince, who charged Eldon with having failed to inform him of the King's condition during the months of April and May, when Eldon had apparently concluded that the King was competent, notwithstanding that the physicians were in constant attendance 'and that so late as the 31st of May mention is made in their report of symptoms still remaining which made them apprehensive of a relapse'.[76] This, however, proved to be the Prince's parting shot, and on 10 July Eldon indicated that the government considered the matter closed. He could not resist a somewhat condescending answer to the charges levelled against him personally.

The Lord Chancellor ... has to lament that he cannot feel it consistent with his duty to His Majesty to enter into a full explanation upon the subject. It is this consideration which compels him to restrain his anxiety to do justice to himself; an anxiety which must be proportioned to the consciousness which the Chancellor asserts, that in the discharge of his duty to the King, he has been actuated only by motives the most pure, and directed, in all circumstances, by the best judgment which he could form with respect to the nature of that duty, considering it with reference both to example and principle.[77]

---

[73] Eldon to Wales, 10 June 1804, BLA (Whitbread papers), W I/2421.

[74] Wales to Eldon, 19 June 1804, *ibid.*

[75] Eldon to Wales, 26 June 1804, *ibid.* See the physicians' report of 23 June 1804, *ibid.* See also Pitt's letter to Eldon of 22 June 1804, in which he reports Dr Simmonds as having found the King 'as well as he ever was in his life'. Encombe (Scott papers).

[76] Wales to Eldon, 2 July 1804, BLA (Whitbread papers). W I/2421.

[77] Eldon to Wales, 10 July 1804, Historical Manuscripts Commission, *Report of the manuscripts of J. B. Fortescue, Esq.* (London, 1912), VIII: 229.

No sooner was the issue of the King's health dropped than it appeared that further trouble, if not outright mischief, was in store for the government, on the subject of the Prince's daughter, Princess Charlotte. The Princess lived with her guardian, the Countess of Elgin, at Warwick House, not far from the Prince's London residence. The King, however, wanted his granddaughter to live at Windsor and be brought up under his direction. On 17 1804 July the Prince, through his friend the Earl of Moira, informed Eldon that 'nothing could be more gratifying to his Royal Highness than to see the Princess Charlotte taken under his Majesty's special direction'. It was, furthermore, hoped that the Princess should be entrusted exclusively to the King.[78] The King immediately understood the Prince to intend that the Princess of Wales should have no access to her daughter, and this wish the King was unwilling to gratify.[79] Nevertheless, Pitt felt that the Prince's conduct warranted, or at least provided an opportunity for, a formal reconciliation between father and son.[80] Shortly thereafter, the King seems to have suffered a mild relapse.[81] By the second week in August, however, Pitt was again describing the King's condition as very satisfactory,[82] and Eldon, accordingly, commenced efforts to arrange a personal meeting between the King and the Prince. The Prince agreed to wait upon the King on 22 August at twelve o'clock, but as late as half past ten on the day in question he changed his mind. In an interview with Eldon, the Prince indicated his conviction that the King had no genuine interest in a reconciliation and, on Eldon's request, he recorded his sentiments in writing. When Eldon read the resulting document, however, which stated that the Prince had 'in the course of two months received no one mark of that returning kindness for which he had so anxiously looked', and that the proposed interview might 'irritate' the King's mind, he refused to present it to the King.[83] Instead, he pressed the Prince to give illness as the reason for declining the interview. Such a message was indeed

[78] Earl of Moira to Eldon, 17 July 1804, Aspinall, *Wales*, V:55.
[79] George III to Eldon, 18 July 1804, *ibid.*, footnote 1.
[80] Eldon to George III, 18 July 1804, *ibid.*, 54; see Colonel McMahon to Northumberland, 25 August 1804, *ibid.*, 88.
[81] See the letters from Pitt to Eldon, of 23 July, 30 July, and 1 August 1804, Encombe (Scott papers).
[82] See the letters of Pitt to Eldon, 6 and 7 August 1804, *ibid.*
[83] See Wales to Eldon, 22 August 1804, Aspinall, *Wales*, V:80, footnote.

dispatched to the King, although at his audience on the following day Eldon informed the King broadly of the actual situation.[84]

Shortly after this setback, the King complicated matters by permitting the Princess of Wales to see Princess Charlotte during a visit to Windsor. When the Prince discovered this he threatened to terminate further negotiations regarding care of his daughter. On receipt of the Prince's letter to this effect, Eldon again informed the Prince of his intention to shield the King from both improper and distressing communications, and he advised the Prince to pursue a less aggressive policy. After pointing out the King's legal authority with respect to the care and education of members of the Royal Family, he suggested that the Prince proceed with the 'delicacy & caution which can alone lead to an arrangement consistent with his Majesty's rights' as well as the personal feelings of the King and Prince.[85] Further negotiations followed, and a meeting was successfully arranged for 12 November.[86] The King described that meeting to Eldon as having been in 'every way *decent*' and negotiations continued cautiously.[87] During the next few weeks, Eldon carried on a difficult and awkward correspondence, reflecting not only the genuinely strained relationship between the Prince and the King, but also the political hostilities of the men advising the two principals. Negotiations continued through Christmas, and by 28 December Eldon was advising the King to resist quibbling about every detail. 'It strikes the Chancellor as being ... exceedingly desireable [*sic*] to profit by the present disposition to secure the great object of the Princess's being well educated.'[88] General agreement was at last reached, and attention turned to the actual appointment of persons to supervise the Princess. Eldon continued to participate in these negotiations, offering his opinion on persons who might and might not be regarded as acceptable by the Prince, and ferrying communications between father and son. In March 1805 a further complication arose when the Prince submitted a proposal

---

[84] George III to Eldon, 22 August 1804, *ibid.*, 80; McMahon to Northumberland, 25 August 1804, *ibid.*, 88.

[85] Eldon to Wales, 30 August 1804, *ibid.*, 94–5.

[86] See the exchange of letters between Wales, Eldon, and George III, 7–11 November 1804, in *ibid.*, 121–124.

[87] George III to Eldon, 13 November 1804, *ibid.*, IV:125 footnote 2.

[88] Eldon's memorandum to George III, 28 December 1804, *ibid.*, V:157.

that the Princess live with him during those months when he resided in London. The King was incensed by this 'very improper paper' both on account of its substance, and by the Prince's attempt to communicate it through the Princess's newly appointed superintendent and governess. Intent on keeping the matter 'in its true channel, the Lord Chancellor's hands' the King instructed Eldon 'to consult with Mr Pitt and prepare a proper answer'.[89] Further negotiations followed, and in late November 1805 a compromise was finally achieved.

The burdens upon Eldon of this prolonged involvement in the affairs of the Royal Family were considerable. Not least was the physical strain of frequent journeys to Windsor and Weymouth when the King was absent from London, as well as attendance at Kensington Palace and Carlton House when the King and Prince wished to communicate with each other. Eldon had likewise acted as the royal channel of information on the ministerial negotiations. In the three-week period between 19 April and 10 May 1804, Eldon obtained at least thirteen audiences with the King.[90] In June of that year, when the King's state of health was still precarious, Eldon complained of the 'afflicting nature of the daily visits' he was obliged to make.[91] His own health suffered during two severe fits of gout, in the autumn of 1804 and the spring of 1805, which undoubtedly made regular travel difficult for him. Such was the value placed upon Eldon's personal communications with the King, however, that Pitt could write,

I am much concerned that you have been so unwell, and under those circumstances I feel very unwilling to say anything to induce you to undertake a troublesome journey. But if you should find yourself able to do so without material inconvenience, I cannot help thinking that your visit to Weymouth is of essential importance.[92]

The emotional strain was even more severe. The King's illness made him a difficult person with which to have regular contact. Certainly Eldon suffered from the petulance and rapid change of mood that characterised this phase of the King's illness. For

---

[89] George III to Eldon, 10 March 1805, Aspinall, *George III*, V:649. See Bishop of Exeter to Eldon, 8 March 1805, Historical Manuscripts Commission, *Fortescue papers*, VII:363.

[90] See *The Times* for this period.

[91] Eldon to Redesdale, 9 June 1804, GRO (Mitford papers), 2002/3/1/23.

[92] Pitt to Eldon, 21 October 1804, Encombe (Scott papers).

example, on 16 May 1804 the King wrote that he 'hopes to see the Lord Chancellor this day at three as he is most thoroughly tired of the unnecessary delays of the Lord Chancellor' while two days later he called Eldon 'his excellent Lord Chancellor, whose conduct he most thoroughly approves'.[93] Moreover, despite regular assertions of Eldon's 'attachment', the King could be not only demanding of the Chancellor's time, but irritable when he did not get it. Christmas Day 1804 was certainly no holiday for Eldon, and after wishing him the compliments of the season, the King required his comments upon the latest correspondence from the Earl of Moira.[94] Similarly, Eldon was expected to hurry from his son's wedding to meet with the Prince of Wales. Sending a report of that discussion to the King by a servant, Eldon explained that he would have 'personally brought [it] down to Kew if it had been possible for him to extricate himself from the engagements of the day'.[95] Nor could Eldon assume that his occasional absences would be lightly tolerated. In September 1804 the King complained to George Rose that the Chancellor's recent prorogation of Parliament had been scheduled so as to avoid holding a Cabinet at Weymouth, and when Eldon wrote to the King in mid-December, expressing his hope that he might wait upon the King when he returned to London, the King replied somewhat ungraciously that having 'banished every spark of irritation & impatience', he 'has with stoickal [*sic*] indifference waited the arrival of some information from his Lord Chancellor'.[96]

Relations with the Prince created further difficulties. The Prince had little cause to regard Eldon with favour, representing as he did not only the interests of his father but also those of his

---

[93] George III to Eldon, 16 May 1804, *ibid.*; George III to Eldon, 18 May 1804, Aspinall, *George III*, V:648.

[94] George III to Eldon, 25 December 1804, Aspinall, *George III*, V:649. In Eldon's reply of the same date, he assured the King that he was in contact with the Earl of Moira, and would see him on the following day. 'Your Majesty may rely upon receiving an accurate account of what has taken place, and shall take place ... probably, in the course of tomorrow or the succeeding day.' Eldon to George III, 25 December 1804, Aspinall, *Wales*, V:153.

[95] Eldon to George III, 22 August 1804, Aspinall, *Wales*, V:79. The King had previously written to congratulate Eldon on his son's marriage. George III to Eldon, 6 June 1804, Twiss, *The public and private life*, I:458; George III to Eldon, 20 August 1804, *ibid.*, 72.

[96] Harcourt, *Diaries*, II:169; Eldon to George III, undated [c.16 December 1804], *ibid.*, 147, footnote 1; George III to Eldon, 16 December 1804, *ibid.*

wife. To the Chancellor, conversely, the Prince was a person coached by opposition politicians who could nevertheless not be treated like one. Undoubtedly, the Prince's demands on the subject of the King's competence caused unease. Following his meeting with the King in November 1804, the Prince expressed shock at the King's condition, and he blamed Eldon for having made possible an inadequate medical regime that 'had removed the only chance of perfect recovery'.[97] That the opposition would attempt such a claim was hardly surprising, yet Eldon was apparently much affected by it. According to Thomas Grenville, 'the Ch[ancello]r Burst into tears, and bewailed himself for having ever accepted a situation which was the misery of his life, as his most conscientious desire of doing the best had ended in doing what was approved of by nobody'.[98] While there is no actual evidence that Eldon ever did improperly obtain the King's signature, the possibility that he might have done must have weighed heavily upon him. As he later confided to Redesdale:

it is impossible for me to represent my own situation, in which I was left much alone, too much perhaps, to determine what duty to the King and the public required to be done: little, if at all assisted, regarded by some with jealousy, and pursued by many with all the malice, that could be engendered by fair dealing ...[99]

Eldon was confident, moreover, that, were the King's health to fail completely, his successors in office would spare little time before subjecting his conduct to official scrutiny.[100]

As the situation of Princess Charlotte drew to a close, Eldon's first Chancellorship was in fact reaching its conclusion, although not as a result of a royal decline. The government would collapse following the death of Pitt in January 1806. For Eldon, however, this public tragedy would be overshadowed by a personal one.

---

[97] See Thomas Grenville to Lord Grenville, 11 November 1804, Historical Manuscripts Commission, *Fortescue papers*, VII:237–8. See Pitt's letter to Eldon of 12 November 1804, Encombe (Scott papers): '[T]he account I have just had of the interview tallies in the main with that sent you, but with the addition of great *lamentation* at having found the King so much *broken in all respects*. I find great efforts may be expected to be immediately made to prevent any further progress towards real reconciliation.' (emphasis in original).

[98] Thomas Grenville to Grenville, 11 November 1804, Historical Manuscripts Commission, *Fortescue papers*, VII:238.

[99] Eldon to Redesdale, 31 December 1804, GRO (Mitford papers), 2002/3/1/23.

[100] *Ibid.*

There is irony in the fact that a term of office so dominated by the health of the royal family should end with Eldon mourning the death of his own eldest son. John Scott died on 24 December 1805 after a short respiratory illness. Eldon was devastated, and in his grief lamented that he had ever consented to hold public office and involve himself in the affairs of government.[101] If the form of expression was somewhat affected by its immediate context, the underlying sentiment was not. Eldon was made miserable by the constant weighing up of the different personal demands placed upon him, and by the knowledge that his resulting conduct, however honestly resolved upon, would be subject to hostile comment. In the autumn of 1803 he had ponderously described his feelings on the conflict of loyalties between the King, Pitt, and Addington in a letter to Redesdale:

[F]eeling as I do that a man stands in a situation, necessarily injurious to character, do what he may, & let his intentions be purity itself, who, on the one hand, may be thought not true to those, to whom he has been attached in former life, & on the other not just to those with whom he may at present be connected, I have not been able to persuade myself that, let Mr P's claims be what they may upon me, let Mr A's be, in comparison, whatever they may be represented to be, that, let my own claims upon myself be whatever they can be stated to be, I can act with justice, or even pardonably towards the King, or with even a decent regard to the kindness, which he has ever shewn to me, of which you know much, if, under the present circumstances of his Government, of the administration, & the country, I was to consult my own ease, or my own wishes, in contradiction to what I sincerely believe to be his pleasure. For the present, therefore, I remain what I was, & I must commit myself to the consequences of my own conduct to such observation, as can be thrown upon it justly.[102]

Such resolution, however, had not made it any easier to bear the general assumption that he had betrayed Addington in the spring of 1804.[103] Relations with the King had exposed Eldon to similar dangers – the possible abuse of his obligations to the King or to the state, and the accusation of failure in one or both of these duties. He would leave office in 1806 before he could quite add to his dilemma the possible complication of a conflict of interest between members of the Royal Family. The next few years would provide opportunities for that as well.

[101]  Eldon to Redesdale, undated [*c.* January 1806], *ibid.*
[102]  Eldon to Redesdale, undated [*c.* autumn 1803] *Ibid.*
[103]  See, e.g., William Horner to John Horner, 14 May 1804, K. Bourne and W. B. Taylor (eds.), *The Horner papers* (Edinburgh, 1994), 332–3

# 11

# THE PRACTICE OF PATRONAGE

Before turning to Eldon's experiences upon leaving office in 1806, it is appropriate to consider an issue that affected the entirety of his public life as Chancellor, but about which little has yet been said. In addition to his own political responsibilities, Eldon had considerable authority with respect to government patronage. This resulted both from the powers of appointment vested in him as Lord Chancellor, and from the opportunity he had to influence patronage vested in the Crown. The areas thus within his sphere of influence were two: legal and ecclesiastical. In conjunction with the King and the Prime Minister, the Lord Chancellor settled judicial appointments. He played a similar role in the appointment of the Crown law officers, the creation of serjeants, and the elevation of King's Counsels, and he confirmed the Lord Lieutenants' nominations to commissions of the peace. Furthermore, he personally appointed over 100 administrative and judicial offices associated with the court of Chancery. Table 11.1 gives some indication of the Lord Chancellor's influence over legal patronage in England and Wales in the early nineteenth century.[1]

His influence in ecclesiastical appointments was of a comparable breadth. He enjoyed considerable practical influence in the appointment to the over 1,000 Crown preferments in England and Wales, as well as having approximately 800 preferments in his official gift. Table 11.2 indicates the extent of ecclesiastical

---

[1] No attempt has been made to include the Crown legal and judicial offices in Scotland, Ireland, and the colonies. Undoubtedly the Lord Chancellor *might* influence these appointments, but probably did so less frequently than those in England and Wales. When Robert Peel was Home Secretary, he sought Eldon's advice on Scottish appointments, but Eldon described this as unusual. See, e.g., his undated letter to Peel [*c.* November 1825] BL (Peel papers), Add. MS 40315 f. 229. Departmental legal appointments have also been excluded.

Table 11.1. *Early-nineteenth-century legal patronage of the Lord Chancellor*

| Westminster judges | Welsh judges | Justices of the Peace | Laws officers | Serjeants | King's counsel and serjeants | Chancery officials |
|---|---|---|---|---|---|---|
| 15 | 10[a] | 19,841/5,002[b] | 5[c] | 15[d] | 39[e] | 135[f] |

[a] Judges of the Welsh circuits, and of the court of Great Session for the County Palatine of Chester.

[b] In 1829, 19,841 persons were enrolled in commissions of the peace, and 5,002 were subsequently sworn. *Parliamentary papers* (1829) XVIII:189–90.

[c] The Attorney and Solicitor General, Advocate General, and the Attorney and Solicitor General of the Queen.

[d] This is the average of the figures provided for serjeants between 1800 and 1820 in R. A. Abel, *The legal profession in England and Wales* (Oxford, 1988), 484.

[e] There were, on average, thirty-four practising silks between 1800 and 1830, and five King's serjeants in 1830. *Ibid.*, 356, 484. Some prominent barristers chose to receive patents of precedence, in preference to taking silk.

[f] For a complete breakdown of Chancery offices, see Table 11.4, p. 211 below.

patronage directly and indirectly influenced by the Lord Chancellor.[2]

The patronage available to a minister such as Eldon consisted of both efficient offices, whose holders performed actual duties, and sinecures. The latter were posts whose duties were no longer performed, were no longer commensurate with their remuneration, or were performed by paid deputies. Sinecures were generally regarded as a species of property whose future as well as their present enjoyment could be conveyed. A reversion to an office conferred the right to succeed upon the termination of the current incumbent's tenure. This typically occurred upon the latter's death, but more complex arrangements were possible. The patronage system could fulfil a number of objectives. First, the absence of strictly merit-based appointments to efficient offices, and the existence of offices for which no particular ability was required, rendered the ability to appoint a source of considerable

[2] These figures have been calculated from the data supplied in 'Ecclesiastical revenues', *Quarterly Review* 29 (1823), 524–60; and *The extraordinary black book: an exposition of the united church of England & Ireland, etc.* (London, 1831). For a more complete breakdown of Church patronage in England and Wales, see Table 11.5, p. 211 below.

Table 11.2. *Early-nineteenth-century ecclesiastical patronage of the Crown and Lord Chancellor*

| Type of preferment | The Crown | | Lord Chancellor | |
|---|---|---|---|---|
| | Number | Percentage | Number | Percentage |
| Bishops | 26 | 100 | 0 | 0 |
| Deans | 28 | 100 | 0 | 0 |
| Prebendaries and canons | 53 | 10 | 21 | 4 |
| Collegiate church officials | 2 | 1 | 0 | 0 |
| Parochial clergy | 1048 | 10 | 780[a] | 7 |
| Total | 1157[b] | 9 | 801 | 6 |

[a] The Lord Chancellor was entitled to grant all the livings listed as having a value of less than £20 per annum in the *Liber regis*, the valuation book compiled in the reign of Henry VIII.

[b] This figure does not take into account the Crown privilege of presentation to all benefices and dignities held by persons nominated to bishoprics, which created the incentive to nominate persons whose promotion would free up several offices. N. Sykes, *Church and state in the eighteenth century* (Cambridge, 1934), 150–1.

political power. By the judicious use of this power amongst politicians and voters, ministers helped to maintain support for the government in Parliament. The practice of patronage could also have more specific consequences for those seeking and those making appointments. Where the basis of appointment was friendship, wealth, or a particular social or educational background, this naturally barred applicants who lacked the requisite credentials and concentrated power and influence within particular groups. Moreover, the right to sell an office, or to appoint one's friends and relations, constituted a valuable source of income for individual ministers. Like the right to collect fees for specific work performed, patronage helped to offset low salaries, which, in the case of the more ancient offices, might not have increased for many years.

Eldon was awake to each of these issues. He opposed abolition of the power to grant offices in reversion, arguing that it had been consistently executed with propriety and demanding evidence that abolition would really contribute to public utility.[3] He advocated

[3] T. Hansard (ed.), *The parliamentary debates from the year 1803 (1ˢᵗ series)*, 41 vols. (London, 1812–20), XIX:713. See Eldon's remarks concerning the Offices in Reversion Bill (1810) and the Sinecure Offices Bill (1812), *ibid.*, XVI:1070; XXIII:893.

the sale of commissions in the military because it prevented 'improper persons' from obtaining high rank.[4] He was perhaps most sensitive, however, to the importance of patronage to individual incumbents, and specifically to those holding senior judicial offices. Appointment to these tended to excite in the holder the expectation of a peerage. At the same time, the official stipend was insufficient to support an aristocratic lifestyle. A Chief Justice or Lord Chancellor lacking inherited wealth, or a great fortune amassed prior to elevation to the bench, could find himself in difficulties were it not for the patronage attached to his office. 'Patronage', affirmed Eldon during a debate in the House of Lords, 'was a main link in the chain that fitted each noble person who preceded him in office ... to have the personal means of holding rank consistently and suitably with others of their lordships.'[5] Consequently, he regarded proposals to reduce patronage as attacks upon vulnerable members of the administration. Replying to Earl Grosvenor's Bill in 1813 to reduce sinecures, Eldon complained:

noble lords who were born to great fortunes, were rather hard on the more laborious part of the community, who, like himself, had nothing but their salaries to subsist on. They were for weighing the public offices of professional men in the nicest balance, and for having them paid with the strictest economy.[6]

When he came to administer his own patronage, therefore, Eldon took into account four factors: personal advantage, political necessity, social prejudice, and the ability of the applicant. The ranking and relative weight accorded to each, however, varied according to whether the appointment in question was an efficient one or a sinecure, and whether it was legal or clerical in nature.

Shortly after he became Lord Chancellor, Eldon was warned by the Archbishop of Canterbury that Church patronage would destroy his peace. Events, Eldon would later acknowledge, had fully justified that warning.[7] The sheer volume of requests for preferments made the task of awarding them burdensome. After only a few weeks in office he was complaining to George Rose of receiving 'as many letters for preferment ... as if every parson in

---

[4] *Ibid.*, XIV:1016.   [5] *Ibid.*   [6] *Ibid.*, XXVI:222.
[7] Eldon to Richard Richards, undated [*c.* 1821], AMA Caerynwch (Richards) papers, Z/DA/64 SB33.

England were dead'.[8] He urged a successful candidate to send the information necessary to complete the appointment 'without delay – for the applications for this living have been infinitely numerous, & they will continue to multiply till a sealed presentation is seen at the office'.[9] In order to limit both the number of disappointed applicants and his own workload, Eldon determined to answer only the request of that person to whom he intended to give the living, to abandon the practice of promising any living not actually vacant, and to ignore all promises made by his predecessors.[10] Nevertheless, the particular pleas, and the identity of the suitor, made the task of sifting through them an onerous one. This was not because Eldon found it difficult to assess the pastoral or intellectual abilities of the men he appointed, because he does not seem to have troubled himself about such matters. Among his considerable surviving correspondence on the subject of Church patronage, there is only one mention of a professional qualification, namely the ability of an incumbent to a Welsh living to speak Welsh.[11] The requests that were easiest for Eldon to deal with, therefore, were those made by persons who had no personal or public demands upon him. Such requests could have only their substance to recommend them. Pertinacity, however, did not endear an applicant to the Lord Chancellor, as evidenced by Eldon's indignant report of a clergyman's attempt to secure a personal interview to discuss a living 'useful to him'.

If Mr V. had explained himself by writing, which he might easily have done, I have very little doubt that I should have been obliged to tell him that there is no piece of vacant preferment, which is not, in some way or other, pledged, but, as to personal interviews with a gentleman, an entire stranger to me, whilst I was in a course of daily employment, intolerably weighty, I really could not think of it . . .[12]

---

[8] Eldon to George Rose, May 1801, L. V. Harcourt (ed.), *The diaries and correspondence of the Rt Hon. George Rose*, 2 vols. (London, 1860), I:376.

[9] Eldon to Hugh Gabell, 8 May 1820, Winchester College Archives (Gabell papers), HG/19, reproduced by permission of the Warden and Fellows of Winchester College.

[10] Eldon to Richards, undated [*c.* 1821] AMA Caerynwch (Richards) papers, Z/DA/64 SB22. Eldon to Henry Reay, undated [*c.* 1801], Newcastle Central Library (Scott papers); Eldon to Lord Pelham, 28 October 1801, BL (Pelham papers), Add. MS 33108 f. 478.

[11] Eldon to Richards, undated [after 1817], AMA Caerynwch (Richards) papers, Z/DA/64 SB36.

[12] Eldon to Lord Lonsdale, 5 October 1815, CRO (Lonsdale papers), D/Lons/L1/2/46, copyright Lowther Family Trustees.

More difficult were the letters written by colleagues, friends, or powerful persons promoting the claims of favourite clergymen. Eldon's letter to Charles Yorke explaining the delay in appointing Yorke's protégé, which begins, '[W]henever I may have the pleasure of seeing you I venture to hope that we shall be better friends, relative to Mr Fox's matter, than I fear we now are', indicates that he understood the effect of his failure upon their relationship.[13] Indeed, when Yorke wrote to thank Eldon for the eventual appointment, he admitted to having felt anxious and disappointed by the Chancellor's inattention: 'I thought myself, in some degree slighted by one, whose colleague I had the honor to have been, for no very short time; & whom I had always considered as my friend.'[14] Moreover, there were various 'local' expectations that Eldon had to recognise, if not accommodate – that livings in Warwickshire should be distributed according to the wishes of the Earl of Warwick – that the family of the Duke of Beaufort should always have a stall in either Bristol or Gloucester cathedral – that the livings attached to Winchester should be awarded only to fellows of that college.[15] Finally, Eldon frequently received communications from various members of the Royal Family with respect to preferments, 'which are commands, that supersede even promises to others'.[16] Princess Mary might request a cathedral stall for a clergyman whose fiancée's mother had been 'unremitting in her attentions & kindness to both my sister and myself' during the Princesses' stay in Weymouth.[17] The Duke of Cumberland, upon noticing 'a place in Liverpool worth

---

[13] Eldon to Charles Yorke, 26 December 1814, BL (Hardwicke papers), Add. MS 45045 f. 130. Eldon wrote in a similarly anxious vein to Lord Wellesley: 'whenever I shall have the pleasure of seeing you, I am sure I shall satisfy you that I had not the power of acting as to the living of Rede, as has been wished.' BL (Wellesley papers) Add. MS 37313 f. 319.

[14] Yorke to Eldon, 30 December 1814, BL (Hardwicke papers), Add. MS 45045 f. 132.

[15] Eldon to John Eardly-Wilmot, 2 October 1810, Yale University Beinecke Rare Book and Manuscript Library (Osborn files) 11.388; Eldon to the Duke of Wellington, undated [c.17 December 1821], SUL (Wellington papers), WP1/688/21; Lord Liverpool to Eldon, 13 September 1813, BL (Liverpool papers), Add. MS 38302 f. 175.

[16] Eldon to Reay, 28 September 1801, Encombe, (Scott papers).

[17] Princess Mary to Eldon, 5 December 1810, A. Aspinall (ed.), *The correspondence of George Prince of Wales (1770–1812)*, 8 vols. (London, 1967–71), VII:95, footnote 1.

£3,000' might drop Eldon a note informing him that it would 'do'
for a clergyman friend of his.[18]

Eldon found all of this 'provoking beyond endurance', because
it reduced the number of livings he could give to his own friends
and relations. That he regarded the opportunity to present clergymen according to his personal preference as a perquisite of his
office and as a moral obligation is clear. While he does not seem
actually to have made a large number of appointments on this
basis, his failure was not the result of disinclination. He lamented
his inability to oblige those 'who have claims upon me', and he
resented the constant stream of requests from persons, 'upon some
such notion as that I cannot myself have in the world a clergyman,
that I can have any personal wishes in favour of'.[19] His troubles
were compounded by the fact that he had, or felt he had, so few
livings at his disposal. Throughout his period as Chancellor,
Eldon complained that very few livings actually became vacant.
Writing to his cousin, Henry Reay, he observed: 'I have been very
unlucky, for the gentlemen who labour to consign others to
immortality seem to cling themselves amazingly to this mortal
world, and the rarity with which I have had vacancies of livings, is
really remarkable: certainly not in the proportion of one to a
dozen.'[20] To George Canning he reported having received
between 800 and 900 applications a year for posts that averaged
two or three vacancies a year. 'You may therefore easily conceive
what a state this Head of Patronage is in.'[21]

While the burden of ecclesiastical patronage was more time-
consuming, that of legal patronage was more complicated. Two
factors account for this. First, Eldon's management of his legal
patronage included a consideration of professional ability. Where
the legal office was a complete sinecure, he awarded it according to
the demands of family, friendship, and politics; but where the
office was an efficient one, a range of professional issues also

---

[18] Duke of Cumberland to Eldon, November 1807, A. Aspinall (ed.), *The later
correspondence of George III*, 5 vols. (Cambridge, 1962), V:582, footnote. The
Duke thought it especially suitable for his friend as 'I understand it may be done
by deputy'.

[19] Eldon to Reay, 28 September 1801, Encombe (Scott papers). See also Eldon to
Liverpool, 31 December 1808, BL (Liverpool papers), Add. MS 38243 f .69.

[20] Eldon to Reay, 28 September 1801, Encombe (Scott papers).

[21] Eldon to George Canning, 7 May 1807, LDA (Harewood papers), HAR GC/
34A.

became relevant. Nor is this surprising, given Eldon's own circumstances and the nature of the offices under his guardianship. He was qualified to assess a lawyer's aptitude, while he had no comparable knowledge with regard to a clergyman. Moreover, his ecclesiastical patronage, particularly those preferments over which he had the greatest control, consisted substantially of parochial livings, and not the great offices of the Church. In contrast, his legal appointments affected the profession at the highest levels. A second factor was the ongoing nature of his involvement. Once he had appointed to a Church living, Eldon's interest in it ended until it became vacant again. The appointee to a senior legal office, however, could expect that his present conduct and future prospects would, in some degree, be under the eye of the Lord Chancellor.

Eldon considered a variety of factors in assessing an individual's capacity to serve as a judge. These included demonstrable skill as an advocate, and evidence of a broad professional knowledge. The dynamics of the particular court were also relevant. For example, a prospective baron of the court of Exchequer had to be conversant with the principles of both the common law and equity.[22] A judgeship in the Great Court of Session at Chester required experience of both Welsh and English circuit practice.[23] Moreover, in filling a judicial vacancy Eldon was obliged to consider the capabilities of the other members of the court, in order to achieve a balanced bench. In a letter to the King in 1807 recommending that George Wood succeed to the Exchequer, Eldon explained:

having only the choice of proposing to your Majesty to place in that Court, ... some gentleman whose professional employment has been principally in a Court of Law, or some gentleman whose professional employment has been principally in a Court of Equity, it is more for your Majesty's service to add to the present three Judges who all practised in Courts of Equity, one eminent Common Lawyer, having an unusually extensive knowledge of the Revenue Laws, than to add to those Judges another, skilled only in matters of Equity: and this the Court itself has strongly felt.[24]

This is not to say, however, that Eldon was oblivious to

---

[22] See, e.g., Eldon to Liverpool, 27 January 1827, BL (Liverpool papers), Add. MS 38302 f. 198.

[23] Eldon to the Prince Regent, 29 January 1818, A. Aspinall (ed.), *The letters of George IV, king of England, 1812–1830*, 3 vols. (Cambridge, 1938), II:242.

[24] Eldon to George III, 5 May 1807, Aspinall, *George III*, IV:574.

political considerations where his profession was concerned. When he appointed Joseph Jekyll to a mastership in Chancery in 1815, Eldon was popularly regarded as having yielded to pressure from the Prince Regent.[25] Sir Samuel Romilly complained in his diary:

If the Chancellor had meant to show with what deliberation he could make a bad appointment to a very important judicial office, and with how strong a sense of the impropriety of it, he could surrender up to the Prince that patronage which it is a duty he owes to the Public to exercise himself, he could not have contrived matters better than he has done.[26]

Eldon's attitude toward the political dimension of legal appointments was actually a complex one. Certainly he felt an appointee's politics were worth mentioning. In a letter to Liverpool on the expected vacancy in the court of King's Bench, Eldon regarded it of 'great importance' to appoint a man 'who has been uniformly acting upon the principles of your administration'.[27] A likely appointee to the court of Common Pleas was 'perfectly sound' on 'his principles as to State and Church'.[28] When suggesting the appointment of Serjeant Copley to a Welsh judgeship, Eldon explained to the Prince Regent, 'as your Royal Highness's servants seem to think it of importance to advance Mr Ser[jean]t Copley, the vacancy of Chester might be useful in that respect'.[29] On the other hand, in 1825 he cited with approval the recent strengthening of the Scottish judiciary, achieved 'by looking more to the professional merit than to the family or clan, to which the intended judge belonged'.[30] Still in the Scottish context, he voiced no objection to appointing a man whose politics 'without being

---

[25] Eldon confirmed the story in his *Anecdote book*, ed. A. L. J. Lincoln and R. L. McEwen (London, 1960), 106. Sometimes, however, Eldon was given a free hand by members of the Royal Family. See, e.g., Queen Charlotte to Eldon, 21 May 1816, H. Twiss, *The public and private life of Lord Chancellor Eldon*, 3 vols. (London, 1844), II:282. When considering the appointment of a new Chief Baron in 1817, the Regent confided to Eldon that: 'Any recommendation from you, you may be certain, my dear friend, ever will and must meet with my entire concurrence and approbation.' *Ibid.*, 292.

[26] Samuel Romilly, *Memoirs of Sir Samuel Romilly*, 3 vols. (London, 1840), III:186.

[27] Eldon to Liverpool, undated [following 8 October 1818] BL (Liverpool papers), Add. MS 38273 f. 205.

[28] Eldon to the Prince Regent, 22 November 1818, Aspinall, *George IV*, II:260.

[29] *Ibid.*

[30] Eldon to Peel, 14 September 1825, BL (Peel papers), Add. MS 40315 f. 202.

vehement, are not favourable to us'.[31] Moreover, he expressed the belief that all members of the bench should not hold the same political opinions. He was less concerned about a genuine narrow-mindedness, however, than that appointments should have the actual and perceived effect of perverting an appointee's independence to a sycophantic adherence to government.[32]

Romilly's belief that the Chancellor was invariably guided by 'party politics', therefore, was only partly true, and also failed to acknowledge Eldon's social bias, which led him to favour men educated at public schools and one or other of the universities, preferably Oxford.[33] On conveying to the King Thomas Plumer's acceptance of a Welsh judgeship in 1805, Eldon could not resist mentioning that Plumer's 'excellent public principles' had been formed 'when this gentleman, after going through a state of tuition in University College, became one of its Fellows'.[34] A university education, Eldon explained to Liverpool in 1818, was even more important for a judge than his professional eminence. Moreover, he thought it 'imprudent' to make appointments 'which will increase a persuasion which our profession rather seems to have adopted, that non-academical men, & strong Opposition men, are preferred to men, educated at the Universities & uniformly acting, in their sphere, with [the] Administration'.[35]

Finding men with the requisite combination of personal, professional, and political qualifications was not the only consideration involved in making appointments, however. Within the senior ranks of the legal profession there existed an unofficial but generally recognised hierarchy of public offices. The Solicitor General was junior to the Attorney General. Depending upon their abilities, both could properly aspire to judicial posts. A well-regarded law officer could expect to succeed to one of the three chief judicial posts in the common law courts, shying away from the King's Bench if he did not fancy criminal work, and leaning

---

[31] Peel to Eldon, 23 October 1823, *ibid.*, f. 95. See Eldon's undated reply, *ibid.*, f. 97.
[32] Eldon to Peel, 14 September 1825, *ibid.*, f. 202.
[33] Romilly, *Memoirs*, III:102.
[34] Eldon to George III, 23 March 1805, Aspinall, *George III*, IV:302.
[35] Eldon to Liverpool, undated [following 8 October 1818], BL (Liverpool papers), Add. MS 38273 f. 205.

toward the Exchequer if he wanted a lighter workload. An Attorney or Solicitor General with less impressive credentials might have to make do with one of the nine junior or puisne judgeships, competition for which would be open to leading silks and serjeants. The ultimate prize for an equity lawyer was the Lord Chancellorship, with the subordinate posts of Master of the Rolls and, after 1813, Vice Chancellor also highly sought. These were also the proper goals for law officers, or for Chief Justices aspiring to greater wealth and political consequence. When a vacancy occurred in a senior judicial office, therefore, this usually created a chain reaction within the profession, as the holders of comparable or inferior posts considered, and expected to be considered for, possible lateral or vertical moves. Orchestrating an appointment, consequently, involved the Chancellor in a series of nice judgments of how best to re-arrange the senior ranks of the profession so as to satisfy individual ambitions, reward faithful service, placate special interests, and maintain professional standards.

An example of the complications faced comes from the autumn of 1818, when Lord Ellenborough, Chief Justice of the King's Bench, indicated a desire to retire. Professional courtesy dictated that the Attorney General, Sir Samuel Shepherd, be offered the post, although it was felt that he would decline on account of his deafness. The Solicitor General, Sir Robert Gifford, was considered too young to be Chief Justice. Eldon and Liverpool meditated on elevating Charles Abbot, a puisne justice of the King's Bench. Abbot, Eldon observed, had previously moved from the Common Pleas in order to support Ellenborough, 'and he was authorised to consider his removal as a sacrifice'. On the other hand, Eldon objected to the appearance of a predetermined arrangement. '[I]n the nature of the thing, a question upon such a situation as C[hief] J[ustice] of [the] K[ing's] B[ench] must always be known to be quite open.'[36] The appointment of Abbot, moreover, might raise particular difficulties in that Ellenborough had so efficiently employed the patronage associated with the office that his successor could not expect to gain much from the appointment beyond the salary. Abbot's own fortune was not suffiiicient to support the peerage that usually accompanied the

[36] *Ibid.*

Table 11.3. *Changes in legal and judicial appointments, 1818–1819*

| | Solicitor General | Attorney General | Justices of the Common Pleas | Justices of the King's Bench | Chief Justice of the Common Pleas | Chief Justice of the King's Bench |
|---|---|---|---|---|---|---|
| 1818 | Gifford | Shepherd | Dallas Park Burrough | Abbot Bayley Holroyd | Gibbs | Ellenborough |
| 1819 | Copley | Gifford | Park Burrough Richardson | Bayley Holroyd Best | Dallas | Abbot |

Chief Justiceship. A further complication occurred at the same time in the collapse of Vicary Gibbs, the Chief Justice of the court of Common Pleas. It was not felt appropriate to move Abbot back into that court, even if Shepherd were to accept the King's Bench, while Gifford refused the Common Pleas on the grounds that he could not yet afford to leave the more lucrative situation of a law officer. In the end, Abbot became Chief Justice of the King's Bench without a peerage. Shepherd left the English bar for the Scottish court of Exchequer, and Robert Dallas, a puisne justice of Common Pleas, replaced Gibbs. Gifford was promoted to Attorney General, and Copley became Solicitor General. The alterations in the English offices between 1818 and 1819 are shown in Table 11.3. As Eldon admitted afterwards to Lord Kenyon: 'Upon the whole, we endeavoured to do the best we could: we could not do what really would have been unexceptional. It was impossible.'[37]

The question of judicial succession arose again in 1824, during the negotiations to bring Charles Wetherell into the government as Solicitor General.[38] Eldon and Liverpool agreed to tell Wetherell that he should not expect an automatic promotion to the judiciary whenever a vacancy occurred.[39] Unfortunately, following separate discussions with the Prime Minister and the

---

[37] Eldon to Lord Kenyon, 14 November 1818, Twiss, *The public and private life*, II:322.

[38] For Wetherell's claims to office, see A. Aspinall (ed.), *The diary of Henry Hobhouse (1820–1827)* (London, 1947), 108–9.

[39] Liverpool to Eldon, 28 December 1823, BL (Liverpool papers), Add. MS 38302 f. 101.

Chancellor, Wetherell understood that the former wished to impose an express stipulation preventing his advancement, which Wetherell felt to be both demeaning and unprecedented. This, Liverpool assured Eldon, had never been his intention.[40] Eldon was obliged to see Wetherell and assure him that while no such stipulation was required, neither ought a law officer to expect his private wishes to take precedence over the interests of the government. Eldon was particularly concerned by the frequency with which men had passed through the offices of Solicitor and Attorney General in recent years. Not only did a brief tenure preclude a thorough understanding of the duties of these offices, but the habit of accepting promotion to puisne judgeships 'has *deeply affected* the dignity of the Law Officers in general estimation'.[41]

Judges too could cause problems over their promotion or workload. Sir William Grant, when Master of the Rolls, demanded to be excused from judicial sessions of the Privy Council, and the government was sufficiently desirous of keeping him in office to accede to his wishes. When puisne judges raised the matter of elevation to chief justiceships in India, however, Eldon was unhappy with the prospect. He warned the King about creating such a precedent:

The Chancellor humbly takes leave to state that, in his judgement, the judicial seats in Westminster Hall ought to be made, in point of emolument, such that a Puisne Judge of those Courts could have no temptation to cease to be such, unless by promotion to the offices of Chief Justices there. Whether such a most desireable improvement does or does not take place it is a matter to which the most serious consideration should be given, before a precedent should be made, which would induce gentlemen in the profession to accept Puisne Judgeships in your Majesty's Courts in Westminister Hall; not with a view of retaining their judicial seats there but in order the more readily to pave the way to their becoming Chiefs in India.[42]

While the senior legal appointments consumed the greater portion of the Lord Chancellor's time, the lesser offices and ranks of the profession were not without their complications. In 1810 Eldon forbade the Bishop of Durham to remove names or omit

---

[40] Liverpool to Eldon, 1 January 1824, *ibid.*, Add. MS 38302 f. 140.
[41] Eldon to Liverpool, undated [January 1824], *ibid.*, Add MS 38302 f. 156 (emphasis in original).
[42] Eldon to George III, 4 November 1824, Aspinall, *George IV*, III:93.

former magistrates from commissions of the peace in that county. The upset caused by the Bishop's conduct is suggested by Eldon's understated report of the matter to Earl Grey:

I further added [to the Bishop] that I was happy in knowing that such a circumstance could not occur again in the county Palatine while the Bishop lived and I held my office; and that as the matter had been matter of great publicity, and the Bishop had my authority to communicate such my sentiments, I hoped no occurrence of the same kind would happen between the magistrates of the county and our successors.[43]

On another occasion Eldon was obliged to defend one of his clerks, when a Cumberland justice, mistakenly omitted from a commission, was 'somewhat intemperate' in his effort to rectify the error.[44] The elevation of barristers to the rank of King's Counsel was always an administrative problem, requiring the Lord Chancellor to consider both the professional pretensions of individuals, and the necessity that each circuit have an appropriate number of silks. Politics, of course, could not be discounted. The most notable occasion of this kind concerned the elevation of Henry Brougham and Thomas Denman. In 1820 Queen Caroline named Brougham and Denman as her Attorney and Solicitor General, respectively. In this capacity they successfully defended her against the charges of adultery made pursuant to the Bill of pains and penalties.[45] While this greatly enhanced their standing with the public, it did little to endear them either to the government or the King, and for eight years the rank of King's Counsel was denied them. Whether the ban was the work of Eldon or the King is unclear. In private, and once notoriously in public, Eldon maintained the latter. In a letter to his daughter, he explained Brougham's parliamentary attacks upon him as the result of misdirected pique. 'No young lady was ever so unforgiving for being refused a silk gown, when silk gowns adorned female forms, as Brougham is with me, because, having insulted my Master, the insulted don't like to clothe him with distinction, honour, and silk.'[46] Brougham, however, certainly thought that Eldon was

---

43 Eldon to Earl Grey, 30 March 1810, W. E. Surtees, *A sketch of the lives of Lords Stowell and Eldon* (London, 1846), 109.

44 See Eldon's letters to Lonsdale of 28 and 31 December 1819, CRO (Lonsdale papers), D/Lons/L1/2/46, copyright Lowther Family Trustees.

45 For the Queen's trial, see chapter 15.

46 Eldon to Lady Frances Bankes, 5 February 1825, Twiss, *The public and private life*, II:537. In an unguarded moment, possibly the result of intoxication, Eldon

behind the ban, and seems to have attempted to bypass him by petitioning the King via Sir John Leach, the Vice-Chancellor. An account of this incident is provided by Henry Hobhouse:

[T]he situation of Mr B. in the profession gave him no pretensions to expect a silk gown, and that his acceptance of the appointment from the Queen gave him no right to ask a favour of the King. Last week however, L[or]d Eldon received from Sir J. Leach (who had probably been persuaded by Mr B. to advise H[is] M[ajesty] to this effect) a message commanding the Chancellor to grant to Mr B. and Mr D. the precedency, of w[hi]ch they were ambitious. The Chancellor was highly offended both by the substance and the channel of this communication, has not obeyed the command, and has not since been at Carlton House.[47]

Whatever his feelings on that occasion, the King was confidently affirming his opposition to Brougham during an audience with the Duke of Wellington in January 1824, and did not relent in favour of either Brougham or Denman until the autumn of 1828.[48] Where appointment did not properly rest with the Chancellor, Eldon declined to involve himself. In 1822 and again in 1826, Peel asked his advice on appointing an officer to act for the Crown in

revealed during a public dinner in June 1825 that the objection to Brougham had come from the King and not the Chancellor. This was made known to Brougham, who stated in the Commons that he had authority to understand that this was not the case. Mrs. Arbuthnot reported the incident in her diary, noting: 'the King is so angry he is wanting to make a number of silk gowns for the purpose of leaving Mr Brougham out.' H. Arbuthnot, *The journal of Mrs. Arbuthnot (1820–1832)*, ed. Frances Bamford and the Duke of Wellington, 2 vols. (London, 1950), I:402. See also G. Peel (ed.), *The private letters of Sir Robert Peel* (London, 1920), 402, footnote 2. In his *Anecdote book*, 142, Eldon claimed that, far from objecting to the claims of Brougham and Denman, he had attempted to advance them. 'My suggestion always was that it did not become the dignity of his Majesty to manifest that the Conduct of Mr B. should so affect him – and I stated the great Inconvenience and Injustice which it occasioned to other Gentlemen at the Bar, as promoting them in their profession was not merely overlooking Brougham, but doing him the Injury, as it would be thought, of making promotions to his prejudice – that it was not merely refusing him a favor by not promoting him in the ordinary course of professional advancement, but degrading him by advancing others.'

[47] Aspinall, *Hobhouse*, 20. See Brougham to Lord Hutchinson, 16 April 1820, Aspinall, *George IV*, II:320.

[48] Wellington's account of the audience is reported in Arbuthnot *Journal*, I:279. Writing to Sir William Knighton on 8 October 1828, Wellington stated: 'I have not yet spoken to the King upon this subject since I have been serving His Majesty as his minister, but I did once before speak to him upon it at the suggestion of Lord Eldon. He then manifested a very strong feeling of repugnance to allow Mr Denman to appear before him.' SUL (Wellington papers), WP1/963/22.

Wales. On both occasions Eldon demurred, on the grounds that the decision rested principally with the Attorney General, and 'The Chancellor does not point out to the A[ttorney] General of the King who should be his representative on the Welsh circuits'.[49]

When the legal appointments were at last settled, the nature of the Chancellor's work shifted from selection to administration, and here too the effort required was substantial. Foremost among Eldon's duties was ensuring that the regular and occasional judicial commissions were adequately manned. This did not always prove an easy task, as judges frequently refused to serve on commissions, on account of age, infirmity, or disinclination. Even when they did agree to serve, the conventions of seniority as between the judges of different courts further complicated the task of empanelling a bench. Eldon described to Lord Sidmouth the difficulties of arranging a special commission in 1812:

I presume the Chief Justices and Chief Baron won't go – & indeed in special commissions in the county it is not usual to insert them. In the King's Bench there is Mr Justice Grose; it is too hard to place him at the head of such a commission, & he must be at the head of it, if he goes. Mr Justice Le Blanc had the hard task of the Lancaster special com[missio]n The other judge of that court is Mr Justice Baily. In the Common Pleas Mr Justice Heath & Mr Justice Chamber are hardly equal to the labour of such a business: If Mr Justice Gibbs goes he must be the junior in the com[missio]n In the Exp[cheque]r. There is Baron Thompson – he had the labour of the Lancaster special com[missio]n – & has had very hard work otherwise lately. Mr Baron Graham – can he be at the head[?] and Baron Wood we can't have with any junior but Gibbs. Upon my word I don't know what to do with these difficulties but I will talk to Lord Ell[enborough].[50]

Eldon was often obliged, in consequence, to draft pleading letters to his particular friends among the judges to fill the gaps. In a letter to Chief Baron Richards regarding service on a commission to try participants in the Luddite riots at Derby in 1817, Eldon explained the awkwardness of his own situation:

The Chief Justice of [the] K[ing's] B[ench] is gone abroad by medical persuasion, to see what dissipation of mind may do, but the body is not

[49] Eldon to Peel, undated [*c.* August 1826], BL (Peel papers), Add. MS 40315 f. 262. See also the exchange of letters in April 1822, *ibid.*, ff. 6, 7.

[50] Eldon to Lord Sidmouth, 14 November 1812, DevRO (Sidmouth papers), 152M/c1818/OH35.

what it was. The C[hief] J[ustice] of C[ommon] P[leas] seems to me also
to be in very indifferent health. It was impossible to put either of them on
these [*obscured*] into the special commission, & Government thought that
there must be a Chief ... I put a fourth judge into the commission in
order that you might be at least relieved as much as possible, if you could
not get attendance dispensed with – and I have felt the more about you,
because of the laborious & anxious time which you had at Lancaster.[51]

An indication of the complexities of judicial management can be
gleaned from Eldon's letter to Liverpool in early 1827:

I fear I cannot suggest any thing preferable to what you propose as to the
Common Pleas. The difficulty – perhaps the strongest – with respect to
that proposal is that it brings to the head of the court of Law & Equity
that judge, whom Ellenboro[ugh] used, in his way, to say was distinguished only by his unparalleled nonscience, and that the Chief Baron is
the only chief who goes the Spring Circuit, and another Chief, I am sure,
won't go for him – Baron Graham has thro' me desired leave to retire. His
successor will be the junior judge of the Court, unless some senior is
removed from some other court. Bailey [*sic*] has desired to go to that court
– but I am sure he can't be spared out of the King's Bench. I have not yet
a successor's name to suggest to you.[52]

With such various concerns as individual ability, court dynamics,
political expediency, and professional ambition, it would not be
surprising that the management of legal patronage should prove
time-consuming. It certainly did so prove for Eldon. His own
caution, when coupled with the complexity of the situation,
resulted in a process that was much protracted, and the source of
complaint at all levels. The diaries of Romilly and Hobhouse
speak of '3 weeks' deliberation' and 'great inconvenience to the
suitors' resulting from Eldon's failure speedily to appoint a Chief
Justice of Common Pleas and masters in Chancery.[53] Sir Joseph
Jekyll observed of Eldon's failure to name new King's Counsels in
time for the spring circuit: 'It is now rumoured he will ponder on
the subject for months.'[54] Nor would royalty always be able to
prod the Lord Chancellor into action. In 1817 the Regent urged

---

[51] Eldon to Richards, 3 September 1817, AMA Caerynwch (Richards) papers, Z/
DA/64 SA21.
[52] Eldon to Liverpool, undated [January 1827], BL (Liverpool papers), Add. MS
38302 f. 196.
[53] Romilly, *Memoirs*, III:186; Aspinall, *Hobhouse*, p. 110.
[54] Joseph Jekyll to Nathaniel Bond, 4 March 1816, DorRO (Bond of East Holme
papers), D/BOH367/C11. In a second letter to Bond on 2 April 1816, Jekyll

Eldon swiftly to name a new Attorney General, lest they both be swamped with applications for the post:

Forgive me also, my dear friend, if I add and bring to your recollection (and I can hardly do so without its forcing at the same time a smile on my countenance), that a snail's gallop is but a bad thing, and a very poor pace at best, in most of the occurrences of life, and I am sure that you would particularly find it such in the present.[55]

When he wished to remind Eldon to appoint a particular individual a commissioner of bankrupts, George IV pointed out that he had put the request in writing 'in order that it may not escape your recollection'.[56]

While he did administer his patronage with part of his attention focused upon factors other than individual ability, Eldon was sensitive about the whole issue of patronage. He was offended when, on the eve of his resignation in 1827, he was overwhelmed with requests for clerical preferment, 'full of eulogies upon my virtues, all of which will depart when my resignation actually takes place, and all concluding with, "Pray give me a living before you go out." '[57] He was also anxious that he not be perceived as having overstepped the mark in exercising his patronage to his personal advantage. When discussing patronage questions generally in Parliament he could not resist including a personal note of vindication. A speech defending the practice of granting offices in reversion must reveal that he 'had procured three or four reversions for his family, without the smallest conception that he was doing any thing wrong'.[58] A plea to raise judicial salaries to realistic levels must contain the observation that 'the office of lord chancellor of England did not produce one farthing more at the present day than it did upwards of a century ago. As for the offices in his gift, he should only say, that he was more sparing in the

---

noted that when Eldon did fill the vacancies, he appointed so many King's Counsel that he failed to obtain the proper political benefits. *Ibid.*

[55] Prince Regent to Eldon, 2 May 1817, Twiss, *The public and private life*, II:293.

[56] George IV to Eldon, 26 March 1823, Encombe (Scott papers). Three months later, pointing out that there were two vacancies, the King sent Eldon a further message on the subject, and including a play on the tag Eldon liked to give as that which guided his professional conduct, *sat cito, si sat bene* (quickly enough, if good enough). The King suggested *bis dat qui cito dat* (he gives twice as much who gives quickly). George IV to Eldon, 1 July 1823, *ibid.*

[57] Eldon to Bankes, undated [April 1827], Twiss, *The public and private life*, II:594.

[58] Hansard, *Parliamentary debates (1st series)*, XV:599.

exercise of that privilege than many of his predecessors.'[59] This self-consciousness got him into trouble when, in retirement, he described criticisms then being levelled against Lord Plunkett, the Lord Chancellor of Ireland, as 'of very trifling importance' when compared with those *he* had endured.[60] This comment provoked an inquiry into Eldon's exercise of patronage, and upon reference to an incomplete Commons Report of 1802, he was, like Plunkett, accused of having improperly advanced the interests of his family.[61] Eldon was furious, and moved an inquiry in the Lords into the appointments he had made as Lord Chancellor. This created yet another opportunity for him to repeat his assertion that he had never wished to be Lord Chancellor, but had been 'drawn forth' by the King and had only complied 'from a sense of that duty which he owed to the commands of the Crown'.[62] The inquiry revealed that Eldon's benevolence to his family had been unexceptional.[63] Both the Duke of Wellington and Eldon's successor, Lord Lyndhurst, defended his conduct in office, the latter

[59]  T. Hansard (ed.), *Parliamentary debates from the year 1803–new (2nd) series*, 25 vols. (London, 1820–30), XIII:1285.

[60]  T. Hansard (ed.), *Hansard's parliamentary debates 3ʳᵈ series*, 365 vols. (London, 1831–91), IV:291. Lord Plunkett was accused of having appointed an excessive number of his relatives to valuable offices, the most notorious instance being the appointment of a second, obviously unqualified secretary, to a post normally filled by a single person, where a competent individual was already in post.

[61]  Referring to the notation in the report that Eldon's son, William-Henry Scott had held six offices in 1802, Spring Rice MP remarked: 'No doubt, had there in the instance which he cited been six sons, thirty-six offices would have been distributed among them.' *Ibid.*, X:1218.

[62]  *Ibid.*, XI:92–3.

[63]  In 1805 Eldon had conferred upon his son the reversions to two Chancery offices which were partially (Clerk of Letters Patent) or completely (Register) in the gift of the Crown. These, Eldon explained, had been pressed upon him by the King as a mark of affection. They were worth £553 and £1,816 per annum, respectively, and the reversions had fallen due at the latest by 1825. In 1813 he had appointed his son Receiver of Fines, an office worth £240 per annum, and in 1816 conferred upon him the reversion to the office of Cursitor, which fell due after six years. In 1826 Scott received a further sum of £3,629 to compensate him for the loss of fee earnings, under the authority of 6 Geo. IV c. 96. Eldon pointed out that in 1813 his own income had been reduced by £2,500 per annum to provide for the salary of the new office of Vice-Chancellor, and he had subsequently given up £1,800 per annum when additional Bankruptcy Commissioners were created. In Eldon's opinion, therefore, he had certainly not enriched his family, and had only gone a small way in restoring what had been lost by various reforms. The above figures are taken from *The extraordinary black book*, 480; the offices are noted in *Parliamentary papers* (1825), XIX:295–6. See also Hansard, *Parliamentary debates 3ʳᵈ series*, XI:93–5.

stating that 'nothing could be more liberal, as well as more correct, than the conduct pursued by his noble and learned friend and those connected with him'.[64]

In assessing Eldon in terms of the issue of patronage, a distinction is helpfully drawn between his actual dispersal of places, and his general views of the system. With respect to the former, his conduct cannot be said to have advanced the career of any great lawyer or divine, or even to have made important artistic or scholarly endeavours possible. On the contrary, his conduct produced results that were probably typical of the system as a whole, whereby ability, privilege, favouritism, and luck all played a part. Eldon's attitude toward ecclesiastical appointment suffers most from a comparison with that of his contemporaries and close successors in public life. Even in his own day, the view that such appointments could be made without much attention to theological and pastoral qualities was challenged, and the stress upon competence increased during the 1830s and 1840s.[65] Eldon's conduct, however, was less a rejection of responsibility than an illustration of his own attitude toward Christianity. Not a man to ponder the intricacies of doctrine, or to assess critically a preacher's oratory, he probably felt that a rather perfunctory statement of orthodoxy and temperament sufficed for any appointment with which he had to deal. Eldon's approach to legal patronage, particularly as regards appointments to efficient offices, was both more sophisticated and more in step with contemporary mores. His focus on ability, political affiliation, and social circumstances continued to characterise judicial appointments throughout the nineteenth century. Most judges were former members of Parliament, if not also former law officers.[66] Moreover, despite the growing professionalisation of the bar, the bench remained largely the province of men with the additional lustre of a university education.[67]

Eldon's attitude toward patronage generally also merits further

---

[64] Hansard, *Parliamentary debates 3rd series*, XI:103–4, 109.

[65] See, e.g., G. Kitson Clark, *The making of Victorian England* (New York, 1982), 155–7.

[66] W. R. Cornish and G. Clark, *Law and society in England 1750–1950* (London, 1989), 21–2.

[67] D. Duman, *The English and colonial bars in the nineteenth century* (London, 1983), 106–13.

consideration. At first glance, Eldon's view appears to exemplify Harold Perkin's 'Old Society', in which bonds of 'vertical friendship' linked persons of different ranks to create a unified, hierarchical, social, political, and economic structure.[68] Indeed, Eldon did support the use of 'influence', and he resisted the attempts both to curb powers of appointment and to reduce the value of sinecures and reversions. Moreover, while it did not happen overnight, the trend which had begun in the late eighteenth century to reduce patronage and raise administrative efficiency continued in the nineteenth. Eldon's attitude reveals more, however, than merely an adherence to an increasingly old-fashioned approach to administration; it suggests a particular habit of mind. He was not inclined, and perhaps not able, to think about this issue on a large scale. When asked to consider the reduction of judicial patronage, he correctly identified the immediate objectionable consequence – an undesirable reduction in judicial income. For him, this was sufficient. He was not inspired to question whether judges *ought* to be maintained by a power to appoint to sinecures, or whether a different compensation scheme should be imposed. When the latter *was* proposed, however, he supported it, nor did he express any wish to maintain older fee structures as they concerned his own income.[69] This suggests, not merely a determination to stand by the old ways, but an inability to think creatively and proactively about them. With such a habit of mind, an adherence to the *status quo* becomes less a dogma than an inevitable consequence.

[68] H. Perkin, *The origins of modern English society 1780–1880* (Toronto, 1981), 44–50.

[69] Eldon supported curbs on judicial patronage and the abolition of fees when these were coupled with a substantial increase in salaries in 1825. Hansard, *Parliamentary debates, new (2nd) series*, XIII:1284. See chapter 16.

Table 11.4. *Chancery offices in the gift of the Lord Chancellor in the early nineteenth century*

| Office | Number of posts in gift of Lord Chancellor | Number of posts filled by relations of the Lord Chancellor |
| --- | --- | --- |
| Accountant General | 1 | – |
| Master in Chancery | 11 | 1 |
| Deputy Register | 2 | – |
| Clerk of the Reports | 1 | – |
| Entering Clerk | 2 | – |
| Cursitor | 24 | 2 |
| Commissioner, Bankrupts | 70 | 3 |
| Register, Bankrupts | 1 | – |
| Commissioner, Lunatics | 5 | – |
| Clerk, Letters Patent | 1 | 1 |
| Examiner, Letters Patent | 1 | – |
| Purse-bearer | 1 | – |
| Principal Secretary | 1 | 1 |
| Receiver of Fines, Cursitors Office | 1 | 1 |
| Secretary, Decrees, Injunctions, Appeals | 1 | 1 |
| Secretary, Commissions Peace, Bankrupts | 1 | – |
| Secretary, Commissions of Lunacy | 1 | – |
| Secretary, Presentations | 1 | – |
| Secretary, Briefs | 1 | – |
| Gentleman of the Chamber | 1 | – |
| Usher of the Hall | 1 | – |
| Persons for keeping order in court | 4 | – |
| Total | 133 | 10 |

*Source: Parliamentary papers* (1825), XIX: 295–7

Table 11.5. *Church of England patronage in the early nineteenth century[a]*

| Source of patronage | The Crown | Lord Chancellor | Bishops | Oxford and Cambridge universities | Cathedrals, collegiate churches | Private individuals |
| --- | --- | --- | --- | --- | --- | --- |
| Total preferments | 1,157 | 801 | approx. 1,600 | approx. 600 | approx. 1,000 | 8,268 |

[a] As the above figures are not exact, the total (13,426) does not tally exactly with the total number of preferments given in the same sources (13,327). Using the lower figure, the Crown still appointed 9 per cent and the Lord Chancellor 6 per cent of preferments.
*Source:* 'Ecclesiastical revenues', 29 (1823), 524–60; and *The extraordinary black book: an exposition of the united church of England & Ireland, etc.* (London, 1831)

# 12

## CUT AND THRUST

On 27 January 1806, having been informed by the remnants of William Pitt's last ministry that they could not carry on after the death of their chief, the King sent for Lord Grenville. In partnership with the long-excluded Charles Fox, Grenville formed the administration known as 'The Ministry of All the Talents'. For Eldon, the prospect of opposition – perhaps of a very lengthy duration – or of retirement, lay before him. In fact, he would be out of office for just over one year, for in May 1807 he returned to the Woolsack in the Pittite ministry of the Duke of Portland. In the years between 1806 and 1810 Eldon became more closely linked with overt political action, as evidenced by his parliamentary conduct, his involvement in Cabinet intrigues, and his relations with the royal family. The King continued to rely on him, and Eldon was not averse to using such political weapons as came his way. Opposition leaders came to see his hand in every scheme, every manoeuvre to thwart their aspirations. This, however, led them both to over-estimate the extent of his power and to misunderstand the direction of his interests. While a fighter of considerable and growing skill, Eldon's experience of political warfare was far from uniformly happy.

In the spring of 1806, with his son's death still fresh in his mind, Eldon professed to have little interest in current public affairs. He wrote to his friend, the Revd Samuel Swire,

At the end of thirty busy years, I have nothing to do, I mean with this world, but the great work of preparing myself for another; and I am afraid that *that* is much to do, when a man has been immersed in this world's business, and such part of its business as I have been engaged in for so many years.[1]

[1] Eldon to Samuel Swire, undated [endorsed 31 March 1806], H. Twiss, *The public and private life of Lord Chancellor Eldon*, 3 vols. (London, 1844), II:4.

He was led inexorably, however, back into politics, both by inclination, and by what he conceived to be his public obligations. The troubles of the Royal Family provided him with his means of entry. On several previous occasions, rumours had spread about the conduct of the Princess of Wales, but these had been officially ignored. In the autumn of 1805, however, the Prince of Wales had insisted upon an examination of the charges levelled by Lady Douglas, a neighbour and former friend of the Princess. Lady Douglas had alleged, *inter alia*, that the Princess had conducted a liaison with Rear Admiral Sir Sidney Smith, and had given birth to a child, perhaps Sir Sidney's, in 1802. In May 1806, therefore, the King appointed a commission of inquiry to investigate the charges. Membership consisted of Lords Grenville, Erskine, Spencer, and Ellenborough, and Sir Samuel Romilly, the Solicitor General.

These events naturally occupied the attention of the Princess. During the commission's deliberations she claimed that her evidence was being withheld, and even after it issued a cautious acquittal, she expressed concern that the King would remain unconvinced of her innocence.[2] Not surprisingly, she turned for assistance to the surviving leadership of the previous government, Eldon among them. He attended a dinner on 15 June 1806, along with George Canning, Lord Castlereagh, and Spencer Perceval, at which they considered how the Princess ought to proceed. They determined that she ought to prepare a defence to be sent to the King, and this document was duly written. Eldon's precise role is uncertain, but he seems at least to have contributed to the drafting. Lord Holland described the Princess's defence as being 'the joint composition of Lord Eldon, Mr Perceval, and Mr Plomer; the first furnishing the law, the second the argument, and the third the prolixity'.[3] Certainly Eldon was to have been the means of its delivery. He could do so because he had been, at about this time, helping the King to revise his will.[4] On 16

[2] See, e.g., the letters of the Princess of Wales to Eldon of 24 June and 25 July 1806, *ibid.*, 23–4. The Commissioners issued their report on 14 July 1806. In it they acquitted the Princess of the specific charge of adultery, but expressed concern about other evidence of indelicate behaviour on her part.

[3] H. R. V. Fox, Lord Holland, *Memoirs of the Whig party during my time*, ed. H. E. Fox, Lord Holland, 2 vols. (London, 1852–4), II:151. See also J. Farington, *The Farington diary*, ed. J. Greig, 8 vols. (London, 1924), II:48.

[4] See, e.g., the exchange of letters between the King and Eldon on this subject in

September 1806, the Duke of Cumberland wrote to Eldon, convinced 'that no one would be properer upon all accounts to present the Princess's papers than yourself ... [T]here is no one for whom the King has a *greater respect and regard* than for you.'[5] In the event, the King declined to receive the document from other than ministerial hands, and Thomas Plumer delivered it to the Chancellor, Erskine.[6] That Eldon had probably involved himself in the affair, however, was generally assumed within the government. Lord Auckland thus observed to Grenville:

I have happened to hear from good authority that Lord Eldon's journey (or journeys) to Windsor was (or were) not relative to the Princess, but professedly on the subject of a new will which the King is making, and on which Lord Eldon had heretofore been consulted. I do not learn, however, that the conference was confined to testamentary discussion.[7]

Eldon certainly remained in contact with the Princess during the autumn and winter.[8] When the Cabinet finally advised the King in January 1807 to receive the Princess at Court, she promptly sought Eldon's help in drafting a suitable answer.[9] She was likewise 'anxious to have Lord Eldon's advice' when she suspected that the King's hesitation in granting her an interview resulted from the machinations of her husband.[10]

Nor was Eldon's interest in public affairs limited to involvement in royal matters. Despite his assertions only a few months previously that he was done with politics, by the autumn he was expressing a renewed attention. In a letter of 10 October 1806 he acknowledged to Lord Redesdale: '[I]f a system embracing all my old friends, and supporting my old principles is adopted I will

---

A. Aspinall (ed.), *The later correspondence of George III*, 5 vols. (Cambridge, 1962), IV:462, 464. See also Earl of Ilchester (ed.), *The journal of Lady Elizabeth Holland 1791–1811*, 2 vols. (London, 1908), II:193.

[5] Duke of Cumberland to Eldon, 16 September 1806, Encombe (Scott papers) (emphasis in original).

[6] Eldon to George Canning, 11 October 1806, LDA (Harewood papers), HAR GC/34A.

[7] Lord Auckland to Lord Grenville, 19 September 1806, Historical Manuscript Commission, *Report of the manuscripts of J. B. Fortescue, Esq.* (London, 1912), VIII:339.

[8] See, e.g., the letters of the Princess of Wales to Eldon of 13 October and 16 November 1806, Twiss, *The public and private life*, II:26, Encombe (Scott papers).

[9] Princess to Eldon, 28 January 1807, Encombe (Scott papers).

[10] Princess to Eldon, 7 February 1807, *ibid.*

take my fair share.'[11] Moreover, his assessment of the political situation since his resignation indicates that he had remained aware of manoeuvres behind the scenes, if he had not been personally involved in them. To Redesdale and to Sir William Scott he wrote of his suspicions that certain of his former colleagues, principally George Canning, were flirting with the government and hoping to be reconciled with Grenville. He lamented the King's failure to make overtures to the opposition following the death of Fox in September, and expressed feelings of guilt at having 'deserted' the King upon Pitt's death.[12] He even began speaking of his own chances of office, albeit in a less than cheerful manner:

I think the Chancellorship would never revert to me, even if things had taken another turn, and it is not on my own account I lament the turn they have taken. As to any other office, I could have no motive, on my own account, to wish for any, and, with a disposition to co-operate for the good of others who have public objects, I have only to pray God to continue to me, if it be His pleasure, the other sources of happiness of a private kind.[13]

By early 1807, moreover, his tone had improved distinctly. In January he wrote to Lord Melville to solicit the latter's views on a Pittite government. He expressed himself willing to take an active part, so long as no move was made to combine with the Foxite elements of the present government. He also claimed to have been playing a more or less active role in attempting to facilitate a unified political opposition. 'I had also, for twelve months past, observed, not without grief, that all my exhortations to plan, to union, to system, had been thrown away upon every body here.'[14] That Eldon was expected to take an active hand in political

---

[11] Eldon to Lord Redesdale, 10 October 1806, GRO (Mitford papers), D2002/3/1/23.

[12] *Ibid.*; Eldon to Sir William Scott, undated [following 24 October 1806], Twiss, *The public and private life*, II:11.

[13] Eldon to Sir William Scott, undated [following 24 October 1806], *ibid.*

[14] Eldon to Lord Melville, undated [January 1807], *ibid.*, 16. Eldon's arguments against a union with Grenville are also found in his letter to George Rose, undated [late January or early February 1807], BL (Rose papers), Add. MS 42774B f. 205. See Canning's letter of 7 February 1807 to Rose on the same subject, L. V. Harcourt (ed.), *The diaries and correspondence of the Rt Hon. George Rose*, 2 vols. (London, 1860), II:311. See Eldon's letter to Canning of 11 October 1806 on the need for organisation among the Pittites. LDA (Harewood papers), GC 34A.

manoeuvres by this time is evident from a letter Canning wrote to his wife in late February. In it he explained how the former ministers had determined to supplant their successors as royal advisers. In his capacity as 'the friend of the K[ing] and the whole family', Eldon was to go to Windsor and discuss a reconciliation with the Princess.[15] Eldon seems to have had his audience on 8 March 1807. Whether it was *intended* that he should use the occasion to criticise the government's plan to extend the Irish Act of 1793 is not clear. Nor is there any proof that they *did* discuss military appointments for English Roman Catholics. Canning mentioned no such plan to his wife, but as he remained in communication with Grenville almost to the moment of the latter's dismissal, he may not have been privy to all the plans of Eldon, Lord Hawkesbury, and Perceval. Certainly Lord Sidmouth, an increasingly uncomfortable member of the coalition government, reversed his advice to the King on the propriety of extending the Act at about this time, and this should not be discounted.[16] It is highly likely, however, that if the King *did* seek Eldon's opinion, any hostility to the government's position was encouraged.

One week after his audience with Eldon, the King informed ministers that he would not countenance any extension of the privilege granted to Irish Roman Catholics in 1793 to hold certain military commissions. On 19 March 1807, following ministers' refusal to accept a royal ban on further discussion of the issue, he dismissed them and sent for Eldon and Hawkesbury. That these two, and especially Eldon, had previously been involved in secret negotiations with the King swiftly became the charge of the late government.[17] When Parliament resumed in mid-April, Lord Howick explained both the steps taken 'to poison the royal mind' and to execute the King's prejudices against his ministers:

On the Saturday before the pledge was required, lord Eldon had an interview with his majesty; what passed at that interview, he [Howick] did

---

[15] Canning to Joan Canning, 28 February 1807, A. Aspinall (ed.), *The correspondence of George Prince of Wales (1770–1812)*, 8 vols. (London, 1967–71), VI:138, footnote 2.

[16] For an analysis of the evolution of Sidmouth's position, see P. Jupp, *Lord Grenville, 1759–1834* (Oxford, 1985), 403–8.

[17] See, e.g., Lord Howick to Grenville, 4 April 1807, Historical Manuscripts Commission, *Fortescue papers* (London, 1915), IX:131–2.

not pretend to state; that he would leave to the house to conjecture. He must also observe, that before he had liberty to state that a new administration was forming, lord Eldon and lord Hawkesbury had been sent for to Windsor.[18]

Such attacks prompted Canning, now Foreign Secretary, to speak on behalf of the newly restored Lord Chancellor:

[D]oes he [Howick] not know what was the cause of lord Eldon's visit to Windsor? Does he or does he not know, that previous to his going to Windsor, lord Eldon waited on lord Grenville, and communicated to him distinctly the subject of his intended interview with the King, adding, at the same time, a solemn assurance, that he would mention no other subject to his majesty. The noble lord may insinuate that lord Eldon did not keep his word. I believe he did, and at least I may safely leave it to the house to determine whether the conduct of lord Eldon, such as I have described it, affords fair grounds for a presumption of insincerity and falsehood?[19]

For his part, Eldon relied upon the 'uniform tenor of his public life' to combat any charges of improper conduct. '[H]e should continue to serve his sovereign to the best of his abilities, without fearing any responsibility that might attach to his official conduct.'[20] Writing after the fact, Lord Holland would suggest that Eldon might have strengthened the King's resolve to act against his ministers.

[P]ossibly some intermediate communication with Mr Perceval or Lord Eldon – the latter of whom on the pretext of private concerns he saw about this time – led him to repent of the concessions he had made, and afforded him a prospect of getting rid of, not only a Bill of which he disapproved, but of a Ministry which he feared and detested.[21]

Restored to the Lord Chancellorship, Eldon did nothing to weaken his reputation for political manipulation in the next sessions of Parliament. Reform of the administration of justice in Scotland and vindication of the Orders in Council to restrict neutral shipping were matters requiring legal and constitutional interpretation, and might have been expected to attract the attention of the Lord Chancellor in debate. While Eldon certainly did not ignore the legal dimension in his remarks, his parliamentary contributions were characterised equally, if not more, by their

---

[18] T. Hansard (ed.), *Parliamentary debates from the year 1803 (1st series)*, 41 vols. (London, 1812–20), IX:639.
[19] *Ibid.*, cols. 343–4.    [20] *Ibid.*, col. 422.    [21] Holland, *Memoirs*, II:194.

reliance on the political dynamics between the government and opposition.

Grenville had previously expressed an interest in reforming Scottish judicial administration, prompted by the frequent appeals from the Scottish Court of Session to the House of Lords. These had proved burdensome for the Lords, and expensive for suitors. Possible remedies offered by Grenville in June 1806 had been an alteration of the structure of the Court of Session, the introduction of civil jury trial, and the establishment of an intermediate court of review.[22] He had repeated these proposals in early February 1807, when he had given notice of his intention to introduce legislation on the subject.[23] On that occasion, Eldon had given cautious support to the principle of reform, and had promised that 'he should most cheerfully contribute all that his experience and humble abilities enabled him to afford towards the advancement of the business'.[24] Whatever he had meant by such benign public expressions, he was soon expressing himself quite forcefully in private. In early March he affirmed to Henry Erskine, the Lord Advocate: 'Taking the purpose of this Bill to be unobjectionable, I have read the Bill with amazement again and again as the worst and most ignorantly and imperfectly drawn legislative composition that I have seen.'[25] He went on, however, and at considerable length, to express his objections to the substance of the proposals. Alteration of the Court of Session from a single, 15–judge chamber into three five-judge chambers would militate against efficient and uniform procedure, and would not increase the number of cases being resolved.[26] The introduction of jury trial in all but very specific classes of cases would prove extremely burdensome, because the Scottish court's jurisdiction included matters whose resolution did not depend upon a specific factual question that could be answered by a

---

[22] Hansard, *Parliamentary debates*, VII:730–5.     [23] *Ibid.*, VIII:602–3.

[24] *Ibid.*, col. 603. See Eldon's similarly bland statement of 16 February 1807, *ibid.*, cols. 792–3.

[25] Eldon to Henry Erskine 4 March 1807, Historical Manuscript Commission, *Report on the Laing manuscripts* (London, 1925), II: 702.

[26] See Eldon to Erskine, 5 March 1807, *ibid.*, 708. The Court of Session's power to regulate its proceedings was confirmed by a statute of 1541. The Court instituted changes in procedure, and sometimes in substantive law, by issuing Acts of Sederunt. O. F. Robinson, *et al.*, *European legal history*, 2$^{nd}$ edn (London, 1994), 233.

jury.[27] Finally, the introduction of an intermediate court of review would violate the Act of Union of 1707, which guaranteed the existence, authority, and privileges of the Court of Session.[28]

Despite these very strong principled objections, however, Eldon's remarks of 16 March in the House of Lords were couched in unnecessary platitudes, prompting an irritated Grenville to reply that he:

thought it unnecessary for the noble and learned lord to remind their lordships that this subject demanded their earnest and anxious attention, as those by whom the measure had been brought forward had not failed to impress upon the house the great importance of the measure, and had earnestly solicited for all the assistance which could be derived for its completion.[29]

Two days later, Eldon was still throwing out innocuous suggestions.[30] No sooner had he resumed the Woolsack, however, than his public conduct with regard to Scottish law reform began to reflect his private sentiments. While keeping quiet about his legal objections he simply obstructed the Bill. First, he wanted to hear the views of the Scottish judges, a request that necessitated loss of time not only in obtaining them, but also in searching the precedents to determine whether, and in what manner, they could be received by the House of Lords. Next, having suggested that a division of the Court of Session into two chambers might be preferable to three, he withdrew from that position and began arguing that the infliction of heavy costs, and not reorganisation of the court structure, would reduce the number of appeals.[31] It is not surprising that, as the Bill's survival looked increasingly unlikely, the friends of the former government abused Eldon for his apparent shift in attitude. He denied both unfairness and inconsistency, claiming 'he had never pledged himself to any further support, than a bare admission that some alteration was necessary in the manner of administering civil justice in Scotland'.[32] Moreover, he blithely refused to state what course he

---

[27] Eldon to Erskine, 4 March 1807, Historical Manuscript Commission, *Laing papers*, pII:703-7.

[28] See 6 Anne c. 11, art. 19. Article 19 also provides that the Parliament of Great Britain may enact regulations for the better administration of justice.

[29] Hansard, *Parliamentary debates*, IX:111.     [30] *Ibid.*, cols. 147-8.

[31] See the debates of 25 March, 8 April, and 17 April 1807. *ibid.*, cols. 188, 281, 481-4, 486.

[32] *Ibid.*, col. 494. In announcing his intention to continue his efforts on behalf of

would take if the Bill were rejected, and when Grenville attempted
to bring in further legislation in June, Eldon professed himself a
friend to the principle of reform, but argued that it was too late in
the session to tackle such a complicated subject.[33]

As an example of an issue upon which he might have taken a
strictly legal view, Eldon's conduct with regard to the Orders in
Council was even more suspect. Like the Scottish courts question,
this issue could be traced to actions of the Grenville government.
In January 1807 it had issued an Order in Council whereby
French ports and those of its allies and satellites had been subject
to a British blockade, as a reply to a series of French decrees
closing French-controlled ports to all vessels coming directly from
British-controlled ports. In November 1807, the Portland government issued more stringent Orders, namely, that all neutral ships
wishing to visit any ports subject to the British blockade must
proceed first to a British port to obtain a licence and pay a re-
shipment duty. The harmful effect of these Orders on neutrals
was increased when the French government ordered the confisca-
tion of those neutral vessels who had submitted to them. In
Britain, the opposition criticised the Orders of 11 November 1807
as contrary to statute and the law of nations, and as likely to drive
neutrals, particularly the United States, into the arms of France.

Eldon did support both the legality and utility of the government's actions. With respect to the effect on the United States, he
hoped that America would be 'sensible of the policy of joining
with us in opposition to the wild and extravagant pretensions of a
power whose object is to crush us both'.[34] During debates in
February and March 1808, however, he increasingly justified the
Orders by reference to what the Grenville government had done
in the previous year. The Orders of January 1807 had recognised
the Crown's right to retaliate against an enemy expressing an
intention to prevent trade in British commodities. The Orders of

the Bill, Grenville announced that *he* 'would not desert his duty and opinions,
  although other noble lords were careless in the performance of the one and the
  recollection of the other.' *Ibid.*
[33] *Ibid.*, cols. 666–7. The following year Eldon did bring in a Bill to divide the
  Court of Session into an inner and outer chamber, the jurisdiction of the inner
  being mainly appellate. At the same time a commission was set up to inquire
  into the efficacy of extending the civil jury trial to Scotland. In 1815 Parliament
  enacted the 55 George III c. 42, which provided for civil juries in Scotland.
[34] *Ibid.*, X:476.

November 1807 had simply exercised that right.[35] Eldon claimed to take for his guide a letter that Lord Howick, the former Foreign Secretary, had written to the Danish minister. This letter,

a most able exposé of the law of nations as applied to the case, clearly marked out the course which the government of this country was justified and bound to pursue under the circumstances which arose out of the extraordinary acts of the enemy.[36]

Grenville called Eldon's speech on this occasion, 'a laboured attack upon the late ministers under cover of an ironical defence', and claimed that while it 'might do very well for a party purpose' it was bereft of both argument and principle.[37] The principle of taunting the ex-ministers with their own policies, however, served Eldon's purposes very well, both on that occasion and subsequently. When Grenville later moved an address to the Crown to rescind the Orders, Eldon again argued that their substance and the principle of retaliation had been recognised in January 1807, and that the address went contrary to the determined views of the House.[38]

Political management of a more overt kind occupied Eldon, together with the other members of the government, in the summer and autumn of 1809. At that time internal disagreements threatened not only to break up the Cabinet, but so to weaken the remnants as to necessitate a complete rearrangement of the government. Disintegration was precipitated by Canning's dissatisfaction with his colleagues, and particularly with Castlereagh's handling of the War Office. In late March 1809 Canning had privately presented his demands to Portland: Castlereagh must give up his department, or Canning would resign. Portland, himself in bad health, and alarmed by the consequences of such a conflict, had offered his own resignation, which the King had refused. There followed instead a period of some five months, during which Portland attempted to impose an arrangement which would satisfy Canning and save Castlereagh from humiliation. Unfortunately, the feasibility of his scheme was never put to the test, because Castlereagh's uncle, Earl Camden, could not be brought to inform him of what was going on. This placed not only Canning, but gradually the remainder of the Cabinet, in an uncomfortable situation *vis-à-vis* their colleague, for while he

---

[35] *Ibid.*, col. 474.  [36] *Ibid.*, col. 972.  [37] *Ibid.*  [38] *Ibid.*, XII:799.

planned what would turn out to be the disastrous military expedition to the Scheldt, they remained silent about his likely political fate. When Castlereagh finally learned the truth on 7 September 1809, he resigned the following day. This did not, however, resolve the situation, but only precipitated the larger problem of Cabinet restructuring. With Portland's health failing, leadership of the government was at stake. It soon became clear that Canning was certainly unwilling to accept subordination in the Commons, and possibly not in the Cabinet. Various constellations of ministers, former ministers, and potential ministers began circling the King in an effort to convince him that they could find him a strong, congenial administration.

Eldon had become aware of the Castlereagh situation in late May and, at Portland's request, had undertaken to discuss Canning's demands with the King.[39] It was upon the threatened break-up in September, however, that Eldon's role seems to have become crucial. On 9 September he presented himself for consultation, an offer which the King accepted, promising that as soon as he discovered the intentions of Portland and Canning, he 'will not fail to apprize the Lord Chancellor'.[40] Within the week Eldon, Liverpool,[41] and Perceval were debating with the King, and among themselves, what ought to be done. Opposition politicians, observing what was going on, considered Eldon the leading force in what was left of the government. In a letter to Earl Grey describing a likely offer of merger, George Tierney affirmed, 'but, as I should suppose the Chancellor cannot expect that this offer will be accepted I look upon the whole game as up with Ministers'.[42] Thomas Grenville likewise warned his brother to be wary of any proposed coalition, which he believed would not be made with any expectation of its being accepted. 'I suspect this

---

[39] Duke of Portland to Eldon, 26 May 1809, Twiss, *The public and private life*, II:79.

[40] See the exchange of letters between Eldon and the King on 9 and 10 September 1809, and again on 12 and 13 September 1809. Aspinall, *George III*, V:336, 342.

[41] Lord Hawkesbury had succeeded his father as Earl of Liverpool on 17 December 1808.

[42] George Tierney to Earl Grey, 13 September 1809, Aspinall, *George III*, V:362, footnote. In a letter of the previous day Tierney had described the situation to Grey thus: 'Matters at last came to such a pass that the King directed the Chancellor to be sent for.' *Ibid.*

the more because I think such a project is very likely for the Chancellor to conceive, and for the King to entertain.'[43]

Thomas Grenville was right to link Eldon's name with that of the King, but his assessment of Eldon's part in any offer of coalition was somewhat wide of the mark. Certainly Eldon's sympathies and loyalty remained firmly with his 'old master', and he considered the evolving situation in terms of its effect on the King. In his private letters to his wife at this time he repeatedly referred to ministers in such terms as 'each of us as the King places any confidence in' and 'such of us as have hearts feeling for the King'.[44] He told the King of 'my likings and dislikings' among the ideas proposed, either by letter or in person, 'for I write constantly when I don't see him'.[45] There can be little doubt that Eldon gloried in the King's reference to him as 'my sheet anchor', and when he learned from Liverpool that the King had 'impatiently, and with great zeal, insisted upon my being retained' he immediately related the fact to his brother.[46] Whether he would consent to continued royal service in a coalition government was another matter. Eldon's attitude toward a coalition was complex, but not quite so machiavellian as the opposition suspected. He firmly opposed treating with Grenville and Grey. In part this was an expression of his long-standing hostility to coalitions. 'I think it never strengthens anybody, and it does nobody credit.'[47] That a coalition would have unpleasant personal consequences, however, he certainly recognised. He admitted to Lady Eldon: 'In the first place, I think nobody, that joins from other parties, would join, unless I cease to be Chancellor.'[48] As

---

[43] Thomas Grenville to Grenville, 22 September 1809, Historical Manuscript Commission, *Fortescue papers*, IX:320.

[44] Eldon to Lady Eldon, 14 September 1809, Twiss, *The public and private life*, II:93; Eldon to Lady Eldon, 15 September 1809, Aspinall, *George III*, V:354, footnote.

[45] Eldon to Lady Eldon, 15 September, 1809, Twiss, *The public and private life*, II:93.

[46] Eldon to Lady Eldon, 15 September, 1809, *ibid.*; Eldon to William Scott, undated [*c*. 20 September 1809], *ibid.*, 97. The King's remarks, delivered at an audience with Perceval, were recorded in a letter from the latter to Liverpool of 19 September 1809. Aspinall, *George III*, V:349, footnote.

[47] Eldon to Lady Eldon, undated [*c*. 14 September 1809], Twiss, *The public and private life*, II:90. See also Eldon's letter of 22 July 1809 to George Rose, in which Eldon reflected again on the damaging effects of a coalition between Pitt and Fox. BL (Rose papers), Add. MS 42774 f. 251.

[48] Eldon to Lady Eldon, undated [*c*. 14 September 1809], Twiss, *The public and*

Perceval and Liverpool tended towards coalition, however, Eldon
found himself in awkward disagreement with his colleagues.
When support for the government within its junior ranks seemed
to fade in late September, the prospects of coalition improved. In
a letter to his brother probably written on 19 September 1809,
Eldon wrote: 'It goes to coalitions in the way I told you I thought
it would. I could see nothing else that could be thought of, and
was obliged to submit. If it is accepted, of course I consider *myself*
as gone.'[49] He refused, however to be 'a negotiator for junction',
and described as the King's the view that Grey and Grenville
would refuse any tender made to them.[50] Far from having been
the advocate of a calculated political gamble, Eldon seems to have
had great difficulty remaining in office at all during the negotiations. He wrote to his brother:

If it [coalition] takes place, there is something horribly offensive, shockingly degrading in it – and feeling *that* most bitterly it was, that I asked
you whether I was right in doing as the King might wish. For in truth, a
sense of duty, even to him, will not bear me quite up in a state which I
feel so disgusted at.[51]

Eldon spoke here of his having remained at his post in accordance
with the King's wishes. Tierney opined that Eldon's conduct in
that respect resulted from a personal fear of royal criticism:

He has not forgotten the reproaches he met with from his master for
having advised the surrender of the Government upon the death of Mr
Pitt, and he will this time endeavour to convince him that he does not
walk off from panic but from the impossibility of staying where he is.[52]

While Eldon's correspondence does mention the King's pleas not
to be abandoned, his own concern seems to have been more that
mental strain would result in another period of illness. Writing to
Lady Eldon after a lengthy audience, Eldon observed of the King:
'His agitation and uneasiness were such as have left me perfectly
agitated and uneasy.'[53] The following day, when he had not

---

*private life*, II:89. His assertion to her that 'upon my own account I do not care a
fig about it' was slightly disingenuous. *Ibid.*, 93.

[49] Eldon to Scott, undated [*c.* 19 September, 1809], *ibid.*, 96.

[50] Eldon to Lady Eldon, undated [*c.* 2 October 1809], *ibid.*, 101; Eldon to Lady
Eldon, undated [*c.* 22 September 1809], *ibid.*, 98.

[51] Eldon to Scott, 25 September 1809, *ibid.*, 101.

[52] Tierney to Grey, 15 September 1809, Aspinall, *George III*, V:363.

[53] Eldon to Lady Eldon, undated [*c.* 21 September 1809], Twiss, *The public and
private life*, II:97.

received the King's promised paper on the coalition question, Eldon worried: 'I infer from this that he is in a most unhappy state of difficulty, and knows not what to do; and I greatly fear that something of the very worst sort may follow upon the agitation.' The news that Canning and Castlereagh had fought a duel 'I have no doubt will create a great deal indeed of additional uneasiness in the King's mind'.[54] In the event, the King did not suffer a breakdown. However, the real possibility of royal illness, when combined with the likely destruction of the government and his own loss of office, made Eldon extremely bitter toward Canning. He was the man 'who has occasioned all this mischief'.[55] Eldon wrote scathingly to his wife of Canning's vanity, ambition, and his attempt to gratify them, which 'have contrived to overthrow himself and all of us along with him: and this is called *serving* the King'. He was particularly affronted by what he believed had been Canning's suggestion to Perceval that Eldon retire and Perceval become Lord Chancellor, thus paving the way for Canning's elevation to premier.[56]

For all his lamentations about the weakness of any government formed from the remnants of the Portland ministry, Eldon's spirits rose following the King's decision to commission Perceval in October 1809. Once again his correspondence featured observations on the likely conduct of the new session of Parliament. He wondered whether accessions of strength might be expected from Lord Lonsdale, what would be the attitude of the Melvilles, and if an understanding could be reached with Sidmouth. Eldon observed to his brother on 4 October: 'As to calling Parliament soon, that will never do. Bets here go twenty guineas to one, that we never face it. But odds are sometimes lost.'[57] The experience of the previous six months, however, was not easily forgotten. It had revealed a willingness among ministers to work behind the back of one of their number, and to cut him adrift if necessary. While Eldon had acquiesced in the treatment of Castlereagh, he felt uneasy about having done so. He defended his conduct as having

[54] Eldon to Lady Eldon, undated [franked 22 September 1809], *ibid.*, 98.
[55] Eldon to Lady Eldon, undated [franked 13 September 1809], *ibid.*, 90.
[56] Eldon to Lady Eldon, undated [*c.* 14 September 1809], *ibid.*, 88.
[57] Eldon to Scott, 4 October 1809, Twiss, *The public and private life*, II:103–4. See also Eldon to Scott, undated [*c.* 25 September 1809], *ibid.*, 101; Perceval to Eldon, 14 October 1809, *ibid.*, 105; Eldon to Scott, 18 October 1809, *ibid.*

been forced upon him by the King, and consequently 'give[s] me a good deal to say for myself', while in same breath he admitted, 'But, in some degree, all who knew it have been – more or less blameable, but blameable.'[58] Moreover, the abortive attempts to achieve a political juncture with Grenville and Grey had shown Eldon that some of his colleagues could also regard *him* as expendable. 'I was hurt to find that, among the old ones, those, whose confidence I thought I had, had been represented to be ready enough to suggest my separation from office and therefore from the King, without even the mention of it to me.'[59]

This sense of political insecurity returned to Eldon at the end of the year in a very different context. In the autumn he had agreed to stand for election to the post of Chancellor of Oxford University, which had become vacant on the death of the Duke of Portland.[60] His principal opponent was to be Grenville, but the contest was kept from being a straightforward one between the government and opposition by the appearance of a third candidate, the Duke of Beaufort. In the event, victory went to Grenville by a narrow margin. He received 406 votes, while Eldon and Beaufort received 393 and 238 votes, respectively. Eldon's chagrin at defeat by a mere thirteen votes was compounded by his sense of having been ill-treated by those 'from whom I had a better right to expect assistance'.[61] When Grenville's supporters had learned of Beaufort's entry, they had assumed that Eldon would withdraw in deference to a candidate presumed to have the backing of the Court.[62] In fact, however, Eldon had regarded his participation, once pledged, as a matter of personal honour. Privately, he had described withdrawal as sacrificing 'the pretensions of a man long labouring for the public, to a fox-hunting Duke'.[63] In a letter to

[58] Eldon to Scott, 4 October 1809, *ibid.*, 103–4.
[59] Eldon to Scott, undated [*c.* 7 October 1809], *ibid.*, 104.
[60] As early as 3 April 1809 Lord Mulgrave was soliciting Lord Lonsdale's support in the event of an Eldon candidacy. CRO (Lonsdale papers), D/Lons/L1/2/16, copyright Lowther Family Trustees. Eldon was already High Steward of the university, a post he had held since 1801.
[61] Eldon to Rose, undated [*c.* late December 1809], BL (Rose papers), Add. MS 42774 f. 273.
[62] See Earl Temple to Grenville, 11 November 1809, Historical Manuscript Commission, *Fortescue papers*, IX:370. Charles Wynne to Grenville, 15 November 1809, *ibid.*, 376, and T. Grenville to Grenville, 30 November 1809, *ibid.*, 391.
[63] Eldon to Scott, undated [*c.* late December 1809], Twiss, *The public and private*

the King following the poll on 13–14 December 1809 he had justified his conduct more delicately: 'After his friends had been numerously engaged, it does not appear to him that he could with honour or with advantage to the general cause retire, unless his friends had thought it proper, voluntarily, to transfer their support to another candidate.'[64] Eldon was gratified to receive the King's approval of his conduct 'throughout the whole course of this business' as well as his sympathy regarding the outcome of the election.[65] This did not, however, alleviate his sense of grievance. He felt that he had been misinformed about the Duke's probable candidacy and placed in a situation which, but for that misinformation, he would never have accepted.[66] Worse than that, both the government and the Court had failed to back him fully. To Redesdale he wrote of having the 'mortification to believe that the King's servants think the Duke of Beaufort's appearance in Easter week & Whitsun week in the House of Lords is of more importance to the administration than all that I have been doing, or am able to do'.[67] Of the treacherous conduct of the Princess of Wales, he complained: 'Think of the Princess canvassing for Grenville! The gout is bad, but these things are more painful.'[68]

In the face of what he considered to be his evident lack of support within official circles, Eldon brooded on resignation. He asked Redesdale: 'Can I possibly remain in office under such

---

*life*, II:111. Writing to his brother-in-law prior to the poll, Eldon maintained that, having consented to stand, he would see the contest out, 'for I cannot be made a fool of with my own consent'. Eldon to Matthew Surtees, undated [*c.* early December 1809], *ibid.*, 109.

[64] Eldon to George III, 15 December 1809, Aspinall, *George III*, V:470.

[65] George III to Eldon, 16 December 1809, *ibid.*, 471. On 21 December 1809 Eldon discussed with his brother the propriety of communicating the substance of the King's letter, to counteract the public perception that he did not support Eldon's conduct. *Ibid.*, 472, footnote.

[66] Eldon described his reliance on Beaufort's not being a candidate in letters to his brother and Redesdale. Eldon to Scott, undated [*c.* late November or early December 1809, *ibid.*, 107; Eldon to Redesdale, undated [late December 1809 or early January 1810, No. 1], GRO (Mitford papers), D2002/3/1/23.

[67] *Ibid.* On 6 January 1810 Eldon complained to his brother that the Paymaster General had canvassed for Beaufort, in ignorance that Eldon was the government candidate. Aspinall, *George III*, V:471, footnote.

[68] Eldon to Redesdale, undated [late December 1809 or early January 1810, No. 2] GRO (Mitford papers), D2002/3/1/23. For the effect of the Princess' conduct upon her reputation, see Farington, *Diary*, VI:204.

circumstances?'[69] He resolved the question for himself in the affirmative, but he expressed a sense of bitterness with which opposition would not have credited him.

If I doubted the King's good faith, I should not hesitate one moment; but considering what we were pledged to, with reference to *him*, before this unfortunate business was engaged in – to stand by him on *his* account, and on *that only* – if he has kept good faith, I doubt whether I can contribute to the *immediate* destruction of the Administration by my resignation.[70]

Sufficient on this occasion, within the year Eldon's commitment to the King would have to stand an even greater strain.

In assessing Eldon's increasing politicisation during this period, it is important to consider two factors: his age, and his relationship with the King. Of the effective members of Pitt's last government who went into a kind of opposition in 1806 and returned to office in 1807, Eldon was the senior figure. Canning, Castlereagh, Hawkesbury, and Perceval were all comparatively young, either in age or experience. Perceval, at 45, had never held Cabinet office. The others were all in their mid-thirties, and while Hawkesbury had been Foreign Secretary in the Addington government, Castlereagh had been a Secretary of State for a total of six months, and Canning's highest office had been Treasurer of the Navy. Eldon, by contrast, turned 56 in 1806, and had held the Great Seal for five years. His professional demeanour, his situation in the House of Lords, and his own temperament militated against actual political leadership, but it is not surprising that he should have been called upon to play a larger political role than he might have among colleagues who were more his contemporaries. In addition to his seniority, his credentials as royal intermediary also contributed to Eldon's political clout. The circumstances of the King, Prince, and Princess of Wales constituted high politics, either in themselves, or in the opportunities that they afforded politicians for raising or lowering government prestige. The man who, whether in or out of office, could legitimately claim to have the royal ear, was a powerful one, and one on whom considerable responsibility could be said to lie. Here, perhaps, was Eldon's

---

[69] Eldon to Redesdale, undated [late December 1809 or early January 1810, No. 1] GRO (Mitford papers), D2002/3/1/23.

[70] Eldon to Scott, undated [late December 1809 or early January 1810], Twiss, *The public and private life*, II:113.

problem. He did not come easily to the political, as opposed to the professional side of government. Circumstances, however, demanded that he assume a political role. Increasingly, he was obliged to rely on his two strengths: his own longevity, and his royal connections. Neither, however, provided a consistently secure base. Seniority was not an unassailable credential in the eyes of younger colleagues, while reliance on the royal family involved reciprocal claims of personal loyalty that were not easy to maintain.

# 13

# A SERVANT MAY SERVE TWO MASTERS

In the autumn of 1812, Eldon wrote to his friend, the Revd Samuel Swire, to apologise for the recent lapse in his correspondence:

I can only assure you that my attention has been utterly distracted, by the events of a year, which, in their extraordinary nature, so far as they respect myself, have surpassed all the extraordinary circumstances which even my chequered life has produced.[1]

Nor was this an exaggeration of the political turmoil from which Eldon had recently emerged, though perhaps a period of eighteen months would have more accurately described its duration. Between November 1810 and June 1812, the different pressures which had hitherto characterised his public life as Lord Chancellor encroached upon him more intensively and with fewer opportunities for relief. Where he had previously considered royal illness, he addressed complete incapacity; where his conduct had elicited political criticism, it provoked accusations of criminality; and where he had responded to ministerial resignation, he witnessed assassination. The King's illness in the autumn of 1810 ushered in a period of unrelenting turmoil for the government, but more particularly for the Chancellor, whose official and personal relations with the Royal Family imposed special burdens and occasioned the exercise of special powers. Eldon's ability to cope with both would determine whether his own career would terminate in a retirement likely to be as permanent as the King's.

Eldon's role as adviser particularly on royal matters had not gone into abeyance following his return to office in 1807. In fact, during the spring and summer of 1809 he had been obliged to

---

[1] Eldon to Samuel Swire, 22 September 1812, H. Twiss, *The public and private life of Lord Chancellor Eldon*, 3 vols. (London: 1844), II:224.

undertake negotiations to settle the debts of the Princess of Wales, and to intervene on behalf of one of Princess Charlotte's preceptors, whose conduct had displeased her father, the Prince of Wales.[2] In the spring of 1810, Eldon had taken it upon himself to write a 'candid statement' to the King regarding the likely outcome of the corruption charge levelled against the Duke of York.[3] None of these, however, had demanded anything like the time and attention given to royal affairs in 1804 and 1805. In the autumn of 1810, however, this would change. Once again the Royal Family would loom large in public affairs, as the pattern recognised in 1788 of royal illness, Regency, and removal from office, looked set to be realised anew.

In the last days of October 1810, the King began to exhibit the symptoms which presaged another period of illness, this time thought to have been triggered by the approaching death of his youngest daughter, Princess Amelia.[4] Parliament had been prorogued until 23 November, and members of the Cabinet, following their meeting on 24 October, had dispersed to the country. Eldon was at Encombe when he received Spencer Perceval's letter apprising him of the situation. His own brief letters to Perceval, written just before and just after his hurried return to London, reveal his initial reactions of the crisis. The first response was a personal one. Explaining that he intended to come straight to Town, he added: 'I should go direct to Windsor, but in the state in which I fear things are, I know the most irritating sight possible w[oul]d be that of me. This is the 3[r]d time.'[5] In his second letter, however, his thoughts were taking a more practical turn –

---

[2] Correspondence between Eldon, the Prince of Wales, William Adam (the Prince's representative), and the Bishop of Salisbury (Princess Charlotte's Superintendent of Education) is collected in A. Aspinall (ed.), *The correspondence of George Prince of Wales (1770–1812)*, 8 vols. (London, 1967–71), VI. In 1810 Eldon acted as the channel of communication between the King and the Prince on the subject of a suitable replacement for the Revd John Nott, Princess Charlotte's subpreceptor, who had retired following the Prince's complaints of over-familiarity with his royal charge. See their correspondence of 8–9 May 1810, *ibid.*, VII:28–9.

[3] See Eldon's letters of 19 February and 10 March 1809 to George III, and George III's of 20 February to Eldon. A. Aspinall, *The later correspondence of George III*, 5 vols. (Cambridge, 1962), V:203–5, 222.

[4] Princess Amelia (1783–1810) suffered from tuberculosis from the age of fifteen, and erysipelas from the age of eighteen.

[5] Eldon to Spencer Perceval, undated [27 October 1810], CUL (Perceval papers), Add. MS 8713 II.D.6.

consideration of the immediate problems thrown up by the King's illness. Having been prorogued, Parliament might not proceed to public business until a new session was opened by the King or his commissioners, nor could the current prorogation be extended except by the King's order. Would the King be in a fit state to perform such an act?[6] Perceval and Eldon saw him on 29 October. Upon learning of their visit, Thomas Grenville concluded that, while the two ministers would 'strain every nerve' to convince themselves that the King was competent, they would not succeed.[7] Whatever the accuracy of his first assertion, he was correct in the second. With Eldon, according to George Rose, 'very strong against putting the Great Seal to the Commission without the King having previously signed it', ministers decided on 30 October that, if the King did not immediately improve, Parliament should assemble and adjourn for a fortnight.[8] The expedient of adjournment, which did not require royal authorisation, served two purposes. First, it vindicated the government from the charge of leaving Parliament in ignorance of the King's condition, as the decision to wait until the legislature was regularly recalled on 23 November would have done. Secondly, adjournment and possibly further adjournment provided the government with a breathing space tailored to the progress of the King's recovery. As had been the case in previous episodes of royal illness, the government wished to avoid the laborious job of initiating a Regency if the period of indisposition was expected to be brief.

Accordingly, on 1 November, after a second visit by Eldon and Home Secretary Richard Ryder established that the King was 'quite incompetent to sign the commission', a thinly attended Parliament agreed to adjourn until the 15 November.[9] In the

---

[6] Eldon to Perceval, 28 October 1810, *ibid.*, Add. MS 8713 II.D.7.

[7] Thomas Grenville to Lord Grenville, 1 November 1810, Historical Manuscript Commission, *Report of the manuscripts of J. B. Fortescue, Esq.* (London, 1927), X:63. The first press report of the King's condition was the cautious statement in *The Times* of 30 October 1810, 3, col. 1, that his Majesty had been 'slightly indisposed with a cold since Friday' and that Perceval and Eldon had held an interview with him on 29 October 1810 'on business'.

[8] L. V. Harcourt (ed.), *The diaries and correspondence of the Rt Hon. George Rose*, 2 vols. (London, 1860), II:450–1.

[9] Lord Colchester, C. Abbot, *The diary and correspondence of Charles Abbot, Lord Colchester*, 3 vols. (London, 1861), II:283.

Lords, Eldon described the King's illness as having 'arisen from the pressure of domestic affliction operating upon his paternal feelings', and claimed to have a 'confident expectation' of recovery.[10] Further adjournments followed on 15 and 29 November, and it was not until 13 December that Lord Liverpool moved that the royal physicians attend the House for interview. The intervening adjournments had not been achieved without a certain irritation on the part of the opposition at the government's conduct. In the Lords this had focused on Eldon's bland assessments of the evolving situation. Lord Grenville had complained that both the hopes expressed for the King's recovery and their own conduct in continuing their sittings, had been based solely on the Lord Chancellor's unsupported pronouncements.[11] Earl Stanhope had accused Eldon of attempting to distract attention from the government's secrecy by an irrelevant plea on behalf of monarchy, while the Marquis of Lansdowne had asserted that the Chancellor's arguments 'proposed to make them commit the crime of abandoning the country while the executive government was totally suspended'.[12] The other important aspect of the debate had been the reference to the King's illness in the winter of 1788–9, and the role that William Pitt had played on that occasion. Grenville, in particular, had invoked 'the great man then at the head of affairs', and had contrasted the open, candid conduct of Pitt's government (in which Grenville had held office) with that demonstrated by the current incumbents. Pitt's status as unassailable defender of the constitution would have a significant influence on what was said, and what was not said, during the succeeding weeks.

The physicians were interviewed by committees of both Houses.[13] In addition to the King's current state of health and

---

[10] T. Hansard (ed.), *Parliamentary debates from the year 1803 ... (1st series)*, 41 vols. (London, 1812–20), XVIII:1–2.
[11] *Ibid.*, cols. 11–13.    [12] *Ibid.*, cols. 74, 75.
[13] The Commons committee consisted of: Ryder, Master of the Rolls, W. Adam, H. Lascelles, R. Dundas, Lord Castlereagh, Lord Milton, Lord G. Cavendish, Attorney General, G. Canning, S. Whitbread, G. Ponsonby, W. Wilberforce, R. B. Sheridan, G. Tierney, W. W. Pole, Sir J. Newport, Sir W. Scott, H. Addington (replacing C. Bathurst), and T. S. Gooch. The Lords committee consisted of: the Archbishop of Canterbury, the Duke of Norfolk, the Archbishop of York, Lord Moira, Grenville, the Duke of Montrose, Lord Ellenborough, Earl Spencer, Lansdowne, Eldon, the Marquis of Wellesley, the Bishop of London, the Earl of Harrowby, Viscount Sidmouth, the Earl Camden, Earl of

prognosis, Eldon's conduct was a particular subject of inquiry. He had seen the King, alone, on 12 December, and the line of questions pursued in the Commons committee bespoke a suspicion that the Chancellor had attempted to gain an unfair influence through his interview.[14] In response to pointed questioning, however, Sir Henry Halford informed the committee that the interview had resulted from *his* decision to use Eldon's name as a means of encouraging the King to restrain himself. Once informed that the Chancellor was coming to Windsor, the King's determination to see him had been such that the physicians had determined that more harm would result from frustrating than from acceding to that wish.[15]

That Eldon's conduct should have aroused suspicion resulted in part from the opposition's growing sense that the government was attempting either to delay or subvert a Regency. On 2 December Lord Moira had reported to Thomas Grenville:

The Chancellor is trying to get the King brought to London, as a procedure which would in general conception imply a marked improvement of the King's health. If any favourable interval will give a plea for asserting the King's being in possession of his intellect for the moment, they will get his signature to a Commission empowering the Prince with others to conduct certain of the ordinary operations of Government. If they cannot get this out of the King, then they will introduce the same provision in form of a Bill to the two Houses.[16]

Accompanying this was a fear that ministers were working to maintain their hold on office even if a genuine Regency were established. Central to this latter fear was the Prince of Wales. Ever since he had almost become Regent in 1789, it had been generally understood that his first executive act would be to dismiss his father's ministers. Now, however, opposition leaders were not so sure. Might not the Chancellor manage to secure the

Westminster, the Marquis of Abercorn, the Earl of Buckinghamshire, the Earl of Powis, Liverpool, and Lord Redesdale.

[14] See, e.g., Hansard, *Parliamentary debates*, XVIII:137–9.

[15] See, e.g., the testimony of Sir Henry Halford and Dr Robert Willis, *ibid.*, cols. 162–4, 174–6. In a letter to the Prince of 13 December 1810, Eldon likewise explained his interview as having been made 'at the request & by the advice of the physicians' and stated that he had gone to Windsor 'without the hope or the intention of seeing his Majesty'. Eldon to the Prince of Wales, 13 December 1810, Aspinall, *Wales*, VII:98.

[16] Lord Moira to T. Grenville, undated [2 December 1810], Historical Manuscript Commission, *Fortescue papers*, X:78–9.

Prince's confidence even as he had secured the King's? In the context of their previously strained relations, the idea of political friendship between Eldon and the Prince seemed fantastic, but more recently, relations between the two had become rather less desperate. From what might be regarded as the nadir in the spring of 1809, when the Prince had been unable to endure a private meeting with Eldon, a modest improvement seems to have occurred.[17] In 1810 the Prince had written very civilly to the Chancellor on the subject of Princess Charlotte's household.[18] He had likewise turned to the Chancellor when he found himself in difficulties over his sister's will, and he had requested that Eldon take sole responsibility for instructing the royal physicians how to field questions from the King on that topic.[19] Consequently, when Eldon had a lengthy audience with the Prince on 9 December, their apparent cordiality, coupled with the perceived influence exerted by Eldon's friend the Duke of Cumberland over the Prince, provoked opposition fears of secret negotiations. Thomas Grenville wrote to his brother:

The little that I hear of C[arlton] House continues to speak the influence of the D[uke] of C[umberland] in those walls, and there was yesterday an audience of *three hours* given to *the Chancellor* at Carlton House, which is *supposed* to have been confined entirely to discussions of *the Princess Amelia's will*. It is probably on the *same business* that the Ch[ancello]r and the D[uke] of C[umberland] have twice in the last week dined *tete a tete* at the St Alban's Tavern.[20]

It was the other species of speculation, however, concerning the King's health, which particularly dogged Eldon during the following weeks. In late December he responded to Grenville's critical assessment of ministerial conduct by protesting that *he* had never attempted to conceal the state of the King's health:

He hoped it would be found that he had acted with all the caution and deliberation which an affair of so much moment demanded, and that he

---

[17] Wales to William Adam, 19 May 1809, Aspinall, *Wales*, VI:387. See also Wales to Adam, 16 May 1809, *ibid.*, 383.
[18] Wales to Eldon, 8 May 1810, *ibid.*, VII:28.
[19] Wales to Eldon, 11 November 1810, *ibid.*, 77. Princess Amelia's will named a single beneficiary, Major General Charles Fitzroy, with whom she had conducted a romantic relationship. Their affair had been kept secret from the King.
[20] T. Grenville to Grenville, 10 December 1810, Historical Manuscript Commission, *Fortescue papers*, X:82. See also T. Grenville to Grenville, 11 December 1810, *ibid.*, 84 (emphasis in original).

had neither over-stated, nor under-rated, what it was his duty to state explicitly to their lordships. He could freely take upon him to say, that to the best of his judgment he had discharged his duty on legal and constitutional grounds.[21]

The question of concealment became an explicit focus of attention in late January 1811, when Eldon was accused, not of conveying misinformation about the *current* state of the King's health, but of having done so during previous periods of royal illness. On 25 January 1811 Lord Grey launched an attack upon Eldon's conduct in 1801 and 1804 that was bitter both in substance and in tone. He mocked Eldon's frequent invocations of conscience, and demanded to know how the government would ever establish that the King had recovered. The mere affixing of the Great Seal to a commission in the King's name was clearly insufficient, 'when it was notorious that the Great Seal had been employed, as if by his Majesty's command, at a time that he was under the care and actual restraint of a physician'. That being the case, 'The noble and learned lord must excuse him then when he said he must have better authority than his [Eldon's] declaration for his Majesty's recovery'.[22] Grey returned to the attack three days later, charging that on several occasions in 1801 and 1804 the government had exercised power in the King's name while the King had been mentally incompetent. Eldon, the minister who had both affixed the Great Seal to commissions signifying the royal assent, and who had informed Parliament that the King was able to perform his public functions, had thereby committed acts of utmost treachery. 'I am bound to arraign the noble and learned lord for an offence little short of high treason ... I shall not hesitate to pronounce his offence to be treason against the constitution and the country.'[23]

These accusations prompted Lord King to object to Eldon's membership of the body created to advise the Queen during the Regency. 'After the unanswerable manner in which the charge had been established against the noble and learned lord', Lord King concluded that Eldon had 'been instrumental in deceiving this House and the country in 1804' and was ineligible to serve on the Queen's Council.[24] Nor were the accusations against Eldon con-

[21] Hansard, *Parliamentary debates*, XVIII:462.    [22] *Ibid.*, cols. 1010, 1016.
[23] *Ibid.*, col. 1052.    [24] *Ibid.*, col. 1085.

fined to the House of Lords. In the Commons, Samuel Whitbread moved a committee to re-examine the evidence relating to the King's condition in 1804. The press too regarded the Chancellor's conduct with suspicion, if not outright condemnation. On 25 January 1811 the *Morning Chronicle* complained:

The state machine should not be perplexed by a wheel within a wheel an *imperium in imperio*, a Baron's Court in the middle of the empire. For we live in Britain, and should wish to see the King a King not *the King a Chancellor, or the Chancellor a King*.[25]

In the wake of Grey's allegations, *The Times* opined that, while all must look forward to the King's recovery, 'recent disclosures have proved the necessity, that the most convincing, open, and daylight evidence should be given' lest 'the joy consequent upon such an occurrence will be deeply tinged with suspicion'.[26]

While it is not possible to evaluate Eldon's conduct conclusively, neither Grey's nor Whitbread's allegations were convincingly presented. The period of allegedly wrongful conduct in 1801 was largely prior to Eldon's assumption of ministerial office, and Grey quickly dropped that charge. Moreover, he based his analysis of the 1804 illness on the equivocal testimony of Dr Heberden before the Lords' committee on 18 December. Not only did Dr Heberden's testimony admit of more than one interpretation, but it actually suggested that the King *had* been judged competent on the relevant dates in March 1804.[27] Significantly, Whitbread did not base his case on the testimony of the physicians, which he admitted was against him. He chose, however, an even more dubious premise, namely, that Eldon's experience of lunacy cases had rendered him more perceptive than the physicians. While they had pronounced the King restored to health, Eldon had known better, and had consciously avoided the issue or

---

[25] *Morning Chronicle*, 25 January 1811, 3, col. 1 (emphasis in original).

[26] *The Times*, 30 January 1811, 3, col. 3.

[27] In his testimony before the Lords, Dr Heberden stated that he considered the 'duration' of the King's illness to have been 12 February to 23 April 1804, on which date he had presided at a Council. He added, however, that 'for some days previous to the 23rd April' the appearances of disorder 'had so far ceased as to make his Majesty's physicians conceive him competent to exercise all the usual functions of his high office'. On the other hand, he noted that the King 'still retained such marks of indisposition about him, as made it expedient that some one of his physicians should be about his person for some months afterwards'. Hansard, *Parliamentary debates*, XVIII:224.

issues that would have revealed the illness. Perhaps Eldon himself had even 'exercised a controull' over the unfortunate monarch.[28]

Arguably the most glaring omission from the attacks on Eldon was the failure satisfactorily to deal with William Pitt's role in 1804. He was either conveniently forgotten or resigned completely to the Regency Crisis of 1788–9. Yet, when Lord Moira posed the rhetorical question, 'Had Mr Pitt attempted to carry on public business in the name of the King when the sovereign was incompetent to discharge the duties of his station?', the answer, according to some of the allegations against Eldon, must have been *yes*. If the King's convalescence during the spring and summer of 1804, and the continued attendance of his physicians until the autumn, were really conclusive evidence of royal incapacity, then Pitt must have returned to office in May of that year and exercised control of the government thereafter without lawful authority. This, however, seems never to have been suggested by Eldon's opponents. Even those men who were arguing for a Regency contrary to that which had been proposed by Pitt were unwilling to appear critical of him. Grey's failure to explain Pitt's conduct was most obviously revealed in his suggestion that Eldon's control over the King had prevented the formation of a Pitt/Fox ministry in May 1804.[29] Unless it was to be supposed that Eldon had beguiled Pitt into taking office and thereafter excluded him from the King's presence, it is difficult to comprehend how events could have occurred as Grey suggested without Pitt's knowledge and compliance.

Both of the actual challenges to Eldon's authority and reputation failed decisively. Lord King's motion to strike him from the Queen's Council was defeated by a vote of 139 to 54.[30] Whitbread's motion to re-examine the physicians relative to the events in 1804 similarly failed by a margin of 198 to 81. This is not to say, however, that Eldon emerged unscathed from his ordeal. He did not appear to advantage during the debates in the Lords. When charged by Grenville with having misled the House into

---

[28] *Ibid.*, XIX:65–6, 68.

[29] See, e.g., Grey's remarks at *ibid.*, XVIII:1076, and Whitbread's remarks at *ibid.*, XIX:61–2.

[30] Robert Plumer Ward noted that Eldon forced the division, by saying that the non-contents were in the majority in the voice vote. E. Phipps, *Memoirs of the political and literary life of Robert Plumer Ward*, 2 vols. (London, 1850), I:369.

thinking that the King's recovery was imminent, he claimed, with what appears to be good grounds, to have been misinterpreted. [31] His further explanation, however, was so odd as to suggest either extreme nervousness or the unreliability of the reported text of his earlier remarks. A speech intended to portray his independence of mind made him appear vacillating and unsure of himself:

> There were many noble lords who now heard him, who knew how well he could justify himself against all the calumnies and accusations urged against him ... [H]e was only one of an administration which acted never against the opinion of the physicians ... He had certainly stated from himself, as from a person ignorant of the medical profession, his confident expectations of his Majesty's recovery within a reasonable time ... If all the physicians on earth were to tell him that his Majesty's recovery would be speedy, he would not believe them. Upon the same grounds, were they to declare that his Majesty's recovery would not be speedy, he would be equally incredulous.[32]

Not surprisingly, Grey thought this admission undermined the government's proposals, all of which had supposedly been grounded on medical evidence.[33] Eldon did eventually go some way to recovering from his gaffe. As he explained:

> [I]t was most important to the sovereign that the Chancellor should not depend wholly on the evidence of the physicians, if he himself thought the King perfectly competent to discharge the functions of royal authority ... If what he had then done was supported by the opinions of all the physicians, it did not follow that he was now guilty of any inconsistency in saying that whatever the report of the physicians might be, he would not consent to dethrone his Majesty upon their report merely, if in his judgment and conscience he believed that the King was adequate to the discharge of his royal functions.[34]

This claim to independence from the physicians came back to haunt Eldon, however, when Whitbread took it up to suggest that he had acted as the King's evil genius.

Frequently Eldon's speeches took on not merely a defensive, but an injured tone. It was 'unfair' that he should be the target of attack. His sense of grievance extended in three directions: against his attackers, who singled him out, against his former colleagues, who distanced themselves, and against the Royal Family, who failed to support their most reliable servant. In none of the three

---

[31] See the remarks of Grenville, Sidmouth, and Eldon, in Hansard, *Parliamentary debates*, XVIII:1001–2, 1043, 1049.
[32] *Ibid.* col. 1049–50.     [33] *Ibid.*, col. 1054.     [34] *Ibid.*, col. 1074.

contexts was his rancour wholly justified. His strongest ground for complaint against Grey and Whitbread was the absence of a strong factual basis for their accusations. If they were going to be made, however, it was not illogical that these accusations should have been made against Eldon. Grey maintained that the constitution did not recognise the institution of the Cabinet, but fastened blame on the individual minister who had committed the wrongful act. Eldon, therefore, was *the* culpable minister who, however innocent his intentions, had 'put the great seal to a commission, at a time when his Majesty was incompetent, and for this he was individually responsible'.[35] Whitbread stated that he did not know whether Charles Yorke and Lord Castlereagh, who had been Home Secretary and President of the Board of Control, respectively, were also 'guilty' of misconduct, because he did not know the extent of their personal involvement in the relevant act.[36] The refusal to consider the events of 1804 as resulting from a decision for which a group of ministers were jointly responsible was certainly not an eccentric one, though in this context Eldon's critics also attempted to portray him as having actually exercised a unique personal authority over the King, and not merely as having performed official acts which devolved technical responsibility on him.

Eldon's complaints against the Royal Family and his political colleagues reflected his own sense of vulnerability more than they did actual failure on the part of others. In an anguished letter to Sir William Scott, Eldon bemoaned that 'the whole Royal Family, whose protestations of gratitude my boxes teem with, are among my enemies'.[37] Yet the evidence is nothing like so damning. When a division on Lord King's motion against Eldon was called, the royal dukes abandoned the opposition, with whom they had voted on the issues relating to Regency restrictions.[38] On 6 February 1811 the Queen included a personal note in her letter acknowledging receipt of information on the King's condition.

She cannot help lamenting that, upon such a melancholy business, which is now finished, and in which the Lord Chancellor has given such strong

---

[35] *Ibid.*, col. 1075.    [36] *Ibid.*, XIX:60.

[37] Eldon to Sir William Scott, undated [end January 1811], Twiss, *The public and private life*, II:162.

[38] Phipps, I:369. Plumer Ward noted that the Dukes of York and Cumberland voted with the government, and the three other royal dukes left the House.

proofs of zeal and affection for his Sovereign and country, his feelings should have been put to such severe trials; but his own conscience, and the King's good opinion, must be his chief support. As to herself, she must always remember, with gratitude, the Lord Chancellor's attention shown her upon this melancholy occasion.[39]

Eldon's complaints against his political colleagues and friends seem similarly misguided. Certainly his assertion that 'every man, who was with me in Administration in 1804 is obstinately holding silent' was far from the case.[40] Lords Liverpool and Sidmouth defended both Eldon and the actions taken in 1804. The King had never been called upon to execute a royal act, Liverpool asserted, 'until it was fully ascertained that he was competent to the discharge of the royal functions'.[41] Sidmouth pledged himself 'ready to answer for all his colleagues, and more particularly for the noble and learned lord'.[42] In the Commons Castlereagh and Yorke were equally supportive of the Chancellor's conduct in 1804. Yorke affirmed that:

although it might be true that Lord Eldon, or Lord Sidmouth, by virtue of their office, might go to his Majesty when the other members of the cabinet were excluded, yet the act alluded to was not done without a full communication with all the confidential servants of the crown, and without their unanimous concurrence as to its strict propriety.[43]

Nevertheless, for someone of Eldon's heightened sensitivity towards any suggestion that he had acted in other than a conscientious, proper, and correct manner, the seriousness of the charges against him undoubtedly aroused feelings of deepest anxiety and unhappiness. Only a man acutely sensitive to slights and accusations could assert his indifference so strongly, as occurred during the debates on the Regency Bill in January 1811:

As to the daily scandal that was poured out against him, he would not condescend to reply to it ... He would discharge his duty to his Sovereign conscientiously and, satisfied that he had done so, he should feel indifferent as to what might be said of him. He had been attacked and reviled, but this he disregarded; actions which he never performed had been imputed to him; and others had been swelled and distorted by calumny and misrepresentation. In the newspapers he might to-morrow read, as he

---

[39] Queen Charlotte to Eldon, 6 February 1811, Twiss, *The public and private life*, II:164.
[40] Eldon to Scott, undated [end January 1811], *ibid.*, 161–2.
[41] Hansard, *Parliamentary debates*, XVIII:1064.
[42] *Ibid.*, col. 1068.    [43] *Ibid.*, XIX:77.

had often before read, sentiments and expressions attributed to him, of which he was perfectly unconscious, and of which he had never heard till he saw them recorded in those newspapers. He assured their lordships that to all this he was insensible, and viewed it without any sentiment of pain.[44]

Given Eldon's genuine, if exaggerated, reputation for political intrigue, the suspicions expressed by the opposition leadership are not surprising. Nor can it have been other than a cause of chagrin for them that, even as he avoided censure for his past conduct, he managed to maintain his current office. Following protracted and difficult negotiations with the opposition leadership, and under contrary pressure from other members of the Royal Family not to dismiss the current ministers, the Prince had begun receiving reports in late January that the King's health was improving.[45] The knowledge that his father might be about to resume his political functions convinced the Prince that he ought not to make any changes that would seem ill-timed and disrespectful. Consequently, when the Regency Bill passed on 5 February 1811, the Prince decided to maintain the *status quo*, at least for the time being.[46] Surprisingly, it was Perceval, and not Eldon, who received credit for such manipulation of the Prince as was believed to have been attempted on this occasion.[47]

As spring passed into summer, and the King's condition seemed rather to decline than to progress, rumours of ministerial changes, coalitions, and dismissals regained currency among ministers and the opposition.[48] Lamenting the Regent's failure to stand firmly behind his former political friends, Thomas Grenville adverted to Eldon's backstage manoeuvres: 'I am afraid the Chancellor has great power, and he employs the Duke of Cumberland, who acts

---

[44] *Ibid.*, XVIII:1018.

[45] For suggestions that the King's condition was improving in late January to early February, see Harcourt, *Diaries*, II:274–81.

[46] See the Queen's letter to Eldon of 6 February 1811, Twiss, *The public and private life*, II:164.

[47] Perceval was credited with having drafted the letter sent by the Queen to the Prince on 29 January reporting the King's much improved condition. C. Hibbert, *George IV* (London, 1976), 360.

[48] See, e.g., Richard Ryder to Earl Bathurst, 30 July 1811, Historical Manuscript Commission, *Report on the manuscripts of Earl Bathurst* (London, 1923), 158, and T. Grenville to Grenville, 25 August 1811, Historical Manuscript Commission, *Fortescue papers*, X:165.

entirely under his directions.'[49] Eldon was, in fact, deeply engaged in royal matters at this time, though they related principally to the King's health. In mid-July the attending physicians pronounced his condition extremely grave, and Eldon badgered his colleagues on the Queen's Council to bring in other medical specialists. '[T]here is not a family in the kingdom, which, in a like case, would not feel it incumbent upon them ... to take the melancholy chance of learning whether other skilful persons, having the means afforded to them of judging, were unable to suggest anything likely to be useful.'[50] Following the Queen's acquiescence to Dr John Willis and Dr Samuel Simmons conversing with the accredited physicians, Eldon next tried to convince her to permit them to examine the King. Her unwillingness to countenance men who continued to advocate physical restraint as a mode of treatment left Eldon questioning the Council's utility. In early September he complained to the Archbishop of Canterbury of the 'fatal effect' of the Queen's intransigence, and made clear his own course of action. 'I shall certainly state to her Majesty my sentiments and apprehensions upon the whole of this business, the present state of which appears to me to leave the Council under very great difficulty.'[51]

When it came to discussing the termination of the Regency restrictions, however, Eldon was less confident. In a letter to Perceval on the subject of future royal finances, he objected to a separate establishment for the Princesses on the grounds that the government's uncertain tenure severely disabled their advocacy of a controversial measure.

[T]ho' it may become, for reasons, unavoidably necessary to propose it, it is a matter of great delicacy, to carry it will I fear be a matter of no small difficulty, if attempted in a state, in which nobody knows what anybody is, or is to be, & will require all the influence & weight in those, who attempt it, of established situation & established known public character.

---

[49] T. Grenville to Grenville, 25 August 1811, Historical Manuscript Commission, *Fortescue papers*, X:166.

[50] Eldon to the Queen's Council, undated [late July 1811], Lambeth Palace Library (Manners-Sutton papers), 2107 f. 102.

[51] Eldon to the Archbishop of Canterbury, undated [franked 9 September 1811], *ibid.*, 2107 f. 183. To Perceval, Eldon complained in an undated letter [*c.* 9 September 1811] that the Queen's decision 'may produce resignations among the Council'. CUL (Perceval papers), Add. MS 8713 II.D.20.

As a matter of such delicacy & difficulty, it is hardly prudent for persons not at present in such established situations to attempt it.[52]

Similarly, he complained to Redesdale that, even if the government were to survive, his own situation was far from secure:

I have no reason to believe that the Regent does or does not contemplate a change in his administration – all you see in the papers is nonsense – no foundation at all for it – but I feel so much with respect to *my own particular* situation as to the King – what it has been & what it is likely to be – that ... I cannot see *my* way through the intricacies & difficulties of the business of the times with any satisfaction.[53]

Eldon's thoughts in the autumn of 1811 still revolved around the King. Noting the doctors' opinion that the limited Regency had had a harmful effect on the King's state, he asked Perceval: 'what must not the Regency, such as it is about to be, effect as to relapse[?]'[54] He admitted to a 'morbid apprehension' that, were the King to recover, he would be 'most deeply affected, if not altogether overset by his reflections' upon any reduction of his station or dignity. For this reason he opposed the creation of a separate establishment for the Queen. '[I]t would have the appearance of separating from him in his utmost need – there would be no arguing with any convincing effect that, because the provisions would cease when he recovered, that *therefore* he was not abandoned as one that never could recover.' Eldon repeated the view he had inelegantly stated in January of how ministers ought to regard the King's condition:

If one could be justified in acting upon the supposition that the King *cannot* recover, the subject would not be of great difficulty – but I think it impossible to *act upon that supposition*, however hopeless the case may be – if *every doctor* said that there was *no* hope, in a case, which ordinarily baffles all reasoning, and that the case of a person, to whom allegiance is due, you must, I think, act, as if there was hope.

Whatever hopes still remained of the King's eventual recovery had sunk to a low ebb by February of 1812, when the Regent was scheduled to assume full executive authority. Precisely what he

---

[52] Eldon to Perceval, undated [*c*. early September 1811], CUL (Perceval papers), Add. MS 8713 II.D.19.

[53] Eldon to Redesdale, undated [autumn 1811], GRO (Mitford papers), D2002/3/1/23.

[54] Eldon to Perceval, undated [*c*. early September 1811], CUL (Perceval papers), Add MS 8713 II.D.19.

intended to do with respect to the government, however, remained unclear. He had himself suffered a serious illness in late November, and this had not helped him to resolve what was proving a most difficult problem – how to placate his old political friends while maintaining the policies of the current government. In particular, the Regent wanted a firm prosecution of the war, and postponement, if not rejection, of constitutional reform on behalf of Roman Catholics. Grey, Grenville, and the other opposition leaders could neither be counted on to pursue the first, nor to give way on the second. On the other hand, the Regent did not want to be seen forfeiting his old Foxite credentials, or abandoning his long-standing political supporters such as Moira and Sheridan. The effect of this conflict was a half-hearted attempt to construct a coalition ministry. Appreciating his usual role as political go-between, Eldon straightaway informed Perceval of his determination 'to take no part' in any negotiation with Grenville and Grey. His frequently expressed objection to coalitions, the absence of sympathy either on specific issues of policy or on general principles of government between himself and the opposition leaders, and their publicly stated objections to his membership of the Queen's Council precluded any such undertaking.[55] He added as a factor complicating, if not explaining, his attitude of non-compliance:

you know how much my heart has been wrung with the difficulties of holding office, when I have been obliged, but I hope justified, in taking the painful part I have had to execute, with regard to the situation of my Sovereign and Benefactor, my reverend Master.[56]

In the event, his services were not needed, for upon being shown the Regent's proposal of junction on 14 February 1812, Grenville and Grey promptly declined.[57] When the Foreign Secretary, Lord Wellesley, immediately suggested an alternative coalition,

---

[55] On 1 February 1811, Lords Grey, Lauderdale, Holland, Erskine, Rosslyn, Derby, Ashburton, and Ponsonby published in the *Morning Chronicle* the protest they had made on 28 January 1811 against Eldon's membership of the Queen's Council. *Ibid.*, XVIII:1086–8. See Plumer Ward's comment in Phipps, *Memoirs*, I:371.

[56] Eldon to Perceval, undated [8 or 15 February 1812], Twiss, *The public and private life*, II:188–9.

[57] For the evolution of the Regent's letter to the opposition leadership, see Historical Manuscript Commission, *Bathurst papers*, 165. The letter is printed at Hansard, *Parliamentary debates*, XXII:40.

however, the Regent did fall back upon the Chancellor. On 17 February Eldon stated that he would not continue in office except under Perceval, but this having been granted, he agreed to hear Wellesley's proposals. These too came to nothing, apart from Wellesley's resignation when Eldon revealed to him that the Regent 'had already fixed Mr Perceval in his seat'.[58] The Regent, who seems to have misled Wellesley on this point, also chose Eldon as the channel through which the resignation was confirmed.[59]

As the spring of 1812 progressed, Eldon began to recover some of his political *sang-froid*. He felt sufficiently confident to indulge in a species of arch humour when opposition back-benchers attempted to move an address in March in favour of further ministerial re-structuring. Referring to opposition he remarked:

Somehow or other they had been for a long time out of humour with him; he was sorry for it, for he really wished them every happiness, and if he knew of any means whereby he could promote their comfort, he would be always ready to use them.[60]

Moreover, he was expressing an interpretation of his own conduct and of his relations with the Regent which, whether or not they constituted an accurate memorial of the previous eighteen months, demonstrated that he had reconciled them in his own mind. In a letter to his friend Samuel Swire, he explained his decision to remain in office in 1811 as an extension of his oft-expressed obligation to the King. So long as the Prince considered it a duty to retain his father's ministers, 'How was it possible . . . his father's servants could refuse to act under him as the representative of his father?' Having thus served the Prince for the year of restricted Regency, Eldon found that the Prince had 'totally altered' his opinion of his father's ministers. Not surprisingly, this political transformation created a new demand on the Chancellor's loyalty. '[H]ow could I possibly refuse to consent to what his entreaty pressed upon me, to remain in the service of a son so conducting himself towards the father to whom I owe so much?' 'Interest, or

---

[58] Marquis of Wellesley to the Regent, 17 February 1812, A. Aspinall (ed.), *Letters of George IV, king of England, 1812–1830*, 3 vols. (Cambridge, 1938), I:9.

[59] See Eldon to Wellesley, 18 February 1812, BL (Wellesley papers), Add. MS 37296.

[60] Hansard, *Parliamentary debates*, XXII:70. The address was rejected, 165 to 72.

ambition, or even private wishes', he maintained, 'have had nothing to do with it.'[61]

Within a few weeks of these satisfied pronouncements, however, Eldon was plunged once more into a situation of political tumult. On 11 May 1812 Perceval was shot dead in the lobby of the House of Commons. Besides causing great personal sadness and grief throughout Westminster, this event precipitated yet another ministerial crisis.[62] For three weeks negotiations involving the government, Wellesley, Moira, Canning, Grenville, and Grey failed to achieve a settlement. On 13 May Eldon drafted a Cabinet minute stating that the government would, if required, 'carry on the administration of the Government under any member of the present Cabinet whom his Royal Highness might think proper to select as the head of it'.[63] The Prince selected Liverpool, and he promptly tried – and failed – to restore Wellesley and Canning. Eldon, who offered his views on the subject to his brother, was wrong in his prediction that the terms would be accepted, but right, ultimately, in judging that the current government would survive.[64] On 21 May a back-bench motion tantamount to no confidence passed the Commons by four votes. Liverpool resigned, and the Regent sent first for Wellesley, and then for Moira. Neither was able to form a government, however, and on 8 June Liverpool was reinstated.

Precisely what had been Eldon's role in this round of negotiations is difficult to assess, and the personal objections entertained by Perceval's friends for Wellesley, the unwillingness of Grenville and Grey to trust the Regent, and the general suspicion with which Canning was regarded on all sides, ought not to be discounted.[65] Nevertheless, Eldon was regarded as having done

[61] Eldon to Samuel Swire, 24 April 1812, Twiss, *The public and private life*, II:196.
[62] For Eldon's sentiments on the death of Perceval, see his letter to Richard Richards, undated [*c.* 12 May 1812] AMA Caerynwwch (Richards) papers, Z/DA/64 SB30; Eldon to Queen Charlotte, 18 May 1812, Twiss, *The public and private life*, II:205–6.
[63] Cabinet minute, Eldon to the Regent, 13 May 1812, Aspinall, *George IV*, I:74–5.
[64] Eldon to Sir William Scott, undated [*c.* 18 May 1812], Twiss, *The public and private life*, II:211.
[65] On 22 May 1812, the *Morning Chronicle* published a statement by Wellesley explaining his reasons for having resigned in February. The statement included very severe criticisms of Perceval's abilities, and these, not surprisingly, caused grave offence. W. Hinde, *George Canning* (Oxford, 1989), 248–9.

his part to keep the opposition out of power. When Grey warned Grenville against being drawn into negotiations in late May, he feared 'a paper from the Cabinet of the Chancellor's composition' as the likely means of ensnaring them.[66] Thomas Creevey saw Eldon as a consummate figure of court intrigue. In a letter to his wife describing the Regent's vacillation he wrote: 'Eldon is always told everything that passes and the Duke of York ... is the unalterable and inveterate opposer of his brother having anything to do with the Opposition. He and Eldon work day and night to keep Prinney in the right course.'[67] Sir Samuel Romilly thought likewise. He noted that Eldon certainly had not 'shown the least symptom of apprehension that he was to resign his office' during the period of official uncertainty. Instead of attempting to clear the Chancery docket for his successor, 'Lord Eldon has been every day closeted with the Duke of Cumberland ... We have even had the Duke of Cumberland coming down to Westminster Hall, and sending for the Chancellor out of court.'[68] Writing long after the event, Lord Holland would absolve ministers from having acted to impede the formation of a new government, 'with the exception of Lord Eldon'.[69] Eldon's own assessment of the failure of opposition was rather coy. To his friend Swire he observed: 'whether Grenville and Grey did not wish to be Ministers, or whether they would not be Ministers unless they could bind kings in chains, I don't know.'[70] To his brother, however, he maintained of his Cabinet colleagues: 'I am mistaken if they do not mainly owe their existence, as such to me.'[71]

Throughout his career, Eldon liked telling people that he had no personal ambition for office. Until the King's final incapacity, loyalty and gratitude to him were the usual reasons Eldon offered to explain his tenure. The King desired his services, and that obliged him to offer them. Once it was acknowledged that the

---

[66] Grey to Grenville, 25 May 1812, Historical Manuscript Commission, *Fortescue papers*, X:274.

[67] Thomas Creevey to Mrs Creevey, 28 May 1812, Sir H. Maxwell (ed.), *The Creevey papers* (London, 1923), 158.

[68] Samuel Romilly, *Memoirs of Sir Samuel Romilly*, 3 vols. (London, 1840), III:42–3.

[69] H. R. V. Fox, Lord Holland, *Further memoirs of the Whig party 1807–1821*, ed. Lord Stavordale (London, 1905), 147.

[70] Eldon to Swire, 22 September 1812, Twiss, *The public and private life*, II:225.

[71] Eldon to Scott, undated [franked 9 October 1812], *ibid.*, 228.

King was unlikely to recover and find *his* Chancellor gone, however, the old argument against retirement no longer sufficed.[72] What, other than ambition, pride, and love of the power and consequence that went with being Lord Chancellor, could explain his remaining in office? Might not his actions appear even more mercenary, given his previous justifications? The advent of the Regency obliged Eldon to ask himself, however secretly, these questions. At first, he had the excuse that the Regent's decision to continue his father's government placed an obligation on ministers to support the King through his son. To a certain extent, that rationale would continue to exist so long as the Regent did not wildly diverge from what had been the King's policies. Eldon's claims that he had won the Regent's respect, however, which he began making once the restrictions ended in February 1812, indicate that his relationship with the Royal Family was evolving.[73] In part this change was an objective one: the Regent's attitude toward Eldon *had* changed, and he was coming to rely on the Chancellor, if he did not (yet) like him. In part, however, the change was subjective. Unwilling to admit to others or to himself that he considered public office other than a duty, Eldon needed to feel that his obligations had been safely transferred. If his 'old Master' no longer required him, his young Master did.

[72] See, e.g., Eldon to Swire, 26 June 1811, *ibid.*, 178.
[73] See, e.g., Eldon to Swire, 22 September 1812, *ibid.*, 225.

# 14

## REFORM AND REVOLUTION

While frequently calling for a considerable expenditure of physical and emotional resources, the affairs of the Royal Family did not constitute the only demand upon Eldon's time. Neither was his attention exclusively focused upon keeping himself and his colleagues in office, whatever the opposition might complain. On the contrary, during his twenty-five years as Lord Chancellor, Eldon played a prominent part in what might be described as the regular political business of the government and Parliament. While he liked to play down his abilities as a politician, he participated fully in parliamentary debates, whether to support government legislation, to challenge the proposals of the opposition, or to steer backbench initiatives into channels helpful to the former and awkward for the latter. In order to examine and assess this aspect of Eldon's political character, it makes sense to focus on his conduct with respect to a particular issue. Reform of the criminal law is appropriate for this purpose. Not only was criminal law an important object of government and opposition legislative programmes during the first decades of the nineteenth century, but it held a particular attraction for Eldon as a former public prosecutor and present royal adviser. Before turning to the specific question of the proper nature and structure of the criminal law, however, it is necessary to examine Eldon's attitude toward legislative reform in general.

Speaking disparagingly of the attempt to disfranchise the borough of Aylesbury in 1804, Eldon announced that he 'was no enemy to real reform, but he would ever oppose that thing called reform, which was founded in injustice'.[1] Despite this apparently

---

[1] T. Hansard (ed.), *The parliamentary debates from the year 1803 ... (1ˢᵗ series)*, 41 vols. (London, 1812–20), II:517.

forthright pronouncement, throughout his public life Eldon gained the reputation of being against every species of reform to which he was exposed. While he might profess himself friendly to the principle of legal amendment, he nevertheless consistently found some objection which forbade his giving the proposal under consideration his support. General measures were too sweeping. Specific proposals encouraged inconsistency. Legislation of any sort was unnecessary, given the existence of common law remedies. This Bill suffered from faulty draughtsmanship. That one required more time for consideration than was available. In his long career, Eldon can be identified clearly with only two reforms: the abolition of an archaic form of trial, and the criminalisation of lethal anti-poaching devices. In 1819 he brought in a Bill to abolish the criminal appeal and trial by battle, whereby a defendant was obliged to prove his innocence in physical combat against his accuser.[2] Eldon expressed surprise, when the measure was discussed in committee, that such a 'gross absurdity' should have 'so long continued a part of our legal system'.[3] In 1825 he supported a Bill to make spring guns illegal, stating that he 'never could defend the practice of setting engines to endanger the life of a fellow-creature for the sake of a partridge or pheasant'.[4] These events are notable, not only in demonstrating that issues existed upon which Eldon could countenance, and even advocate, reform, but as providing exceptions to his more typically expressed attitudes towards society. He tended to defer to institutions rather than criticise them, while support of property and exemplary punishment of wrongdoers formed a significant part of his social creed.

Eldon was generally hostile to what he perceived as attacks upon institutions or recognised sources of authority. Such attacks might take the form of actual proposals for change, or merely criticisms of an established practice. For example, in 1811 he opposed an

---

[2] 59 George III c. 46.

[3] Hansard, *Parliamentary debates (1st series)*, XL:1207. Removal of this 'gross absurdity' was due to no reforming zeal on Eldon's part, but was prompted by a litigant's having invoked the moribund process in the previous year by appearing in the court of King's Bench and issuing his challenge. *Ashford* v. *Thornton*, (1818) 1 B. & Ald. 405. For a summary of the history of the appeal, see J. H. Baker, *An introduction to English legal history*, 3rd edn (London, 1990), 574–6.

[4] T. Hansard (ed.), *The parliamentary debates from the year 1803 ... new (2nd) series*, 25 vols. (London, 1820–30), XII:940.

inquiry into the Attorney General's use of *ex officio* informations as a means of prosecution. While defending the actual conduct of his learned colleague, Eldon objected to the principle of an inquiry, 'because the very adoption of it would in some degree sanction a suspicion that there was something improper in the administration of justice'.[5] He argued that it was in the public interest that individuals in positions of trust should be presumed to execute them properly. Consequently, 'no clamours should be excited against them, except in cases of such aggravated misconduct as called for the severest reprobation'.[6] Eldon reacted similarly to a prisoner's petition complaining that his letters had been opened by the gaolers, and that he had been denied access to legal advice. Eldon grudgingly acknowledged that there 'might be a regulation of the magistrates about letters which might possibly be wrong', but in the main he praised both magistrates and gaoler, the latter of whom 'was one of the best officers in his situation in Great Britain'.[7] Nor were persons in official situations uniquely deserving of protection. Eldon opposed legislation in 1819 to regulate mental asylums because of the potential effect upon doctors. The Bill aimed to strengthen the regimes of visitation and inspection for all asylums, and to impose particular regulations on those institutions that treated paupers. Eldon gave qualified support to the principle of regulation, and particularly to the measures relating to care of the poor.[8] He objected, however, to the scheme by which one half of any penalty imposed upon an institution went to the individual who had exposed the wrongful practices. These individuals, Eldon argued, would invariably be the 'attendants and servants' employed in the asylum, 'who would thus be made the judges of the conduct of the physicians', their superiors. If this kind of informing were encouraged by the prospect of financial reward, physicians would find their work much hindered, if not impossible.[9]

Eldon also complained that putative reforms promoted disorder and confusion, as when long-established ways of doing things were departed from, or rendered more complicated. This fear lay at the heart of Eldon's objection to Bills in 1814 and 1815 relating

---

[5] Hansard, *Parliamentary debates (1st series)*, XIX:160.

[6] *Ibid.* The motion proposing an inquiry was defeated, 24 to 2.

[7] *Ibid.*, XXVIII:94.     [8] *Ibid.*, XL:1346.

[9] *Ibid.*, col. 1345. The Bill failed to receive a second reading, by a vote of 21 to 14.

to debts contracted by persons in possession of freehold estates. The Bills would have made those estates liable for the simple contractual debts of the deceased freeholder.[10] Eldon preferred to leave responsibility for obtaining security with the individual creditor, rather than to encourage imprudent lending by the promise of statutory protection.

[I]t was much better that he [the creditor] should be left to use his own caution and discretion upon this point, than that he should sit down in apathy and carelessness, under the impression, that the legislature would take care of his interests.[11]

A reform involving a recognised authority could nevertheless be productive of disorder. Lord Lansdowne's Liberty of the Subject Bill in 1815 would have allowed judges to issue writs of *habeas corpus* during the vacations, and to free persons where it was shown that the reason given for incarceration was false. Eldon could and did imagine various examples of the mischievous consequences of such legislation, from lunatics being discharged from mental institutions to seamen departing their ships in wartime. 'The whole would be an endless scene of litigation, confusion, and mischief to all the parties concerned.'[12] Legislation to shift responsibility for the education of poor children away from the clergy and onto the parish was objectionable because it would give rise to all the confusion and mischief of an election.[13] Measures to regulate the employment of children in specific trades and industries could not be supported because such piecemeal legislation would not impose a uniform standard of conduct upon employers. '[I]t might happen that a particular law, applicable only to children in one trade, might expose them to greater evils than those from which it was intended to protect them.'[14] Attempts to alter the existing law regulating silk manufacturing threatened to upset a *status quo* directly or indirectly recognised in

[10] For Eldon's criticisms of the 1814 and 1815 versions of the Freehold Estates Bill, see *ibid.*, XVIII:749–50, XXXI:1038.
[11] *Ibid.*, XXVIII:750. Both Bills were defeated.
[12] *Ibid.*, XXXI:219. The Bill failed to receive a second reading.
[13] *Ibid.*, IX:1176. Eldon said he 'never would agree to any [bill] that left matters of this nature to be judged or decided by the majority of the inhabitants of a parish'.
[14] *Ibid.*, XXXIX:654. Eldon was speaking against the Cotton Factories Bill in February 1819. See also his remarks on the similar Bill of the previous year, and on the Chimney Sweep Bill of May 1819. *Ibid.*, XXXVIII:795, XL:669.

legislation for at least fifty years. 'The question was, whether acts which had been so long in force should now be repealed at once?'[15]

In addition to reforms that threatened recognised authority or produced disorder, Eldon opposed reforms that failed to afford due protection to private property. Proposals laudable in their general social or political aims were resisted where the economic interests of individual property owners would suffer. Speaking in opposition to a Bill to increase financial support for poor London clergymen, Eldon protested against 'this general principle, that because it is right to provide for a great public good, you may do so by taxing the property of individuals'.[16] He consistently attempted to derail legislation hostile to slavery and the slave trade, out of sympathy for the West Indian sugar planters. Arguing against abolition in 1804, he urged the House to consider the slave owner as entitled to sympathy. While wealthy statesmen might wish to 'indulge their benevolence and humanity' on behalf of the slaves, they ought not to act 'at the expence [*sic*] and total ruin to other classes, equally entitled to consideration and to justice'.[17] He feared for planters and ship owners, not merely because they would incur higher production costs or lose business, but also because their losses would serve no purpose. Eldon professed that 'There was no man more inclined to the abolition of the slave trade than himself', but he could not support a ban ruinous to British economic interests where there was no guarantee that international compliance would actually end the practice.[18] As late as 1826 he was repeating his appeal for a sympathetic treatment of the slave-owning interests, describing it as unfair that those who had acted in accordance with a long-established practice should suffer merely because Britain no longer supported it. While slaves were the victims of the original decision to sanction and promote slavery, slave owners were equally the victims of the latter decision to abolish it.[19]

---

[15] Hansard, *Parliamentary debates, new (2ⁿᵈ series)*, IX:1532.

[16] Hansard, *Parliamentary debates (1ˢᵗ series)*, II:1106. Eldon considered it disgraceful that many clergymen had such scanty incomes, but felt 'It is the public, and not individuals, that should be taxed, to provide more decently for them.' *Ibid.*, col. 1107. The Bill in question aimed to increase the amount paid by residents in parishes where clerical contributions had been capped by legislation following the Great Fire.

[17] *Ibid.*, col. 932.    [18] See, e.g., *ibid.*, VII:231, VIII:257–8, 670.

[19] Hansard, *Parliamentary debates, new (2ⁿᵈ series)*, XIV:1157–8.

Just as, in practice, Eldon advanced the economic rather than the moral argument in the context of slavery, he feared the loss of property resulting from disfranchisement more than the political dangers posed by electoral corruption. He consistently opposed legislation to disfranchise particular constituencies, typically because he did not find the relevant behaviour sufficiently objectionable. For example, the Bill in 1814 to disfranchise Helston alleged 'illegal practices' rather than 'notorious corruption' as was usual. Eldon 'did not mean to say, that bribery and corruption were not included under the expression, illegal practices; but there were many illegal practices which would not warrant them in disfranchising a body of electors'.[20] Even where illegal election practices had clearly been proven, Eldon felt that individual, honest voters ought not to be punished by losing their capacity to vote. In arguing that 'The right of franchise was always considered as sacred in the eye of the law', Eldon was conceiving the vote as a species of private property.[21] In contrast to Lord Liverpool, who described the franchise as 'more in the nature of a public trust' which was forfeit whenever circumstances suggested that it could not be executed properly, Eldon considered the franchise as adhering primarily in the individual voter, to be expressed according to his personal wishes and protected absent proof of individual misconduct.[22]

The three foundations upon which Eldon opposed reform (deference to authority, avoidance of confusion, and protection of private property) combined to form the basis of his attitude toward law reform in the criminal context. Eldon was not the most vociferous opponent of Sir Samuel Romilly's campaign to ameliorate the criminal law – that title must go to Lord Ellenborough, the Chief Justice of the King's Bench. Eldon's admission that he had limited professional experience in this area of the law militated against his pursuing an uncompromising position.[23] Nevertheless,

---

[20] Hansard, *Parliamentary debates (1st series)*, XXVIII:676.  [21] *Ibid.*, II:681.
[22] *Ibid.* Cf. the respective positions of Liverpool and Eldon on the Bill to disfranchise Grampound in 1821. Liverpool argued: 'The elective franchise was conferred on the corporation, not for the benefit of individuals, but as a public trust; and when parliament should be of opinion that this trust was abused, it became their duty to withdraw it.' Eldon, conversely, felt that: 'The right of voting was given to the corporation, but the benefit belonged to individuals.' Hansard, *Parliamentary debates, new (2nd series)*, V:695–6.
[23] During the debates on Romilly's 1810 Bill, Eldon remarked that, having spent

his voice, especially when raised in sympathy with the senior criminal judge in the land, was undoubtedly influential.[24] Eldon rejected the views of theorists such as Count Beccaria, that moderate, but certain punishment most effectively discouraged criminal behaviour.[25] On the contrary, he was convinced that the criminal law must remain extreme in principle, and disparate in application. He was, in part, influenced by his desire to keep discretion in the hands of the judges. No specific formulation of crime and punishment was adequate for every situation, he believed, and a rule which obliged judges to impose one, typically moderate, punishment for a particular crime would not provide for circumstances either aggravating or mitigating the offence. Where the legislature imposed punishments of maximum severity upon criminal actions broadly defined, however, it provided judges with the full quantum of discretion. Having heard the specific facts of a case, they could impose the utmost penalty allowed, or recommend the offender to the Crown's mercy, 'in cases of great doubt, or where the shade of crime was comparatively very light.'[26]

Perhaps surprisingly, Eldon's support of the discretionary principle also reflected the value he placed upon certainty in the criminal law. Following the precepts of William Paley, Eldon argued that the certain fear of capital punishment deterred criminal behaviour.[27] Despite the fact that the death sentence was but

---

much of his career in Chancery, he was 'not competent to form so satisfactory an opinion, upon subjects of this sort' namely, the matters of concern to the common law criminal courts. Hansard, *Parliamentary debates, (1st series)*, XIX:cx.

[24] See, e.g., P. Medd, *Romilly* (London, 1968), 222–3.

[25] Beccaria's work was published in England as *Of crimes and punishments* in 1767, and influenced the ideas of, among others, Sir Samuel Romilly, who led the movement for amelioration of the criminal law in the House of Commons until his death in 1818.

[26] Hansard, *Parliamentary debates (1st series)*, XIX:cxi. Eldon particularly used the example of cases of sheep and horse stealing, and compared the defendant who stole one sheep to feed his family, with the defendant who, upon being apprehended with a stolen horse, was found to possess the keys to various turnpikes, in order to facilitate horse stealing on a large scale. See, e.g., *ibid.*, XVII:199*, XX:301, Hansard, *Parliamentary debates, new (2nd) series*, II:495. For the range of opportunities afforded judge and jury to exercise discretion in criminal cases, see T. A. Green, *Verdict according to conscience* (Chicago, 1985), 276–80.

[27] Paley's *Principles of moral and political philosophy* was published in 1785. See

infrequently enforced, convicted criminals nevertheless strongly believed that they would be executed, and potential wrongdoers likewise believed that nothing would save *them*, were they to fall afoul of the law.[28] Certainty, therefore, resulted from the individual's subconscious fears, rather than from the actual functioning of the penal system.

There is no felon, I think, on whom the sentence of death is pronounced, that does not firmly believe at the time, that the punishment must sooner or later be inflicted. Therefore, I am rather of the opinion that it is not from the circumstances of the severity of the law being put into execution to the fullest extent, so much as the imaginary terrors of it on the mind, that produces the abhorrence of crime.[29]

Even a single execution could produce certainty of punishment, and could, therefore, deter criminal conduct. As part of his argument in support of a Bill on corrupting members of the armed forces, he pointed out that, under previous legislation, only one person had been executed in almost twenty years. Since that execution, however, carried out shortly after the law had been enacted, 'no instance of this crime had occurred'. He was therefore 'decidedly of opinion, that this law would operate by intimidation to prevent the offence'.[30]

This certainty in the mind of the potential wrongdoer was jeopardised if the threat of capital punishment was removed. Eldon asked rhetorically: 'Was it an encouragement or discouragement ... in the eyes of any man of common sense, to commit a crime, that instead of being hanged, if he committed it, he could, at the most, be transported?'[31] In fact, he believed that levels of crime increased when it was generally understood that an amelioration of the criminal law was about to be enacted.[32] That Eldon would not have approved an indiscriminate or general application

---

L. Radzinowicz, *History of English criminal law and its administration from 1750*, 5 vols. (London, 1948–86), I:248–59.

[28] In 1805 one of every five persons convicted of a capital offence was executed. This rate fell to one to nine in 1811, and in 1818 one out of twelve. A. L. Manchester, A *modern legal history of England and Wales 1750–1950* (London, 1990), 240.

[29] Hansard, *Parliamentary debates (1ˢᵗ series)*, XIX:cxii.

[30] *Ibid.*, XXXV:904. The Bill under debate aimed to extend the provisions of the 37 George III c. 70. While Attorney General, Eldon had obtained the conviction of Richard Fuller, but had recommended him to the Crown's mercy. See chapter 7.

[31] Hansard, *Parliamentary debates (1ˢᵗ series)*, XXV:525.    [32] *Ibid.*

of the capital sanction, however, seems clear. He took very seriously his responsibility to review all capital cases decided by the Recorder of London, and to advise the King whether to grant a pardon. To Robert Peel he observed of one report: 'from the Recorder's communication to me, he is much more bloody-minded than I am after three times reading all the cases.'[33] On another occasion he predicted that the meeting with the King would be lengthy, because one defendant was entitled to have the verdicts in several related cases taken into consideration.[34] As late as 1830, during debate on a Bill to abolish the death penalty for forgery, Eldon would claim never to have recommended an execution unless persuaded of its absolute necessity.[35]

He also sympathised with the victim, particularly the victim of economic crimes, which were the prime targets of reformers. While acknowledging the apparent harshness of execution for 'stealing privately in a shop to the amount of five shillings', he urged the House to consider the 'men of small property, who could not so well protect themselves'. The loss of what might seem like a trivial amount 'might effectually [*sic*] ruin many shop-keepers'.[36] Eldon's advocacy of the property-owning victim went further. It was frequently argued, in support of Bills to remove the death penalty from various forms of theft, that victims forbore prosecuting out of a disinclination to expose the offender to capital punishment. Eldon disagreed.[37] '[A]nger and a desire to prosecute more often possess the prosecutor's breast, than the amiable qualities of charity and philanthropy.'[38] He opined that parsimony alone deterred most private prosecutions. Already 'sore' at the loss of property, victims were unwilling to bear the expense of prosecution, especially in cases where proof was difficult. Eldon

[33] Eldon to Robert Peel, undated [*c.* October 1822] BL (Peel papers), Add. MS 40315 f. 63.

[34] *Ibid.*, f. 276.     [35] Hansard, *Parliamentary debates, new (2^{nd}) series*, XXV:856.

[36] *Ibid.*, II:493. Eldon described the proposed legislation as a 'merciful experiment' to which he would make 'no very strenuous objection'. He added, however, that 'if hereafter it should be found, that shop-lifting became universal, and that many persons were reduced to misery by this crime, he hoped it would be remembered that he had suggested the consideration, whether this law which had so long existed was not wise and politic'. *Ibid.*

[37] Eldon argued, however, that if fear of capital punishment *did* work upon victims, it must work even more strongly upon criminals and potential criminals. *Ibid.*

[38] Hansard, *Parliamentary debates (1^{st} series)*, XIX:cxiii.

suggested that the public ought to bear the expense of such prosecutions, in order to encourage victims to come forward.[39]

Given Eldon's general interest in protecting private property, it may seem surprising that he did not exercise a comparable deference in the context of the crime of treason. He strongly objected to any change in the law, under which all property of the convicted traitor was forfeit, and which prevented his innocent heirs from inheriting any property from him.[40] Treason and sedition, however, struck a particular chord with Eldon, and his attitude toward their frustration was both more profound and more passionate than his attitude towards criminal law reform generally. This was because, where treason and sedition were concerned, Eldon could and did draw upon his own experiences. When the nation had been poised on the precipice of revolution, he believed that he had actively prevented the fatal step into anarchy. For Eldon, then, his experiences as Attorney General not only qualified him to identify the threats posed by public meetings, marches, and provocative publications, but entitled him to ground almost any defence of current government conduct upon the actions taken during the 1790s. The invocation and justification of his work as prosecutor and exponent of repressive legislation during that period became a familiar ingredient to Eldon's speeches. When the Habeas Corpus Act was suspended in Ireland, Eldon felt obliged to recall his own experience of a similar suspension in England.[41] When the frequency of prosecution by *ex officio* information since Eldon's time became the subject of an opposition motion, he reflected upon his own conduct in that respect as a law officer.

He believed that no Attorney General had prosecuted more libels than it had fallen to his lot to prosecute when he held that office. He acted on a conviction at that time, certainly, that the publication of libel was one of the most formidable weapons then wielded against the constitution; and that it was an engine which was directed to the subversion of the government of the country. It was grateful to him to reflect that he had, by his conduct then, done his part towards its preservation.[42]

---

[39] *Ibid.*, col. cxiv. The Royal Commission on Criminal Law reported in 1845 that private prosecutors were deterred by the necessity of expending 'time, labour, and money'. See Manchester, *History*, 227.

[40] Hansard, *Parliamentary debates new (2nd) series*, XIII:836.

[41] Hansard, *Parliamentary debates (1st series)*, III:582.     [42] *Ibid.*, XIX:158.

Certainly if persons or incidents actually involved in events of the 1790s came under discussion, even obliquely, Eldon could be counted upon to make his contribution. He prefaced a lengthy comparison of jury trial and summary proceedings for contempt with a vindication of his conduct in the treason trials of 1794, because Earl Grey had referred briefly to the activities of the Society for Constitutional Information in his motion for an address to the Crown on the state of the nation.[43] As part of his defence against the charges that he had misled Parliament on the state of the King's health, Eldon could not resist referring to his conduct during the 1790s, when he had acted 'in conjunction with some noble lords over the way, at the most critical moment that this country ever experienced'.[44] He continually invited his audience to view again the abyss so fortunately avoided through the government's (and his) actions.

The period of 1816–19, which was characterised by severe, if intermittent, unrest, called forth Eldon's particular bogies. Following the end of the long continental war, various sections of British society came under severe economic stress. The damaging effects of poor harvests, unemployment, and government economic policies culminated in strikes and protest meetings, as well as events more threatening and sinister. In December 1816 a public rally in Spa Fields in London, at which revolutionary banners were displayed, ended in an attempt by some participants to march into the City after breaking into a gun shop. The following January the window of the Regent's coach was broken as he returned from opening Parliament. This was not the first time in recent memory that economic crisis had provoked violence. In 1811 business failures and unemployment, particularly in the iron and textile industries, had led to organised machine-breaking and the creation of Luddite societies.[45] On that occasion, the situation

---

[43] *Ibid.*, XVII:591.

[44] *Ibid.*, XVIII:1017. This reference was not quite so inapt as it might appear. In mentioning the conduct of the government in the 1790s Eldon not only emphasised the Pittite pedigree of one section of the opposition, but endeavoured to show that protection of the King was a prerequisite to the maintenance of the constitution.

[45] The economic distress of 1811 had also inspired radicals of more 'middle class' sensibilities. Sir Francis Burdett chaired the Hampden Club, founded to resume the process of political agitation and education undertaken by the Society for Constitutional Information (SCI) and the London Corresponding Society

had been largely diffused by the trade revival in 1812. In the spring of 1817, however, comparable relief was not forthcoming, and the government determined to act.[46] Committees of secrecy were formed in both Houses of Parliament, and these examined the evidence for the existence of revolutionary conspiracies. Bills to suspend the Habeas Corpus Act and to restrict public meetings were swiftly enacted.

As Home Secretary, Lord Sidmouth was primarily responsible for these measures, but Eldon provided strong support, often concluding the debate in the Lords for the government. Reports of marches and rallies at which democratic symbols were displayed, suggestions that reform clubs and societies were being founded, and the evidence that cheap publications were questioning not only the conduct of government but the very structure of society, were for him particularly threatening. He could not regard them as other than a repetition of those assaults upon the state and the constitution which he believed he had helped to repulse two decades earlier. Eldon's attitude to the threat took two forms, both based on his previous experiences. First, he looked for malevolent external influences. Fears that foreign agitators would promote unrest in England had already been evident in Eldon's support of the Alien Bill in 1816. He had considered this Bill, which allowed the Crown to deport aliens who had failed to abide by registration and residence requirements, necessary to counter the continuing threat from abroad. He had found it 'astonishing' that after twenty-five years of war anyone could imagine that a peace treaty would remove the danger of contamination.[47] In the debates on the Seditious Meetings Bill in March 1817 he took a similar line, warning that he 'had only to cast his eyes abroad, and see mischiefs threatening, evil designs at work, and disaffection active, sufficient to call for additional means of protection'.[48] While France remained the most potent source of revolutionary

---

(LCS). Men like Eldon, who had prosecuted these organisations, undoubtedly regarded their resurrection as a worrying development.

[46] On the contrary, establishment fears were further roused by the abortive attempt by Jeremiah Brandreth to lead an uprising in Nottingham. The scheme was thwarted through the activities of a government spy. Nineteen persons were sentenced to death for their part in the conspiracy, and of these, four were executed. J. W. Hunt, *Reaction and reform 1815–1841* (London, 1972), 49–50.

[47] Hansard, *Parliamentary debates (1ˢᵗ series)*, XXXIV:1066.

[48] *Ibid.*, XXXV:1240.

ideas, Ireland too posed a danger, as a breeding ground for riotous, undisciplined conduct. In a letter to his brother, Eldon lamented the influence of Irish forms of wrongdoing and their consequences for the English government:

[A]t the time of the union with Ireland, I told Mr Pitt that I thought the great objection to it was that it would perhaps introduce into this country sedition and treason in their Irish modes and forms; that, if such should be the case, we should have to attempt passing, at Westminster, such laws as Ireland had enacted; that my belief was that no Parliaments at Westminster ever would pass such laws; that, if they would not, Great Britain, as a land of anarchy, would be a land in which it would be impossible to exist; and, if they would pass such laws, it would be a land of necessary tyranny, in which existence would not be to be wished. Treason and sedition do now appear in such modes and forms.[49]

The expression 'necessary tyranny' reflects a second tendency in Eldon's arguments. He repeatedly emphasised the need to forego certain liberties in order to preserve the larger quantum of liberty inherent in the constitution. This was particularly his justification of interference with such cherished ideals as the Habeas Corpus Act. Speaking on that subject during debate on the Seditious Meetings Bill, Eldon remarked that if the House 'wished to secure the inestimable blessings the country enjoyed, they would ... imitate what had often been done by their ancestors, namely, to suspend their liberties for a short time, in order to have the full enjoyment of them for ever after'.[50] The notion of necessary tyranny also applied in respect of other activities. He regretted the use of 'spies', those persons who infiltrated radical clubs and assemblies and informed the government about their activities, and admitted that the spies themselves often deserved opprobrium. Where dangerous plots had been discovered, however, the government was obliged to use such individuals for the greater good.[51] Even the prosecution of libels, he argued, only occurred when they were part of a systematic plot against the nation. *Ad hoc* attacks upon individuals or the government were left alone. He explained that: 'It had never been his disposition to regard the case of an ordinary libel on the government of the country with

---

[49] Eldon to Sir William Scott, undated [*c.* September 1819), H. Twiss, *The public and private life of Lord Chancellor Eldon*, 3 vols. (London, 1844), II:346.

[50] Hansard, *Parliamentary debates (1ˢᵗ series)*, XXXV:1217.

[51] *Ibid.*, XXXVI:1063. Eldon was defending the use of spies to report on the activities of the Spa Fields rioters.

any particular jealousy or vigilance.'[52] Similarly, he affirmed that he 'cared not two-pence' for any of the libels published against himself personally.[53] However, when evidence existed of a 'system', 'the object of which was, by means of these libellous publications, to overthrow the government', then it was necessary to suppress it 'with a strong hand'.[54] In circumstances of such national peril, the individual who suffered a loss of liberty must 'bear the hardships of his fate' rather than obtain redress.[55] Indeed, repressive government measures ought not to be regarded as unjust, but as 'essential to the preservation of a constitution, under which more practical liberty and happiness was enjoyed by the subject than any other under the canopy of heaven'.[56]

The threat of unrest leading to active insurrection seemed to reach its peak in the summer of 1819. As a means of protesting against their exclusion from the political process, radicals in the Midlands determined to elect their own representatives, who would then assemble in London to 'pass' 'legislation' on issues of economic and political reform. One such election meeting was held in Birmingham. Following a pronouncement by the Home Secretary that actions of this kind were unlawful, a meeting was publicised in Manchester with the avowed purpose of the lawful petitioning of Parliament. On 16 August 1819 approximately 50–60,000 people assembled in St Peter's Fields, the site of a similar mass meeting two years earlier which had ended in magistrates using troops to disperse the crowds. Amongst the speakers was the famous radical orator, Henry Hunt, who had previously attended the meeting in Spa Fields. On this occasion, drilling took place among the participants, some of whom included women and children, but no firearms were in evidence. Nevertheless, the magistrates present attempted to arrest Hunt, using a contingent of the local yeomanry. Accounts of what followed differed, but the yeomanry proved unable to execute their orders in either an efficient or a non-violent manner. The

---

[52] *Ibid.*, col. 503.
[53] *Ibid.*, XXXV:1240. Eldon expressed himself similarly in private correspondence with his brother. Eldon to Scott, undated [*c.* 1813], Twiss, *The public and private life*, II:237. See also Eldon to Scott, undated [*c.* 1813], *ibid.*, II:235.
[54] Hansard, *Parliamentary debates (1st series)*, XXXVI:503.
[55] *Ibid.*, XXXVII:657.    [56] *Ibid.*, XXXVI:505.

appearance of a troop of cavalry swiftly resolved the situation, but the consequences of panic, crowding, and undoubted acts of violence by the soldiers, horses, and crowd were 11 persons killed and approximately 400 injured.

The after-effects of the Peterloo massacre, as it was soon called, were dramatic. On 13 September 1819 Hunt made a flamboyant entry into London, having been freed on bail. In the capital and across the country, meetings of opposition and radical sympathisers questioned and frequently condemned the actions of the Manchester magistrates. Cartoons and pamphlets were published depicting Peterloo as the latest assault by the government on traditional English liberties. Hampered by the fact that fewer than half the Cabinet was in easy reach of London in August and September, the government nevertheless responded with firmness. The authorities in Manchester received strong official support, and Earl Fitzwilliam was relieved of his office of Lord Lieutenant after having supported a meeting of freeholders in the West Riding of Yorkshire that resolved to seek an inquiry into the events of Peterloo.[57] Parliament was recalled early, and met on 23 November 1819. Within a month the government had successfully enacted legislation designed to deal with the state of crisis which many felt to be at hand. These were the so-called 'Six Acts'. They specifically forbade unauthorised military drilling, penalised seditious libels, restricted public meetings, authorised magistrates to search private property for weapons, streamlined the mechanism for indicting and trying persons charged with seditious or public order offences, and extended the stamp tax to previously exempt publications.[58]

Eldon's sentiments with regard to these events are not difficult to imagine. In letters to his brother and to Sidmouth he spoke generally of his anxiety at the threat faced by society, and specifically of how situations like Peterloo ought to be dealt with, in terms suggesting that he feared the lessons of revolutionary

---

[57] Sidmouth wrote indignantly to Eldon on 17 October: 'Lord F[itzwilliam] ought to be instantly removed; and so I have said to Lord Liverpool.' Twiss, *The public and private life*, II:347.

[58] 60 George III c. 1 (Training Prevention Act); 60 George III c. 2 (Seizure of Arms Act); 60 George III c. 4 (Misdemeanors Act); 60 George III c. 6 (Seditious Meetings Prevention Act); 60 George III c. 8 (Blasphemous and Seditious Libels Act); and 60 George III c. 9 (Newspaper Stamp Duties Act).

insurrection had yet to be learned. To his brother he stated the case openly, describing the 'better sort' of people as afflicted with a kind of insanity, which rendered them incompetent to recognise the danger they faced:

The one insane, and manifesting that insanity in perfect apathy, eating and drinking, as if there was no danger of political death, yea even to-morrow: the other ... hallooing on an infuriate multitude to those acts of desperation and fury, which will first destroy those who encourage the perpetration of them.[59]

More dangerous than either of these, however, was the radical press, which inflamed the common man against the government and established institutions. Writing from Encombe, Eldon informed Sidmouth of the locals being 'inundated with newspapers &c of a most wicked & seditious kind – with no publications to counteract their effects'.[60] Subjected to such influences, it was not only 'impossible to hope that ... the minds of the lower classes can for any time resist the seduction constantly applied to them', but 'we shall find no juries, whose minds are not alienated by the boldness & sophistry' of these publications.[61] One means of counteracting this invidious flow, Eldon suggested, would be the distribution of 'small works for general information' such as had been circulated between 1793 and 1796 to educate people on the legal sanctions available against those who engaged in activities inimical to the state.[62] As regards the specific assembly in Manchester, Eldon supported, although not unreservedly, the actions taken by the authorities. With a cautious regard for the reports he had read of the events of 16 August, he opined that, while the magistrates seemed to have been justified in using reasonable force to disperse the assembly, whether 'force was used beyond what was reasonable, & therefore not justifiably and in excess, may be another question'.[63] To his brother he expressed some concern

---

[59] Eldon to Scott, undated [*c*. August 1819], Twiss, *The public and private life*, II:340.

[60] Eldon to Sidmouth, 20 September 1819, DevRO (Sidmouth papers), 152M/c1819/OH86.

[61] Eldon to Sidmouth, 16 September 1819, *ibid.*, 152M/c1819/OH84.

[62] Eldon to Sidmouth, 20 September 1819, *ibid.*, 152M/c1819/OH86.

[63] *Ibid.* In his letter to Sidmouth of 4 October Eldon added a somewhat confusing postscript: 'When I use the words *reasonable force* I use them, doubting whether force was not used in excess at M[anchester] – if the papers are to be believed – I may add the testimony of witnesses, however, as I read it, is such, as to its

that, if the meeting were held to have been merely an unlawful assembly, justification of the magistrates' actions 'will be difficult enough in sound reasoning'.[64] His own opinion, however, was that the meeting ought not to be so designated, and that the circumstances of inflammatory language and provocative banners made it a 'rebellious riot'.[65]

Of more concern to Eldon, however, was the basis of any prosecution of individuals responsible for holding the ill-fated meeting. He admitted to Sidmouth to have been 'plaguing *myself* in every hour's ruminations on account of the Manchester prosecutions not being for treason'.[66] Even prior to the determination of the law officers to proceed with the lesser charge of sedition, Eldon had not doubted the outcome of their deliberations. '[T]he case is as large and complicated as mine was in 1794, and nobody has the spirit to attempt it.'[67] He was convinced, however, both that the events in Manchester constituted overt acts of treason, and that a prosecution for that offence ought to have been attempted. On the first point Eldon grounded his arguments on the statute of 36 Geo. III c. 7, which he referred to as 'my act'.[68] This provided that a conspiracy to levy war, to kill, depose or force the King 'to change his measures or counsels', or 'to put any force or constraint upon, or to intimidate or overawe' Parliament, constituted treason. 'Can any man doubt, connecting Birmingham and Manchester together, that these meetings are overt acts of conspirators, to instigate [*sic*] to such specific acts of treason or some of them? I cannot doubt it.'[69] The link between Birmingham and Manchester was significant, as the former had nominated

general nature, that it is [difficult] to give any credit to it.' *Ibid.*, 152M/c1819/OH96.

[64] Eldon to Scott, undated [*c.* August 1819], Twiss, *The public and private life*, II:338.

[65] Eldon to Sidmouth, 20 September 1819, DevRO (Sidmouth papers), 152M/c1819/OH86. Nor, according to Eldon, did it matter whether the Riot Act had been read (accounts differed on this point, but it seems clear that if they did read the Act, the magistrates did not wait the requisite hour before attempting to disperse the assembly). Eldon pointed out that riot existed at common law, and need not be based on the statute. *Ibid.*

[66] *Ibid.*

[67] Eldon to Scott, undated [*c.* August 1819], Twiss, *The public and private life*, II:336.

[68] For the events leading up to the enactment of this statute, see chapter 6.

[69] Eldon to Scott, undated [*c.* August 1819], Twiss, *The public and private life*, II:339.

delegates to attend the proposed legislative assembly in London, while the latter had not.[70] Despite his confidence in the strength of his legal argument, however, Eldon did not advocate prosecutions for treason because he considered convictions likely. On the contrary, he regarded them as 'wholly inefficacious' in that respect, presumably because of the corrupting influence of the radical press upon likely juries. He supported prosecutions for treason for the same reason that he advocated the occasional infliction of capital punishment, because of their salutary effect on the public temperament. Unlike sedition, which must await the next assizes, a prosecution for treason could be commenced speedily. Given the 'unremitting efforts which will be made to inflame the public mind upon all these topics from this hour till the next spring assizes', it was desirable to deny the press that opportunity. Moreover, the gravity, not to say awe, with which the average person would regard a trial for treason, must help to restore a proper respect for the legal authority of the state. '[S]uch prosecutions would, in the interim, have kept the public mind in a much more serious state, and in a state, much better suited to the real nature of the transactions which have passed.'[71]

As he had been in the 1790s, Eldon was convinced that, ultimately, legislation and not prosecution must check the dangerous tendencies revealed by recent events. He strongly advocated the early recall of Parliament, both to enact the necessary legislation, and to demonstrate resolution in the face of 'that revolutionary system now in prosecution'. Precisely what constituted appropriate legislation would take time for consideration. In September, he mentioned to Sidmouth the political dimension of any legislative proposals:

The measures proposed, if they are not strong measures, will be more mischievous than leaving things as they are: if they are strong, if in fact they break in upon, or can be represented to the conviction of the multitude, however fallaciously, as breaking in upon the right of public

---

[70] Eldon did not believe that the professed aim of the Manchester assembly was the genuine one. 'When one sees bodies of men, & corporations, representing Manchester meetings as meetings for petitioning parliament, when all intention of petitioning had been previously publickly disavowed, what may not be represented or rather misrepresented, with fatal effect, to an ill-inclined multitude?' Eldon to Sidmouth, 20 September 1819, DevRO (Sidmouth papers), 152M/c1819/OH86.

[71] Eldon to Sidmouth, 16 September 1819, *ibid.*, 152M/c1819/OH84.

meetings, for petitions &c and the liberty of the press – and I can think of
no measures, which may not be so represented, that can be resorted to,
those, who best know the temper of the House of Commons, will be best
able to judge whether the members of that House will adopt them.[72]

Nor were his concerns only those of the practical politician. He
did not forget his creed of doing, at least according to his own
lights, only what was necessary to preserve the greater liberties of
the constitution. To Sidmouth he warned:

Great care must be taken not further to break in upon habits, founded in
constitutional English liberty, than is necessary to secure the direct object
of the English constitution and the law of England – the happiness, safety,
& liberty of the public. So far as it is necessary for that purpose, the
necessity might be met, & provided for effectually.[73]

At the same time, however, he proposed several general measures
to the Home Secretary, namely, facilitating the swift processing of
criminal trials as required by public safety, preventing unauthorised military drilling, regulating more strictly the conduct
of public meetings, and restricting cheap political publications.
The similarity between this list and the legislation enacted by
Parliament in December is clear.

Accordingly, when the various Bills were debated, Eldon supported them strongly. He charged that the current practices of
mass meetings, military drilling, and, above all, the publication of
cheap political cartoons and pamphlets, were part of a new
attempt to overturn English society, and the proposed legislation
was no more than what was strictly necessary to defeat this undertaking. It could hardly be objectionable to ban so-called 'monster'
meetings, which were simply occasions for inflaming the passions
of the crowd. 'Was it possible that these multitudes could carry on
any thing like debate, that they could calmly discuss their grievances, or make any rational progress toward their removal?' The
Bill still authorised men to meet 'in a manner calculated to answer
the purposes of debate, and to enable them to come to a right
conclusion'.[74] How could a ban on military drilling be deemed
coercion, when no man had the right to keep arms other than for
his own defence?[75] Eldon repeated his warning of the insidious
effect of publications that undermined public confidence in estab-

---

[72] Eldon to Sidmouth, 20 September 1819, *ibid.*, 152M/c1819/OH86.
[73] Eldon to Sidmouth, 16 September 1819, *ibid.*, 152M/c1819/OH84.
[74] Hansard, *Parliamentary debates (1ˢᵗ series)*, XLI:1588.          [75] *Ibid.*

lished institutions, focusing particularly on the link between blasphemy and sedition:

The publications he was adverting to were made up of seditious blasphemy, and blasphemous sedition. By no other means could a people who for fifty years had shown themselves to be the most moral and religious in the world, be seduced into a conspiracy for overthrowing the constitution of their country. It was necessary that their religion and their morals should first be undermined.[76]

Speaking in support of the Blasphemous Libel Bill he trusted that: 'When attempts were made to undermine religion, morals, law, property, in short everything held most dear ... they would not withhold their concurrence from this Bill, which was intended to support them.'[77]

In what might be described as his 'mature' attitude toward reform, as expressed during his years as Lord Chancellor, Eldon was dominated by a conservative sensibility operating at three levels. Together, these resulted in hostility to the idea of change, preference for an old-fashioned mechanism of change, and an increasingly outdated sensitivity for what constituted important matters demanding change. At the most basic level, Eldon valued the certainty of that which *is* over the uncertainty of that which *might be*. This was not because he could not perceive that current practices or institutions were other than flawless (although he generally thought them very nearly perfect), but because he believed flaws were inevitable and any change would introduce new and probably worse ones. If change were inevitable, he preferred to see it occur slowly, specifically, and internally. Thus, his preferred engines of reform were the institutions in which social, legal, or political practice was already being carried out, with the best example being the exercise of judicial discretion. A parliamentary engine of reform, by contrast, provided for a pace of change that was unacceptably fast, and a quantum of change that was unacceptably large. It was, moreover, an engine that imposed change upon an institution, often without sufficient attention to the unique and complex rules, problems, and traditions of that institution. Sometimes, of course, Eldon recognised that the larger needs of society required the swift, powerful intervention afforded by parliamentary action. Significantly, he

[76] *Ibid.*, col. 1589.    [77] *Ibid.*, col. 729.

looked to Parliament to meet the threat of political revolution. In the 1790s his conduct had been dictated by the failure of prosecutions to stem the tide, and in 1819 he needed no further proofs. Where a 'system' existed to undermine the institutions and values of society, society could not be expected to combat it via ordinary mechanisms. Rather it must draw on the resources of Parliament for enhanced powers. The almost unique status Eldon gave to political revolution meant that he was increasingly out of touch on substantive issues. He did not, for example, recognise the existence of an overriding moral imperative for change in such issues as capital punishment, slavery, and child labour. These, for him, were not so important as to justify parliamentary intervention, but could safely be left to tentative, piecemeal, or occasional alterations, and only undertaken after a careful weighing up of contrary interests. It is easy to describe Eldon simply by reference to the *substance* of his views on such issues as these. For example, his unwillingness to regard a regular working week of 72 hours as proof that children employed in cotton factories were being overworked shows an insensitivity to the humanitarian attitudes of the time.[78] It is important to remember, however, that, while his views were becoming increasingly outdated in the course of his career, his was not a lone voice in the House of Lords. What was more fundamental to Eldon's political character, and more at odds with what would become the dominant feature of the nineteenth-century constitution, was his attitude towards parliamentary change. For him, it remained an extraordinary source of exceptional powers, little needed because the existing structures and practices were sound. A growing dissatisfaction with those structures, combined with a confidence in parliamentary intervention, by contrast, would initiate a pace and degree of change with which Eldon would have had no sympathy.

---

[78] Liverpool, by contrast, argued that 'it was morally impossible such labour should not have those injurious effects which called for the interference of the legislature'. *Ibid.*, XXXVIII:795.

# 15

# THE SPEAKER SPEAKS

Eldon's work in the House of Lords was not confined to speeches of an overtly political nature. Among his duties as Lord Chancellor, he presided over debates in the capacity of Speaker. The office of Speaker was concomitant with that of Chancellor, and, if the latter was vacant, the Speakership was held by the Keeper of the Great Seal. Unlike his counterpart in the lower House, therefore, the Speaker of the House of Lords was named by the government, rather than elected by his colleagues in the legislature. Another crucial distinction between the two Speakers was their attitude towards debate. While the Speaker of the House of Commons did not participate other than in matters of form, his counterpart in the Upper House might do so under certain circumstances. By means of a fiction which enabled a commoner to conduct the business of their lordships' House, the Speaker's seat, known as the Woolsack, was not considered to be part of that place. Therefore, a Speaker confined to the Woolsack by his lack of a title of nobility was obliged to remain silent during debates. If the Speaker were a peer, however, he could 'enter' the chamber by vacating the Woolsack and standing some few paces from it, and he performed this manoeuvre when he wished to contribute to proceedings in his personal capacity. In the normal course of events, the Lord Chancellor officiated over matters of procedure and privilege as the servant of the House, and participated in debates as a minister.

Because of the difference in his physical posture, it was easy for those present to determine when the Chancellor was at least professing to speak without political bias. It is rather more difficult to make this determination from the early nineteenth-century reports, however, as they do not always indicate when the Chancellor was speaking from the Woolsack. Sometimes, of course, this is evident from the substance of the speech, as when Eldon notified the House of a breach of privilege associated with the admittance of strangers with umbrellas.[1] Similarly, he was clearly speaking as a member of the government when he coloured his remarks on the Alien Act in June 1818 with the reflection that he 'rejoiced that the course of his politics had been quite different' from that of Earl Grey.[2] In other circumstances, however, the case is less clear. Nor, indeed, can it be assumed that political considerations did not creep into the Chancellor's remarks when he addressed the House as its Speaker. Eldon seems to have been aware of the likelihood of such a suggestion during a discussion of whether the Standing Orders permitted Lord Melville to appear before a Commons committee investigating accusations against him. In stating his opinion, Eldon assured his listeners that:

For his own part, in such a case, did every subject in his majesty's dominions think he was acting wrong, he should perform his duty to himself, to all their lordships, and to the house in general, and, therefore, to the country, in strenuously recommending, nay, even in insisting ... it should be referred to the committee of privileges to enquire what had been the former practice of the house upon such occasions.[3]

The difficulty of maintaining and appearing to maintain an unbiased view of procedures was probably one frequently faced by Speakers. Eldon's treatment of petitions addressed to the House illustrates his own conduct in this respect. On some occasions his reluctance to admit a petition seems genuinely to have resulted from a view that the document was objectionable on its merits. For example, he complained that a petition opposed to the general theory of a pending Bill failed to allege a specific injury. If all such petitions were allowed, he observed: 'Their bar might be thus perpetually occupied by debating upon general principles.'[4] In the same way, he had little sympathy for a petitioner who possessed a judicial remedy but had failed to make use of it. '[I]f, under the circumstances stated in the Petition, the petitioner had remained in prison, it was entirely his fault; for on application to any judge, he would immediately have been liberated.'[5] In situations where

---

[1] T. Hansard (ed.), *The parliamentary debates from the year 1803 ... new (2ⁿᵈ) series*, 25 vols. (London, 1820–30), XVII:35.
[2] T. Hansard (ed.), *Parliamentary debates from the year 1803 ... (1ˢᵗ series)*, 41 vols. (London, 1812–20), XXXVIII:1003.
[3] *Ibid.*, IV:590–1.    [4] *Ibid.*, XXX:243.    [5] *Ibid.*, XXVIII:841.

Eldon's complaint related purely to a formal inadequacy, his *bona fides* is harder to judge. On one hand, of course, the Chancellor was notoriously punctilious in his regard for form. A simple attention to form can be assumed in Eldon's objection to a petition referring to an *unpublished* House of Commons report, and to a petition which consisted of two separate documents, one containing the prayer for relief and the other containing the supporting signatures.[6] On the other hand, a pedantic attachment to terminology can suggest a less defensible tendency. Eldon's announcement that a prisoner's petition did not contain the word 'humble', or his observations regarding the tendency of Quakers to address their petitions to 'the Upper House', 'Peers', or 'Lords in Parliament assembled' rather than 'the Lords Spiritual and Temporal now in Parliament assembled' seem small-minded, if not worse.[7] In the case of the Quakers, at least, Eldon did not press his objections strongly. It is difficult, however, to read Eldon's objections to petitions against the conduct of attorneys in the Lord Mayor's Court as other than an attempt to block these complaints on technical grounds. When the petitions were presented by Earl Stanhope, Eldon requested a determination whether the House was the proper forum for such matters. When this was agreed to, Stanhope expressed a wish to read one of the petitions aloud. Eldon acquiesced, but upon hearing the House designated 'the Upper House of Parliament, denominated the lords spiritual & temporal' he immediately objected on the grounds of informality of address.[8]

For the most part, however, Eldon seems to have performed the tasks of Speaker with both propriety and skill. He guided debates gently, and sometimes with humour. For example, during the discussion of a Bill to regulate voting by Scottish peers, the question of legitimacy under Scottish law was raised. Eldon remarked that:

he was aware that there were many modes of contracting marriage in Scotland. He had heard, he believed, three or four hundred ways pointed out by counsel at their lordships' bar, who descanted on the subjects as learnedly as if they had three or four hundred wives themselves.[9]

[6] Hansard, *Parliamentary debates (1ˢᵗ series)*, XXXV:491; *ibid.*, XXX:258. See also *The Times*, 24 January 1811, 2, col. 2.
[7] *Ibid.*, XXXVII:438–9; XXXIII:543; XXVIII:609.   [8] *Ibid.*, XXXIII:300.
[9] Hansard, *Parliamentary debates, new (2ⁿᵈ) series*, I:1046.

He described his as a judicial station, whereby he notified his colleagues of the legal issues arising from their arguments, and attempted finally to weigh up those arguments and declare his opinion when he had heard 'all those noble lords who were disposed to speak upon the question'.[10] On those occasions when he considered his own legal knowledge suspect, however, he sought the 'indulgence' of the House. This was particularly so in matters involving current criminal legal practice. Describing himself as not 'so great an adept in the criminal law as to be always prepared to give their lordships a satisfactory opinion upon every difficulty that might be stated', he gave his opinion 'for which such allowances should be made as his practice confined to courts of equity required'.[11]

An issue upon which Eldon expressed himself strongly was attendance. A peer with a poor record on that score could expect little sympathy from the Lord Chancellor. When Earl Grosvenor protested in January 1811 against the House having received petitions in advance of the Bill for supplying the deficit of royal executive power, Eldon observed: 'If the noble earl was so anxious to protest against the reception of petitions, as inconsistent with their lordships' duty in their present situation, why did he not attend his duty on other days in that House, and, upon the principles he had urged tonight, protest ...?'[12] Similarly, when the Earl of Suffolk moved to put off consideration of the University Advowsons Bill in May 1805 because of the thin attendance of lay peers, Eldon pointed out that the Bill had been discussed 'again and again' and that the considerable exodus from the House only ten minutes earlier indicated a lack of opposition. He added that 'there might be some peers who preferred their dinner to their duty'.[13] Not surprisingly, Eldon took his own obligations in this respect very seriously. Replying to Suffolk's observation about the cost of litigation before the House of Lords, Eldon went on the attack. He remarked that *he* could not be blamed:

who sat on that woolsack for two or three hours day after day, without being able to get the attendance of noble lords sufficient to make a House

---

[10] Hansard, *Parliamentary debates (1ˢᵗ series)*, X:1153.

[11] *Ibid.*, XXXVII:716, 717.    [12] *Ibid.*, XVIII:1030–1.    [13] *Ibid.*, IV:634.

and proceed on any business. That expense, therefore, was more imputable to the noble earl and others, who declined their assistance.[14]

After his retirement from office, Eldon would remind his successors of their obligation to put attendance first among their many public obligations. When Lord Brougham begged to excuse himself in order to attend in the court of Chancery, Eldon observed that the Standing Orders required the Lord Chancellor's attendance in the House.[15] Noting that individual's absence during a debate on a Bill to increase the Chancellor's authority over the parochial clergy, Eldon pointed out that the practice was to seek permission from the House before absenting oneself. He opined, moreover, that, as a royal summons had not always been deemed a sufficient excuse for non-attendance, he doubted that bankruptcy business 'however excellently done' could suffice.[16] While it is tempting to see Eldon's remarks as the particular result of Brougham's previous criticisms of Eldon's management of his judicial and parliamentary responsibilities, they also accord generally with his views on what was owed to the House by any Chancellor.[17]

In any assessment of the duties of a Lord Chancellor, the job of Speaker would, under normal circumstances, not rank as among the most onerous. Peers, when they attended, conducted themselves decorously,[18] and both the government and opposition expected important or controversial measures to be settled largely in the House of Commons. During Eldon's tenure, however, the Lords were thrust on one occasion into the political foreground in a way that increased significantly the role of its presiding officer. This was the so-called trial of Queen Caroline. More specifically, it was a Bill to punish her for adulterous intercourse, consideration of which occupied the attention of the upper House in the late summer and autumn of 1820.

The domestic problems of Caroline of Brunswick were long-

---

[14] *Ibid.*, XVII:470.

[15] T. Hansard (ed.), *Hansard's parliamentary debates 3rd series*, 356 vols. (London, 1831–91), VI:454.

[16] *Ibid.*, VII:590–2. See also *ibid.*, XXIV:600.

[17] See, e.g., Eldon to George IV, 10 April 1827, A. Aspinall (ed.), *The correspondence of George IV, king of England, 1812–1830*, 3 vols. (Cambridge, 1938), III:217. For Brougham's criticism of Eldon, see chapter 16.

[18] For evidence of Eldon's ability to keep order, see his rebuke of the Duke of Gloucester in Hansard, *Parliamentary debates (1st series)*, XXX:243.

standing, and the chronology of events leading up to the legal action against her deserve further consideration. Following the cautious vindication of her conduct by the Commission of Inquiry in 1806, her public reputation had, to a degree, strengthened. Living primarily at Montague House in Blackheath, she had maintained a link with Court and government resulting from the King's sympathy and ministers' recollection of their former support. Her circumstances, as well as her political importance, however, had changed following the creation of the Regency in 1811. While the Regent's animosity had increasingly barred her from the first circles of society and had hardened ministers against her, his failure to bring his old political associates into office had transformed them into her enthusiastic supporters. The resulting political warfare had led to the publication in 1813 of the old charges and counter-charges, while London newspapers had become vehicles for propaganda on either side. At last, pestered by her new friends and snubbed by her old ones, the Princess had gratified her own wishes and those of the Regent by leaving England. In the summer of 1814, she had set off for Brunswick, and from there had embarked upon an extensive foreign tour. Over the next two years her itinerary had included Milan, Naples, Tunis, Athens, Constantinople, and Jerusalem. Thereafter she had settled near Milan, on an estate she had purchased near Lake Como. She had continued to travel, albeit on a smaller scale, visiting Munich, Innsbruck, and Vienna between 1817 and 1819.

Unfortunately, the Princess's life abroad had not been unexceptionable. Reports and rumours of indiscreet, improper, and even outrageous behaviour during her European sojourn had not failed to reach the Prince Regent. [19] In June 1816 and July 1817 he had pressed the Cabinet for an opinion on the evidence, but ministers had refused to commit themselves.[20] Finally, in the autumn of 1817 the Regent had laid the accumulated materials before his friend and adviser, Sir John Leach. Leach had opined that a judgment resting solely on the existing evidence would result in 'the most unfavorable conclusion' and had advocated further

[19] There is evidence that the Hanoverian envoy at the Vatican had been collecting evidence and passing it on to the Foreign Office since 1815. J. E. Cookson, *Lord Liverpool's administration* (Edinburgh, 1975), 202.

[20] For the Cabinet minutes, see BL (Liverpool papers), Add. MS 38368 f. 312; Add. MS 38267 f. 203.

inquiries regarding the Princess's travels in Italy and beyond.[21] While unwilling to sanction an oficial inquiry, the government had undertaken to pay the expenses of the three-member commission Leach assembled. This panel had been despatched to Milan in September 1818.[22] There, with the assistance of the Austrian government, they had begun to assemble the case against the Princess.

The decision to commence an investigation, closely following the death of Princess Charlotte, had convinced Princess Caroline's friends that they ought likewise to resume an active interest in her affairs.[23] One of these, Henry Brougham, had sent his brother to Italy in the spring of 1819 to discuss with her the advantages of a negotiated separation from the Regent. Meanwhile, the Milan Commission had been collecting a formidable dossier, consisting largely of the testimony of the Princess' former servants. This had focused on the Princess' allegedly adulterous relationship with one Bartolommeo Bergami, formerly her courier and more latterly her chamberlain. He had accompanied her on her eastern tour, and James Brougham had found him and various members of his family living with the Princess at Villa Cassielli, the estate she had purchased for him. At this point, the four parties most closely concerned in the matter – the Regent, the Princess, Henry Brougham, and the government – had found themselves in a difficult position. The Regent wanted to divorce the woman whom he described to Eldon as 'a woman who has ... not alone been the bain [*sic*] & curse of my existence, but who now stands prominent in the eyes of the whole world characteriz'd by a flagrancy of abandonment unparalell'd in the history of woman, & stamp'd with disgrace & dishonour'.[24] The Princess likewise was coming to regard a mere separation as unacceptable. Brougham

---

[21] Leach's memo on the Milan Commission, 4 February 1821, Aspinall, *George IV*, II:411.

[22] The so-called 'Milan Commission' consisted of John Powell, solicitor; William Cooke, a Chancery barrister; and Major (subsequently Colonel) Thomas Browne.

[23] It was felt that, while the Regent might have been willing to forego a divorce so long as his daughter remained his heir, her death removed any wish to protect her, and might have encouraged him to contract a second marriage for dynastic reasons. See, e.g., the discussion in C. Hibbert, *George IV* (London, 1976), 541.

[24] The Prince Regent to Eldon, 1 January 1818, A. Aspinall (ed.), *The correspondence of George Prince of Wales (1770–1812)*, 8 vols. (London, 1967–71), VIII:426.

wished to avoid the public revelation of the Princess' conduct that divorce proceedings must entail, while the government both suspected the strength of the evidence collected against the Princess and feared that any proceedings against her would result in equally unfavourable revelations about the Regent.

The situation had altered swiftly from uncertain deadlock to certain confrontation following the death of George III in January 1820. The new King had straightaway made his wishes known to the government: a divorce, and Caroline's exclusion from that part of the Anglican liturgy in which prayers were said for the Royal Family.[25] Ministers had acquiesced only to the second demand, despite the King's threat to dismiss them and retire to Hanover if they would not get him the divorce.[26] Having judged that no more compliant replacements were obtainable, and that the threat of retirement was not to be relied upon, ministers had instead advised that Caroline be offered a sufficiently generous financial settlement to induce her to part with her royal title and to remain abroad.

The decision to exclude her from the liturgy seems to have provoked the new Queen to return to England to assert her rights. She rejected the cautious overtures made to her by Henry Brougham and the King's representative Lord Hutchinson, and took her cue instead from Matthew Wood, the radical MP and former Lord Mayor of the City of London. On 29 May she informed Liverpool of her imminent arrival. After the government failed to make any arrangements for her, she obtained passage on the ordinary packet, and arrived at Dover on 5 June. From there she set out with Wood for London and the confrontation that would decide her political future. The consequences of her arrival convulsed London for most of the month of June. On 7 June, the King deposited with Parliament the evidence of her misconduct, and recommended that appropriate action be taken. Ministers scrambled to avoid, even at that stage, the necessity of a full-scale inquiry. Eldon wryly observed: 'Cabinets are quite in fashion;

---

[25] A third demand, also rejected by ministers, was for an augmentation of the King's revenues under the Civil List. See Eldon to Mrs Edward Bankes, 26 April 1820, H. Twiss, *The public and private life of Lord Chancellor Eldon*, 3 vols. (London, 1844), II:362–3. See also Hibbert, *George IV*, 546–7.

[26] See Eldon to Liverpool, undated [February 1820], BL (Liverpool papers), Add. MS 38283 f. 155.

daily, nightly, hourly Cabinets are in fashion.'[27] As efforts were made to reach a compromise between the royal couple, the King put out feelers to the opposition leadership and to those members of the government he hoped were more sympathetic to his wishes. Eldon thus described the situation:

The bulk of those who are in Parliament are afraid of the effect of the disclosures and discussions which must take place, if there is not some pacific settlement: the Queen is obstinate and makes no propositions tending to that – at least as yet; the King is determined, and will hear of none – of nothing but thorough investigation, and of what he, and those who consider *themselves* more than him, think and talk of – thorough exposure of the Q[ueen], and divorce. To this extent Parliament will not go – but, amidst this mess of difficulties, something must arise in a few days, or it will happen, I think, in a few days, that the K[ing] will try whether he cannot find an Administration which can bring Parliament more into his views than the present Ministers; I don't see how matters can go on a week longer with the present Administration remaining; I think no Administration, who have any regard for him, will go the length he wishes, *as* an Administration – and if they will, they cannot take Parliament along with them.[28]

While the politicians were thus engaged, the general populace of the capital took up the Queen's case with considerable vigour. She was loudly cheered whenever she appeared in public, while public illuminations, the publication of pamphlets and cartoons, and the unfriendly reception generally afforded to the King and ministers, attested to her popularity. In the end, it was she who rejected the compromise urged by William Wilberforce on behalf of the Commons. Acknowledging that they had no choice but to go forward, ministers put in train the procedures that would result in the Queen's trial. On 26 June the Commons adjourned in deference to the Upper House, which had previously named a secret committee of inquiry. On 28 June this committee met and examined the documentary evidence; six days later it reported to the House, and on 5 July Liverpool introduced a Bill of Pains and Penalties. The effect of this measure would be to deprive the Queen of all royal titles and privileges, and to effect a divorce.

Parliament could impose criminal sanctions upon an individual following an impeachment or a legislative enactment, the former

---

[27] Eldon to Bankes, undated [June 1820], Twiss, *The public and private life,* II:372.
[28] *Ibid.*

being a wholly judicial process in which the House of Commons brought its charges before the House of Lords, and the latter being partly a legislative and partly a judicial process involving both Houses. Bills of attainder for treason or felony, or Bills to inflict pains and penalties 'beyond or contrary to the common law'[29] were couched as regular legislative acts. They proceeded through each House according to the usual stages of first and second reading, committee, and third reading, and required the royal assent. Unlike most pieces of legislation, however, consideration of the Bill conformed more closely to a trial than to a debate. Witnesses could be sworn[30] and examined by counsel, and MPs and peers could participate in cross-examination. This 'trial', typically at the second reading stage, would determine whether the Bill would be passed or rejected.

In the case of Queen Caroline, the decision to proceed by a Bill of pains and penalties commencing in the House of Lords was based on several factors. First, it made a divorce practically possible. If the King had simply sought a Bill of divorce, Parliament would have required a judgment in his favour from an ecclesiastical court, to which his own record of marital misconduct made him distinctly ineligible. So-called 'recrimination' evidence, however, was technically irrelevant to a Bill of pains and penalties, which aimed to relieve a public rather than a private grievance.[31] Secondly, a Bill of pains and penalties was preferable to a Bill of attainder, despite the fact that the Queen was accused of having committed adultery while Princess of Wales, which would ordinarily constitute treason.[32] Because the alleged adultery had occurred abroad and with a man owing no allegiance to the laws of Great Britain, it could not constitute treason by the Queen. Her liability

---

[29] W. Blackstone, *Commentaries on the laws of England*, 4 vols., 1st edn facsimile (Chicago, 1979), IV:256.

[30] This applied only to the House of Lords.

[31] The weakness of this argument is revealed by Cookson, *Lord Liverpool*, 246, who states that the public grievance against the Queen would have been fully satisfied by her loss of royal status and privilege, as contained in the first clause of the Bill. The second clause, granting a divorce, remedied the King's private grievance.

[32] Under the Act of 25 Edw. III c. 2, it was accounted treason 'if a man do violate ... the King's companion, or the King's eldest daughter unmarried, or the wife of the King's eldest son and heir'. As Blackstone *Commentaries*, IV:81, observed: 'and this is high treason in both parties, if both be consenting; as some of the wives of Henry the eighth by fatal experience evinced.'

rested in consenting to a treasonable act, and Bergami's alleged conduct could not be treasonous. Avoidance of a charge of treason meant that two important procedural safeguards associated with that offence were unnecessary. The prosecution was not obliged to prove each wrongful act by the testimony of two witnesses, nor was the defence entitled to a list of the prosecution's witnesses prior to trial.[33] Finally, while the Bill could originate in either House, the decision to begin in the Lords was both reasonable and particularly attractive to the government. Generally speaking, the upper House could be regarded as less partisan than the lower House, as well as having the benefit of considerable legal talent in the persons of several serving and former judges.[34] The Lords' considered decision could, therefore, carry great weight if they approved the Bill and sent it down to the Commons.[35] Moreover, from the government's point of view, this tactic at least postponed the imposition of a considerable burden on the Treasury Bench. Already less than formidable in terms of debating strength, it was soon to be depleted further by the withdrawal of George Canning to the continent for the duration of the Queen's trial.

Introduction of the Bill in the House of Lords did, however, place considerable responsibility upon Eldon. As Speaker, he would be obliged to preside over what promised to be highly charged proceedings, and in which his political and legal deportment would be subjected to close scrutiny. Even before the Bill was introduced the pressures on him had commenced. He described 26 June as 'a teazing day'. First, he had received a communication from the Queen stating her intention to attend the debates. Judging that this would result in the appearance not merely of the Queen but also of an unruly crowd of her supporters, Eldon had informed her that he could not admit ladies without the consent of the House; therefore an application to him was misdirected. Next, he had been requested to deliver a message from her, which he had likewise declined on the grounds that the House

---

[33] These were required in cases of treason by 1 Edw. IV c. 12, 5 & 6 Edw. VI c. 11, 1 & 2 Ph. and M. c. 10 (two witnesses); 7 Ann. c. 21 (list of witnesses).

[34] In addition to those peers who were judges, the Lords could summon members of the judiciary to advise and assist them.

[35] See Blackstone, *Commentaries*, IV:258. But see Cookson, *Lord Liverpool*, 247, who points out that the more overtly partisan nature of the Commons made it less suited to act as the final decision-maker with regard to controversial Bills.

only received messages from the King.[36] Finally, he had received the Queen's petition, begging that her counsel be heard in support of her request to delay all proceedings for two months. Having excused himself from the task of presenting the petition, Eldon had explained to the House that 'due regard for the situation in which he stood' had convinced him to search for precedents for the postponement. Having been unable to find any, he had felt obliged to demur.[37] Privately, he admitted, 'I am resolved I will not be employed in any way by this lady', but he was sufficiently conversant with the details of protocol to rebuff her in accordance with the dictates of accepted practice.[38]

Debates during the month of July provided further opportunities for skirmishes with the Queen and her adherents. On 6 July, she petitioned that her counsel be permitted to state her case immediately, rather than upon the second reading. Eldon's motion to restrict the scope of any such argument by counsel at that stage of the Bill was carried without a division.[39] A week later, he deflected motions by Lord Erskine that would have required the prosecution to produce a list of witnesses.[40] Eldon similarly rejected the treason parallel put forward in the Queen's petition of 24 July, in which she asked for the dates and places of all alleged adulterous conduct. Eldon described this request as 'unsupported by any principle, and unsanctioned by any precedent'.[41] It would be wrong to suggest, however, that Eldon relied primarily on technicalities to avoid difficult questions, or that he steadily impeded the progress of the Queen's defence. That he should have felt called upon to *assert* his impartiality and his earnest desire to see justice done is not surprising, and almost from the moment that a full parliamentary investigation became inevitable he began to make professions of that kind. He announced to the House on 27 June that no punishment would be too severe if he 'during the prosecution of the inquiry into which they were about to enter, holding the high judicial situation which he held, willingly lost sight of the great principles of English justice'.[42] To his daughter he wrote in a similar vein: 'I am

---

[36] Eldon to Bankes, 27 June 1820, Twiss, *The public and private life*, II:376.

[37] Hansard, *Parliamentary debates, new (2nd) series*, I:1325.

[38] Eldon to Bankes, 27 June 1820, Twiss, *The public and private life*, II:377.

[39] Hansard, *Parliamentary debates, new (2nd) series*, II:231–236.

[40] *Ibid.*, cols. 440–5.    [41] *Ibid.*, col. 577.    [42] *Ibid.*, col. 25.

determined to look neither to the right nor to the left – to court no favour from any party, but, doing my duty faithfully and to the best of an unbiassed [*sic*] judgment, to preserve that state of comfort in my own mind which I have hitherto laboured not to forfeit.'[43] Moreover, having made such assertions, he generally adhered to them during the next few months. The Queen's 'trial' essentially commenced on 17 August, when counsel were heard on the second reading of the Bill. The prosecution concluded on 7 September, and following an adjournment of two weeks, the defence lasted until 24 October. Closing arguments occupied part of a further week, and proceedings were brought to a close on 30 October.[44] Throughout Eldon's conduct was characterised by tolerance, good humour, and fairness.

These were qualities demanded though not encouraged by the circumstances. In the main, Eldon's problems were two. First, he had to manage the proceedings at the procedural level. Early on he won approval for his suggestion that, in so far as was possible, the House should follow the practices of the courts of common law. While providing a good foundation, this resolution did not foreclose either conflict or uncertainty, because strict adherence to common law principles was not always possible or desirable. The second problem was more difficult – management at the personal level. Peers lacking legal training and suspicious of legal technicalities frequently posed questions or advocated modes of action that violated regular judicial standards. The principal advocates involved, the Attorney and Solicitor General in support of the Bill, and Henry Brougham and Thomas Denman against it, were not inclined to forego an opportunity to press an advantage if either the strength of the law or the forbearance of the House seemed to warrant it. Then again, the nature of the case was such as to involve foreign witnesses, many of whom did not understand English, let alone English justice.

An important ingredient to Eldon's *modus vivendi* was that the participants have confidence in each other. In the matter of the degree to which counsel ought to press a witness, Eldon pleaded

[43] Eldon to Bankes, undated [June–July 1820], Twiss, *The public and private life,* II:380–1.
[44] In addition to the contemporary accounts published by shorthand writers, a modern account of the trial in its entirety is provided in R. Fulford, *The trial of Queen Caroline* (London, 1967).

for mutual tolerance. Replying to peers' complaints that some witnesses needed protection against improper questioning, he 'felt great difficulty in interfering with Counsel, on the ground that these questions were not material. Their Lordships must trust Counsel with looking more forward into the case than any Court could do, and therefore rely on them not to abuse the privileges with which this opinion clothed them.'[45] Intervening in a dispute between the advocates, he tried to 'impress on the minds of the Counsel on both sides, that the House was sincerely and conscientiously endeavouring to do justice in the case; and they ought to be careful not to press any question upon it which they did not believe absolutely necessary, and within the limits prescribed.'[46] When applied to the issue of how the cross-examination ought to be structured, Eldon's policy of deference caused some difficulties. Following the examination, cross-examination, and re-examination of a prosecution witness, Brougham announced that he wished to recall the witness and conduct a further cross-examination. He defended his request by stating that the lack of prior notice of the identity of prosecution witnesses prevented the defence from conducting a proper cross-examination in the first instance. While objecting in principle to a 'piece-meal' cross-examination, Eldon observed that 'their Lordships would be guided by a sense of justice how far the Counsel should be indulged'. When Brougham promised to limit himself to three to five questions, Eldon thought that 'with such a pledge, their Lordships ought not to refuse the application', and Brougham thereupon indulged in a rather more extensive questioning session.[47] Eldon soon realised the inevitable complications that would result from such leniency.[48] Two days later, the House was again plunged into a lengthy debate on the degree of freedom afforded the defence in recalling prosecution witnesses. When would the prosecution re-examine a witness, if the full cross-examination were to spread across several potential sessions? How would examination by peers be accommodated? Would they be entitled to question a witness after each segment of his cross-examination or only after the first? Various models of procedure were proposed, including a basic preliminary cross-examination to

[45] Anon., *Trial of Queen Caroline*, 2 vols. (London, 1821), I:122.
[46] *Ibid.*, 202.     [47] *Ibid.*, 64.     [48] *Ibid.*, 174.

elicit details followed by a full cross, and a full cross-examination with an optional second cross upon proof of need. Both models seem to have been accepted in the course of the debate. For his part, Eldon was influenced by his liking for the procedures of the Westminster courts, and his wish not to be seen as forcing a particular procedure on the House. In the course of a none too clear speech he remarked:

I feel a great difficulty on this, not on account of the importance of the present question, but as to the consequences likely to result from permitting such a procedure. With reference to a former opinion, if I am not out of order in mentioning it, I have to say circumstances have since arisen that have led considerably to alter it ... If this House has really adopted the right mode, for God's sake abide by it. But if it would be doing injustice to one of the parties, and to that one most interested, do not let any notions of inconsistency prevent your retracing your steps and do what is right ... Your Lordships must lay down some rule beyond which you will not go, as to what may be the safest limit you will determine as to the cross-examination of witnesses.[49]

Contrary to Eldon's hesitant advice, the House resolved to allow the defence to cross-examine 'according to the mode proposed by them at the bar of the House'. Intermittent wrangling on the subject continued for the next few days, however, with Eldon intervening to assure the House of his own *bona fides*. In offering his own opinion he did no more than to honour a 'solemn obligation', but 'if their superior wisdom should adopt another course, he would endeavour to struggle through it'.[50]

Despite the potential for such complications, Eldon generally maintained his policy of letting the counsel conduct the case as they wished. For his own part, this meant intervening to protect Brougham when he conducted himself less than tactfully toward peers. Following complaints about the peremptory nature of Brougham's objection to a question posed by Lord Donoughmore, Eldon remarked that he was 'certain' that Brougham had meant only to act upon the allowance granted to counsel to intervene 'if Noble Lords should put any questions to a witness which they [counsel] considered to be improper'. He similarly diffused the irritation caused by Brougham's description of Lord Colville's question as 'droll'. 'The Lord Chancellor observed it might be expected that expressions would sometimes fall from the Counsel

---

[49] *Ibid.*, 207.    [50] Hansard, *Parliamentary debates, new (2<sup>nd</sup>) series*, II:1058.

in the hurry of the moment that were not quite appropriate.'[51] When the lawyers fell out amongst themselves, Eldon generally adopted a conciliatory tone. During a discussion of the propriety of mentioning the person with whom the witness had allegedly held a conversation, in which discussion the Solicitor General Sir John Copley and Brougham described each other as 'ignorant of all the rules in the Courts of Justice', Eldon offered a mild opinion. 'In the time when he sat at *Nisi Prius* it was customary to have names mentioned, and he thought it would also be proper in the present instance.'[52] On the occasion of a heated exchange between Denman and Copley as to a witness's description of the chain of command on board the Princess' boat, Eldon likewise intervened:

It struck me, but I may be wrong, that there might be a different construction put by different persons on the word 'management.' I understood that what the Learned Counsel in support of the Bill intended to ask, was what the witness meant by the word 'management.' I apprehend the question might well be put in this way.[53]

Likewise, when John Williams, one of the junior defence counsel, seemed to be working himself up to a passion over a perceived interference, Eldon acted to pacify him:

MR WILLIAMS: My Lords, I submit I have a right to ask this question.
THE LORD CHANCELLOR: Nobody says you have not, Mr Williams, but some of their Lordships have observed you have put that question three times, and are now putting it for the fourth.
MR WILLIAMS: I humbly submit I have a right – (go on).
THE LORD CHANCELLOR: No objection is made by the Counsel on the other side, nor is any taken here; you are at liberty to proceed therefore.
MR WILLIAMS: But I trust, my Lord – (go on, go on).
THE LORD CHANCELLOR: We are not now arguing any objection, you are therefore at liberty to proceed. You are at liberty to go on, Mr Williams.
MR WILLIAMS: Then I must take a little time to consider myself, with the permission of your Lordships.[54]

---

[51] *Trial*, II:212–13; see also *ibid.*, 323.    [52] *Ibid.*, 167.    [53] *Ibid.*, 201.
[54] *Ibid.*, 284. Shortly thereafter, Eldon replied in a similar manner on Williams' complaining that the witness's silence infringed upon counsel's right. 'Mr Williams nobody is disputing your right. (a laugh) If the witness does not answer satisfactorily any question you put to her, you have a clear right to persist in your question till you get a proper answer.' *Ibid.*, 288.

Counsel could exceed the limit of Eldon's patience, but his severity on such occasions was only moderate.[55] In an exchange about the readiness of the defence to proceed with their case, Eldon managed admirably in the face of what looks suspiciously like Brougham's intentional misunderstanding. The prosecution having concluded, Eldon inquired whether the defence intended to proceed fully on the following day, or merely to open their case and seek a further delay. Brougham thereupon entered into a long discussion of what *he* asserted were his alternatives. These were either to make an immediate address and call no witnesses, or to state nothing at present in order to preserve the option of calling witnesses. He, not surprisingly, found both objectionable and perilous to the Queen's case.[56] Eldon 'disclaimed any intention of throwing a difficulty in the way of the Queen's Counsel by his question. He only wished to have him asked what he meant to do, and what course he would take?'[57] Brougham complained again that if he elected to open his case, he might wish to seek a delay, and would be unable to do so. Eldon 'was still afraid the Learned Counsel had not understood the question. The question was only as to the mode which the Counsel meant to follow in his defence; but it by no means followed, if he made his election to open his case, that he should be obliged to go on.'[58] Brougham thereupon announced his wish to proceed, but to do so after a period of two weeks, and this was granted. Eldon also dealt with misbehaviour in an even-handed manner.[59] On Brougham's addressing the House after having been ordered to withdraw from the bar, Eldon sternly remarked: 'Counsel were ordered to withdraw, Mr Brougham, and if they cannot appreciate that courtesy, with which the House is accustomed to treat them, by not requiring that they should leave the House, the regulation will, for the

---

[55] Writing long after the event, Eldon would affirm that he had determined at the outset of the trial, 'that no provocation should disturb my Temper, being aware that this was intended to be severely tried'. Lord Eldon, J. Scott, *Lord Eldon's anecdote book*, ed. A. L. J. Lincoln and R. L. McEwen (London, 1960), 114.

[56] *Trial*, I:438.     [57] *Ibid.*, 439.     [58] *Ibid.*, 439.

[59] The fact that Eldon intervened more frequently to check the defence counsel is not surprising. Not only was Brougham a more provocative speaker than either Gifford or Copley, but it was the nature of the defence's case to push lines of argument that were more controversial. Eldon made a point of refusing to speak to either the Attorney or Solicitor General outside of the House during the trial. E. Phipps, *Memoirs of the political and literary life of Robert Plumer Ward*, 2 vols. (London, 1850), II:80.

future, be strictly enforced.'[60] Later in the same debate, he cut
short an attempt by the Attorney General, Sir Robert Gifford, to
answer a straightforward question with a peroration. Eldon 'did
not apprehend that the House wished the Learned Gentleman to
argue the case; but were desirous that he should state simply, as he
was perfectly authorized to do, whether or not he withheld his
consent'.[61]

If his general level of tolerance for others was high, Eldon's
sense of his own abilities was modest. Despite his acknowledged
pre-eminence in the law, he did not attempt to impress upon the
House the deference with which they ought to receive his professional opinions. In fact, the reverse was true. Typical of the tone
in which he offered his views was the following, offered in preface
to a discussion of the admissibility of agency evidence. He
thought:

these declarations could not, in the present stage of this proceeding, be
admitted: and, if any noble lord could entertain an opinion, that,
according to the course and practice of the Courts below, the view which
he (the lord Chancellor) took of the subject could be so far contradicted as
to have it shown that the practice of those Courts would let in such
evidence, it would be competent to that noble lord to have the advice of
the learned judges on the question, and he would feel obliged to the noble
lord who called for that opinion, in order that he might thereby correct
his own.[62]

Eldon frequently sought the opinions of the judges on complicated
questions relating to oral evidence. When he did venture an
opinion, he did so with considerable diffidence. Commenting on
the extent to which a conversation between a witness and a third
party was admissible, Eldon explained:

My lords, with respect to any opinion I may have formed upon this point,
I do not set a very great value upon it, because, as I have before stated to
your lordships, it has not occurred to me of late years to attend to this
subject of cross-examination, and therefore I think it much safer, upon
the whole, to act upon the general opinion of those who have been
conversant with such matters, than to act upon what would have been my
own opinion before I heard what I have now heard; but I must confess to
your lordships I have been long in an error, if the rule with respect to re-
examination or cross-examination, does not go the whole length of

---

[60] *Trial*, I:437. See also *ibid.*, 389.      [61] *Ibid.*, II:142. See also *ibid.*, I:314.
[62] Hansard, *Parliamentary debates, new (2^{nd}) series*, III:705. See also *ibid.*, cols.
745, 748.

entitling a witness to have the whole of that conversation stated, I have no hesitation in expressing that opinion.[63]

Despite the fact that Eldon's legal opinions, even those based on a common law practice almost twenty years old, were consistently vindicated by the judges, he remained extremely cautious throughout the proceedings.

Only occasionally did Eldon appear to lapse from the standard of rigorous objectivity that he had set for himself. Where the lapse was in the nature of political bias it is fair to describe Eldon's language as *tending* toward his own political interests, for he committed no obvious egregious gaffes. For example, the voice of the minister can be detected in Eldon's commentary upon the defence's failure to seek Foreign Office assistance in producing certain witnesses. He swept aside Brougham's point that the defence had observed the obstructionist tactics of the Austrian government and had concluded that intervention by the Foreign Office would prove nugatory:

Although they had no means of summoning foreign witnesses by any thing which could have the power or force of a *subpoena*, yet it appeared that there was a mode to be made use of by applying for the interposition of our own government. This was a point that should not be forgotten; and as that was the only means that could be used, and as her Majesty's Counsel had not made use of, or applied for these means, he could not see what claim they could have to the indulgence of their Lordships.[64]

Discussing allegations by the defence of a conspiracy to suborn witnesses, Eldon spoke on the effect of proof of such a conspiracy. Despite having begun well, the disinterested tone had distinctly wavered by the end of his speech:

A conspiracy might be formed to subborn [*sic*] witnesses, and yet no witnesses might be suborned. The conspiracy might be, nevertheless, of the most mischievous description. If they should find, that such a conspiracy had been formed – if this fact were once established, they must look with suspicion at all the evidence, even of that part of it to which the conspiracy did not appear to apply. But, to argue, as some of their lordships had done, that because some of the witnesses had been suborned, or attempted to be suborned, there was an end of the case, though it was supported by purer testimony on the part of the prosecution, and, as often happened, by evidence brought forward in support of the defence, was, in his judgment, a very inconclusive way of reasoning.[65]

---

[63] *Ibid.*, II:1310. See also *ibid.*, III:50; *Trial*, I:301.     [64] *Trial*, II:84.

[65] Hansard, *Parliamentary debates, new (2ⁿᵈ) series*, III: 849.

More striking, if no more frequent, were Eldon's digressions into matters of personal interest. When considering whether a particular witness could be described as an agent of the Milan Commission, in order to link that individual's questionable conduct to the commissioners, Eldon broke into a defence of one of them. While this tribute might be judged an attempt to vindicate the Commission, to which the government was generally linked in the public mind, it is more likely to have been a personal tribute from one old Chancery hand to another. Hansard reports:

> Upon reading the name of Mr Cooke, his lordship said, that when that name fell first from his lips, in the course of this proceeding, he must state, that he had known that gentleman for nearly half a century, and knew him to be one of the most honourable men. A higher character for integrity and honour, he declared upon his honour and veracity, he had never known.[66]

The best example of Eldon's giving vent to personal considerations was the rather extraordinary argument that took place between himself and Erskine. Still on the subject of a possible conspiracy against the Queen involving the Milan Commission, Eldon opined that the defence had not sufficiently established any basis for a particular line of questioning. This prompted an altercation between the two former opponents in the *Hardy* trial of 1794, as Erskine asserted that, in that case, Eldon had been permitted to pursue a similar line of argument with respect to an allegation of conspiracy. In reply, Eldon stated that he had re-read *Hardy* and disagreed. Eldon's mood seems to have been one of good humour at the start of the exchange, as he observed that the *Hardy* case had occurred so long ago that, prior to refreshing his memory, 'he had forgotten all the circumstances, excepting that he made a tedious speech'.[67] When Erskine pressed his point, however, arguing that the Chancellor's account was incomplete, Eldon coolly suggested that 'it might perhaps be as well if his noble and learned friend would take an opportunity of again reading the arguments in that case'.[68] Erskine maintained 'that he remembered all the main features of the case as well as if they had occurred yesterday', upon which Eldon pressed the judges to state the current law on conspiracy evidence. They duly affirmed his analysis.[69] This dispute over a case argued more than twenty-five

---

[66] *Ibid.*, col. 585.          [67] *Ibid.*, col. 840.          [68] *Ibid.*, col. 841.          [69] *Ibid.*

years previously assumed a rather comic aspect the following day when the defence submitted that they had wished to advance their line of questioning for a reason quite different from that supposed by Eldon and Erskine. Consequently, the various reminiscences and the disputed application of *Hardy* to the instant case had been irrelevant, and counsel requested permission to resume. Eldon responded with his usual aplomb, observing: 'no man who acted as a judge could expect to be treated with respect, unless he showed respect to others. He therefore thought it right to state, that having found he had misunderstood the object of Mr Williams, he was sorry that he had interrupted him.'[70]

With the trial phase of the proceedings having been brought to a close on 30 October, the House adjourned and resumed on 2 November. A succession of peers then gave their individual opinions on the evidence, starting with the Lord Chancellor.[71] On 6 November the vote on the second reading of the Bill was taken. It was approved, but the margin in favour, 123 to 95, was smaller than had been expected.[72] Ministers discussed abandoning the Bill, but decided to persevere.[73] On the following day the House went into committee, and approved retention of the divorce clause by a vote of 129 to 62. Supporters of both the King and the Queen voted in favour, the first wanting the Bill approved in its entirety and the second believing that inclusion made ultimate approval of the Bill less likely. Government supporters, who thought likewise and consequently voted against the clause, found themselves in a minority. Peers subjected the Bill to its final test on 10 November. On the vote for the third reading, the majority in favour fell to nine, 108 to 99. Ministers had decided that if support fell to ten, they would conclude that the Bill was incapable of succeeding in the Commons. Liverpool's motion effectively to abandon the Bill passed without a division.

What was Eldon's conduct during these final stages? When he

---

[70] *Ibid.*, cols. 843–5, 848.

[71] Eldon observed that he would not make a summation in the manner of the judge at the conclusion of a case, 'for we are all here, my lords, as judges and jurors; and we must proceed, not on any principle of summing up the evidence, but on that of communicating to one another our opinions, and discussing the grounds upon which those opinions have been formed'. *Ibid.*, col. 1441.

[72] Eldon had predicted a majority of between 45 and 50. Phipps, *Memoirs, II:69.*

[73] A. Aspinall (ed.), *The diary of Henry Hobhouse (1820–1827)* (London, 1947, 38.

departed the Woolsack to address the House on 2 November, and in his subsequent contributions to debate on the Bill, he maintained something of the remote, deliberative manner that had characterised his conduct since the trial began. He judged the charge against the Queen to have been made out, but he declined to undertake a full-blown argument of the case. Rather, confining himself only to that testimony which had neither been contradicted nor shaken, he found this sufficient 'to lead a plain man' to infer that adultery had taken place, and pointed out that the law required nothing further.[74] Characteristically, he not only mentioned his determination to perform his 'public duty', but he urged his colleagues to do likewise. This duty consisted of making a decision without reference to popularity, and in so doing to preserve the true liberties of the constitution.[75] Eldon's failure to speak out more strongly in favour of the Bill did not please all his ministerial colleagues. The Duke of Wellington described it as 'an admirable speech as far as it went', but he considered that it did not go far enough.[76] Lord Camden criticised it as indecisive.[77] Decision was also lacking in Eldon's assessment of the divorce issue. Debate centred on whether, if the Queen were to suffer legal degradation, she *could* be degraded without also being divorced, and if adultery were proven, she *could* be divorced without consideration of the King's conduct. On 7 November Eldon presented information that seemed to support alternative views of the matter without resolving them: on the one hand, Parliament required that a petitioner seeking relief have clean hands, and on the other, degradation without divorce would actually bind the Queen more closely to the King, as the loss of royal privileges would transform her from a *femme sole* to a *femme covert*.[78] On the

---

[74] Eldon's speech in favour of the Bill is found at Hansard, *Parliamentary debates, new (2nd) series*, III:1439–58.

[75] While Brougham was not mentioned by name, his warning to peers that approval of the Bill could provoke a civil cataclysm, came in for pointed censure from the Chancellor. He adjured the House to ignore the 'threat', and declared that 'an address of such a nature, such an address of intimidation, to any court of justice, was never until this hour considered to be consistent with the duty of an advocate.' *Ibid.*, cols. 1457–8. 2 November 1820. For Brougham's speech, see *ibid.*, col. 210.

[76] H. Arbuthnot, *The journal of Mrs Arbuthnot (1820–1832)*, 2 vols., ed. F. Bamford and the Duke of Wellington (London, 1950), I:49.

[77] Phipps, *Memoirs*, II:81.

[78] Hansard, *Parliamentary debates, new (2nd) series*, III:1716–17.

following day he appeared ready to fall in line behind Liverpool, but proceeded to describe the Bill as incoherent without either the existing divorce clause or an alternative, and actually voted in favour of retention.[79] It is not surprising that Liverpool should have rounded on Eldon at the Cabinet called to discuss government tactics on the third reading, for not having supported him.[80]

Robert Plumer Ward recorded an incident that occurred just after the conclusion of the Queen's trial:

> Returning from riding in the Park, I joined the Chancellor, who was walking home after the House. He asked me what people thought; and hoped they at least gave him credit for impartiality in the conduct of the trial. I told him (as I could truly) what satisfied him on that point.[81]

Eldon's evident concern, not only that he should have behaved with propriety, but that he should be perceived as having so behaved, is interesting. A review of his actual conduct bears out the former, so anxiety on the latter point suggests either a lack of confidence in public opinion or a suspicion about his own personal prejudices. Certainly the Bill was popularly identified with the government, and even the most self-possessed minister presiding over the trial could expect a rough handling by the radical press. Eldon's own circumstances, however, made him more susceptible both to public examination and self-analysis. More than other senior members of the government, he was the King's minister, expected by the King to sympathise with his troubles as 'my dear friend', and expected by colleagues to smooth royal feathers when they became ruffled. Had he let the King down by a too rigorous attention to formal impartiality? Conversely, had the Bill failed in spite of his unconscious efforts to disadvantage the Queen's case? And did memories of his previous assistance to the Queen, dating from the time when her husband had been a burden to George III and a threat to the government, linger in the Chancellor's mind? Eldon's personal correspondence from the period of her trial and

---

[79] Eldon suggested that some legal device might be formulated that would dissolve the civil contract of marriage while preserving the religious one. Given his admiration of fictions, a solution such as this would have been particularly appealing to him, both as a subject for rumination and as a solution to the particular difficulties of the King and Queen. See *ibid.*, col. 1721.

[80] Aspinall, *Hobhouse*, 39–40. Liverpool apologised to Eldon on the following day. Twiss, *The public and private life*, II:398–9.

[81] Phipps, *Memoirs*, II:69.

subsequently until her death the following year indicates no surfeit of tenderness. Yet he recognised the unsatisfactory nature of the proceedings against her. In a letter to his daughter Eldon observed:

The Bill should either have been rejected or passed. But to have upon our Journals four different resolutions, all founded upon our avowed conviction of her guilt, and then neither to withdraw those resolutions, nor to act upon them, appears to me perfectly absurd, and, both to the country and to her, unjust. To her surely it is so. We condemn her four times; she desires at our bar that we will allow her to be heard in her defence before the Commons; we will neither do that, nor withdraw our condemnations; for, though the Bill is withdrawn, the votes of condemnation remain upon our journals. This is surely not pretty treatment for a lady.[82]

The obligation of fairness, particularly when conceived as demanding both an outward and inward objectivity, was a draining one. The period of the Queen's trial was an occasion for Eldon to speak generally of his age, his exhaustion, and his willingness to retire. Perhaps the burdens of such a proceeding, both those imposed externally and those which he imposed upon himself, were at last rendering the office of Lord Chancellor too much for him.

[82] Eldon to Bankes, undated [*c.* November 1820], Twiss, *The public and private life*, II:400.

# 16

## LORD ENDLESS

On 24 February 1824 the Home Secretary, Robert Peel, announced to the House of Commons that the government supported the appointment of a royal commission to inquire generally into the practice of the court of Chancery, and to consider whether removing any or particular matters from the Lord Chancellor's jurisdiction would improve that practice. The government's decision, Peel affirmed, was based on advice from the Chancellor, recommendations of a House of Lords committee, and the recognition that members opposite 'had made out a case of complete justification for inquiry'.[1] The Home Secretary's speech provoked an apparently curious response. MPs who had been the firm advocates of reform for the past several years were extremely sceptical. Eldon, in contrast, who opposed most if not all of the substantive reforms then being considered, wrote gratefully to Peel on the following day: 'I cannot go forth this morning to my work and labour without having expressed to you how very much I feel myself obliged to you.'[2] The divergence in these expressions reflects the complexity of the issue of Chancery reform. The length of the agitation for change, the complexity of the subject-matter, and the personalities involved, all demand further analysis, particularly as debate on the subject dominated Eldon's last years in office.

In the early nineteenth century, the judicial authority of the Lord Chancellor existed in two contexts. He presided over the judicial business in the House of Lords as its Speaker, and he sat as judge in the court of Chancery. The House of Lords had both

---

[1] T. Hansard (ed.), *The Parliamentary debates from the year 1803 ... new (2$^{nd}$) series*, 25 vols. (London, 1820–30), X:410.
[2] Eldon to Robert Peel, 25 February 1824, BL (Peel papers), Add. MS 40315 f. 119.

an original and an appellate jurisdiction. It was the proper forum for impeachments and trials of peers. As a Committee of Privileges, their lordships resolved disputed peerage claims and could institute advisory proceedings on private Bills before they went to the floor of the House. The House of Lords heard appeals from English, Scottish, and Irish common law and equity decisions. At least in theory, this judicial work was the responsibility of peers generally, and the Lord Chancellor presided over their deliberations as he presided over debates – lending the weight of his legal knowledge and experience, but not otherwise exercising a superior authority. In fact, however, many peers were not interested in hearing cases, particularly those which did not immediately concern themselves, and by the beginning of the century the Lords' appellate jurisdiction had become largely the province of the Chancellor and such other legal peers as could be cajoled into attending.

The Chancellor's work in the court of Chancery requires greater explanation. Arising from Chancery's medieval foundation as a centre of royal administration, the Chancellor had acquired the authority to resolve disputes relating to the issuance of commissions, letters patent, and other enabling documents that must pass the Great Seal. Complaints against the king, or against royal officers or ministers, were also cognisable on the so-called 'Latin' or 'legal' side of Chancery. The more important area of the Chancellor's jurisdiction, however, lay on the 'English' or 'equity' side. This grew out of the authority of the medieval royal Council, of which the Chancellor was a member, to dispense justice where relief was not possible in the regular royal courts. Gradually petitioners sought redress not from the Council, but from the Chancellor, who undertook to intervene where corruption, ignorance, or the technicalities of the common law would have barred recovery by the otherwise deserving litigant. The substantive issues raised before the Chancellor came to be focused largely, although not exclusively, in the area of real property. His jurisdiction also extended, sometimes through statute, to the protection of infants, 'idiots', and 'lunatics'; the superintendance of charities; and to matters relating to bankruptcy.

The Chancellor presided over a considerable administrative apparatus in Chancery. His primary assistants were the twelve Masters, to whom particular factual issues could be delegated for investigation and decision. The chief of these officials, called the Master of the Rolls, had gradually acquired greater judicial duties, and from the seventeenth century had been allowed to hear and decide causes in the Chancellor's absence.[3] Beneath the Masters were a clerical staff. The most senior were the Six Clerks. Once the effective intermediaries between litigants and the court, their actual duties had come to be simply the keeping of certain records associated with the litigation. They were assisted in this work by the Sixty Clerks. In addition, registers, cursitors, secretaries, and clerks were employed to record the orders and decrees of the court, to draw up writs, to file the different classes of documents, and to collect the various fees that attached to each stage of the litigation. The Chancellor's particular authority with respect to bankruptcy and lunacy had resulted in the creation of a further class of commissioners, upon whom various investigative and judicial responsibilities were devolved.

Delays in the hearing and resolution of causes in Chancery had long been recognised. Together with complaints of official abuses, the inadequacy of the judicial staff had formed the basis of many pamphlets and parliamentary debates in the early seventeenth century. Substantial reforms had been advocated during the Interregnum, and while these had been abandoned upon the Restoration of Charles II, complaints about Chancery had not been laid to rest.[4] Delay in the House of Lords was a more recent problem, and this is what first attracted parliamentary attention during Eldon's tenure as Chancellor. By the beginning of the nineteenth century, the upper House was 'creaking' beneath the burden of its appellate jurisdiction, which consisted largely of Scottish appeals.[5] These cases were particularly burdensome to the House as they were heard *de novo* and not, as was true of appeals from English common law courts, on the record as produced below. Moreover, the resolution of complex problems of Scots law was a task for which few of even the legally trained peers

---

[3] The Master of the Rolls' authority was recognised by statute in 1729, when it was enacted that his judicial decisions were valid, subject to an appeal to the Lord Chancellor. 3 Geo. II c. 30.

[4] For a summary of the specific subjects of dispute in this period, see W. Holdsworth, *A history of English law*, 17 vols. (London, 1903–72) I:423–42.

[5] R. Stevens, *Law and politics, the House of Lords as a judicial body, 1800–1976* (London, 1979), 15. In 1808 there were 139 Scottish cases pending in the House of Lords, as compared to 31 English and 27 Irish cases.

were qualified. As a consequence, attendance was extremely light, and the burden on the Chancellor extremely heavy. An attempt was made to stem the flood of Scottish appeals in 1808, following the recommendations of a Commons committee, but it had little effect.[6] In March 1811, therefore, Eldon himself moved the appointment of a select committee in the Lords to consider such measures as would expedite appellate proceedings. The problem of Chancery arrears was not expressly included within the committee's remit, but Eldon acknowledged that the effect upon Chancery of greater judicial time being spent in the Lords 'would most probably come under the cognisance of the committee'.[7] The committee was duly appointed, and it produced a report in May. Among its recommendations were that the House increase the time spent hearing appeals from two to three days a week. Furthermore, since this would inevitably encroach upon the Lord Chancellor's time, an additional Chancery judge should be appointed with a rank comparable to that of the Master of the Rolls.[8]

A Bill to give effect to the latter recommendation was introduced by Lord Redesdale in 1812, and it reached the Commons in February 1813. There, however, the Bill ran into difficulties, resulting from the far from quiescent attitude of a small but vocal minority. Since March 1811, this group had been calling for a Commons inquiry focusing more directly on the court of Chancery. The chief advocate of inquiry was Michael Angelo Taylor.[9] His motions of 7 March and 17 May 1811 had been defeated, the government arguing that the proposed committee would merely duplicate the work already undertaken in the Lords.[10] Following

---

[6]  For previous efforts to reduce Scottish appeals, see chapter 12.

[7]  T. Hansard (ed.), *The Parliamentary debates from the year 1803 ... (1st series)*, 41 vols. (London, 1812–20), XIX:232. The current arrears in the House of Lords were stated by Earl Stanhope as follows: 35 cases from the English common law courts, 43 from the English and Irish courts of Chancery, and 195 from Scottish courts. *Ibid.*, col. 233.

[8]  *Parliamentary Papers* (1810–11), III:2–3.

[9]  Called to the bar in 1774, Taylor gave up a legal career for politics at an early age. Attached to the Prince of Wales' 'friends', he had hoped to be appointed Judge-Advocate or Irish Secretary, but was obliged to abandon these hopes when the Prince decided to retain his father's ministers in 1811. R. G. Thorne (ed.), *The history of Parliament: the House of Commons (1790–1820)*, 5 vols. (London, 1986), V:341.

[10]  The motion of 7 March 1811 was defeated 87 to 47, and that of 17 May 1811 was defeated 40 to 19. Hansard, *Parliamentary debates (1st series)*, XIX:269, XX:207.

the production of that committee's report, however, Taylor had repeated his call for a Commons inquiry.[11] With the seventy-two MPs present equally divided, the Speaker had cast the deciding vote in favour of a committee to consider the arrears in Chancery and the House of Lords, as well as the fees and emoluments received by the Lord Chancellor. The committee had produced reports in July 1811 and February 1812, and its work had helped to re-orient the approach of MPs towards the issue of Chancery reform. Rather than regarding it simply as a consequence of improvements in House of Lords procedure, they had been encouraged to understand it primarily in relation to failings within Chancery itself. When, consequently, Lord Castlereagh moved the second reading of the Vice-Chancellor Bill in February 1813, he found the debate shifting from the Bill's avowed purpose. MPs wanted to consider whether appointment of a Vice-Chancellor would improve the situation in Chancery, and whether some re-allocation of work between the Chancellor and the Master of the Rolls might be preferable. Taylor proposed that the Chancellor be relieved of his bankruptcy jurisdiction; more than one Member doubted whether the creation of a Vice-Chancellor would not merely increase the number of appeals. When the question of expedition in the House of Lords was discussed at all, MPs expressed little sympathy for their lordships' plight. Arrears were blamed primarily on poor attendance, which led to the Lord Chancellor 'pacing up and down the House for three or four hours before there was an attendance'.[12] Moreover, it was argued that any measure that 'estranged' the Chancellor from Chancery would have the dangerous consequence of rendering future Chancellors more political and less legal in character. Despite these several objections, however, opposition was neither sufficiently numerous nor sufficiently united to defeat the measure. It gained its third reading on 11 March 1813 by a comfortable majority, 127 to 89.

Following what might be described as the first phase of parliamentary agitation for Chancery reform, the subject faded from view for a period of five years. In March 1819, however, it resurfaced through Taylor's efforts. He wished to discover, he announced, whether the creation of the office of Vice-Chancellor had been a success, and to that end he moved for an account of the

[11] *Ibid.*, XX:444.    [12] *Ibid.*, XXIV:542.

total amount of suitors' effects tied up in Chancery from 1756 to the present. Such an accounting would establish whether and to what extent the business of the court was increasing, and the effect of an additional Chancery judge on the despatch of business. This motion was agreed to without a vote, but thereafter Taylor's efforts met with consistent and potent government opposition. In May he proposed that a committee be appointed to consider depriving the Chancellor of his bankruptcy jurisdiction. He argued that lengthy delays and the lack of provision for appeals made the current system iniquitous, and when account was taken of the vast amount of property involved in bankruptcy litigation, the argument for reform was compelling. 'In 1752 the Bank of England had £3 million belonging to suitors; in 1819 it was £34 million. And one-third of all landed property was decided in a court from which there was no substantive appeal.'[13] Sir Robert Gifford, the Solicitor General, disputed both Taylor's premise – that arrears in bankruptcy litigation had increased since creation of the Vice-Chancellor – and his recommendation – that a new bankruptcy court would assist litigants and ease the pressure on Chancery. The House supported Gifford, and Taylor's motion was defeated, 151–49. Two years later, Taylor again urged Parliament to consider the present state of Chancery and the appellate jurisdiction of the House of Lords. The court of Chancery as presently constituted, he argued, could no longer cope with the amount of legal business that it was called upon to bear. Moreover, the complexity of the law had so increased that untrained peers were longer fit to resolve disputes.[14] In the brief debate that followed, however, Lord Londonderry and Gifford, now Attorney General, again defended the *status quo*, and the motion was defeated, 56 to 52. Despite these rebuffs, Taylor submitted a third motion in June 1822, that a committee be appointed to consider the Vice-Chancellor Act. He had ample evidence, he claimed, to prove that this statute had failed to reduce the size of Chancery arrears, and had merely shifted the bottle neck, from trial before the Vice-Chancellor to appeal before the Lord Chancellor. Once again the Attorney General pointed to the dedication and ability of the relevant judicial officers, and the motion was defeated, 108 to 51.

---

[13]  *Ibid.*, XL:564.
[14]  Hansard, *Parliamentary debates, new (2ⁿᵈ) series*, V:1036.

Despite the fact that the reformers based their arguments upon what they argued were real defects in the court of Chancery, Eldon did not fare badly at their hands. At the start of his campaign, Taylor avoided open condemnation of the Chancellor. In moving for a committee in March 1811 he 'assured the House he meant nothing invidious to the Noble Lord. He asked merely for justice to the public.'[15] Sir Samuel Romilly too was unwilling to speak harshly of the Chancellor, professing that Eldon 'never had his equal, in point of anxiety, to do justice to the suitors of the court'.[16] If anything, Eldon was treated more kindly during the period 1819 to 1822. Taylor himself, who had previously questioned whether the business of the court had actually increased under Eldon, was now convinced that it had, and was willing to attribute delays 'to the pressure of business, which no human strength could perform'.[17] The fault, Taylor argued, lay with the structure of Chancery, whereby a single man, even of acknowledged abilities, carried an intolerable burden. Moreover, this professional burden, when coupled with the Chancellor's political obligations, was beyond 'even the discriminating faculties of lord Eldon'.[18]

Whatever might have been the effect of continued agitation at this level of intensity, it was succeeded in the summer of 1823 by a new, more virulent strain. Taylor acquired the assistance of John Williams, recently returned for Lincoln, and together they transformed their attack on Chancery into an attack on the Chancellor's ability and integrity.[19] On 4 June Williams moved the appointment of a select committee to consider the arrears in Chancery and in the appellate jurisdiction of the Lords. The inclusion of the appellate jurisdiction was somewhat surprising, given that a select committee had been appointed in the Lords in 1822, but may have reflected the lack of confidence in their lordships' deliberations previously expressed by Taylor and his colleagues. Both Williams and Thomas Denman were sharply critical of Eldon, and when Gifford rose to defend him, the proponents of inquiry further argued that such conduct only strengthened the suspicion that

---

[15] Hansard, *Parliamentary debates (1st series)*, XIX:262.     [16] *Ibid.*, col. 268.
[17] *Ibid.*, XL:560.     [18] Hansard, *Parliamentary debates, new (2nd) series*, V:1032.
[19] Williams maintained an active legal practice, and had been junior counsel for Queen Caroline in the Bill of Pains and Penalties brought against her. See chapter 15.

fault lay primarily with the Chancellor.[20] The government still possessed the votes to defeat the motion, though it was felt necessary to rebut suggestions of stonewalling. George Canning, the recently appointed Foreign Secretary and leader of the House, pointed out that the Lords were already taking steps to improve their appellate procedure. Moreover, while *he* did not believe that members opposite intended to attack Eldon personally, he 'was convinced that the House could not go into the inquiry without its being considered, in the eyes of the public and of all mankind, as an accusation against the lord Chancellor'.[21] While the reformers contrasted Canning's attitude toward Chancery reform when out of office with that now being expressed, they lacked the voting strength to do other than slightly embarrass him.[22] The motion was defeated, 174 to 89.

The Lords committee had not, in fact, shirked its responsibilities. In June 1823 it recommended several measures to improve the conduct of judicial business, including the abolition of interlocutory Chancery appeals, removal of both the lunacy and bankruptcy jurisdiction from the Chancellor, and alteration of the Chancery fee structure.[23] Peers also adopted a Standing Order extending the time spent upon judicial business from three to five days in the week. Eldon pledged to take the Chancery recommendations forward in consultation with his brother judges and Chancery officials, though he made clear his objections to several of these as well as to the proposed separation of the Chancellorship from the Speakership.[24] In the months that followed, a certain amount of discussion seems to have occurred between Eldon and his officers on the issue of fees, and he came around to the idea of a Deputy Speaker to preside over appeals in the absence of the Chancellor.[25]

---

[20] See, e.g., the remarks of James Scarlett, Hansard, *Parliamentary debates, new (2nd) series*, IX:773–4.

[21] *Ibid.*, col. 793.

[22] Canning had previously opposed the Vice-Chancellor Act.

[23] The committee also made specific recommendations with respect to Scottish appeals. See Hansard, *Parliamentary debates, new (2nd) series*, IX:1246–53. These became the subject of further inquiry, and some were given legislative effect in 1825. Stevens, *Law and politics*, 18–19.

[24] Eldon's objections are found in Hansard, *Parliamentary debates, new (2nd) series*, IX:1327. Writing in February 1824, Lord Colchester noted Eldon's promise of eight months previously. Lord Colchester, C. Abbot, *The diary and correspondence of Charles Abbot, Lord Colchester*, 3 vols. (London, 1861), III:311.

[25] Eldon referred to the fee issue in a letter to Robert Peel of 15 February 1824. BL

A formal rota system came into effect in the Lords in February 1824, whereby four peers, including the Chancellor or Deputy Speaker, were assigned to attend appeals on a daily basis. Failure to attend resulted in a £50 fine.

Williams also returned to the subject of Chancery delays in February 1824. Again he chronicled instances of lengthy delays and excessive charges, and he repeated his assertion that many practitioners feared retribution by Chancery officials if they criticised the court. Williams suffered from no such anxiety. He listed eight specific grounds of complaint, encompassing the conduct of the Chancellor, Vice-Chancellor, Masters, and clerical staff, and the court's jurisdiction. Retreating somewhat from his previous attack on Eldon, he nevertheless argued that praise of the Chancellor must result in condemnation of the Chancery system:

If under the management of a man so perfectly wise as the noble and learned lord was represented to be, such bitter proofs of delay and expense had been produced, what must the system be that had given birth to them? Let him ask them also to consider in what a luckless condition would the people of England be, if, without any amelioration, this system should be handed over, at some remote period, to a chancellor of inferior talents and virtue – since all men could not be the best? It would seem that the more the present agents were extolled, the more the system would be depressed.[26]

On this occasion Williams was answered by Robert Peel, who entered into the most comprehensive defence of Eldon's conduct to date. He went on, however, to propose that a royal commission of Chancery lawyers and judges – rather than MPs – should inquire into Chancery practice. Peel described his proposal as resulting from the suggestions of the Lords committee and Eldon himself. James Abercromby probably spoke for more than himself, however, when he described the government's action as 'a capitulation at the opening of the second campaign'.[27] Certainly his objection to membership consisting of judges named by the Chancellor was strongly echoed. Williams noted that judges habitually opposed changes to their profession, while Henry Brougham was amazed by the suggestion that Eldon should be

(Peel papers), Add. MS 40315 f. 117. See Eldon's letter of 16 September 1823 to Lord Liverpool in which he discusses the Speakership. BL (Liverpool papers), Add. MS 38296 f. 308.

[26] Hansard, *Parliamentary debates, new (2nd) series*, X:401.      [27] *Ibid.*, col. 419.

involved.[28] Despite these objections, however, Williams withdrew his motion.

The fourteen-member committee was appointed on 26 April 1824.[29] Over a period of eighteen months, it questioned fifty-three persons, including barristers and solicitors practising in Chancery, and many of the court officers and staff.[30] A report, consisting of 187 propositions, was produced on 2 March 1826. Given the recent history of reform agitation in Parliament, however, it is not surprising that the work of the commission had occasioned considerable interest, speculation, and criticism long before it was completed.[31] In the spring and summer of 1825, the question of Chancery reform was very much alive in the House of Commons. Brougham, Williams, and Sir Francis Burdett complained that the real purpose of the commission was to preserve the *status quo* and to vindicate the Chancellor. Consequently, witnesses were asked the wrong questions for the wrong reasons. Peel and Sir Charles Wetherell, the Solicitor General, urged the House against a premature condemnation of the inquiry, while Canning and Stephen Lushington, the sole opposition member of the commission, complained that some MPs seemed to expect a criminal investigation of the Chancellor's conduct.

An investigation of the Chancellor did seem to lie behind the petition presented by Joseph Hume in April 1826 on behalf of a man imprisoned for contempt of Chancery. In the course of his remarks, Hume described Eldon and the court of Chancery as 'the greatest curse that ever fell on any nation'.[32] Back-benchers, as well as ministers, objected to this language. Taylor, however,

---

[28] *Ibid.*, cols. 436, 425.

[29] Members of the commission were Eldon, Redesdale (formerly Lord Chancellor of Ireland), Gifford (Master of the Rolls), Sir J. Leach (Vice-Chancellor), Sir C. Wetherell (Solicitor General), S. C. Cox (Chancery Master), W. Courtenay (Chancery Master), A. Hart (Chancery Master), R. P. Smith (barrister), J. Littledale (barrister), J. M. Merivale (barrister), N. C. Tindal (barrister), J. Beames (barrister), and S. Lushington (Doctor of Civil Law).

[30] The range of witnesses was as follows: the Chief Baron (one); King's Counsel (five); barristers (two); solicitors (thirteen); Master's Clerks (twelve); Six Clerks (one); Examiners (two); Registrars (three); Commissioner of Bankrupts (six); Secretary of Bankrupts (one); Secretary of Lunatics (one); Account General's Clerk (one); Clerk in Court (one); Messenger (one); Secretary at the Rolls (two); Deputy Sergeant at Arms (one).

[31] For the campaign in favour of Chancery reform as carried on outside of Parliament, see the *Edinburgh Review*, vols. 39, 45.

[32] Hansard, *Parliamentary debates, new (2nd) series*, XV:299.

greeted the episode with flippancy, advising the Chancellor's friends to take comfort from the effect that the offensive remark could have no effect on him:

[T]he noble lord against whom it was aimed, was determined to brave his enemies to the last, and had long since made up his mind to quit office and life at the same time ... Let it not, therefore, be feared that praise or censure would at all operate to produce an effect so fatal and alarming; for the noble and learned lord was not so easily vanquished.[33]

When Hume returned to the subject of particular miscarriages of justice a few days later Wetherell described his conduct as part of a 'system of running down the lord chancellor' rather than a *bona fide* topic of discussion.[34]

On 18 May 1826, the Attorney General, Sir John Singleton Copley, brought in a Bill to give effect to the commission's recommendations. It focused on improving Chancery procedure at three stages: parties would be obliged to appear and answer complaints more quickly, to advance their claims more responsibly, and to appeal decisions more circumspectly. Limits were imposed on both the number of counsel appearing for a party, and the number of motions each lawyer could file. Masters were given increased powers to compel attendance and to render binding decisions. The work of the Chancellor was likewise affected in three ways. He would be relieved of *habeas corpus* petitions, he would hear appeals from the Vice-Chancellor only on receipt of a sworn statement of sufficiency filed by counsel, and he would lose his original jurisdiction over bankruptcy matters.[35] The reformers greeted this measure with grudging support. They approved of the changes proposed, but they found the Bill a poor result of a long-delayed and unsatisfactory inquiry. Williams maintained that 'almost the whole of the abuses mentioned might have been remedied by the court five and twenty years ago'. Why had Eldon not exercised his vaunted 'acuteness and intelligence' to correct them?[36] Taylor objected to the proposed reorganisation of the bankruptcy jurisdiction, whereby decisions of a new bankruptcy commission would remain subject to appeal to the Lord Chancellor. Brougham lamented the failure to examine the relationship between the Chancellor's professional and political responsibil-

---

[33] *Ibid.*, col. 315.    [34] *Ibid.*, col. 538.    [35] *Ibid.*, cols. 1213–26.
[36] *Ibid.*, col. 12300.

ities. Despite these criticisms the Bill went forward, but administrative and financial complications required that it be abandoned
for that session. When Copley, lately elevated to the office of
Master of the Rolls, re-submitted the Bill in February 1827, he
found its progress again impeded by calls for further inquiry and
more radical reform. He, Peel, Canning, and Wetherell, then
Attorney General, fended off what had 'swelled into nothing less
than a direct attack' on Eldon.[37] Chancery and the Chancellor
continued to occupy the Commons in March and early April, but
events were soon to rob both attack and defence of their primary
focus. In April Eldon and half the cabinet resigned, and while the
advent of a new Lord Chancellor would not put an end to the
debate on the Chancery, it would cause politicians to re-examine
their views on the subject.[38]

During the long campaign for Chancery reform, complaints
focused both upon the institutional weaknesses of the court and
upon the personal failings of the current Lord Chancellor. Often
these complaints were kept separate, but in some cases they
merged, as when institutional deficiencies were allegedly ignored
or facilitated by its presiding officer. The charges against Eldon
linked him to the unacceptable length and cost of Chancery
litigation, and can be summarised as distortion, inefficiency,
delay, intransigence, and manipulation. These charges were complicated, and need to be explained in turn.

The first complaint charged that the Chancellor's portrayal of
his workload was distorted. Chancery business had *not* increased
during Eldon's time in office, it was argued, or, if some areas had
experienced growth, these were either insignificant or had been
offset by decreases elsewhere. Delays, therefore, must be the
Chancellor's fault. Alternatively, it was admitted that appeals
from decisions of the Vice-Chancellor to the Chancellor had
increased, but for this Eldon was again held indirectly and directly
responsible. The very creation of the office of Vice-Chancellor
must have tended to increase litigation in the form of appeals, and
the appointment of an inept Vice-Chancellor, in the person of
Thomas Plumer, had made that tendency absolute. As Eldon had

---

[37] The remarks are Canning's. *Ibid.*, XVII:264.
[38] The government argued that it was only reasonable to allow the new Lord
Chancellor (Copley, elevated to the peerage as Baron Lyndhurst) time to settle
into his office and attempt to reduce arrears, before forcing changes upon him.

been behind both creation and appointment, he had severely weakened an already precarious structure.[39] Moreover, it was argued that Eldon's very style of adjudication actually encouraged appeals from his junior colleague. His willingness to re-hear and re-consider arguments prompted losing counsel to try their luck a second time.[40]

Quite apart from the issue of growth, Eldon was accused of delaying Chancery litigation. His habit of decision-making was described as slow, hesitant, even non-existent, and as creating a vast backlog of cases awaiting a final decision. Williams acknowledged that, while the Lord Chancellor was possessed of both ability and practical knowledge:

> [Y]et, unfortunately, those high qualities stood combined with one defect, which destroyed and defeated almost all their usefulness – with a degree of learned doubtfulness – that *dubitandi patientia* ... which, indulged too far, degenerated into habit, into weakness, and even into vice. Unfortunately, those great and estimable talents were joined to a degree of indecisiveness and over caution which neutralized, and he might almost say annihilated, the high advantages which should have resulted from them.[41]

For the most part this tendency was ascribed to a generous intention – that of being absolutely just to the individual parties. However laudable in the abstract, the practical consequence of that intention was injustice to litigants as a class. Romilly said of Eldon: 'his fault was over anxiety to do justice in each particular case, without considering how many other causes were waiting to be decided.'[42] Only Denman attempted to link the Chancellor's ability to make up his mind to the political ramifications of the decision. He observed that Eldon had speedily recognised the King's right to exclude the late Queen from the liturgy, and just as promptly had refused to afford her the status of Queen consort at her trial.[43] He

---

[39] For the view that Eldon was responsible for Plumer's appointment, see Jeremy Bentham to Etienne Dumont, 7 June 1811, S. Conway (ed.), *Correspondence 1809–1816*, vol. 8 of *The collected works of Jeremy Bentham*, 10 vols., general eds. J. R. Dinwiddy and F. Rosen (Oxford, 1988), 164.

[40] Hansard, *Parliamentary debates, new (2nd) series*, XVI:740.

[41] *Ibid.*, IX:709.

[42] S. Romilly, *Memoirs of Sir Samuel Romilly*, 3 vols. (London, 1840), II:369. See too his speech of 7 March 1811, found in Hansard, *Parliamentary debates (1st series)*, XIX:268.

[43] Hansard, *Parliamentary debates, new (2nd) series*, IX:750, 751.

had been unable, however, to render a speedy decision on the Portsmouth lunacy petition.

[T]he fact of the petitioner having, as a member of that House, commonly voted against the ministers, and of the unfortunate nobleman, who was the object of the petition, having constantly lent his proxy in the House of Lords to the friends of the ministry, might have unconsciously exercised an influence on his mind.[44]

Denman likewise explained the alacrity with which the Chancellor had refused to grant Lord Byron an injunction to prevent pirated publication of his work. '[I]t would not be considered unnatural that the lord chancellor should have been somewhat influenced, whose whole life had certainly not been devoted to discovering modes of preserving the liberty of the press.'[45]

The accusation of intransigence related to Eldon's undertaking to perform a range of functions beyond his, or anyone's, capacity. His unwillingness to admit that his duties must be reduced if any were to be performed satisfactorily provoked very hostile comment. On more than one occasion he was accused of clinging particularly to those parts of his jurisdiction which were most lucrative. Taylor claimed that Eldon regularly gave bankruptcy petitions top priority: 'What was the reason? Simply because the profits attending those petitions were too great to be parted with.'[46] D. W. Harvey spoke even more bluntly: '[W]as it at all likely that the Chancellor would give up the £15 or the £20 which each bankruptcy case produced him?' Harvey 'firmly believed that the Chancellor derived not less than £20,000 a year from the bankruptcy cases alone'.[47] Alternatively, Eldon was charged with neglecting his judicial duties generally, in order to maintain and increase his political authority. Taylor remarked that: 'somehow or other, whenever any question, whether of foreign or domestic policy was agitating in the cabinet, the lord chancellor could never be easy in that court, but shut up his note-book and went to Carlton House.'[48]

Nor was Eldon's conduct said to be limited to a personal opposition to reform. Rather it extended to actual manipulation of other likely agents of change. The government, it was charged, had long relied on Eldon for its survival, and dared not advocate

---

[44] *Ibid.*, IX:752.    [45] *Ibid.*, cols. 752–3.    [46] *Ibid.*, col. 735.
[47] *Ibid.*, XVI:721.    [48] *Ibid.*, VII:1376–7.

any measures contrary to his wishes. Indeed, ministers even feared to permit criticism of the Lord Chancellor to go unanswered. Taylor claimed: 'the lord chancellor is the individual who keeps the whole government together. If he is molested he will give up the seals; and there is an end to the government.'[49] If the government suffered from the overt exercise of the Chancellor's political clout, the Chancery commission was allegedly undermined by a more subtle assault. This was Eldon's particular authority, as well as his ready charm and polished manners. His very membership proved that the inquiry must be unsatisfactory. Knowledge of his views would effectively gag any officer or practitioner appearing before the committee. So too the presence of commissioners such as Redesdale, 'the noble lord's old and tried friend ... who had mounted the ladder of political preferment with his lordship, but always a step behind', Sir John Leach, 'an officer of the noble lord's own court', Gifford, 'who owed his advancement to the favour of the lord chancellor', and others 'who expected to be Masters' would ensure that only questions favourable to Eldon were asked.[50] Brougham accused the Chancery commission of having 'slumbered' over the crucial question of fundamental reform, and the cause of this lethargy was Eldon himself, whose 'fascinating manners' had lulled the commissioners rather than obstructed their work.

Thus the case against Eldon made him out to be a man who negligently, if not wilfully, overloaded an already failing institution. He facilitated a growth in business which made him enormously rich and impoverished a significant segment of the public, and he would neither reform his own habits nor tolerate an enforced alteration of his official duties. The available evidence does not quite bear out these accusations. Neither, however, does it vindicate the Lord Chancellor. Rather, each charge has some merit, albeit subject to qualifications. To assess the various charges against him, it is necessary to re-examine the issues of Chancery growth, delays, and remedies more closely.

Chancery arrears had been a problem before Eldon became Chancellor.[51] In his first year in office he admitted having to wade

---

[49] *Ibid.*, IX:733. See also *ibid.*, col. 738.
[50] *Ibid.*, XIII:1090–1091. See also *ibid.*, XV:1261.
[51] *Parliamentary papers* (1826) XV:306. See also the testimony of Thomas Raynsford, Chancery Registrar, *ibid.*, 495.

through a considerable number of cases left undecided by his predecessor. '[H]ard as I have worked, after being *chancellor three months*, it was not till Saturday that I had got through arrears so far as to approach the very *first* petition presented to myself.'[52] Moreover, during Eldon's time the judicial business of both Chancery and the House of Lords does seem to have increased. Even sceptics like Romilly admitted that the number of bankruptcy cases had grown, and most observers, including Eldon, argued for a more general increase. Peel maintained that the rise in litigation principally resulted from the significant growth in population and in funded property since 1800.[53] The effect of the Napoleonic wars upon commerce, investment, and production must also have affected the business of Chancery during that period. The Lords committee of 1811 and its immediate successor in the Commons both produced figures comparing current Chancery litigation with that undertaken in the middle of the eighteenth century. This data introduced two complications to any assessment of Eldon's workload. First, the data itself was subject to different interpretations. In absolute terms, the number of original causes heard by Eldon had declined sharply as against the number heard by Lord Chancellor Hardwicke (see Table 16.1). The number of petitions and motions, however, had risen substantially in the same period. Whether the increase in motions and petitions offset the decline in causes was the subject of much debate. Secondly, the data presented was incomplete. Chancery officials reported to the Commons committee that many more petitions and motions were actually heard by the Chancellor than were recorded as having been heard or than appeared on the accounts.[54]

The knowledge that absolute numbers could not provide other than a very impressionistic picture of a court's business did not inhibit MPs from stating, relying upon, and demanding the production of, further tables of figures. The Chancery commission produced detailed accounts of the various classes of judicial work undertaken by the Chancellor, the Master of the Rolls, and the Vice-Chancellor, although the testimony of witnesses suggested

---

[52] Eldon to Henry Addington, 16 June 1801, DevRO (Sidmouth papers), 152M/c1801/OZ137.
[53] Hansard, *Parliamentary debates, new (2nd) series*, IX:405.
[54] *Ibid.*, II:43, 54.

Table 16.1. *Chancery business, 1745–1755 and 1800–1810*

| Date | Causes | Petitions | Motions |
|---|---|---|---|
| 1745–6 | 202 | 198 | 3769 |
| 1746–7 | 178 | 178 | 3787 |
| 1747–8 | 193 | 198 | 3732 |
| 1748–9 | 181 | 170 | 4060 |
| 1749–50 | 178 | 205 | 4073 |
| 1750–1 | 120 | 128 | 2981 |
| 1751–2 | 140 | 157 | 3935 |
| 1752–3 | 170 | 153 | 4091 |
| 1753–4 | 139 | 143 | 4066 |
| 1754–5 | 137 | 123 | 3386 |
| 1800–1 | 87 | 333 | 4684 |
| 1801–2 | 52 | 262 | 4745 |
| 1802–3 | 60 | 296 | 4748 |
| 1803–4 | 87 | 337 | 5160 |
| 1804–5 | 58 | 318 | 6050 |
| 1805–6 | 42 | 275 | 5674 |
| 1806–7 | 56 | 253 | 6001 |
| 1807–8 | 41 | 257 | 6909 |
| 1808–9 | 54 | 207 | 6362 |
| 1809–10 | 33 | 180 | 6730 |

*Source: Parliamentary papers* (1810–11), III: 4–5, Appendix B

that these figures were not only incomplete, but overly simple. Thomas Walker, Chancery Registrar, informed the commission that entire days were taken up with business before the Chancellor that was not included in the court registry.[55] Eldon's supporters consistently objected to simple numerical comparisons, but this did not stop Peel and Gifford from producing lists of figures with an enthusiasm to rival that of Williams and Taylor.[56]

To predict that the creation of the Vice-Chancellor would almost necessarily increase the number of appeals to the Chancellor does not take much imagination. Knowledge of that tendency need not condemn the decision to create a subordinate judgeship, however, as it was assumed that the increase in appeals would be smaller than the increase in final decisions in original causes. That the appointment of Plumer to the office in 1813 failed to give satisfaction seems not to be doubted. Many of his

---

[55] *Parliamentary papers* (1826) XV:475–6.
[56] See, e.g., Gifford's remarks in the debate of 4 June 1823, reported in Hansard, *Parliamentary debates, new (2nd) series*, IX:725–8.

decisions were appealed, probably resulting from a combination of what Londonderry called 'the desire which every man felt to have his case decided by the great talents and learning' of Eldon, and a corresponding lack of confidence in Plumer.[57] Eldon must take some responsibility for the appointment, since Plumer was his friend and in no way forced upon him. Plumer was not, however, the only Vice-Chancellor to fall afoul of the profession. His successor, Leach, who achieved his place through friendship with the Prince Regent, was criticised for his impatience and unwillingness to listen to arguments. In a letter to Sir William Scott, Eldon admitted: 'Half my time has been spent in hearing complaints that the V[ice]-C[hancellor] would hear no counsel, party, &c., nor give ear to anything he ought to listen to. This has produced scenes very indecent, and I have done my best, ineffectually often, to put an end to them.'[58] While such information may tend to rehabilitate Plumer, it likewise strengthens the objection to the office *per se*, as likely to promote dissatisfaction regardless of the incumbent. It was perhaps unlikely that practitioners would not find fault with the junior in circumstances when they could complain to the senior, or that the public would believe 'that the decision of a Vice-Chancellor will have as much weight as the decision of a Lord Chancellor'.[59] Eldon must also take some responsibility for the creation of the office in the first place. While he argued in 1823 that the office had not been established 'at my instance', it is also true that ten years earlier the Vice-Chancellor Bill had been described in the Commons as having Eldon's support, and he had affirmed in the Lords that he 'would not have suffered the measure to have gone on to its ultimate stage, had he not been thoroughly convinced of its absolute necessity, for the assistance of suitors'.[60] Eldon drew a

---

[57] *Ibid.*, V:1038. See the testimony of barrister and commissioner of bankrupts, Basil Montague, before the Chancery commission. *Parliamentary papers* (1826), XV:412.

[58] Eldon to Sir William Scott, 28 August 1819, H. Twiss, *The public and private live of Lord Chancellor Eldon*, 3 vols. (London, 1844), II:337–8.

[59] The expression is that of Basil Montague, testifying before the Chancery commission. *Parliamentary papers* (1826) XV:411. Montague also pointed out that with the Chancellor and Vice-Chancellor sitting at the same time, the Chancery bar was necessarily divided between them, and considerable time was lost when matters were obliged to be put back in one court because the barristers were arguing another case elsewhere. *Ibid.*, 410.

[60] Hansard, *Parliamentary debates (1ˢᵗ series)*, XXIV:246. The remarks are Castle-

distinction between creating a Vice-Chancellor in order to relieve the Chancellor, and creating a Vice-Chancellor to accommodate litigants whose Chancellor had been called away on other business, but the result was the same.

That Eldon failed to resolve the growing number of cases promptly was an observation not confined to the Chancery reformers in Parliament. The artist Joseph Farington recorded a conversation in 1803 with two back-benchers, William Praed and Robert Fellowes, in which 'The Lord Chancellor was spoken of with[ou]t approbation. [H]is *indecision* was felt a grievance in the Court of Chancery'.[61] Jeremy Bentham frequently referred to Eldon as 'Lord Endless.'[62] Nor was Eldon oblivious to the charge of tardiness. On the contrary, he sometimes joked about it. In a letter to Sir William Scott he remarked that men such as Leach, who 'talk, and sometimes judge, so quickly, their conduct imposes great hardship upon such a dull, slow, plodding, deliberating dog as I am'.[63] The cause of Eldon's indecision seems to have been three-fold. First, the issues concerned in the cases before him were frequently complex and wide-ranging. Litigation arising out of the management of an estate, for example, might involve diverse questions of real property, trusts, taxation, employment, inheritance, and family settlements. Lunacy petitions required consideration of medical evidence on the dimly understood issue of mental illness. Undoubtedly, Eldon's considerable intellect enabled him to appreciate the potential significance of details that other judges would have overlooked.[64] Secondly, Eldon was obsessed by the desire to give the 'right' decision in each case. He felt obliged, therefore, to weigh up each detail as it occurred to him. Together, these two factors must have resulted in a tendency to delay judgment, but this was enhanced by the third, Eldon's lack of self-confidence. George Rose recorded in his diary a

reagh's. *Ibid.*, col. 533. Eldon would continue to argue that the Vice-Chancellorship had not been his creation. See his remarks during a debate on Brougham's bankruptcy reforms in 1831 in Hansard, *Parliamentary debates 3^rd series*, VII:252.

61  J. Farington, *The Farington diary*, ed. J. Greig, 8 vols. (London, 1924), II:81.

62  See, e.g., Bentham to J. F. Gwynn, 31 July 1818, S. Conway (ed.), *Correspondence 1817–1820*, vol. 9 of *The correspondence of Jeremy Bentham*, 230.

63  Eldon to Scott, 14 October 1815, Twiss, *The public and private life*, II:273.

64  For a tribute to the breadth and depth of Eldon's analysis, see *Legal Observer* 1(14) (1831), 209.

conversation with George III, in which the King lamented the Chancellor's 'want of decision, occasioned by his not having sufficient confidence in himself, particularly in protracting the determination of causes'.[65] Abercromby likewise described the Chancellor's 'great infirmity of mind' as 'a want of confidence in his own judgment'.[66] Thus Eldon, seeing the genuine complexity of the issues facing him in a given case, and wanting to do justice to the parties concerned, would both examine the case from every possible perspective, and then do so again and again through fear of error. An exasperated Romilly complained: 'He thus condemns all the other impatient suitors to continue waiting in anxious expectation of having their causes decided, till he shall have made quite sure ... that he has not been already three times mistaken.'[67] Witnesses before the Chancery commission testified to many instances of these traits combining to result in serious delay. The Chancellor was 'too good-natured in allowing other business to interrupt the usual course, in consequence of the representations of the hardship of particular cases'.[68] Having thus agreed to hear disputes irregularly presented, the Chancellor heard counsel 'to much greater length than previously' or found them ill-prepared. The latter failure obliged him 'to postpone his judgment until he has had an opportunity of reading or looking into the pleadings and documents relating thereto, and by such means ascertaining what are the real facts of the case'.[69] When the documentation revealed disputed or inconsistent facts, the Chancellor would attempt to resolve them, rather than passing them on to the Masters.[70] In lunacy matters he required doctors to explain their findings to him, or interview the alleged lunatic, under a belief that 'the case was so interesting to the individuals concerned, and their feelings and interests were so much involved, that it was his duty to give a preference to that business'.[71]

Undoubtedly, Eldon was generally averse to altering either the

---

[65] L. V. Harcourt (ed.), *The diaries and correspondence of the Rt Hon. George Rose*, 2 vols. (London, 1860), II:178.

[66] Hansard, *Parliamentary debates, new (2nd) series*, IX: 761.

[67] Romilly, *Memoirs*, II:372.

[68] Testimony of John Bell, K. C. *Parliamentary papers* (1826) XV:249. See also the observations of the barrister G. B. Roupell, *ibid.*, 332.

[69] Testimony of W. Leake, solicitor, *ibid.*, 451.

[70] See the testimony of John Pensam, Secretary of Bankrupts, *ibid.*, 501.

[71] Testimony of Thomas Carr, Secretary of Lunatics, *ibid.*, 502.

office of Chancellor or the practice of Chancery. He opposed creation of a separate bankruptcy court, a separate lunacy jurisdiction, and a separate office of Speaker, and he had little faith that the peers' rota would facilitate appeals in the House of Lords. In his later years, he sometimes acknowledged that he had simply grown too old to countenance change. In a letter to Liverpool in 1821 he observed that law 'has its reformers – young men think they can do better than old ones – the old ones don't like innovation – and get crusty'.[72] Hostility to change did not simply come with old age, however. Eldon opposed change because he genuinely believed in the strength, if not the perfection, of the existing structure. He noted the experience of his predecessors in a letter to Peel:

I have intimately known most of those who have had the Seals since 1778. I have known none of them, who did not project alterations in practice, which they confidently thought would be beneficial. Hardly an alteration have been made by any of them. And I *know* that a year or two's experience taught them that the alterations they had projected would be mischievous changes – and, therefore, they were content to stand *super antiquas vias*.[73]

Moreover, Eldon had a great desire to see the office preserved for the future. At the start of his first term in office he opposed dividing the offices of Chancellor and Speaker – for fear of diminishing the Chancellorship for future incumbents.[74] For his own emoluments he was not jealous, expressing himself willing to surrender his fees and to suffer a reduction in income upon the appointment of a Deputy Speaker. On the latter point he wrote to Liverpool in 1823 that he would agree to any reduction 'that may be thought reasonable, it being understood that this is not to be drawn into precedent as to my successor'.[75]

The charge that Eldon gave preference to particular categories

---

[72] Eldon to Liverpool, undated [*c.* April 1821] BL (Liverpool papers), Add. MS 38289 f. 134. Two years later Eldon wrote to Liverpool in a similar vein: 'change is itself a sore evil to man, grown old enough to be wedded to things as they have been, and as they are.' *Ibid.*, Add. MS 38296 f. 308.

[73] Eldon to Peel, undated [*c.* February–March 1824], BL (Peel papers), Add. MS 40315 f. 122.

[74] Harcourt, *Diaries*, II:178–9.

[75] Eldon to Liverpool, undated [*c.* mid-September 1823] BL (Liverpool papers), Add. MS 38296 f. 308. On Eldon's later hostility to the principle of fees, see Hansard, *Parliamentary debates 3rd series*, VII:253.

of judicial business to maximise his fees is certainly unproved. Despite the fact that he provided a breakdown of his annual salary and fees on several occasions during his public career, the suspicion of enormous wealth persisted. Eldon's income was regularly rumoured to stand at £30–40,000 per year, rather than the true figure of £15–20,000. The figure produced by Harvey of £15–20,000 per year in fees from bankruptcy petitions at a rate of £15–20 per petition was similarly inflated. In fact Eldon received £1.02.00 per petition, totalling £3–5,000 per annum.[76] That Taylor should have raised the spectre of the Chancellor's love of fees in 1823 was disingenuous, given his admission in 1813 that the same had been 'much exaggerated by general and vulgar report'.[77] On that occasion Taylor had not only confirmed the lower figure, but had admitted that Eldon was far from committed to a fee-based income. On the contrary, when the Commons committee of 1811–12 had advocated replacing fees with a salary, Eldon had 'approved of such an arrangement, and acquiesced in the average of the last five years being taken as the standard, amounting to about £16 or 17,000 a year'. Taylor had thought it 'only doing fair justice to the noble lord to state, that on this occasion they found him as liberal as any principle of fairness or equity could require'.[78] In an undated letter to Liverpool, probably written around 1821, Eldon affirmed that he had 'not the least objection' to making his income known. The figure that Liverpool supposed, of £13–14,000 per year, Eldon thought low, '& desired it to be looked into'.[79] The particular charge that Eldon

---

[76] See, e.g., Hansard, *Parliamentary debates, new (2ⁿᵈ) series*, XVI:722. On 22 May 1827 Harvey admitted that his previous assertions regarding Eldon's bankruptcy fees had been incorrect, and that he had known this at the time. 'He knew very well at that time, that the whole amount of them [the fees paid in to the Chancery] did not go to the lord Chancellor; but he certainly thought a much larger portion of them found their way to his lordship than he now found did.' *Ibid.*, XVII:958. On 27 February 1827 Brougham also admitted that his previous description of Eldon's fortune as standing at £1.5 million had merely been intended to reflect common rumour, and that the Chancellor's income 'never exceeded £18,000 annually, and that the bankruptcy portion of it did not amount to a fourth that sum'. *Ibid.*, XVI:757.

[77] Hansard, *Parliamentary debates (1ˢᵗ series)*, XIV:681.          [78] *Ibid.*

[79] Eldon to Liverpool, undated [*c.* 1820–1822], BL (Liverpool papers), Add. MS 38577 f. 64. The figures provided in this letter for the Chancellor's annual emoluments over a three-year period were as follows:  £12,925.19.08, £12,774.19.06, £13,012.09.08, an average of £12,904.09.07. A previous four years produced an average of £13,405.

spent all his time dealing with bankruptcy business is also misplaced. On the contrary, his usual course seems to have been largely to ignore bankruptcy petitions during term, and then to hear them all at the end of his sittings. This practice was objected to, both as extremely fatiguing for the lawyers, and as failing to provide the bankruptcy court with a consistent practice.[80] Joseph Marryat MP, a West Indies merchant and chairman of Lloyds, complained, 'at present the Chancellor visited them like a comet, once in a century, and with inconceivable velocity'.[81]

It is clear that Eldon did take a great interest in both Court and Cabinet dynamics. Moreover, management of the affairs of the Royal Family was particularly burdensome during his time in office, while the very length of his tenure brought involvement in several political crises. Assessing his ability to balance his different roles is more problematic. He certainly did write letters while presiding in Chancery, though whether he missed important arguments of counsel thereby is questionable. Further, the practice of terminating his judicial sittings in order to attend to other business was already established when Eldon entered office.[82] While he undoubtedly curtailed sittings to attend to political matters, he also did the reverse. Several letters survive in which Eldon excused his absence from a Cabinet or private meeting with George III, the Prince Regent, Liverpool, or Peel on the grounds of professional business in Chancery or the House of Lords.[83] Moreover, in absolute terms Eldon spent many hours, year in and year out, on Chancery business. The Chancery Registrars testified that Eldon typically held longer sittings during term time and the vacations than his predecessors had done.[84] Moreover, he looked

---

[80] Romilly complained of his end-of-term 'slavery', when the Chancellor might hear and decide upwards of 300 bankruptcy petitions in a fortnight. Romilly, *Memoirs*, II:405–6, III:149.

[81] Hansard, *Parliamentary debates (1ˢᵗ series)*, XXV:20.

[82] See, e.g., Eldon to Addington, 16 June 1801, DevRO (Sidmouth papers), 152M/c1801/OZ137.

[83] See, e.g., Eldon to George III, 12 August 1802, A. Aspinall (ed.), *The later correspondence of George III*, 5 vols. (Cambridge, 1962), IV:49–50; Eldon to the Prince Regent, 31 March 1813, A. Aspinall (ed.), *The letters of George IV, king of England*, 1812–1830 3 vols. (Cambridge, 1938), I:237; Eldon to Liverpool, undated [possibly 1812], BL (Liverpool papers), Add MS 38251 f. 102; Eldon to Peel, undated [possibly 1822], BL (Peel papers), Add. MS 40315 f. 82.

[84] See, e.g., the testimony of Thomas Raynsford before the Chancery commission on 20 December 1825. *Parliamentary papers* (1826) XV:495.

out for opportunities to supplement the time spent in the business of his court. He would hear matters in his rooms before the usual hour, and sit on days outside the usual judicial calendar. As late as August 1826 Eldon was holding Chancery sittings during the Long Vacation until counsel begged to be excused on the grounds of exhaustion.[85] On the occasion of an unexpected adjournment of Parliament, Eldon undertook to fill up the time that would have been spent on appeals in the Lords on Chancery matters, trusting that he would redress the balance when Parliament resumed.[86] On those occasions when he escaped London for his home in Dorset, Chancery business regularly followed him. It was not uncommon for solicitors or Chancery officers to present him with documents requiring his immediate attention.[87] In a note to Peel, Eldon declined an invitation to a day's shooting, so that he would be available if called upon to perform any professional functions. '[T]he uncertainty at what hour the Seal may be wanted hardly leaves me any option as to that.'[88]

Taylor's statement of 30 May 1821, that the Lord Chancellor's opposition to Chancery reform 'could not but influence the government', has real merit.[89] It would be surprising if feelings of loyalty and respect did not lead ministers to support their colleague, particularly upon issues which his professional knowledge uniquely qualified him to speak. That they did not defer to his judgment, but acted only to prolong their stay in office, is much harder to prove. It is probably easiest to posit in the case of Canning. Out of office he had opposed the Vice-Chancellor Bill in 1813, and even spoken flippantly on the likely relationship between Eldon and his subordinate. At the time, Castlereagh had accused Canning of political opportunism, and that charge was repeated by opposition speakers when Canning defended Eldon

---

[85] See Eldon to Peel, August 1826, BL (Peel papers), Add. MS 40315 f. 264.

[86] Hansard, *Parliamentary debates (1ˢᵗ series)*, XXVII:328.

[87] See, e.g., Eldon to Liverpool, 5 October 1824, BL (Liverpool papers), Add. MS 38299 f. 135; Eldon to Liverpool, undated [*c*. April 1821], *ibid.*, Add. MS 38289 f. 134; Eldon to Lord Sidmouth, undated, DevRO (Sidmouth papers), 152M/c1824/OZ.

[88] Eldon to Peel, undated [possibly November 1822], BL (Peel papers), Add. MS 40315 f. 78.

[89] Hansard, *Parliamentary debates, new (2ⁿᵈ) series*, V:1027–8.

from the government front bench in 1823.[90] Certainly in private Canning complained of Eldon's habit of indecision, and inquired in Cabinet why a Chancery inquiry should *not* go forward.[91] Moreover, the measured tone of his support in the Commons suggests that it was the product of ministerial solidarity, rather than personal sympathy. In the same way, it is difficult to acquit the law officers of exercising a certain degree of self-interest. Indeed, it would have been the brave Attorney or Solicitor General who provoked the displeasure of the leader of the profession, and chief source of past and future advancement. On the other hand, the law officers were particularly well placed to refute stories of incompetence and injustice which they knew to be incorrect, and their assessments of 'notorious' cases should not be dismissed as mere servility.[92] The motives of Eldon's staunchest defender, however, are unquestionable. Peel's support was firmly based on friendship and respect: friendship for a colleague with whom he sympathised on the issue of religious reform, and respect for an elderly man of established ability and long service. While far from opposed to alterations in Chancery practice, Peel conducted the government's policy so as to spare the Chancellor unnecessary pain. Writing to Eldon in February 1824 to assuage his anxiety over upcoming debates, Peel affirmed:

Every consideration arising out of my sincere esteem for you, and the knowledge of the motives of those who attack you, would induce me zealously at least to co-operate with more able and competent defenders in resisting these attacks. Depend upon it, my dear Chancellor, they can make no impression. Men ask themselves who is the ablest and honestest [*sic*] man who ever presided in the Court of Chancery; and the decisive answer to that question, if it does not silence malignity and political hostility, at least disarms them of the power to rob you of your hardly earned and justly acquired honours.[93]

Peel, significantly, was the minister upon whom Eldon came to

---

[90] For Castlereagh's remarks, see Hansard, *Parliamentary debates (1ˢᵗ series)*, XXV:21.

[91] See, e.g., Canning's letter to Liverpool of 7 March 1824, on Eldon's failure to approve a treaty with the United States. E. J. Stapleton (ed.), *Some official correspondence of George Canning*, 2 vols. (London, 1887), I:47. Eldon referred to Canning's unwelcome Cabinet inquiry in a letter to Liverpool, probably written in the autumn of 1823. BL (Liverpool papers), Add MS 38296 f. 308.

[92] See, e.g., the remarks of Wetherell and William Courtenay on 5 June 1823, in Hansard, *Parliamentary debates, new (2ⁿᵈ) series*, IX: 756–7; 767–70.

[93] Peel to Eldon, 10 February 1824, BL (Peel papers), Add. MS 40315 f. 114.

rely most. He did not trust Canning, and he felt that the law officers did not support him as they ought. His reaction to what he considered the neglect of his colleagues, however, was to beg, rather than to demand, support. His letters to Liverpool during their last years together in office certainly express his conviction that, without support, he must resign. They do not, however, convey anything like a threat to weaken or incapacitate the government. Even as he complained of Burdett's motion having passed without government opposition he assured Liverpool: 'Don't suppose that I am at all out of humour about that.'[94] To Peel he wrote of the same incident: 'I am aware that it might be mere inattention that the matter passed *sub silentio* – and confidently believe that no unkindness was meant.'[95] Moreover, while taking steps to retire from office, he did not mean to turn his back upon the obligations that high office would continue to demand of him. He stated publicly his belief that retiring Chancellors should be obliged to give their attendance to appeals in the House of Lords.[96]

That Eldon could exert an influence upon the proceedings of the Chancery commission is a not unreasonable assumption. His actual conduct seems to have been beyond reproach. Lushington affirmed that the Chancellor invariably absented himself when potentially hostile witnesses came forward, and only afterwards attended the commissioners to answer their questions.[97] That is not to say, however, that he did not exert a more subtle influence, both on the commissioners and on those who testified before them. Undoubtedly some members of the commission were his friends and others were his appointees, and both might have been looking to acquit him of any wrongdoing. While it is not possible to determine the identity of individual commissioners from the transcripts of witness interviews, sometimes these reveal what looks like a questioner attempting to portray the Chancellor in a favourable light. For example, the solicitor Thomas Hamilton asserted that 'frequently months' and 'sometimes years' elapsed between Eldon hearing a case and rendering a decision. This prompted the following line of questions.

[94] Eldon to Liverpool, November 1825, The Rare Book, Manuscript and Special Collections Library, Duke University, (Liverpool papers), MS 2836.
[95] Eldon to Peel, 30 July 1825, BL (Peel papers), Add. MS 40315 f. 200.
[96] Hansard, *Parliamentary debates, new (2^{nd}) series*, IX:1322.
[97] *Ibid.*, XIII:1085.

Q. 108: Is not the Chancellor much occupied in hearing appeals?
Q. 114: Is not the Chancellor very much occupied during the session of Parliament in hearing causes in the House of Lords?
Q. 117: Is the Chancellor much occupied now in hearing cases in bankruptcy?

All of which must be seen as intending to counter the negative image created by Hamilton's observation. When Hamilton observed that lunacy petitions did not generally consume much of the Chancellor's time, he was asked:

Q. 112: Was not the Portsmouth case one of great length?
Q. 113: Did not the case of Sir Gregory Page Turner occupy considerable time?[98]

At which point Hamilton was obliged to yield. Not only commissioners, but certain of the witnesses probably also wished to avoid criticising the Chancellor. The barrister George Heald, for example, was unwilling to commit himself when asked about Chancery arrears:

Q. 160: Has there been a considerable delay in the Lord Chancellor's court? – *Many matters have been heard before the Lord Chancellor, upon which he has not given judgment for a considerable time.*
Q. 161: Do you attribute the not giving of judgment to the great engagements of the Lord Chancellor in the House of Lords and elsewhere; or to what other cause? – *I do not attribute it to any cause specifically. The Chancellor's engagements, alluded to by the question, must have their effect.*

On being questioned further as to whether delay between hearing and deciding a case was injurious, Heald observed that it depended, 'as it appears to me, upon the question, whether the Chancellor can or cannot satisfactorily make up his mind sooner. It is obvious that, if judgment is unnecessarily delayed, the suitors are injured.'[99] Such studied reticence may have resulted simply from self-interest – a sense that it was unwise to attack the most powerful legal officer in the land. It is more likely, however, that witnesses were made uncomfortable by the prospect of attacking the individual behind the office. More than one witness acknowledged Eldon's great kindness, patience, and good nature, often expressed during a long professional acquaintance. In such cir-

---

[98] *Parliamentary papers* (1826) XV:95 (Appendix A).
[99] *Ibid.*, 361 (emphasis added).

cumstances, it was difficult to make what might appear to be cold-blooded observations about this or that failing.

At the start of the agitation for Chancery reform Eldon does not seem to have been much affected. At least, no substantial evidence of his views survives. He did complain to Perceval in the spring of 1812 that the Chancellor, rather than the increased business of Chancery, had become the subject of inquiry, while in the autumn he told his brother that ministers took 'not the slightest notice' of his request for professional support in the Commons.[100] These points were to be repeated more frequently in the 1820s. The fact that they were not a more common feature of Eldon's earlier correspondence probably indicates that he did not consider them especially pressing concerns. When the accusations against him began to bite, his thoughts turned naturally to them. Even then, he sometimes affected not to care what was said about him in Parliament. In a letter to his daughter in the spring of 1825 he described himself as 'easy and callous', and he urged Liverpool and Peel to believe that, as a personal attack, the consequences of the annual assault upon him were trivial.[101] He was even able, occasionally, to joke about his troubles. In the spring of 1824 he mentioned to his old friend, Sir Matthew White Ridley, the proposed legislation to prevent bull-baiting and bear-baiting, adding: 'Will no kind man introduce a measure to prevent Chancellor-baiting?'[102] He made light of Hume's assertion that the Chancellor was the curse of the country, in a letter to his grandson. Having come upon the Bishop of London, recently designated a firebrand by Hume, 'I told him that *the curse of the country* was so very cold that I hoped he would allow him to keep himself warm by sitting next to *the firebrand*; and so we laughed, and amused ourselves with this fellow's impertinence.'[103]

It would be wrong, however, to conclude from these remarks that Eldon did not mind the severe and often bitter criticisms levelled at him. On the contrary, he resented them tremendously. He acknowledged that some of the criticisms were valid. 'I am as much aware as any other person can be, of my defects as a judge,

---

[100] Eldon to Perceval, undated [April–May 1812], Twiss, *The public and private life*, II:201; Eldon to Scott, 9 October 1812, *ibid.*, 228.
[101] Eldon to Lady Frances Bankes, 3 June 1825, *ibid.*, 556.
[102] Eldon to Sir Matthew White Ridley, undated [*c.* March 1824], *ibid.*, 504.
[103] Eldon to Viscount Encombe, 8 May 1826, *ibid.*, 568 (emphasis in original).

and I am so often angry at myself that I ought not to be surprised to find that others are not pleased with me.'[104] While admitting that some degree of neglect might be attributed to him over the course of his professional career, however, he did not believe that his 'lazy moments' detracted significantly from 'a long industrious life'.[105] Nor did he feel that his achievements suffered when compared to his predecessors. To his brother-in-law, Matthew Surtees, he protested: 'I have done more business in the execution of my public duty than any Chancellor ever did; yea, three times as much as any Chancellor ever did.'[106] He felt, therefore, that the extent of the attacks upon him were unjust. He viewed them as inspired largely by political animosity, and led by men with professional grievances against him. Opposition, he asserted, was striving to force him out of office by repeatedly placing before the House evidence of what seemed to be his professional incompetence – evidence which most members were not qualified to assess. He summarised the inevitable consequences in a letter to Peel:

[D]id it require great exertion of mind to be satisfied that the first Law Officer of the Crown could possibly be maintained in the respect that was due to him for the sake of the public if attorneys, solicitors &c, perhaps those whom, in due execution of his duty, he had had to reproach, were day by day, laying complaints before Taylor's committee for the dishonor of the Chancellor, and if, in almost every year since that committee was defunct, all the officers and dissatisfied suitors of the court, in which the Chancellor presides, have been employed in getting together the material in obedience to the order of the Commons founded on the motion of some discontented lawyer, who had obtained a seat in Parliament, which materials were to be used to his disgrace[?] How can the court go on with the magistrate so disgraced at the head of it in the opinion of all the officers, of his court, who should have no feeling towards him but that of unqualified respect?[107]

Reflections such as these, he admitted, made him miserable, and his misery was compounded by the belief that his political colleagues were failing to defend him. His letters to Peel reveal a touching gratitude to the only senior politician on whom he felt he could rely in these matters. In the same letter he wrote: 'experi-

[104] Eldon to Peel, 24 June 1826, BL (Peel papers), Add. MS 40315 f. 257.
[105] Eldon to Bankes, 25 February 1824, Twiss, *The public and private life*, II:488.
[106] Eldon to Matthew Surtees, 28 February 1824, *ibid.*, 490. See also Eldon to Peel, undated [*c*. 10 September 1826] BL (Peel papers), Add. MS 40315 f. 270.
[107] Eldon to Peel, 10 September 1826, BL (Peel papers), Add. MS 40315 f. 270.

ence has taught me that you will do what is right, and I most gratefully acknowledge the protection your kindness has hitherto thrown around me.'[108] He did not respond passively to the attacks, however. During a debate on judicial salaries he warned his critics that they would not achieve their ends by seeking to discredit him.

Perhaps it was thought that this mode of calumnious misrepresentation was the way to get him out of office: they were mistaken who thought so; he would not yield to such aspersions, nor shrink from asserting what he owed to himself.[109]

Moreover, he provided both Peel and Canning with performance figures, information on Chancery practice, and details of controversial cases, in order to strengthen their efforts on his behalf in the Commons.[110] On evenings when hostile motions were being debated in the Commons, Eldon is said to have waited in his private rooms in the House of Lords, receiving reports of the speeches. 'Walking rapidly through the room, he could not command the ardent expression of his indignation, and at last he would sink into a chair overcome by his feelings.'[111] Once his frustration demanded a more immediate expression. Goaded by a newspaper report of a Commons debate, which incorrectly attributed some offensive remarks to Abercromby, Eldon described the MP's remarks as 'utter falsehood' in Chancery on the following day. A motion censuring him for a breach of privilege was defeated by a vote of 151 to 102, and Eldon swiftly recovered his self-control.[112] In a penitent letter to Peel he professed himself willing to offer a public apology to Abercromby, noting: 'In my situation I ought not to have any difficulty in setting myself right in matters of this sort.'[113]

In the end, Eldon resigned and Chancery reform remained undone. Brougham, who would follow Lord Lyndhurst to the Woolsack in 1830, would take up the challenge that he had repeatedly cast before Eldon. Despite his efforts, however, Chancery practice and the duties of the Chancellor would remain a

---

[108] *Ibid.*

[109] Hansard, *Parliamentary debates, new (2^{nd}) series*, XIII:1378–9.

[110] See, e.g., Eldon to Peel, 23 March 1824, BL (Peel papers), Add. MS 40315 f. 137; Eldon to Canning, undated [*c.* early May 1826], LDA (Harewood papers), HAR GC/75.

[111] *Legal Observer* 1(13) (1831), 195.    [112] Colchester, *Diary*, III:313–314.

[113] Eldon to Peel, 1 March 1824, BL (Peel papers), Add. MS 40315 f. 125.

subject for debate and inquiry for much of the century. In retrospect, Eldon can be seen as one of many Chancellors who allowed the old institution to survive. If he was not oblivious to its inadequacies then at least he was unwilling to remove them. The unique length of his tenure in office, however, makes his indifference to reform more blameworthy. It could legitimately be argued that the day-to-day work of the Lord Chancellor was too onerous for him to undertake a major reform. Certainly this was true for a Chancellor like Eldon so deeply involved in both the political and professional sides of his office. With the partial exception of the Vice-Chancellorship, however, Eldon does not seem to have been willing to contemplate the *principle* of reform, even if undertaken by others. There is no evidence that he raised the issue with Addington, Peel, Perceval, or Liverpool as worthy of discussion. He failed to consider the consequences for government or for the legal system of current or likely levels of strain on the one person upon whom so much depended. Eldon's critics would have said that this was because he could not tolerate rivals, and would not allow others to tinker with *his* office or authority.[114] This is a fair comment, but not on account of an overweening ambition on Eldon's part. Rather, the natural ambition of a man in high office was transformed by Eldon's particular combination of reverence for the political and legal establishment and his anxiety about his own conduct. He was hardly likely to advocate sweeping institutional change, being convinced that institutions kept back the flood waters of anarchy. Moreover, perhaps *because* of his many years in office and his unique status as the caretaker of two very difficult kings, he often felt isolated, embattled, and unappreciated in government. Under these circumstances, it was hardly likely that he would suffer, let alone promote, an inquiry into the conduct of his office. Admit that *he* was the Chancellor who could not cope with the burdens borne by his predecessors? Never. His only solution to the problem was to work harder. Significantly, this was the strongest reply that he and his supporters offered, when reform was mentioned, and it failed to address the more important issue. While he had indeed worked hard, that fact did not establish why such a degree of effort should be expected of one man.

[114] See, e.g., Brougham's remarks in Hansard, *Parliamentary debates, new (2nd) series*, XVI:743.

# 17

# FAITHFUL DEFENDER

On the morning of 17 February 1827, Lord Liverpool suffered a severe stroke which left him paralysed on one side. Irrespective of his very survival, his professional life was swiftly recognised as having come to an end. '[A]s an official man, he is no more', Eldon reported to his daughter on the following day.[1] The identity of Liverpool's successor, consequently, occupied the attention of the political world. The King was informed, and while he forbade any unseemly haste in replacing the stricken premier, the *status quo* could not long be maintained.[2] After a period of intense speculation, meetings between ministers, and summonses to Brighton and Windsor, the King sent for the Foreign Secretary, George Canning. Canning was asked to form a government based on the same principles as those of his predecessor. He received his commission on 10 April. Within two days half the Cabinet had resigned, including Eldon, Robert Peel, and the Duke of Wellington. Thus collapsed a ministry that had governed for fifteen years, some of whose members had been in office far longer. For Eldon it was the end of almost thirty-eight years in government, with twenty-five of these spent as Lord Chancellor of England. In keeping with his long career of royal service, he alone of his colleagues tendered his resignation to the King in person.

The reasons for Eldon's resignation were several. First, he was nearly seventy-six years of age, and he had been speaking of retirement for some time. While his critics regularly accused him

---

[1] Eldon to Lady Frances Bankes, 18 February 1827, H. Twiss, *The public and private life of Lord Chancellor Eldon*, 3 vols. (London, 1844), II:583.

[2] The King felt it would be extremely unfortunate for Liverpool to recover his health and learn that his colleagues had been engrossed by the problem of replacing him. W. Hinde, *Canning* (Oxford, 1989), 435.

of having resolved to part with life and office together, it is extremely likely that he would have made good his representations but for the unexpected death of the Vice-Chancellor, Lord Gifford, in the autumn of 1826. On that occasion he had been prevailed upon to remain in office so as not to subject the country to the awkwardness that must result from the appointment of two new equity judges.[3] Nor was this the only instance in which Eldon's personal wish to resign had given way to what he conceived as his public duty. In the autumn of 1822 he had also remained at the behest of the King. This event, coupled with a much longer association, provides a second reason for Eldon's conduct in 1827, namely that he declined to remain in office under Canning. Eldon had mistrusted Canning since they had served together in the Portland government twenty years earlier. Along with other colleagues, Eldon felt Canning lacked principle and was dominated by self-interest. Upon hearing of Liverpool's collapse, Eldon even remarked that he supposed Canning's own poor health would not admit of his succeeding as premier, but 'ambition will attempt anything'.[4] Eldon had previously sought to avoid serving with Canning. During the negotiations to bring Canning back into office in the summer of 1821, Eldon had advised the King to request Lord Sidmouth, the Home Secretary, not to retire and create an immediate opening.[5] On that occasion the efforts to secure Canning had been abandoned, but upon their revival in the late summer of 1822, Eldon had again stood opposed. The suicide of Lord Londonderry had made Canning's inclusion essential to the government, and Wellington had urged the King to approve the offer of the Foreign Office. Acknowledging that 'no arrangement ought to be adopted which should oblige the Lord Chancellor to withdraw from Y[our] M[ajesty]'s Councils,' Wellington had not believed that Eldon *would* insist upon resigning and so prevent this 'arrangement otherwise bene-

---

[3] See, e.g., Eldon to George IV, undated [*c.* 10 September 1826], A. Aspinall (ed.), *The letters of George IV, king of England*, 3 vols. (Cambridge, 1938), III:156–7; Eldon to Robert Peel, undated [*c.* 10 September 1826], BL (Peel papers), Add. MS 40315 f. 270. Peel opined to Eldon on 10 September: 'I doubt whether under present circumstances you could overcome the King's reluctance to lose your invaluable services – I really doubt whether he would accept the Seals from your hands.' Twiss, *The public and private life*, II:576.

[4] Eldon to Bankes, 18 February 1827, *ibid.*, 538.

[5] A. Aspinall (ed.), *The diary of Henry Hobhouse (1820–1827)* (London, 1947), 61.

ficial to your service'.[6] That Eldon had taken some persuading, however, is evident from the King's letter of 9 September. Here he spoke of his 'unbounded affection and regard for your conduct towards me', and affirmed that 'I *look forward with confidence* (what I will venture to use as a *command*) namely, that you will not surrender up the Seals'.[7] The King remembered Eldon's previous conduct when he came to reflect upon the mass resignations in the spring of 1827. 'The Chancellor, to do him justice, has acted right and consistently for he staid in before against the grain at my entreaty and I can say nothing to him.'[8]

Eldon's objection to Canning was not, however, primarily a personal one. It was, rather, that Canning was a strong and committed proponent of removing the political disabilities from Roman Catholics. The 'Catholic question', which had long existed in the Liverpool Cabinet as a subject upon which ministers were allowed to differ, had finally broken it apart. The 'Protestant' members did not believe that the government would maintain the *status quo* when led by a man who not only supported Catholic political equality but had himself introduced a Bill to that effect in 1822.[9] In defending his resignation to the House of Lords, Eldon maintained that his 'whole life had been devoted to the defence of that constitution, and to the resistance of the concessions now proposed to be given to the Catholics', and in consistency to that belief he could not remain in the Canning government.[10]

---

[6] Wellington to George IV, 7 September 1822, H. Arbuthnot, *The journal of Mrs Arbuthnot (1820–1832)* ed. F. Bamford and the Duke of Wellington, 2 vols. (London, 1950), I:188.

[7] George IV to Eldon, 9 September 1822, Aspinall, *George IV*, II:538 (emphasis in original).

[8] Marquis of Londonderry to Wellington, 13 April 1827, SUL (Wellington papers), WP1/887/18. The King sent Eldon a 'token' of his regard, consisting of a silver tankard with an accession medal, and bearing the inscription: 'The gift of his Majesty King George IV. To his highly-valued and excellent friend John earl of Eldon, Lord High Chancellor of England etc. upon his retiring from his official duties in 1827.' Twiss, *The public and private life*, II:603.

[9] See Eldon to George Canning, 12 April 1827, A. Aspinall, *The formation of Canning's ministry, February to August, 1827* (London, 1937) 65.

[10] T. Hansard (ed.), *The parliamentary debates from the year 1803 ... new (2nd) series*, 25 vols. (London, 1820–30), XVII:454. Peel defended the Chancellor's conduct in the Commons. Answering charges that the 'Protestant' ministers had resigned in concert in order to thwart Canning, Peel remarked: 'As to the lord Chancellor's decision, what could be more natural? It must, indeed, have been expected. I have heard the sarcasms uttered in this House, that if Catholic emancipation were made a point in the formation of an administration, the lord

As it existed in 1827, the British constitution envisaged a union between Church and State, whereby participation in local and national government was restricted to communicant members of the Established Protestant Church. This restriction had its origins in legislation enacted in the reign of Charles II. The Corporation Act of 1661 required all members of municipal corporations to swear the oaths of allegiance and supremacy, and to have taken the sacrament according to the Anglican rite within the previous year.[11] The Test Act of 1673 provided that all persons holding offices of trust and emolument under the Crown must likewise swear the oaths of allegiance and supremacy, and take Anglican communion within a prescribed period following their appointment. Moreover, they were obliged to declare their rejection of the doctrine of transubstantiation.[12] A second Test Act in 1678 extended the oaths, the sacramental test, and the declaration to all sitting peers and members of the House of Commons.[13] These statutes barred both Roman Catholics and members of some Protestant sects. The restrictions did not weigh equally upon both groups, however, as indemnity Acts had regularly been passed during the eighteenth century for the benefit of non-Anglican Protestants who had not adhered to the sacramental provisions.

Legislation had been enacted in 1793 and 1794 to remove certain restrictions from Irish and Scottish Roman Catholics upon their swearing the oath of allegiance. William Pitt had planned to couple Catholic emancipation generally with the Act of Union in 1801. Upon George III's refusal to countenance such a step, Pitt had resigned. Thereafter, however, a small and diverse group of English and Irish politicians committed to emancipation had kept it a regular feature of the parliamentary year. Eight specific Bills had been introduced between 1807 and 1825. In the Lords the Earl of Donoughmore had moved for the appointment of committees to consider the state of the law with regard to Roman Catholics in 1810, 1811, 1812, 1816, 1817, and 1819. Slowly the principle of reform had won approval in the Commons. In 1819 a

---

Chancellor would accede to it rather than give up his place; and I do think it a little hard, now that he adheres to his principles, and refuses office rather than concede them, that he should be charged with joining in a cabal.' *Ibid.*, col. 447.

[11] 13 Car. II st. 2 c. 1. The Anglican rite was laid down in the Act of Uniformity, 14 Car. II c. 4.

[12] 25 Car. II c. 2.     [13] 30 Car. II st. 2 c. 1.

Bill had been defeated by two votes. Two years later a similar measure had been approved by a margin of seventeen votes, and in 1825 this had increased to twenty-one. At the same time, the agitation out-of-doors, and particularly in Ireland, had been gaining momentum. The activities of the Catholic Association had brought the mass of Irish Catholic popular opinion into the struggle for reform, and had added a political element to the existing economic, social, and religious instability of that country.

The House of Lords, however, had stood firm against concessions, and Eldon had been one of the leading exponents of that view. He had opposed every Bill and motion in favour of Catholic political emancipation.[14] He had differed with Pitt on the subject in 1801, and three years later he had confided in Lord Melville: 'I cannot foresee the circumstances, in which ... I could ever be brought to give my consent to what I understand he [Pitt] thought of proposing.'[15] Eldon's objection to Catholic emancipation was complex. He consistently argued that the existing constitution 'had been introduced into this country upon protestant principles', namely, the requirement of a Protestant sovereign, government, and national church.[16] It had not been founded on the belief that all men were equally entitled to exercise political power, but upon the belief that political power must be limited to those most likely to exercise it for the good of the state.

Toleration and power were very different. The British constitution gave toleration to every class of its subjects; but the very nature of the thing rendered it necessary that that power should be vested where it was most calculated to produce and to preserve the good of the whole. If persons who by refusing to qualify themselves for offices of power and trust, had still complete toleration allowed them, they had the benefits of the British constitution.[17]

The aim of the revolution of 1689 had been to concentrate political power in Protestant hands. The government of James II had demonstrated that Roman Catholicism inspired civil and religious

---

[14] He had not opposed the legislation in 1817 to extend the privilege of holding military commissions, already granted to Roman Catholics in Irish regiments, to Catholics in English regiments.

[15] Eldon to Henry Dundas, Viscount Melville, undated [*c.* 1804], University of Michigan, William Clements Library (Melville papers).

[16] T. Hansard (ed.), *The parliamentary debates from the year 1803 ... (1ˢᵗ series)*, 41 vols. (London, 1812–20), IV:783.

[17] *Ibid.*, IX:780.

tyranny, and therefore specific legal bars to future participation by Roman Catholics had been erected. Not only was the sovereign's religion mandated, but he was forbidden Catholic advisers, 'lest they should taint his mind with their pernicious counsels', and protected from Catholic privy councillors and members of Parliament, 'lest they should sow dissension in the great assemblies of the nation'. Nor were Catholics to serve as judges, in order that the 'fair and impartial administration of justice' should be ensured.[18]

Given his veneration for the nation's legal and political inheritance, it is not surprising that Eldon wished to pass on the confessional element of the constitution 'in as much purity as we had received it from our ancestors'.[19] Moreover, he felt that his status as Lord Chancellor imposed upon him a particular obligation to preserve the constitutional *status quo*.[20] He also particularly believed that an established religion was fundamental to the well-being of the nation, because it would imbue the practice of government with a moral component. 'The object of such an establishment was not to make the Church political, but to make the state religious.'[21] He viewed with grave suspicion, consequently, the American separation of the institutions of Church and State.[22] The religion most advantageous to the State was, he believed, the Protestant religion, and specifically that species of Protestantism practised in the Anglican Church. He considered the doctrines of Anglicanism 'the purest in the world', and consequently entitled 'to be favoured by the state in a higher degree than any other religion'.[23] He did profess himself willing to accept a national Church encompassing doctrines 'less pure' rather than lose the moral benefits of a religious establishment.[24] He believed that such an expansion must not embrace Roman Catholicism, however, because the tenets of the Catholic faith remained dangerous. They still required obedience in all matters to the papacy, whose programmes and policies had consistently resulted in political absolutism and religious repression. Nor did the

[18] *Ibid.*, XL:408.     [19] *Ibid.*, IV:783.
[20] *Ibid.*, XXIII:835; see also Hansard, *Parliamentary debates, new (2nd) series*, XI:839.
[21] *Ibid.*, V:291.     [22] *Ibid.*, XIII:764.
[23] Hansard, *Parliamentary debates (1st series)*, XXIII:834.
[24] Hansard, *Parliamentary debates, new (2nd) series*, V:291.

various securities offered by reformers to protect the State convince Eldon that emancipation could be undertaken safely. *A distinction was drawn between the Crown's temporal authority and the Pope's spiritual authority.* Eldon doubted the reality of such a distinction, and therefore doubted that any conscientious Catholic could swear to support and obey the Crown and British government. *The government was to assume responsibility for the payment of Catholic priests.* Eldon described as 'preposterous' the hope that payment would secure loyalty. 'Would the boon of fear produce the return of affection?' he demanded of the equally intransigent Lord Redesdale.[25] *The Crown was to exercise a veto over the appointments to Roman Catholic bishoprics.* Eldon denied that *bona fide* Catholics would submit to such an invasion of the rights of their Church. Moreover, if they did accept such terms, 'they would be worse subjects than if they refused them, inasmuch as dishonest men could not be good subjects'.[26] *Certain offices of state were to be reserved exclusively to Protestant appointees.* Eldon scorned the notion that the presence of a Protestant Lord Chancellor would prevent any invidious policies being pursued. 'Those who know the state in which a Protestant chancellor would stand in a cabinet of Roman Catholic ministers, will readily believe that, if he had either sense or honesty, he neither would remain there, nor be permitted to remain there an hour.'[27]

For all these reasons, therefore, Eldon looked upon a Canning government with grave foreboding. In the event, however, this government did not survive long enough to launch a threat to the constitution. Worn out by the pressure of simultaneously occupying the posts of Prime Minister, Chancellor of the Exchequer, and Leader of the House, as well as retaining a guiding influence in the Foreign Office, Canning succumbed to an inflammation of the lungs and liver on 8 August 1827. Ministers carried on for a few months under Lord Goderich, but he found himself unequal to the task and resigned on 8 January 1828. On 9 January the King sent for Wellington. He formed a ministry that combined Canningites with seceders from the Liverpool government and the odd Whig. Eldon was not among them. The question of his return to

[25] Eldon to Lord Redesdale, undated [*c.* summer 1803], GRO (Mitford papers), D2002/3/1/23.

[26] Hansard, *Parliamentary debates (1st series)*, XVII:406.

[27] Hansard, *Parliamentary debates, new (2nd) series*, V:307.

office had been raised in mid-August, when observers realised that a Wellington–Peel ministry was both inevitable and imminent. Following informal discussions, Eldon had indicated his wish to support 'cordially' from the back-benches, but 'never be in the way'.[28] The Chancellor, Lord Lyndhurst, however, had mentioned Eldon for the largely honorific post of Lord President of the Council. Sir Henry Hardinge had noted that the former Chancellor's 'experience and support would place Lord Lyndhurst at his ease in the Lords'.[29] When Wellington came to discuss the Cabinet with Eldon in early January, however, Eldon surrendered any claim to the Lord Chancellorship, and no other office was mentioned.[30] Whether Eldon wanted to become Lord President is uncertain. That he wanted to be asked is not. He felt deeply hurt that he had largely been ignored by his former colleagues during the process of Cabinet-formation, and that neither his views nor his participation had been sought. He took some consolation from the fact that, once his unhappiness was known, Peel, Wellington, and Lords Bathurst and Melville each took steps to placate him. Peel hastened to 'express to you my deep regret that any circumstances should have occurred carrying with them the remotest appearance of a separation from you in public life'.[31] Wellington accounted for Eldon's exclusion by referring to the former Chancellor's own political views. As Eldon explained their second meeting to his daughter:

He stated in substance that he found it impracticable to make any such Administration as he was sure I would be satisfied with, and, therefore, he thought he should only be giving me unnecessary trouble in coming near me, or to that effect.[32]

Eldon seems to have come round to this explanation; at least their relationship was sufficiently cordial that the Duke asked him in February to help resolve a conflict between the Attorney General,

---

[28] Sir Henry Harding to Charles Arbuthnot, 14 August 1827, C. Arbuthnot, *The correspondence of Charles Arbuthnot*, ed. Arthur Aspinall (London, 1941), 90.

[29] Hardinge to Wellington, 11 August 1827, SUL (Wellington papers), WP1/985/15.

[30] Eldon to Bankes, 30 January 1828, Twiss, *The public and private life*, III:29.

[31] Peel to Eldon, 26 January 1828, BL (Peel papers), Add. MS 40315 f. 316.

[32] Eldon to Bankes, 30 January 1828, Twiss, *The public and private life*, III:31. See also Lord Colchester, C. Abbot, *The diary and correspondence of Charles Abbot, Lord Colchester*, 3 vols. (London, 1861), III:544; Eldon to ?Duke of Cumberland, undated, Free Library of Philadelphia (Carson papers).

Sir James Scarlett, and his predecessor, Sir Charles Wetherell, over a point of professional etiquette.[33] As late as March, however, Eldon was still feeling sore at what he regarded as his colleagues' neglect:

[T]hey might have given me an opportunity of offering my services to the country . . . It is not because office was not offered me that I complain – it is because those with whom I had so long acted and served did not, candidly and unreservedly, explain themselves and their difficulties to me.[34]

Soon, however, Eldon's attention would be taken up with what he considered a far more important matter. In the House of Commons a campaign was being launched to remove the political disabilities from non-Anglican Protestants.

Eldon viewed removal of the political disabilities from Dissenting Protestants as he did similar moves in favour of Roman Catholics: both were unwarranted constitutional innovations. He had consistently opposed the series of Bills in 1823, 1824, 1825, and 1827 regarding the marriages of Unitarians and of non-Anglican Protestants. Under Lord Hardwicke's Act, a valid marriage could only be performed by an Anglican minister, in accordance with the Anglican rite. Moreover, publication of the intended marriage was required in the parish church of each party, and registration of the completed ceremony was demanded of the officiating clergyman.[35] Eldon had opposed each proposal to alter some or all of these requirements. He had disliked the broadly based measures because of the prospective danger posed by 'all those religious opinions which might hereafter be promulgated'.[36] Narrowly drawn provisions had failed to win his approval because he considered the Unitarians 'a sect the most adverse in their opinions to the doctrines of the established Church', and he

---

[33] The dispute concerned whether Wetherell or Scarlett was entitled to undertake certain litigation in the King's interest soon to come to trial in the King's Bench. For the correspondence on the subject, see Wellington to George IV, 7 February 1828, SUL (Wellington papers), WP1/920/18; Wellington to Eldon, 8 February 1828, *ibid.*, WP1/920/24; Eldon to Wellington, 8 February 1828, *ibid.*, WP1/917/4; Eldon to Wellington, 17 February, 1828, *ibid.*, WP1/917/27.

[34] Eldon to Mrs Henry Ridley, 3 March 1828, Twiss, *The public and private life*, III:35.

[35] 26 Geo. II c. 33 (1753).

[36] Hansard, *Parliamentary debates, new (2nd) series*, IX:969.

resented any attempt 'to make the Church of England the servant and handmaid' to such persons.[37]

When faced with a more fundamental reform in favour of dissenting Protestants, therefore, Eldon was adamant in his opposition. On 26 February 1828, Lord John Russell introduced a Bill in the Commons to abolish the sacramental requirements for office-holding and corporate membership, as these affected non-Anglican Protestants. He argued that religious liberty protected the Established Church more effectively than did exclusion, and that the Bill did away with the reprehensible practice whereby the most sacred rite of the Christian faith was used for a purely secular purpose. Peel opposed the Bill as unnecessary, given the practical freedom enjoyed by non-Anglican Protestants, and as potentially disruptive of the good relations among Protestants generally. Upon rejection of this view, however, the government tactics changed.[38] Together with a number of leading Churchmen, Peel formulated a declaration whereby a future office-holder or member of a municipal corporation would undertake not to use his position to damage the interests of the Established Church. This declaration was approved at the committee stage, and the amended measure was sent up to the Lords.

Eldon opposed the very principle of the Bill. He felt the union between Church and State as presently provided for was an important guarantor of the nation's political security, and that it had long been regarded as such. He acknowledged that both Charles II and William III had hoped that the religious establishment could be expanded to comprehend a broad spectrum of Protestantism, but pointed out that Parliament had not given effect to those sentiments. Instead, the passage of annual indemnity Acts to disable but not abrogate the existing legislation constituted 'acknowledgements and recognitions on the part of the legislature, that the Corporation and Test-acts ought not to be dispensed with'.[39] During the years of republican fever, Eldon recalled, the Established Church had come under threat. Perhaps the only positive consequence of those troubled times had been

---

[37] Eldon to Wellington, undated [*c*. March 1828], SUL (Wellington papers), WP1/980/10; Hansard, *Parliamentary debates, new (2nd) series*, XI:79.

[38] For Peel's strategy, see G. I. T. Machin, 'Resistance to repeal of the Test and Corporation Acts, 1828', *Historical Journal* 22(1) 1979, 115–39.

[39] Hansard, *Parliamentary debates, new (2nd) series*, XVIII:1501.

Parliament's realisation of the danger posed by such a threat, and its consequent resolution to defeat it.[40] While acknowledging that the present Parliament was not bound by the decisions of their predecessors, he warned against altering laws 'which were understood to be the fundamental laws of the country'.[41]

Despite such sentiments, Eldon did not speak against the Bill until well into the debate on the second reading, on 17 April. He was convinced that the Bill would pass, and therefore hoped only to limit its application.[42] He objected to the replacement of the sacramental test by the proposed declaration to avoid injuring the Anglican Church as being an insufficient barrier against non-Protestants. This was partly because members of municipal corporations were not also obliged to swear the oath against transubstantiation, and partly because a member might truthfully say that he did not act to the detriment of the Established Church by virtue of his position, but 'by virtue of his conscience'.[43] Moreover, the declaration was not required of all persons holding offices of trust and emolument under the Crown, but was imposed at the sovereign's discretion.[44] Eldon concentrated his attention on the first objection, and offered a series of amendments. He moved variously that the declaration should be made an oath, that the swearer should make a profession of faith more closely tied to Protestantism, and that greater protections should be afforded to Anglican practice, institutions, and discipline. Each amendment, like those proposed by the other 'ultra' Tories, was defeated by a substantial margin.[45] The Bill itself

---

[40] *Ibid.*, cols. 1501–2.     [41] *Ibid.*, col. 1575.

[42] See, e.g., Eldon to Bankes, 12 April 1828, Twiss, *The public and private life*, III:38.

[43] Hansard, *Parliamentary debates, new (2nd) series*, XIX:160.

[44] *Ibid.*, XVIII:1498–9.

[45] The government argued, *inter alia*, that Roman Catholics considered the oath of supremacy 'highly obligatory', and this would bar them from membership in municipal corporations. The existence of the oath against transubstantiation would continue to bar them from Parliament and Crown appointments. See, e.g., Hansard, *Parliamentary debates, new (2nd) series*, XIX:118. A point not raised by Eldon in debate, but which features in his correspondence with Peel, was that some Roman Catholic noblemen, named in Commissions of the Peace out of courtesy, had actually acquired an acting capacity when the various oaths were not administered. See, e.g., BL (Peel papers), Add. MS 40315 ff. 156, 158, 160. An amendment proposed by the Bishop of Llandaff, that the declaration be made 'on the true faith of a Christian' was accepted. Hansard, *Parliamentary debates, new (2nd) series*, XVIII:1609.

received its third reading on 2 May, and passed the royal assent the following week.[46]

Eldon's conduct during the debates was called 'mischievous' and 'inconsistent', and his recommendations were described as 'failing to serve any good purpose and likely to cause irritation'.[47] Remarks such as these, especially when coming from the government and the leadership of the Church, were particularly galling and provoked Eldon to displays of temper. Referring to Lyndhurst, Eldon 'trusted that the learned lord having now yielded his opinions of the subject to those of others, would not attack the motives of those who still maintained that opposition, which it was his original intention to offer to this Bill'.[48] He likewise suggested that the bishop of Chester 'attend to his own consistency rather than to be talking about that of others'.[49] Eldon was particularly disappointed by what he considered the 'dormant apathy' of the bishops. He scorned the view, espoused by several, that they were merely bowing to public opinion. On the contrary, Eldon felt that they had been swayed by petitions which they 'could not possibly have *read*', and whose size merely reflected a determined campaign by a few individuals.[50] Again recalling his own experiences with revolutionary groups in the 1790s, he remarked that, to produce a successful petitioning campaign, 'nothing more was necessary than to establish a committee in London, and to open communications with the various Dissenters throughout the country'.[51]

A further and critical basis of Eldon's position was his belief that any liberties won would be extended to Roman Catholics. Even before debate on the Bill began, Eldon was predicting gloomily to his daughter:

[46] A protest against the Bill was signed by the following peers: Eldon, Kenyon, Brownlow, Walsingham, Boston, Beauchamp, Malmesbury, Newcastle, Falmouth, Howe, Mansfield, and Stanhope. *Ibid.*, XVIII:1609–10.

[47] See, e.g., the remarks of Lyndhurst at *ibid.*, XIX:115, 118.

[48] *Ibid.*, col. 129.     [49] *Ibid.*, XVIII:1159.

[50] Eldon to Bankes, undated [late April or early May 1828], Twiss, *The public and private life*, III:47.

[51] Hansard, *Parliamentary debates, new (2^{nd}) series*, XIX:130. Eldon further described the petitions as 'founded upon revolutionary principles'. *Ibid.* Recalling the earlier attempts of Drs Price and Priestly to lay 'a train of gunpowder under the Church', Eldon noted bitterly to his daughter: 'The young men and lads in the House of commons are too young to remember these things.' Twiss, *The public and private life*, III:37.

sooner or later – perhaps in this very year – almost certainly in the next – the concessions to the Dissenters must be followed by the like concessions to the Roman Catholics. That seems unavoidable, though, at present, the policy is to conceal this additional purpose.[52]

At first it seemed that even this prediction might prove overly optimistic. The Bill received the Royal Assent on 9 May, one day after Sir Francis Burdett had successfully moved that the laws on Catholic political disabilities be taken into consideration. On 9 June Lord Lansdowne introduced a comparable motion in the upper House, but peers rejected it by 181 votes to 137. The result of the Clare by-election in July, however, seemed likely to break this stalemate. Daniel O'Connell, the leader of the Catholic Association and one of the most vocal advocates of Catholic emancipation, defeated the government candidate by a large majority. O'Connell's success increased dramatically the pressure on the government to remove the disabilities that prevented him from taking his seat. As the political temperature in Ireland hovered around the boiling point, the leadership of both the British and Irish executives became convinced that emancipation was inevitable.

The King, however, was still opposed to emancipation, and in the months that followed he had to be convinced, and remain convinced, to think otherwise. His references to Eldon in late 1828 and early 1829 reflect his anxious mood. Eldon was again brooding about his exclusion from office.[53] To his brother-in-law he acknowledged that the strength of his views on the Catholic question was unlikely to endear him to ministers, but it was just this attribute that the King identified when he proposed a Cabinet reshuffle to Wellington in October 1828.[54] The King repeated his suggestion in January 1829, when he asked Wellington to 'turn your thoughts for a moment to Lord Eldon upon the present occasion'.[55] On 4 March

---

[52] Eldon to Bankes, undated [*c*. April 1828], Twiss, *The public and private life*, III:37–8.

[53] See, e.g., Eldon to Stowell, undated [*c*. September 1828], *ibid.*, 56.

[54] See Wellington to George IV, 14 October 1828, SUL (Wellington papers), WP1/963/36. The correspondence is also referred to in H. Arbuthnot, *Journal*, II:213. The King was possibly influenced by his brother, the Duke of Cumberland, who described Eldon as 'that great pillar of Protestantism' and suggested to the King's friend Sir William Knighton that the former Chancellor be brought back as Lord President. Aspinall, *George IV*, III:438.

[55] George IV to Wellington, 30 January 1829, SUL (Wellington papers), WP1/992/12. The King also echoed Cumberland's view that Eldon would provide

the King informed Wellington that he reluctantly agreed to emancipation, and on 10 March Peel presented the Catholic Relief Bill to the Commons. As late as 28 March, however, the King was still hoping to avoid committing himself irrevocably, and he accordingly sent for Eldon. Only after a four-hour session, during which Eldon assured him that no credible alternative ministry could save him, did the King finally submit.[56]

Eldon was convinced that the Bill would succeed, but he was determined to do battle against it nevertheless. He had proclaimed his views in dramatic form on 5 February, during the debate on the King's Speech. Asserting that no man had an abstract right to political office save where his participation would serve the public interest, he maintained that 'if ever a Roman Catholic was permitted to form part of the legislature of this country, or to hold any of the great executive offices of the government, from that moment the sun of Great Britain would set'.[57] Nor would he hesitate to resist such a cataclysm, whatever the consequences. 'His country might send him to his grave covered with all the obloquy that could blast the reputation of a public man; but to this declaration he would adhere.'[58] In the days that followed, Eldon became the focus for anti-Catholic petitions up and down the country. He would later claim to have presented over 800 petitions between early February and early April, some containing many thousands of signatures. For the most part, the exchanges between peers on the topic of petitions were good-natured. When attention turned to the Catholic Relief Bill itself, however, the tone of the debate altered for the worse. This was particularly true of the speeches of Eldon, Lyndhurst, and Wellington. The reasons for this descent into angry, and sometimes aggressive, condemnation were several. First, Eldon was generally recognised as the leader of the anti-Catholic camp, and it would have been

---

invaluable assistance to the Lord Chancellor. On both occasions Wellington declined to bring Eldon into the government. In a letter of 14 October he remarked that Eldon was not one to put himself forward in Parliament to support a measure agreed upon by the majority of the Cabinet (when the majority presumably did not include himself). *Ibid.*, WP1/963/36. In January he told the King that Eldon was unlikely to accept office, and his refusal would reflect badly on the King's government. *Ibid.*, WP1/1000/1.

[56] Eldon's meeting with the King is referred to in H. Arbuthnot, *Journal*, II:261, 262; and P. W. Wilson (ed.), *The Greville diary*, 2 vols. (London, 1827), I:203.

[57] Hansard, *Parliamentary debates, new (2nd) series*, XX:17.    [58] *Ibid.*, col. 21.

surprising if his remarks had not particularly drawn his opponents' fire. Lord Darnley described Eldon as the only person in the House 'remarkable for learning and talent' who opposed the Catholic claims.[59] Secondly, debates on the Bill took place in an atmosphere of great political tension. Not only were many persons convinced that success was essential to prevent violent rebellion in Ireland, but peers found their very discussions the focus of intense scrutiny. Hansard's reporter thus described the scene on 2 April, the first day of debate on the second reading:

> The interest excited by the expected discussion of the Roman Catholic Relief Bill collected a great crowd round the doors of their lordships' House at an early hour. Although there was a great number of constables, they could with difficulty keep order. The House was much crowded when the reporters were admitted; the space below the Throne was completely filled, as well as the space allotted to the public.[60]

It was an atmosphere conducive to hasty tempers and sharp words. Fundamentally, however, the exchanges between Eldon and ministers were undertaken on both sides at a very personal level. While Eldon continued to state his old reasons for opposing Catholic reform, he also raised the issue of ministerial inconsistency, both in introducing the measure at all, and in 'surprising' the country by the manner of introduction. At least some of Eldon's complaints in this respect were understandable. Ministers *had* profoundly changed their position on the Catholic question and Eldon, knowing himself to be in an embattled minority, undoubtedly felt betrayed by his former colleagues. His claim that Ministers had not been candid about their intention to bring forward a Bill at this time is less credible. Certainly Eldon had known of or strongly suspected such an undertaking as early as the previous July.[61] Eldon's language toward Wellington and Peel in this respect was not particularly violent. He said that he imputed no improper motive to either man, but rather the conscientious performance of what they considered their duty.[62] Nevertheless,

---

[59] *Ibid.*, col. 673.     [60] *Ibid.*, XXI:33.

[61] Eldon's point seems to have been that the consequence of a leaked correspondence between Wellington and the Revd Patrick Curtis, Catholic Archbishop of Armagh, had been to suggest that a measure was forthcoming before such an intention had been expressed in Parliament. This had led to public surprise or, perhaps more accurately, confusion.

[62] See, e.g., Hansard, *Parliamentary debates, new (2nd) series*, XXI:349–50, 392, 625–6.

the frequency of such remarks, as well as Eldon's more critical private observations, rendered Wellington exasperated by 'the personal attacks upon me and upon my right hon. friend in the other House of parliament'.[63] He also felt that Eldon's criticism of the government's policy against the Catholic Association was unseemly. Government action was based upon legislation enacted in 1825, and Eldon and Wellington bickered over what precisely had been Eldon's attitude toward that legislation *then*, and whether that should disqualify Eldon from complaining about it *now*.[64]

The character of Eldon's exchanges with Lyndhurst was even more antagonistic. Aware of the vulnerability of the government, and himself in particular, to a charge of trimming, the Chancellor went on the offensive in a more general attempt to undercut Eldon's authority to criticise. Eldon, he claimed, was one of those men who had stood by for twenty-five years, observing the 'distracted state of Ireland' and allowing it to degenerate still further. The very acceptance of the Catholic question as an open subject in the Cabinet had been 'blameably inconsistent with his duty' and on Eldon's part might have been done 'merely for the purpose of upholding the preponderance of a party'.[65] Moreover, the present champion of the Protestant constitution had not been

---

[63] *Ibid.*, col. 688. Mrs Arbuthnot thus described the meeting in late March between the King and Eldon: 'Lord Eldon, it seems, talked pretty freely of the Duke & said he was not a man of *reason* but of determination, that argument was thrown away upon him, that, when he made up his mind to insist upon having a thing, he *w[oul]d have it*'. H. Arbuthnot, *Journal*, II:262. Lord Colchester recorded a conversation with Eldon in February, in which Eldon complained of the 'mysterious concealment' by Wellington, and stated that Peel ought to have resigned from the government and should lose his Oxford seat. Colchester, *Diary*, III:596–7.

[64] Wellington maintained that Eldon had approved of the legislation when it was discussed in Cabinet in 1825, and had not stated a preference for common law prosecutions. Eldon argued that he had said that legislation would prove ineffectual unless coupled with common law prosecutions, but that he had supported such prosecutions. The lack of prosecutions, he supposed must have reflected the decision of the Irish law officers, or a failed communication with ministers. Hansard, *Parliamentary debates, new (2$^{nd}$) series*, XX:1041, 1044–5. Eldon contributed sparsely to the debates on the Bill in 1825, professing non-involvement in its drafting and ignorance of its effect upon Irish common law. *Ibid.*, XII:867, 944–5. His correspondence with Peel, however, reveals a consistent advocacy of prosecution, certainly between 1824 and 1827. See, e.g., BL (Peel papers), Add. MS 40315 ff. 180, 274, 297.

[65] *Ibid.*, XXI:193, 194.

quite such a stalwart defender of Protestant interests in the past. On the contrary, he had stood by while previous legislation had been enacted to remove Catholic disabilities.[66] Of Eldon's present stance Lyndhurst was curtly dismissive – his arguments were 'too extravagantly absurd to be entertained by any reasonable man'.[67] He further accused Eldon of urging objections in an 'insinuating and mystifying manner', and warned the House against being 'overborne by the talent, the learning, and the name of the noble and learned lord'.[68] While severely bruised by these remarks, Eldon was no stranger to sarcasm or to bitter invective. He observed in reply that, if it was the duty of a minister to resign when he differed with his colleagues, then Lyndhurst was fortunate in his ability to change his mind so readily as to avoid that difficulty.[69] Eldon's explanation of his previous tolerance of legislation to remove Catholic civil or military, as opposed to political, disabilities included a dig at Lyndhurst's ignorance of Scottish law.[70] He responded furiously, however, to Lyndhurst's warning to the House:

I have been … twenty-seven years in this House, and I have, on all public questions spoken the opinions I entertained, perhaps in stronger language sometimes than was warranted; but I have now to tell the noble and learned lord on the woolsack, that I have never borne down the House, and I will not now be borne down by him nor twenty such.[71]

When not trading insults with ministers, Eldon attempted to restate and expand upon his objections to the proposed legislation.

---

[66] *Ibid., col.* 202; see also col. 203.      [67] *Ibid.*, col. 510.

[68] *Ibid.*, cols. 209, 510.      [69] *Ibid.*, col. 352.

[70] *Ibid.*, col. 354. The Act of 33 George III c. 21, enacted by the Irish Parliament in 1793, allowed Irish Roman Catholics to vote, bear arms, take degrees at Trinity College, become members of corporations, and hold commissions in Irish regiments below the rank of general. The Act of 57 George III c. 92 extended this last provision to Catholics in English regiments. The Act of 31 George III c. 32 protected Roman Catholic religious practices and prevented the forfeiture of Catholic land, and was extended to Scotland in the 33 George III c. 44. In 1828 Eldon asserted: 'in no part of these discussions had he ever stated his objections to go further than to resist the giving of political power to the Roman Catholics, by bringing them into parliament, and allowing them to fill the great offices of state.' Hansard, *Parliamentary debates, new (2^{nd}) series*, XXI:355. Speaking in support of the Catholic Bill in 1791, he had expressed the wish that 'toleration, when granted, might be as extensive as possible'. W. Cobbett (ed.), *The parliamentary history of England … to 1803*, 36 vols. (London, 1806–20), XXVIII:1375.

[71] *Ibid.*, col. 512.

Constitutional innovation, he argued, should only be undertaken when the benefits of change clearly outweighed the dangers. The dangers inherent in the government's plans were several. In general, alteration of a venerated system and theory of government weakened public confidence in the state, producing 'doubt, alarm, and discontent among the people'.[72] More specifically, Catholic emancipation threatened the goal of a national English church governed by 'the best and purest system of Christianity possible', as any challenge to the established Church in Ireland would also undermine the Protestant establishment in England.[73] Emancipation would also vindicate and strengthen the Catholic Association. Eldon likened the Catholic Association to the rebellious groups in 1798, for whom the claim of Catholic rights had been a cover for full-scale insurrection, and 'In our own day the cry for civil and religious liberty has ... been mixed up with the folly of universal suffrage, and all the mischief of radical reform'. Finally, he argued that constitutional change in a particular context signalled acceptance of the principle of change generally, and, in approving one change, 'you may pull down and destroy the whole structure of the constitution'.[74]

Despite Eldon's pleas, and the various blocking motions attempted by like-minded colleagues, the Bill sailed through the Lords in ten days, receiving its third reading on 10 April by a margin of 213 votes to 109. His knowledge at the outset that his efforts would not succeed had been confirmed by the heavy defeat of each amendment. Nevertheless, he was bitterly disappointed by the result. He criticised public apathy on such a seminal issue of national well-being, and he blamed the clergy for having failed to rouse the public from its torpor. The government, too, had surrendered both its principles and its responsibility for moral leadership. Finally, the King had proven unable to fill the vacuum created by ministerial weakness. Eldon observed to his daughter, after having attended a royal levee at the end of April: 'He is certainly very wretched about the late business. It is a pity he has not the comfort of being free from blame himself.'[75]

---

[72] *Ibid.*, col. 357.    [73] *Ibid.*, col. 359.    [74] *Ibid.*, col. 361.
[75] Eldon to Bankes, undated [c. late April 1829], Twiss, *The public and private life*, III:88. Precisely what Eldon thought the King should have done is not clear. Eldon stated publicly his unwillingness to discuss what effect the Coronation Oath ought to have on the King. Hansard, *Parliamentary debates, new (2nd)*

The significance of Eldon's conduct and the defeats in 1828 and 1829 for an understanding of the British political climate is a matter of historical debate. J. C. D. Clark has argued that Eldon represented a traditional view of the Church–State relationship that was not an extreme or isolated reaction away from the 'common ground' of English society. Clark has described the gradual erosion of public faith in the old regime, but has disputed the characterisation of the public mood as clearly settled in favour of reform. The ultra-Tory attitude, he suggests, has not been fairly reported because it was defeated and stigmatised by the victors as reactionary.[76] Linda Colley has described Catholics in the 1820s as having resumed their status as bogey in the English consciousness, after being displaced during the war by the French menace. Anti-Catholic fears again provided a sense of identity, particularly among the uneducated, albeit less violently expressed than in the latter part of the eighteenth century.[77] As one, if not *the*, recognised leader of the fight against religious reform, it would be helpful if Eldon could shed some light on the question – what was the state of the Anglican constitution out-of-doors? Unfortunately, neither his conduct nor his correspondence provides an unequivocal answer to this question. He did introduce many petitions hostile to reform, but as both he and his opposite number Lord Holland regularly complained that signatures were falsified and numbers inflated, it is difficult to place much faith in petitions. His private correspondence and public statements do indicate that Eldon believed he was not an isolated figure, but that he did not regard the public as reliable. He seems to have felt that the

*series*, XXI:356. In a private minute to George IV, he offered more detailed advice on a proper response to an objectionable Bill. Parliament might be dissolved, in an attempt to effect the return of a legislature less likely to pass such a measure. If this failed, and a Bill was produced, loyal addresses could be sought, evidencing support for the King. Thereafter, if the King sincerely felt that assent was contrary to his oath, this oath being interpreted as that which first bound William III, he would be justified in withholding assent. Aspinall, *George IV*, III:117–23. In 1795, Scott had opined that the decision whether a particular Bill would destroy the settlement of Church and State must rest with the King, 'being constitutionally advised'. The exercise of judgment, he believed, was a consequence of the nature of the Oath, which prescribed maintenance generally, but did not define the threat. Colchester, *Diary*, III:510.

[76] J. C. D. Clark, *English society 1688–1832* (Cambridge, 1991), 408–9.

[77] L. Colley, *Britons, forging the nation 1707–1837* (London, 1992), 330–1.

public's latent sympathy for the old constitution had atrophied, so that they failed to regard an Anglican establishment as necessary to the maintenance of their political well-being, or no longer saw Dissent or Catholicism as significant threats to the national health. He had recognised these dangerous tendencies in 1824, when he became aware of Roman Catholic noblemen, included in the lists of justices of the peace out of courtesy, who had acquired an acting capacity through the oath of supremacy not being administered. This laxness on the part of persons entrusted to maintain the essential constitutional safeguards, noted Eldon, could signal the end of the old regime. '[I]t seems to be that all is over – for if this can be done with Justices of the Peace ... the whole policy in England of supporting the King's supremacy is gone, or may be gone.'[78] Here was a threat, not of conscious assault, but of ignorance or indifference.

For Eldon, however, the question of popularity, at whatever level, was ultimately less important than that *he* maintain the true course. In the wake of his great defeat in 1829, he took comfort from the fact that he had remained stalwart, that he had not 'ratted'.[79] He had concluded his final speech on the Catholic Relief Bill stating:

I would rather hear that I was not to exist to-morrow morning, than awake to the reflection, that I had consented to an act, which had stamped me as a violator of my solemn oath, a traitor to my church, and a traitor to the constitution.[80]

The possibility of his own isolation, moreover, had never seemed to trouble him, at least as it might have reflected upon the justice of his position. He had consistently professed himself ready to maintain his stance alone, and took some pride in having declined to follow even Pitt, without proof that the nation would be safe in Catholic hands. He had been ready, too, to expose the cynical side of certain elements of the pro-emancipation camp. Those who argued that Catholics posed no realistic threat because none would ever be appointed to an important office of state, offered 'an insult towards them, more

---

[78] Eldon to Peel, undated [August–September 1824], BL (Peel papers), Add. MS 40315 f. 158.
[79] For Eldon's condemnation of 'lordly rats', see Eldon to Revd W. Bond, undated, DorRO (Bond of Tyneham papers), D.1141:1/2.
[80] Hansard, *Parliamentary debates, new (2^{nd}) series*, XXI:640.

intolerable than ineligibility'.[81] He had likewise objected to
coupling Catholic emancipation with measures to disfranchise
the mass of Irish Catholic voters.[82] He declined to support the
Bill to disfranchise the mass of Irish Catholic voters, 'looking at
it as a sort of hush-money, to pass the Catholic Bill'.[83]

This is not to say, however, that this long and fruitless opposition was easy. Almost from the start, Eldon's views had subjected
him to a good deal of parliamentary criticism. He had been
accused of religious bigotry, and with stirring up anti-Catholic
feelings in the country. The allegations of bigotry he had found
hard to bear. He repeatedly protested that he was 'no enemy' to
the Catholics, and opposed the extension of political power solely
because of the consequences for the state.

[H]e could not see that such a charge ought to be made merely because
the lord high chancellor did what all the King's ministers had done;
namely, declare in his individual and ministerial capacity, that he could
not consent to a measure from which he apprehended the greatest danger
to that supremacy of the Crown, which he felt it to be his duty to
maintain.[84]

During his years in office he had been taunted with the division in
the government on the Catholic question. In 1817 Donoughmore
had observed that the Chancellor must find it 'most painful ... to
find himself surrounded by a number of brother privy counsellors
and cabinet ministers, who are in favour of the measure, and who,
he conceives, are aiming blows at the vitals of the constitution'.[85]
Out of office, he had been called to account for what he had or had
not done while in office. During the debates on the second reading
of the Relief Bill he had reflected wistfully that 'it did seem to be
thought a very pleasant thing in parliament to have a dash at the
old chancellor'.[86] Finally, the outcome of the Catholic question
had confirmed his political isolation. It is hard to avoid ascribing
some of his fervour against repeal to personal disappointment and
ill-feeling against the government, and this fervour had, in turn,

[81] *Ibid.*, V:308. Eldon argued that such an outcome would have the more
objectionable consequence of refocusing Catholic discontent against the King.
*Ibid.*
[82] *Ibid.*, XIII:765.    [83] *Ibid.*, XXI:469.    [84] *Ibid.*, XI:840.
[85] Hansard, *Parliamentary debates(1ˢᵗ series)*, XXXVI:604. During the previous
week the Commons had debated Henry Grattan's motion regarding Catholic
disabilities, and both Castlereagh and Canning had spoken in favour.
[86] Hansard, *Parliamentary debates, new (2ⁿᵈ) series*, XXI:354–5.

rendered him even less palatable to them. Not merely the ex-minister whose advice was not sought, he had become a positive irritant. For a man who had spent his adult life at the heart of politics, making the decisions that guided the nation, it was not the way he would have liked to bring his political career to a close. Moreover, if he were proven wrong about the consequences of Catholic emancipation, he would have shown himself no political patriarch, but merely a relic of an old, rejected order. If he were proved right, he could only look forward to grave political turmoil. Neither was an attractive prospect.

# 18

# TWILIGHT OF THE STATE

Eldon remained politically active for another four years; his last recorded speech in the House of Lords occurred in July 1834. By then, however, he was no longer a potent force in the upper House. Ill health restricted his attendance, and when he did participate in debate, his tone was frequently rambling and querulous.[1] He often referred to his approaching demise, undoubtedly made more real to him by the deaths of his wife, brother, and son. While contributing to the struggle for the next seminal political issue, the Reform Act of 1832, he did not lead the opposition forces as he had done in 1829. Nevertheless, the debates on electoral and religious reform in his last years called forth from Eldon a clear expression of his vision of the State. As ever, the perception of danger provoked an answer, and as he perceived the danger of equality, he tried to rekindle support for government based on rank and responsibility.

Fundamental to Eldon's view of the good society was the notion of inequality. He described the English State approvingly as 'like a great and glorious pillar – the people formed its base; then came those of a little higher rank; then still a little higher, until it reached the apex, on which stood the Monarch of the country.'[2] Rank, in its several layers, was based on a combination of wealth, ability, and virtue. Wealth rendered a man's judgment independent; ability enabled him to exercise his judgment logically, and virtue obliged him to apply it on behalf of others. Focusing political power in the hands of individuals so equipped, therefore, ought to be the goal of the State. Equality, by contrast, was

---

[1] See, e.g., Lord Ellenborough's diary of 27 February, 1832, A. Aspinall (ed.), *Three early nineteenth century diaries* (London, 1952), 203.

[2] T. Hansard (ed.), *The parliamentary debates from the year 1803 ... new (2nd) series*, 25 vols. (London, 1820–30), XXIII:499.

undesirable for two reasons. It robbed men of the incentive to improve themselves, and prevented anyone from exercising effective control or leadership. Thus was the State plunged into anarchy, and society restricted to a subsistence level.

The glory of the English constitution, according to Eldon, was the opportunity for great advancement, made possible by the access to, and protection afforded, different species of property. He included in that term not only real and personal wealth, but titles, privileges, and rights of appointment and election. He referred to his own history, as evidence that 'any man of this country, possessing moderate abilities, improved by industry may raise himself to the highest situations in the country'.[3] These 'situations' conferred upon the individual levels of wealth, authority, and fame entirely beyond his original circumstances. Fundamental to Eldon's own rise, moreover, had been the voluntary exercise of property rights by others on his behalf. He had received a good primary education because his father had achieved the status of freeman of the borough of Newcastle, which entitled his sons to attend the local grammar school. Entry into Parliament had been possible because a seat managed by a patron had been conferred on him. Nor was his own case unique. The operation of the constitution had rendered Englishmen generally 'happier than any other people on God's earth' and given England 'a lustre and a glory that did not belong to any other nation in the world'.[4]

The mere amassing of wealth and status did not, of course, ensure political justice or social tranquillity, absent virtuous conduct. All property, according to Eldon, imposed upon the recipient the obligation of its proper application. Religion rendered fulfilment of the obligation more likely. In England, membership of the Anglican Church impressed upon persons of wealth and status the duty to employ their riches in accordance with Christian principles. The first responsibility of the governing class was to undertake policies of general benefit. Peers and MPs 'were the trustees of the people, and bound to act the best for their interests'.[5] If this occasioned suffering, they were obliged to take the appropriate steps to alleviate it. In 1830 Eldon repeatedly

---

[3] T. Hansard (ed.), *Hansard's parliamentary debates, 3rd series*, 356 vols. (London, 1831–91), VIII:214.
[4] *Ibid.*, XII:398.    [5] *Ibid.*, col. 392.

supported parliamentary inquiry into current conditions among the labouring poor, and a failure to do so 'was neither more nor less than a total abandonment of all the duties of Parliament'.[6] Moreover, if an amelioration of conditions proved impossible, justices of the peace should be dispatched to calm and reassure. It was an act of mercy to explain to the people 'the law of the land, and the reasons of the law, and the reasons why it was for their interest, and to the interest of the community at large, that it should remain the law of the land'.[7] Eldon believed that a love of the constitution would inspire great endurance among the poor. When ignorance or malevolence goaded them to violence, however, it was the responsibility of government to take a firm hand. This was particularly true with regard to unrest in Ireland where, presumably, the identification with English sensibilities was less strong. Speaking on conditions in Ireland in 1832 Eldon opined:

> To leave matters of this kind to be settled by the progress of good sense and of calm reflection was, in critical circumstances, rather an unsafe mode of proceeding, for if calm good sense had been absent for so many centuries, it was not very likely to return in time enough to be useful.[8]

He regarded the different electoral reform Bills that reached the House of Lords in 1831 and 1832 as unwarranted assaults upon propertied society. He acknowledged that, if the presently vested rights of election were abused, they ought to be taken away. Forfeiture, however, must result from actual proof, and not the general assumption of abusive practice. He did not believe that persuasive evidence of misconduct existed and, consequently, he lamented the opprobrium cast upon the present franchise regime and those who acted under it.[9] He feared too, for the consequences of electoral reform. No property would be secure if 100 boroughs were swept away 'because we have a notion that those who are connected with them have not executed their trust properly'.[10] The threat to create new peerages to guarantee acceptance of the reform Bill constituted a further assault on property. If the King agreed to circumvent the determined decision of the House of

---

[6] Hansard, *Parliamentary debates, new (2$^{nd}$) series*, XXIII:497.

[7] Hansard, *Parliamentary debates, 3$^{rd}$ series*, I:680.

[8] *Ibid.*, XIII:1226. Repression in Ireland, moreover, would prevent the danger spreading to England. *Ibid.*, X:756.

[9] *Ibid.*, VIII:215.      [10] *Ibid.*, col. 211.

Lords, it would constitute not only 'a departure from the proper exercise of the prerogative, but a most abominable exercise of it'.[11]

Nor did he believe that constitutional change would stop at the single, controlled, expansion of the electorate then advocated. On the contrary, the proposed reform was 'at war' with the principle of the constitution, and would open the floodgates to more profound changes. '[T]he Bill will be found, I fear from my soul, to go the length of introducing in its train if passed, Universal Suffrage, Annual Parliaments, and Vote by Ballot. It will unhinge the whole frame of society as now constituted.'[12] Certainly that was the hope of the lower orders – the persons Eldon identified as constituting the most significant support for the reform Bill.[13] Already their destructive influence could be identified in the conduct of MPs. Rather than making a reasoned and, if necessary, strong rejection of these demands, some MPs were willing to regard themselves pledged to advocate them. Regarding, as he did, a policy of levelling as essentially prejudicial to the interests of society, Eldon found the conduct of these individuals 'a perversion of one of the best principles of the Constitution', namely, that each MP ought to represent the 'whole of the Commons of England'. If a member of Parliament were willing to be called to account by a particular constituency, he ought not to sit in the legislature.[14]

The attacks on property were not limited to property in the hands of private persons. The Irish Church Temporalities Bill of 1833 abolished the vestry-cess, a tax to pay for church repairs, and redistributed the wealth of Protestant livings to promote equality of income. Not only did such a measure expose the Church to the dangerous consequences of levelling, but abolition of the tax practically and symbolically severed the ties between the Established Church and the individual. Because the Establishment served as a 'prop' to the State, 'the State itself would sink' if it were weakened or removed.[15] Eldon demanded: 'if the obligations

---

[11] *Ibid.*, XII:1089. Such conduct was, in Eldon's view, comparable to James II's exercise of the dispensing power. *Ibid.*, col. 395.

[12] *Ibid.*, VIII:220.

[13] See, e.g., *ibid.*, XII:397. Writing after the passage of the Reform Act, Eldon complained of the 'dormant apathy' of those well disposed to the old constitution. Eldon to Richard Burdon-Sanderson, 15 September 1832, NLS (Sanderson papers), MS 6102 f. 120.

[14] Hansard, *Parliamentary debates, 3$^{rd}$ series*, XII:391.     [15] *Ibid.*, XX:115.

of religion were loosened, then every man might be told to think as he pleased on religion, and what, he would ask, could be expected to result from such a licence?'[16] Clearly, the result he foresaw was immorality which, when coupled with a general loosening of the bonds of social, economic, and political rank, would lead to anarchy. As with political upheaval, Eldon feared that misguided policies in Ireland would inevitably spread to England. Objecting to the abolition of Irish tithes in 1832, he had observed: 'It was perfectly absurd to suppose that what would take place in Ireland in this instance would not be sure afterwards to take place in England also.'[17]

Defeat on the issue of electoral reform left Eldon disheartened. At a political dinner at the Duke of Wellington's in 1833 he complained that the new House of Commons 'was neither elected by gentlemen nor composed of gentlemen'.[18] He did not cast aside what he considered his own obligations, however. In 1835 and 1836 he was writing to Wellington, promising to oppose the English and Irish Municipal Corporations Bills, and the further regulation of the Irish Church.[19] His last years afforded him some comfort, moreover, in respect of his personal circumstances. Not only were friendly relations with Wellington restored, but Peel sent a respectful letter upon accepting office in 1835, in which he expressed a 'constant hope that the administration over which I preside, will entitle itself by its acts, to your support and confidence'.[20] Eldon also received important evidence of the respect in which he was held within communities whose opinion he valued. In December 1833 he was subpoenaed to appear in a matter in Chancery. On his entering the court, the Bar rose, and the Solicitor General 'expressed in the name of his brethren the satisfaction they felt at seeing him once more among them'.[21] A similar tribute was paid him by his old university, when he attended the Oxford convocation in the following June in his capacity as High Steward. John Wilson Croker described the 'astounding' applause occasioned by his appearance, 'next, if not

---

[16] *Ibid.*, XIX:924.      [17] *Ibid.*, X:1299.

[18] Aspinall, *Three diaries*, 294.

[19] Eldon to the Duke of Wellington, 25 July 1825, SUL (Wellington papers), WP2/34/122; Eldon to Wellington, ?22 June 1836, *ibid.*, WP2/39/87.

[20] Robert Peel to Eldon, 1 January 1835, BL (Peel papers), Add. MS 40315 f. 327.

[21] P. W. Wilson (ed.), *The Greville diary*, 2 vols. (London, 1927), I:183.

equal' to that given Wellington.[22] Such tributes undoubtedly went some way to assuring Eldon that, albeit latterly in a series of losing causes, he had consistently done his duty.

Throughout his career Eldon maintained that he was guided by what he considered his duty. To what, or to whom, however, did this duty lie? Two of his contemporaries described Eldon's essential allegiance to 'Toryism'. For Henry Brougham this term referred to the particular political creed based on support for the monarchy and the established Church. Having 'imbibed' this dogma during his university days, Eldon had remained absolutely true to it for the rest of his life, whatever the cost in personal effort or integrity.[23] For William Hazlitt, Eldon's Toryism was rather more self-serving. As a man dedicated to his own comfort, he offered unending propitiation to ministerial prejudice and princely whim because he could not bear to cause upset, either to himself or to those with whom he had become allied in public life. 'Common humanity and justice are little better than vague terms to him: he acts upon his immediate feelings and least irksome impulses.'[24]

Hazlitt was right to mention Eldon's conciliating manner as a prominent element of his personality. He was no bully, and did not thrive in situations demanding that force be answered with force. A portrayal that depicts indifference to the substance of the Anglican constitution, however, fails significantly to comprehend Eldon's political character. Brougham wrote more accurately of the 'perfect sincerity' of Eldon's belief that monarchical government, as limited by the Revolution settlement, and political life as shaped by inequalities of rank, power, and access, were eminently suited to English society. The fact that Eldon's skills made unnecessary the advocacy of his views from the back-benches did not render their expression from the Woolsack any less genuine. As the barrister Charles Butler noted in 1824:

[22] L. Jennings (ed.), *The Croker papers*, 3 vols., 2nd edn (London, 1885), II:227, 226. A law scholarship at Oxford had been created in Eldon's honour, founded upon public subscriptions, in 1830. See *Gentleman's Magazine* 163 (1838), 317.

[23] Lord Brougham and Vaux, H. Brougham, *Sketches of statesmen of the time of George III*, 3 vols. (London, 1855), II:56.

[24] W. Hazlitt, *Spirit of the age, or contemporary portraits*, 2 vols. 2nd edn (Paris, n.D.), II:183.

He has almost always supported administration, but has never been subservient to any minister; and, among those, who by the public opinion of the worth and dignity of their individual character, attach the people to the government, and thus assure its stability, his lordship is universally allowed to be eminently conspicuous.[25]

While thus closer to the mark, Brougham's analysis does not go far enough to capture the essential motivation of Eldon's public life and conduct. His duty, clearly, lay with the Crown, the Established Church, and the other legal and political institutions that comprised the constitution. The crucial expression of that duty, moreover, was in personal loyalty. Eldon was loyal to those individuals whom he perceived following the true course. For this reason he repeatedly counselled William Pitt against risking his own political purity by uniting with Charles Fox. Better a ministry completely devoted to Foxite principles than one in which policies were sacrificed in a spirit of accommodation.[26] When Pitt deviated from what Eldon considered a consistent political path, he declined to follow. Pitt's overall integrity, however, imposed a duty of loyalty that lasted beyond his lifetime. Eldon remained a constant attendant at the annual Pitt dinners, and he expressed disapproval at the lack of a similar dedication among his former colleagues. His loyalty to George III and George IV was partly personal and partly institutional. George III inspired both strands of loyalty; both as man and king he too was wholly dedicated to the right course, and his debilitation through illness strengthened, rather than weakened, the bonds of service. While weakness, vacillation, and political inconsistency made George IV a less inspirational figure, the requirement of loyalty to the sovereign helped to bridge the gap.

The political writer James Grant observed of Eldon: 'Though every one else, from the king on the throne down to the humblest subject in the land, had abandoned Toryism, Lord Eldon would have clung to it with all the tenacity and with all the fondness with which he would have clung to life.'[27] Such a fixed loyalty could spring from practical, intellectual, or emotional influences or, as with Eldon, a combination of all three. The effect of French-

---

[25] C. Butler, *Reminiscences of Charles Butler Esq.*, 2 vols. 4th edn (London, 1824), I:136.

[26] Eldon to George Rose, 22 July 1809, BL (Rose papers), Add. MS 42774 f. 251.

[27] J. Grant, *The bench and the bar*, 2 vols. (London, 1837), I:94.

inspired radicalism upon his sensibilities is both clear and highly significant. Having faced the spectre of revolution in the 1790s, he could never escape its toils. Not only did comparisons feature in his subsequent analyses of diverse social and political issues, but the 1790s became, in retrospect, his finest hour – the epitome of pure political service. He could never afterwards conceive of acting inconsistently with the values that had, in his view, saved the nation from ruin. In addition to the fear of change inspired by experience, Eldon's intellect made him hostile to change. His was a mind that delighted in fine discrimination and detailed analysis, but it was not creative in the sense of transcending received structures or modes of thought. His 'metaphysics' demanded a predefined legal, political, or religious universe. Within those confines, his intellect was extremely lively, subtle, and energetic. He was thus happy to consider how existing systems worked, but he could not conceive of dismantling and reconstructing the fundamental systems of the State. Finally, the religious dimension to Eldon's political character imparted an emotional power to his loyalty. He repeatedly told his critics that, having supported the Anglican constitution for the whole of his adult life, he could not do other than to continue. This was not mere intransigence on his part, but a conviction that a system grounded on religious principles could not be altered according to human whim without the risk of dire consequences. He acknowledged that he might be wrong in affording such authority to the English political system, but that he was either completely wrong or completely right, and that tinkering with the *status quo* afforded no safe option. For Eldon, of course, the way was clear; he was convinced that the political world he entered in 1783 was grounded as firmly as possible on a strong foundation. Fifty years later his views had not changed, and he only lamented that others had failed to guard the citadel. In 1830 he complained to his brother-in-law: 'This country is certainly in a worse state than you and I have ever known it – and I see no signs of improvement.'[28] In the face of human failure, therefore, he was obliged to place England's political salvation in the hands of God. At the age of eighty-one he

---

[28]  Eldon to William Surtees, 27 December 1830, W. Surtees, *A sketch of the lives of Lords Stowell and Eldon* (London, 1846), 167.

wrote to his nephew: 'That mighty control can alone now save the men of property, the men of sound religious character, the men of rank, the nobility and the Crown in this disordered country.'[29]

---

[29] Eldon to Burdon-Sanderson, 20 August 1832, NLS (Sanderson papers), MS 6102 f.118.

# BIBLIOGRAPHY

*All books are published in London unless otherwise stated.*

MANUSCRIPTS

*Archifdy Meirion Archives (Gwynedd)*
Caerynwch (Richards) papers

*Bedfordshire and Luton Archives*
Whitbread papers

*Beinecke Rare Book and Manuscript Library, Yale University*
Osborne files

*British Library*

Hardwicke papers
Liverpool papers
Peel papers
Pelham papers
Rose papers
Wellesley papers

*Cambridge University Library*
Perceval papers

*Centre for Kentish Studies*
Camden papers

*William Clements Library, University of Michigan*
Lee papers
Melville papers

*Cumbria Record Office (Carlisle)*
Lonsdale papers

*Devon Record Office*
Sidmouth papers

*Dorset Record Office*
Bond of East Holme papers
Bond of Tyneham papers

*East Sussex Record Office*
Sheffield papers

*Encombe, Dorset*
Scott papers

*Free Library of Philadelphia*
Carson Collection

*Gloucester Record Office*
Mitford papers

*Inner Temple Library*
Mitford Collection of Legal Manuscripts

*House of Lords Record Office*
Peerage reports

*Lambeth Palace Library*
Manners-Sutton papers

*Leeds District Archives*
Harewood papers

*Middle Temple Library*
Scott papers

*National Library of Scotland*

Sanderson papers

*Newcastle-upon-Tyne City Library*

Scott papers

*Northumberland Record Office*

Barington papers

*Public Record Office*

Board of Trade: law officer correspondence
Chatham papers
Colonial Office: law officer correspondence
Customs Office: law officer correspondence
Durham Chancery records
Exchequer posting book
Home Office: law officer correspondence
Privy Council: law officer correspondence
Treasury: law officer correspondence
Treasury solicitor papers

*Rare Book, Manuscript and Special Collections Library, Duke University*

Liverpool papers
Wilberforce papers

*Scottish Record Office*

Melville papers

*Southampton University Library*

Wellington papers

*Winchester College*

Gabell papers

LEGAL AND PARLIAMENTARY DOCUMENTS

Anon., *The extraordinary black book: an exposition of the united church of England & Ireland etc.*, 1831
Anon., *Trial of Queen Caroline*, 2 vols., 1821

*Brown's Chancery Reports*

Cobbett, W. (ed.), *The parliamentary history of England ... to 1803*, 36 vols., 1806–20

Debrett, J. (ed.), *The parliamentary register ... 1780–1799*, 54 vols., 1782–99

*English Reports*

Hansard, T. (ed.), *Parliamentary debates from the year 1803 ... (1ˢᵗ series)*, 41 vols., 1812–20

   *Parliamentary debates from the year 1803 ... new (2ⁿᵈ) series*, 25 vols., 1820–30

   *Hansard's parliamentary debates 3ʳᵈ series*, 356 vols., 1831–91

Helmholz, R. H. (ed.), *Select cases on defamation: to 1600*, 1985

Howell, T. J. (ed.), *A complete collection of state trials and proceedings for high treason and other crimes and misdemeanours*, 33 vols., 1816–26

Lambert, S. (ed.), *House of Commons sessional papers of the eighteenth century*, 147 vols. Wilmington, DE, 1975–6

*The Old Bailey proceedings*, 38 micro film reels Brighton, 1984

*Parliamentary papers* (1810–11) II, III

*Parliamentary papers* (1825) XIX

*Parliamentary papers* (1826) XV

*Parliamentary papers* (1829) XVIII

Parry, C. (ed.), *Law officers' opinions to the Foreign Office*, 97 vols., 1970–73

PAMPHLETS

Holcroft, T., *A narrative of facts relating to a prosecution for high treason*, 1795

Wakefield, G., *A letter to Sir John Scott*, n.p., 1798

NEWSPAPERS AND PERIODICALS

*Cumberland Pacquet*
*Edinburgh Review*
*General Evening Post*
*Gentleman's Magazine*
*Legal Observer*
*London Chronicle*
*Morning Chronicle*
*Public Advertiser*
*St James' Chronicle*
*The Times*
*Tribune*
*Whitehall Evening Post*
*World*

BIOGRAPHIES, MEMOIRS, CORRESPONDENCE, AND DIARIES

Arbuthnot, C., *The correspondence of Charles Arbuthnot*, ed. A. Aspinall, 1941

Arbuthnot, H., *The journal of Mrs Arbuthnot (1820–1832)*, ed. F. Bamford and the Duke of Wellington, 2 vols., 1950

Arnold, R., *The unhappy countess*, 1957

Aspinall, A., *The formation of Canning's ministry, February to August 1827*, 1937

(ed.), *The letters of George IV, king of England, 1812–1830*, 3 vols. Cambridge, 1938

*The correspondence of George Prince of Wales (1770–1812)*, 8 vols., 1967–71

*The diary of Henry Hobhouse (1820–1827)*, 1947

*The later correspondence of George III*, 5 vols., Cambridge, 1962

*Three early nineteenth century diaries*, 1952

Bennet, W. H., *Select biographical sketches from the note-books of a law reporter*, 1867

Bourne, K. and Taylor, W. B. (eds.), *The Horner papers*, Edinburgh, 1994

Brady, F., *James Boswell, the later years, 1769–1795*, 1984

Lord Brougham and Vaux, H. Brougham, *Sketches of statesmen of the time of George III*, 3 vols., 1855

Duke of Buckingham and Chandos, R. Grenville, *Memoirs of the court and cabinets of George III*, 4 vols., 1853–55

Butler, C., *Reminiscences of Charles Butler, Esq.*, 2 vols., 4th edn, 1824

Lord Colchester, C. Abbot, *The diary and correspondence of Charles Abbot, Lord Colchester*, 3 vols., 1861

Derry, J., *Charles James Fox*, 1972

Dinwiddy, J. R. and Rosen, F. (general eds.), *The collected works of Jeremy Bentham*, 10 vols., 1981, and Oxford, 1984, 1988, 1989; vol. V: *Correspondence 1794–1797*, ed. A.T. Milne; vol. VI: *Correspondence 1798–1804*, ed. J. R. Dinwiddy; vol. VIII: *Correspondence 1809–1816*, ed. S. Conway; Vol. IX, *Correspondence 1817–1820*, ed. S. Conway

Ehrman, J., *The younger Pitt*; vol. I, *The years of acclaim, 1969*; vol. III, *The consuming struggle*, 1996

Lord Eldon, J. Scott, *Lord Eldon's anecdote book*, ed. A. L. J. Lincoln and R. L. McEwen, 1960

Farington, J., *The Farington diary*, ed. James Greig, 8 vols., 1924

Foss, E, *Judges of England*, 9 vols., 1864

Grant, J., *The bench and the bar*, 2 vols., 1837

Harcourt, L. V. (ed.), *The diaries and correspondence of the Rt Hon. George Rose*, 2 vols., 1860

Hazlitt, W., *The spirit of the age, or contemporary portraits*, 2 vols., 2nd edn, Paris, n.d.

Hibbert, C., *George IV*, 1976

Hinde, W., *Canning*, Oxford, 1989

Historical Manuscript Commission, *14th Report Appendix, Pt IV (the manuscripts of Lord Kenyon)*, 1894

    *Report on the manuscripts of Earl Bathurst*, 1923

    *Report on the Laing manuscripts Vol. I*, 1914

    *Report on the Laing manuscripts Vol. II*, 1925

    *Report of the manuscripts of J. B. Fortescue, Esq., Vol. VIII*, 1912

    *Report of the manuscripts of J. B. Fortescue, Esq., Vol. IX*, 1915

    *Report of the manuscripts of J. B. Fortescue, Esq., Vol. X*, 1927

Hobhouse, C., *Fox*, 1934

Lord Holland, H. R. V. Fox, *Memoirs of the Whig party during my time*, ed. H. E. Fox, Lord Holland, 2 vols., 1852–4

    *Further memoirs of the Whig party 1807–1821*, ed. Lord Stavordale, 1905

Earl of Ilchester (ed.), *The journal of Lady Elizabeth Holland 1791–1811*, 2 vols., 1908

Jeaffreson, J., *A book about lawyers*, 2 vols., New York, 1867

'John Scott, Earl of Eldon', *Oxford University Record* (1951–2), 16–25

Jupp, P., *Lord Grenville, 1759–1834*, Oxford, 1985

Laprade, W. T. (ed.), *Parliamentary papers of John Robinson, 1774–1784*, 1922

Lustig, I. S. and Pottle, F. A. (eds.), *Boswell, the English experiment 1785–1789*, 1986

Maxwell, Sir H., (ed.), *The Creevey papers*, 1923

Medd, P., *Romilly*, 1968

Peel, G. (ed.), *The private letters of Sir Robert Peel*, 1920

Phipps, E., *Memoirs of the political and literary life of Robert Plumer Ward*, 2 vols., 1850

Romilly, Sir S., *Memoirs of Sir Samuel Romilly*, 3 vols., 1840

Russell, Lord J. (ed.), *Memorials and correspondence of Charles James Fox*, 4 vols., 1853

Scarlett, P. C., *A memoir of the right honourable James, first Lord Abinger*, 1877

Earl Stanhope, *The life of William Pitt*, 3 vols., 1879

Stapleton, E. J. (ed.), *Some official correspondence of George Canning*, 2 vols., 1887

Surtees, W. E., *A sketch of the lives of Lords Stowell and Eldon*, 1846

Twiss, H., *The public and private life of Lord Chancellor Eldon*, 3 vols., 1844

Walpole, S., *The life of the Rt Hon. Spencer Perceval*, 2 vols., 1874

Wilberforce, R. and Wilberforce, S. (eds.), *The life of Samuel Wilberforce*, 5 vols., 1838

Williams, J., *Satires and biography*, 1795

Wilson, P. W. (ed.), *The Greville diary*, 2 vols., 1927

Wraxall, N., *Historical and posthumous memoirs 1772–1784*, ed. H. B. Wheatley, 5 vols., 1884

    *Historical memoirs of my own time*, ed. R. Askham, 1904

Wynne, E., *Strictures on the lives and characters of the most eminent lawyers of the present day*, Dublin, 1790

SECONDARY SOURCES

Abel, R. A. *The legal profession in England and Wales*, Oxford, 1988

Aspinall, A., *Politics and the press*, 1949

Baker, J. H., *An introduction to English legal history*, 3$^{rd}$ edn, 1990

Beedell, A. V., 'John Reeves's prosecution for a seditious libel, 1795–6: a study in political cynicism', *Historical Journal* 36(4) (1993), 799–824

Bellot, H., 'The origin of the Attorney-General', *Law Quarterly Review* 25 (1909), 400–11

Blackstone, Sir W., *Commentaries on the law of England*, 4 vols., 1st edn facsimile, Chicago, 1979

Boylan, H. (ed.), *A dictionary of Irish biography*, 2nd edn, Dublin, 1988

Chambers, Sir R. and Johnson, Sir S., *A course of lectures on the English law delivered at the university of Oxford 1767–1775*, ed. T. M. Curley, 2 vols., Oxford, 1986

Christie, I. R., *Wars and revolutions: Britain 1760–1815*, 1982

Clark, J. C. D., *English society 1688–1832*, Cambridge, 1986

Coke, Sir E., *The third part of the institutes of the laws of England*, 1797

Colley, L., *Britons, forging the nation 1707–1837*, 1992

Cone, C. B., *The English jacobins*, New York, 1968

Cookson, J. E., *Lord Liverpool's administration*, Edinburgh, 1975

Cornish, W. R. and Clark, G., *Law and society in England 1750–1950*, 1989

Davies, C. C., *Warren Hastings and Oudh*, Oxford, 1939

Derry, J., *The regency crisis and the Whigs*, Cambridge, 1963

Duman, D., *The English and colonial bars in the nineteenth century*, 1983

*The judicial bench in England 1727–1785: the reshaping of a professional elite*, 1982

'Ecclesiastical revenues', *Quarterly Review* 39 (1823), 524–560

Edwards, J. L. J., *The law officers of the crown*, 1964

Elliott, M., *Partners in revolution: the United Irishmen and France*, New Haven, 1982

Emsley, C., 'An aspect of Pitt's *terror*: prosecutions for sedition during the 1790s', *Social History* 6(2) (1981), 155–84

*British society and the French wars, 1793–1815*, 1979

'The Home Office and its sources of information and investigation 1791–1801', *English Historical Review* 94 (1979), 532–61

'Repression, *terror* and the rule of law in England during the decade of the French revolution', *English Historical Review* 100 (1985), 801–25

Foster, Sir M., *A report of some of the proceedings of the commission of oyer and terminer and gaol delivery for the trial of the rebels in the year 1746 in the county of Surrey, and in other crown cases to which are added discourses upon a few branches of the crown law*, 1762

Fulford, R., *The trial of Queen Caroline*, 1967

Goodwin, A., *The friends of liberty: the English democratic movement in the age of the French revolution*, 1979

Green, T. A., *Verdict according to conscience*, Chicago, 1985

Hale, Sir M., *Historia placitorum coronae: the history of the pleas of the crown*, ed. G. Wilson, 2 vols., 1778

Hamburger, P., 'The development of the law of seditious libel and the control of the press', *Stanford Law Review* 37 (1985), 661–765

Hayes, R., *Biographical dictionary of Irishmen in France*, Dublin, 1949

Holdsworth, W. S., *A history of English law*, 17 vols., 1903–72

Hunt, J. W., *Reaction and reform 1815–1841*, 1972

Kitson Clark, G., *The making of Victorian England*, New York, 1982

Knox, T. R., ' "Bowes and Liberty": the Newcastle by-election of 1777', *Durham University Journal* 77(2) (1985), 149–64

Lobban, M., 'From seditious libel to unlawful assembly: Peterloo and the changing face of political crime c. 1770–1820', *Oxford Journal of Legal Studies* 10 (1990), 307–52

Machin, G. I. T., 'Resistance to repeal of the Test and Corporation Acts, 1828', *Historical Journal* 22(1) 1979, 115–39

Manchester, A. L., *A modern legal history of England and Wales 1750–1950*, 1990

May, Sir T. E., *Erskine May's treatise upon the law, privileges, proceedings, and usage of Parliament*, ed. Sir C. Gordon, 20th edn, 1983

Melikan, R. A., 'Mr Attorney General and the politicians', *Historical Journal* 40(1) (1997), 41–69

Mitchell, L. G., *Charles James Fox and the disintegration of the Whig party, 1782–1794*, Oxford, 1971

Namier, Sir L., *The structure of politics at the accession of George III*, 2nd edn, 1957

Namier, Sir L. and Brooke, J., *The history of Parliament: the House of Commons 1754–1790*, 4 vols., 1964

Odgers, W. B. and Ritson, R., *Odgers on libel and slander*, 6th edn, 1929

Perkin, H., *The origins of modern English society 1780–1880*, Toronto, 1981

Philips, C. H., *The East India Company, 1784–1834* (reprint), Manchester, 1961

Phillips, J., 'Parliament and southern India, 1781–3: the secret committee of inquiry and the prosecution of Sir Thomas Rumbold', *Parliamentary History* 7(1) (1988), 81–98

Porritt, E., *The unreformed House of Commons*, 2 vols., Cambridge, 1909

Porter, R., *English society in the eighteenth century*, 1982

Prochaska, F. K., 'English state trials in the 1790s: a case study', *Journal of British Studies* 13(1) (1973), 63–82

Radzinowicz, L., *History of English criminal law and its administration from 1750*, 5 vols., 1948–86

Rickword, E. (ed.), *Radical squibs and loyal ripostes*, Bath, 1971

Robinson, O. F. *et al.*, *European legal history*, 2$^{nd}$ edn, 1994

Simeon, J., *A treatise on the law of elections in all its branches*, 1789

Stephen, J. F., *A history of the criminal law of England*, 3 vols., 1883

Stevens, R., *Law and politics, the House of Lords as a judicial body, 1800–1976*, 1979

Stoljar, S. J., *A history of contract at common law*, Canberra, 1975

Sykes, N., *Church and state in the eighteenth century*, Cambridge, 1934

Thorne, R. G. (ed.), *The history of Parliament: the House of Commons 1790–1820*, 5 vols., 1986

Watson, J. S., *The reign of George III, 1760–1815*, Oxford, 1960

Wells, R. A. E., *Insurrection: the British experience 1795–1803*, Gloucester, 1983

# INDEX

Abercromby, Hon. James, 1st Baron
  Dunfermline (1776–1858), 303,
  314, 324
Abinger, Lord, see Scarlett
Act of Union (1801), 161, 262, 329
Addington, Henry, 1st Viscount
  Sidmouth (1757–1844), 118, 216,
  241, 261, 264 n. 57
  Prime Minister, 168, 171, 176, 178,
  189
Alvanley, Lord, see Arden
Anglican Church, see Established
  Church
Arden, Sir Richard Pepper, 1st Baron
  Alvanley (1745–1804), 21, 27, 30,
  71
Attorney and Solicitor General, 38–40,
  199–200

Bentham, Jeremy (1748–1832), 42–3,
  313
Blackstone, Sir William, 91
Brougham, Henry, 1st Baron Brougham
  and Vaux (1778–1868), 203–4,
  353
  Chancery reform, 303–4, 305, 309,
  316 n. 76, 324
  Queen Caroline's trial, 275, 277–8,
  283–9, 292 n. 75
Burdett, Sir Francis (1770–1844), 159,
  260 n. 45, 304, 338
Burke, Edmund (1729–97), 63 n. 10,
  68, 71–2, 73, 74, 83

Cabinet crisis (1809), 221–5
Camden, Lord, see Pratt
Canning, George (1770–1827), 247,
  281, 332, 346 n. 85, 326, 327–8
  Chancery reform, 302, 306, 318–19,
  320

politics (1807), 213, 215, 216, 217,
  228
politics (1809), 221–2, 225
Caroline, Princess of Wales
  (1786–1821) 184, 185, 203,
  276–9
  Bill of Pains and Penalties against,
  280–1, 283–91, 292–3
  investigation of (1806), 213–4
  relationship with Eldon, 173,
  213–14, 227, 231, 281–2, 293–4
Castlereagh, Lord, see Stewart
Catholic Association, 330, 338, 341,
  343
Catholic emancipation, 161, 175, 245,
  328–32, 337–8
Catholic Relief Act (1829), 339–43
Cavendish-Bentinck, William Henry,
  3rd Duke of Portland (1738–1809),
  25–6, 57–8, 119, 221–2
Chancery, 296–7, 298–9, 299–300,
  301–4, 304–6
Chancery commission (1824), 295,
  303–4, 309, 310–11, 314, 320–2
Chancery Reform Bill (1826), 305–6
Charlotte Augusta, Princess
  (1796–1817), 184–6, 231, 277
Charlotte Sophia, Queen (1744–1818),
  67–8, 240–1, 243
Clark, J. C. D., 344
Coke, Sir Edward, 104, 105
Colley, Linda, 344
Constitution, 65–6, 138, 262–3, 268,
  292, 348–50, 353
  see also Established Church
Copley, Sir John Singleton, 1st Baron
  Lyndhurst (1772–1863) 201, 209,
  333, 341–2
  Chancery reform, 305, 306
  Queen Caroline's trial, 283, 286

Crossfield, Robert, prosecution of (1796), 120, 121–3
Cuthell, John, prosecution of (1799), 132–3

Denman, Thomas, 1st Baron (1779–1854), 203–4, 283, 301, 307–8
Dundas, Henry, 1st Viscount Melville (1742–1811), 35, 55, 101, 119

East India Company, 23, 33–4, 69
East India Declaratory Act (1788), 33–5
Eaton, Daniel Isaac, prosecution of (1793), 87, 90–1, 94–5, 96
Ecclesiastical Courts Act (1787), 29–30
Eldon, Lord, *see* Scott
Encombe, Lord, *see* Scott
Ernest Augustus, Duke of Cumberland (1771–1851), 195–6, 214, 235, 242, 248, 338 n. 54
Erskine, Sir Thomas, 1st Baron Erskine (1750–1823), 15, 213, 282, 290–1
    MP, 74, 78, 80, 85
    trial advocate, 76 n. 69, 92, 108, 110, 112–13, 117 n. 87, 121, 135
Established Church, 328–32, 334–6, 339, 343–5, 351–2, 355
*ex officio* informations, 90, 92, 136, 252, 259
Eyre, Sir James (1734–99), 106–7, 109, 111

Foster, Sir Michael, 88, 89, 103–4, 105
Fox, Charles James (1749–1806) 32, 70, 74, 85, 178, 180, 212
    Libel Act debates, 78–80
    Regency debates (1788–1789), 62, 64, 66, 68
    *see also* Fox's India Bill; Westminster election scrutiny
Fox, Henry Richard Vassal Holland, 3rd Baron Holland (1773–1840), 213, 217, 248, 344
Fox's India Bill (1783), 23–5
Fox's Libel Act (1792), 75, 77–81, 87, 90, 91, 94
Francis, Philip (1740–1818), 31–2, 35, 68, 70, 71
Frederick, Duke of York and Albany (1763–1827), 231, 248

Frost, John, prosecution of (1793), 87–90, 96–7

*Gentleman's Magazine*, 30, 36, 114–5
George III (1738–1820), 25, 115, 159, 221, 278, 329
    assessment of Eldon, 21, 173, 314
    illness (1788), 62, 64
    illness (1801), 168–72, 236–7
    illness (1804), 177–84, 186–8, 236–8, 241
    illness (1810–11), 143, 231–4, 242, 243, 244
    relationship with Prince of Wales, 182–6
George IV (1762–1830), 62, 169, 198, 203–4, 231, 326
    marriage, 173, 185, 213, 276–9
    politics (1812), 242, 244–6
    relationship with Eldon, 187–8, 207, 234–5, 246–7, 249, 327–8, 338–9, 354
    relationship with George III, 182–6
Gifford, Sir Robert, 1st Baron (1779–1826), 200–1, 327
    Chancery reform, 300, 301, 309
    Queen Caroline's trial, 283, 288
Grenville, Thomas (1755–1846), 222–3, 232, 235, 242–3
Grenville, William Windham, 1st Baron Grenville (1759–1834), 178, 218–20, 226, 233
    political negotiations, 222–4, 245, 247, 248
    *see also* 'Ministry of All the Talents'
Grey, Charles, 2nd Viscount Howick and 2nd Earl Grey (1764–1845), 216–17, 236–40, 245, 247, 248

Habeas Corpus Act, suspensions—
    (1794) 101–2
    (1795) 113–14
    (1798) 131, 132
    (1800) 161–2, 176
    (1817) 261
Hale, Sir Matthew, 64–5, 104, 105
Hardy, Thomas, prosecution of (1794), 103 n. 22, 106–9, 113, 119, 290–1
Hastings, Warren (1732–1818), 31, 68–75
Hawkesbury, Lord, *see* Jenkinson
Hazlitt, William (1778–1830), 353

Hobhouse, Henry (1776–1854), 204, 206
Holland, Lord, *see* Fox
Holt, Daniel, prosecution of (1793), 87, 92, 93, 96
House of Lords jurisdiction 295–6
  complaints about, 297, 298–9, 300, 301–3
Howick, Lord, *see* Grey
Hume, Joseph (1777–1855), 304, 305, 322
Hunt, Henry (1773–1835), 263

Impey, Sir Elijah (1732–1809), 31–3
Irish Act (1793), 216, 329

Jekyll, Sir Joseph (1754–1837), 198, 206
Jenkinson, Robert Banks, 1st Baron Hawkesbury, 2nd Earl of Liverpool (1770–1828), 201–2, 216, 233, 241, 247, 255, 270 n. 78, 326
  politics (1809), 222, 224, 228
  Queen Caroline's trial, 279, 291, 293

Kenyon, Lloyd, 1st Baron (1732–1802) 4, 27, 29, 166
  judge in sedition trials, 89–90, 91, 94
King, Peter, 7th Lord, King, Baron of Ockham (1776–1833), 236, 238

Lambert, John, prosecution of (1793), 87, 92–5, 97
Lansdowne, Lord, *see* Petty-Fitzmaurice
Law, Sir Edward, 1st Baron Ellenborough (1750–1818), 200, 206, 213, 255
Leach, Sir John (1760–1834), 204, 276–7, 309, 312, 313
legal opinions—
  conventions regarding, 45–8, 49–51
  corpus produced by Scott, 43–5
  re Canada Act, 53–6
  re colonial judiciaries, 56–60
Liverpool, Lord, *see* Jenkinson
*London Chronicle*, 24–5, 30
London Corresponding Society, 83, 99, 100–1, 128, 260 n. 45
  prosecutions of Hardy and Tooke, 106, 107–11
Londonderry, Lord, *see* Stewart

Lord Chancellor—
  history of office, 167
  judicial authority, 295–7
  patronage, 190–2, 211
  *see also* Speaker of the House of Lords
Loughborough, Lord, *see* Wedderburn
Lushington, Stephen (1782–1873), 304, 320
Lyndhurst, Lord, *see* Copley

Macdonald, Sir Archibald (1736–1814), 21, 47, 48, 52, 72, 84
Melville, Lord, *see* Dundas
Milan commission, 277, 290
'Ministry of All the Talents', 212–17, 220–1
Mitford, Sir John, 1st Baron Redesdale (1748–1830), 41, 110, 117 n. 87, 154, 161
  Chancery reform, 298, 309
  legal opinions, 47, 48–59 *passim*, 125–7, 130, 137 nn. 74–5
Moira, Lord, *see* Rawdon-Hastings
*Morning Chronicle*, 29, 237
  *see also* John Lambert

Namier, Sir Lewis, 20
Newspapers Regulation Act (1798), 127–8

O'Coigly, James, prosecution of (1798), 128–9, 135, 161, 162
O'Connell, Daniel (1775–1847), 338
Orders in Council (1807), 220–1
Oxford University election (1809), 15, 226–8

Paine, Thomas (1737–1809), 83, 84, 90, 92, 107
Pains and Penalties, Bill of, 279–81
patronage—
  ecclesiastical, 190, 192, 211
  Eldon's employment of, 192–3, 196–9, 207–10
  legal, 190–1, 205, 211
Peace of Amiens (1802), 174–5
Peel, Sir Robert (1788–1850), 190 n. 1, 326, 327 n. 3, 335, 339
  Chancery reform, 295, 303–4, 306, 310, 319
  friendship with Eldon, 295, 319, 328 n. 10, 333, 352

Perceval, Spencer (1762–1812), 213, 228, 242, 246, 247
King's illness (1810), 231, 232
politics (1809), 222, 224, 225
Perkin, Harold, 210
Peterloo Massacre (1819), 263–7
Petty-Fitzmaurice, Henry, 3rd Marquess of Lansdowne (1780–1863), 233, 338
Pitt, William (1759–1806), 28, 69, 83, 101, 119, 148, 329
Regency debates (1788), 62–4, 233, 238
return to office (1804), 178–81
supporting Scott in debate, 32, 35, 72, 80
Plumer, Sir Thomas (1753–1824), 213–14, 306, 311–12
Portland, Duke of, *see* Cavendish-Bentinck
Pratt, John Jeffreys, 2nd Earl and 1st Marquis Camden (1759–1840), 221, 292
*Public Advertiser*, 25, 27

Rawdon-Hastings, Francis, 2nd Earl of Moira (1754–1826), 184, 234, 238, 245, 247
Redesdale, Lord, *see* Mitford
Reeves, John, prosecution of (1796), 116–17, 120, 123–4
reform, 250–5, 269–70
criminal, 255–60
electoral, 255, 350–1
political, 80–4, 97, 99–103, 263
Regency debates—
(1788–9), 41, 62–8, 233
(1811–12), 236–42
Revolution, threat of—
(1790s), 83–5, 99–103, 114–16
(1816–19), 260–70, 352, 354–5
effect on Eldon, 175–6, 259–60, 264–6, 354–5
Romilly, Sir Samuel (1757–1818), 41 n. 10, 48, 213, 248, 255, 256 n. 25, 310, 317 n. 80
assessment of Eldon, 9, 42, 198, 206, 301, 307, 314
Rose, George (1744–1818), 168, 170, 181, 232, 313–14

Scarlett, James, 1st Baron Abinger (1769–1844), 9, 10, 334

Scott, Elizabeth (Repton) (b. 1783), 147
Scott, Elizabeth Surtees, Countess of Eldon (1754–1831), 139–42, 146, 148, 151
Scott, Francis Jane (1798–1838), 146–7
Scott, Henry (1748–99), 145
Scott, Sir John, 1st Earl of Eldon (1751–1838):
attitude toward George III, 174, 189, 223–5, 227–8, 244–5, 248–9, 354
attitude toward George IV, 188, 246–7, 248–9, 293, 354
attitude toward Pitt, 159–60, 161, 165, 171, 176–7, 178–81, 189, 354
health, 10–11, 153, 173, 186
income, 3–8, 154, 208 n. 63, 308, 315–16
indecision, 42–3, 47, 206–7, 292, 307–8, 313–14, 319
insecurity, 10, 12, 115–16, 226–8, 293–4, 313–14, 325, 339–42
intellect, 8–9, 156, 313, 355
judicial temperament, 155–9, 274, 283–91
prosecutorial temperament, 94–7, 112–13, 124–5, 136–8
*see also* Robert Crossfield; John Cuthell; John Frost; Thomas Hardy; James O'Coigly; William Stone; John Horne Tooke; Revd Gilbert Wakefield
religion, 17–19, 209, 212, 215, 331, 355–6
Scott, Hon. John (1774–1805), 16, 146, 147–8, 187, 189
Scott, John, 1st Viscount Encombe, 2nd Earl of Eldon (1805–1854), 149–50
Scott, Sir William, 1st Baron Stowell (1745–1836), 1, 3, 54, 142–5, 148, 151
Scott, Hon. William-Henry (1795–1832), 146, 147, 149, 208 nn. 61 and 63
Scottish judicial reform (1807), 218–20, 297–8
sedition, 103 n. 22, 116, 130, 259, 266–7
seditious libel, 75–7, 84, 116, 127, 259, 262–3, 264–5, 269
*see also* John Cuthell; Daniel Isaac

seditious libel (*cont.*)
Eaton; Fox's Libel Act; Daniel
Holt; John Lambert; John Reeves;
John Vint; Revd Gilbert Wakefield
seditious Meetings Act (1817), 261, 262
seditious words, 86, 131, 137 n. 8
*see also* John Frost
Sheridan, Richard Brinsley
(1751–1816), 25, 63 n. 10, 150,
245
Ships in Mutiny Act (1797), 125–7
Sidmouth, Lord, *see* Addington
'Six Acts' (1819), 264, 268
slave trade, 254, 270
Society for Constitutional Information,
83, 99, 100, 101, 260
prosecutions of Hardy and Tooke,
106, 110, 111
Speaker of the House of Lords, 271
*St James Chronicle*, 86 n. 12
Stanhope, Charles, 3rd Earl
(1753–1816), 233, 273
Stephen, Sir James, 105
Stewart, Robert, 2nd Viscount
Castlereagh, 2nd Marquess of
Londonderry (1769–1822), 213,
221–2, 228, 327, 346 n. 85
Chancery reform, 299, 312, 318
Stockdale, John, prosecution of (1789),
76 nn. 69–70, 84 n. 3
Stone, William, prosecution of (1796),
103 n. 20, 119–21
Stowell, Lord, *see* Scott

Taylor, Michael Angelo (1757–1843),
298–301, 304–5, 308, 309, 316,
318
Test and Corporation Acts, repeal of,
335–7
Thanet, Earl of, prosecution of (1799),
135–6
Thurlow, Edward, 1st Baron
(1731–1806), 5, 21, 47, 63 n. 10,
169–70
Thynne, Thomas, 3rd Viscount
Weymouth and 1st Marquess of
Bath (1734–96), 21, 22
Tierney, George (1761–1830), 222, 224
*Times, The*, 21 n. 3, 30, 75, 86, 114,
121 n. 6, 156, 232 n. 7, 237
complimenting Scott's parliamentary
speeches, 31, 32, 33, 66
Tooke, John Horne, prosecution of

(1794), 41, 103 n. 22, 109–11, 113,
119
Traitorous Correspondence Act (1793),
85–6
treason, 103–6, 118, 137 n. 74, 259,
266–7, 280–1, 282
*see also* Robert Crossfield; Thomas
Hardy; James O'Coigly; William
Stone; John Horne
Tooke; Treasonable Practices Act
'Treason trials' of 1794, 114–16, 119,
132, 260, 266
Treasonable Practices Act (1795),
115–16, 118, 266

Vice-Chancellor Act (1813), 298–300,
312–13
Vint, John, prosecution of (1799), 134–5

Wakefield, Revd Gilbert, prosecution
of (1799), 132–4
Ward, Robert Plumer (1765–1846),
238 n. 30, 240 n. 38, 293
Watson, Stephen, 119
Wedderburn, Alexander, 1st Baron
Loughborough (1733–1805), 47,
61, 63 n. 10, 167, 168
Wellesley, Sir Arthur, 1st Duke of
Wellington (1769–1852), 204,
208–9, 292, 326, 327–8, 332–4,
338–9, 341, 352
Wellesley, Richard Colley, 1st Baron
Wellesley, 1st Marquess of
Wellesley [Ire] (1760–1842),
245–6, 247
Westminster election scrutiny (1784),
26–8, 36
Wetherell, Sir Charles (1770–1846),
201–2, 304, 306, 334
Weymouth, Lord, *see* Thynne
Whitbread, Samuel (1758–1815),
237–8, 239, 240
*Whitehall Evening Post*, 24, 25
Wilberforce, William (1759–1833), 37,
42, 61, 159, 279
Williams, Sir John (1777–1846), 286,
301, 303–5, 307
*World*, 75, 79 n. 83
Wraxall, Sir Nathaniel (1751–1831), 21
n. 4, 24, 35–6, 67

Yorke, Charles Philip (1764–1834),
241